REMEMBERING THE REFORMATION

This stimulating volume explores how the memory of the Reformation has been remembered, forgotten, contested, and reinvented between the sixteenth and twenty-first centuries.

Remembering the Reformation traces how a complex, protracted, and unpredictable process came to be perceived, recorded, and commemorated as a transformative event. Exploring both local and global patterns of memory, the contributors examine the ways in which the Reformation embedded itself in the historical imagination and analyse the enduring, unstable, and divided legacies that it engendered. The book also underlines how modern scholarship is indebted to processes of memory-making initiated in the early modern period and challenges the conventional models of periodisation that the Reformation itself helped to create. This collection of essays offers an expansive examination and theoretically engaged discussion of concepts and practices of memory and Reformation.

This volume is ideal for upper level undergraduates and postgraduates studying the Reformation, Early Modern Religious History, Early Modern European History, and Early Modern Literature.

Brian Cummings is Anniversary Professor of English at the University of York and a Fellow of the British Academy. He edited *The Book of Common Prayer* (2013) and his book *Mortal Thoughts* (2013) won the Dietz Prize of the Modern Language Association of America. With Alexandra Walsham, he co-directed the AHRC project 'Remembering the Reformation' between 2016 and 2019.

Ceri Law has worked at Queen Mary University of London, Cambridge University, and the University of Essex. She is the author of *Contested Reformations in the University of Cambridge, c.1535–84* (2018). She was a Postdoctoral

Research Associate on the AHRC 'Remembering the Reformation' project between 2016 and 2019.

Karis Riley has degrees in Philosophy, Classics, and English Literature and is currently completing a book on Milton and the passions. She was a Postdoctoral Research Associate on the AHRC 'Remembering the Reformation' project between 2018 and 2019.

Alexandra Walsham is Professor of Modern History at the University of Cambridge and a Fellow of the British Academy. She has published five books, including *The Reformation of the Landscape* (2011), which won the Wolfson History Prize in 2012. With Brian Cummings, she co-directed the AHRC project 'Remembering the Reformation' between 2016 and 2019.

REMEMBERING THE MEDIEVAL AND EARLY MODERN WORLDS

REMEMBERING THE REFORMATION

Edited by Brian Cummings, Ceri Law, Karis Riley, and Alexandra Walsham

Routledge
Taylor & Francis Group

LONDON AND NEW YORK

First published 2020
by Routledge
2 Park Square, Milton Park, Abingdon, Oxon OX14 4RN

and by Routledge
52 Vanderbilt Avenue, New York, NY 10017

Routledge is an imprint of the Taylor & Francis Group, an informa business

British Library Cataloguing-in-Publication Data
A catalogue record for this book is available from the British Library

Library of Congress Cataloging-in-Publication Data
A catalog record has been requested for this book

ISBN: 978-0-367-15075-4 (hbk)
ISBN: 978-0-367-15076-1 (pbk)
ISBN: 978-0-429-05484-6 (ebk)

Typeset in Bembo
by Taylor & Francis Books

In memory of two eminent and generous scholars. Margaret Aston (1932–2014) and Irena Backus (1950–2019)

CONTENTS

FIGURES

ACKNOWLEDGEMENTS

This volume arises from the interdisciplinary project, 'Remembering the Reformation', based jointly at the Universities of Cambridge and York. The project ran from January 2016 to September 2019. We gratefully acknowledge the support of the UK Arts and Humanities Research Council: the funding it has provided has facilitated a wonderful collaboration which has shaped the scholarship of all members of the project team in transformative ways.

The essays in this volume emerged from a major conference held at the University of Cambridge in September 2017. We would like to thank all those who attended, offered papers, and participated in the stimulating and fruitful discussions that took place over these three days. We thank our contributors for responding so constructively to comments on earlier drafts and for their patience as this volume has evolved. Bronwyn Wallace, postdoctoral research associate on the project, played a vital part in organising the conference and in planning the programme. We owe her our immense thanks.

The final preparation of the volume for submission to the press was undertaken by Matthew Rowley: we are indebted to him for his meticulous and excellent work. Heartfelt, but completely inadequate gratitude goes to our Project Administrator, Tom Taylor, without whom the collection could not have been brought to completion. We thank Routledge for inviting us to publish this volume in its 'Remembering the …' Series and we are very grateful for the support of Laura Pilsworth and Morwenna Scott.

Brian Cummings, Ceri Law, Karis Riley, and Alexandra Walsham
York and Cambridge, January 2020

CONTRIBUTORS

Andrew Atherstone, Latimer Research Fellow, Wycliffe Hall, University of Oxford.

Philip Benedict, Professor Emeritus, l'Institut d'histoire de la Réformation, University of Geneva.

Brian Cummings, Anniversary Professor of English, University of York.

Dagmar Freist, Professor of Early Modern History, Carl von Ossietzky University of Oldenberg.

Phillip Haberkern, Associate Professor of History, Boston University.

Kat Hill, Lecturer in Early Modern History, Birkbeck College, University of London.

Geert H. Janssen, Professor of Early Modern History, University of Amsterdam.

Isabel Karremann, Professor of Early Modern Literature, University of Zurich.

Ceri Law, former Postdoctoral Research Associate, AHRC 'Remembering the Reformation' project.

Carolina Lenarduzzi, Visiting Member of Staff at the Institute for History, University of Leiden.

David van der Linden, Assistant Professor in Early Modern History, Radboud University, Nijmegen.

Natalia Nowakowska, Professor of European History and Fellow and Tutor, Somerville College, University of Oxford.

Katrina B. Olds, Associate Professor of History, University of San Francisco.

Judith Pollmann, Professor of Early Modern Dutch History, University of Leiden.

Tarald Rasmussen, Professor of Church History, University of Oslo.

Karis Riley, former Postdoctoral Research Associate, AHRC 'Remembering the Reformation' project.

Sarah Scholl, Lecturer, Faculty of Theology, University of Geneva.

James Simpson, Donald P. and Katherine B. Loker Professor of English, Harvard University.

Stefano Villani, Associate Professor of History, University of Maryland.

Alexandra Walsham, Professor of Modern History and Fellow of Emmanuel College, University of Cambridge.

Róisín Watson, Departmental Lecturer in Early Modern History, University of Oxford.

ABBREVIATIONS

EHR	English Historical Review
HistJ	Historical Journal
HLQ	Huntington Library Quarterly
JBS	Journal of British Studies
JEH	Journal of Ecclesiastical History
ODNB	Oxford Dictionary of National Biography
P&P	Past and Present
RenQ	Renaissance Quarterly
SC	The Seventeenth Century
SCJ	Sixteenth Century Journal
StCH	Studies in Church History
TRHS	Transactions of the Royal Historical Society

1

INTRODUCTION

Remembering the Reformation

Brian Cummings, Ceri Law, Karis Riley, and Alexandra Walsham

It was said that Theodore Beza, the great theologian of Geneva, after he reached the age of eighty, could say 'perfectly by heart' — in Greek — any verse from St Paul's epistles, or indeed anything 'he had learned long before', but whatsoever he was newly told, he forgot straightaway.[1] The anecdote appears in a miscellany written by members of the family of Sir Marmaduke Rawdon (1583–1646), a Yorkshire merchant and Civil War soldier, where it is used to illustrate the commonplace topic 'Of Memory'. Memory, the writer states, following classical theories of psychology still in vogue, is constructed like a 'treasure house'. This metaphor goes back to the oldest surviving Latin book of rhetoric, *Rhetorica ad Herennium*, where memory is defined as a natural quality, yet one that can be perfected by artificial techniques. Through training and discipline we can overcome our cognitive deficiencies: for example by imagining each of the things we are trying to recall as a room within a house.[2] This helps the mind to retrieve information in an orderly way from within its vast storage system. Elsewhere, however, Cicero warns of a storehouse that has become too large for its own good. He recalls the view of Themistocles, from the time when the science of mnemonics was first being introduced. Informed that it would enable him to remember everything, Themistocles replied that 'it would be a greater kindness' if he were taught how to forget.[3] Likewise, in the Rawdon family's commonplace account of Beza's extraordinary powers of memory, the reader is urged to be wary: like a purse, if the memory store becomes over full, it cannot shut; and its contents will spill out. Beza, it is implied, tried to remember too much, and so forgot how to forget.

For a modern reader, Beza's reported experience is an agonisingly accurate rendition of the characteristic symptoms of dementia. Some way that this is described in a seventeenth-century manuscript reminds us that memory was understood very differently in previous periods, less in terms of neuroscience or medicine, and more in terms of an art or craft. A characteristic way of imagining memory in the Middle Ages, Mary Carruthers shows, is rhetorical.[4] For example, Peter of Ravenna's *Phoenix, sive artificiosa memoria* (Venice, 1491) encourages his readers to organise subjects in their heads by reference to imaginary *loci* (or 'places') to remember them by. Peter claimed to have devised one hundred thousand 'places' in his mind as a young man, enabling him to locate different memories at will. Memory is thus a process of conscious visualisation as much as a neural network. Peter's work was published in many editions in many countries, and translated and abbreviated by others, making it the best-known memory text of the Renaissance.[5] When looking back to the past, it is worth recalling that people remembered differently then.

The history of memory

The distinctive historical formation of remembering and forgetting is the subject of this book: how the experiences of the tumultuous years of the Reformation are reflected in complex and often contradictory processes of memorialisation. This is a two-way process: the Reformation transforms public and private experiences of memory; in turn, the processes of memory affect the way that the events and people of the Reformation are interpreted and analysed. Raphael Samuel has identified how religious memory has been 'the crucible of the national idea'.[6] At a local level, Samuel remarks how places of religious worship form centres of memorial emotion.[7] The Reformation lies at the heart of these contested religious identities. This is by no means limited to the enforcement of establishment traditions: puritanism and non-conformity, Samuel claims, are equally significant codes of cultural incorporation. Memory is the home of dissent as much as official tradition. The Reformation is thus a complex 'theatre of memory'.

History, of course, is not the same thing as memory. The records of Beza's life speak to the concerns of this volume in both trajectories, in suggesting how memory informs and invades the writing of history, and how history reshapes and revisits the materials of memory. Beza was born in Vézelay in Burgundy in 1519 in the heart of Catholic France, the nephew of a Cistercian Abbot, before a single writing by Martin Luther had yet appeared in his native country. At the time of his death in Geneva in 1605, however, Beza was the most celebrated surviving figure of the combined Protestant revolutions in doctrine, belief, and behaviour.[8] His scholarship in ancient languages analysed the society and beliefs of the Biblical epochs in order to challenge every aspect of his own childhood faith. His life therefore speaks eloquently of divisive memory: of the reinvention of the past in the name of the profoundest social change. Indeed, Beza contributed to the history of the Reformation by writing a *Life* of Jean Calvin as a preface to Calvin's Commentary on Joshua in 1564, published separately as the *Discours de la vie et mort de Maistre Jean Calvin* and translated into many languages.[9] Brief though it is, it succeeds in shaping the memorial record of biography into the pattern of Calvinist doctrine. 'What was hys lyfe', asks Beza, 'other than a continuall doctrine, as wel by worde as by writing, and by all his manners and order of lyfe?'[10] In Irena

Backus's words, Calvin's doctrine becomes (in Beza's account) 'both the way he lived, and what he taught in his struggle to establish orthodoxy'.[11] Catholic lives of Calvin, unsurprisingly, adopted an opposing narrative. Jerome Bolsec, a double convert, who began as a Carmelite friar, then joined the Reformation in Geneva, then recanted again, re-established his Catholic credentials with *Lives* of Calvin in 1577 and subsequently of Beza in 1582. In contrast to Beza's exemplary tale of austerity and chastity, Bolsec presents Calvin repenting on his death-bed, tormented by crab lice, and disowning his own writings, especially the *Institutes*, which was the foundational text of Calvinists.[12] To match these final moments of Protestant heresy with earlier patterns of behaviour, he accuses Calvin of secret sins: adultery and sodomy. Bolsec repeats this trope in his *Life of Beza*, who also appears in this light as a serial sexual predator.[13] What is significant is not the obvious back and forth of lurid fantasy, but the way that history is subject to controversial acts of remembering. Despair in dying is equivalent to changeableness of doctrine, depravity to heresy. To counteract this, Protestant biographers turned Calvin's last moments into an exemplary tale of steadfast faith. There is no better instance of the importance of remembering, and of the difficulty of verifying it.

At the heart of *Remembering the Reformation* is the experience of historical change. This collection of essays traces how what we now recognise as a complex, protracted and unpredictable process came to be regarded, recorded, and commemorated as a transformative event. It also probes the enduring, unstable, and divided legacies that it engendered. It examines the Reformation not as a finite set of events in the past, but as an extended idea that has embedded itself in the modern historical imagination. In chronology it ranges from the late Middle Ages to the present day. The essays underline in different ways the extent to which modern historiography of the Reformation is indebted to (and enriched by) processes of memory-making initiated in the early modern period itself. The volume is designed to break out of the paradigms of nationalist historiography in order to explore the memory of what may be seen as alternative and plural Reformations (Protestant, Catholic, and radical). It seeks to stimulate discussion of how memory cultures are associated not only with magisterial and state-led Reformations, but also with religious communities that were thwarted, or threatened. From local versions of memory and religion the volume moves outwards into patterns of global memory which transcend and cross territorial boundaries, and which are diasporic and mobile in character. Likewise, it challenges the periodisation that the Reformation itself helped to create, breaching conventional divides between medieval, early modern, and modern. In this way, concepts of memory and religion are used to question each other, moving from past contexts into the processes by which Reformation consciousness has been and is reframed in modernity.

Theories of memory

This book is informed by the surge of important interdisciplinary work in the last few decades on how societies remember. This has reflected a shift from the ancient and Renaissance concentration on memory as the cognitive faculty of an individual, towards an ethical concept of collective memory framed within the concerns of sociology and anthropology. Mary Douglas has commented on how the work of Émile Durkheim and Marcel Mauss led to a perception of time 'not as an intuition, but as a social construct'.[14] From here we are but a step away from the term *mémoire collective*, first used as the title of the last, posthumously published book by Maurice Halbwachs, who died at Buchenwald in 1945. In an earlier work in 1925, Halbwachs argued that 'the individual calls recollections to mind by relying on the frameworks of social memory'.[15] Following from this perception, Pierre Nora, the French-Jewish historian, began in 1978 a series of highly influential seminars on memory, arguing that it is never a neutral historical space, the product of spontaneous reflection.[16] Rather, it is through a conscious effort that archives are collected, anniversaries celebrated, or monuments maintained. Modernity, Nora holds, has a compulsion to remember, in a world felt to be transformed irrevocably. If Nora sees this as an effect of secularisation, it is worth pointing out the entry of the Reformation into collective or national conceptions of memory as a significant event. Whatever happened on 31 October 1517 was quickly lost with the individual memory of the participants.[17] It was subsumed into public anniversaries of Luther's posting of the Ninety-Five Theses, the first of which took place in 1617. Only at this point did a visual iconography for the original 'event' come to exist.[18] In 1817, a national festival was organised by students all over Germany: Luther was hailed as a freedom fighter; medals were struck with images of the Reformation events; in more sinister fashion, Napoleonic books were burned.[19] The 400th anniversary was more muted, taking place as it did in 1917 in the midst of the First World War. In 2017, by contrast, the themes for the 500th anniversary were reconciliation and globalism. Anybody who visited Wittenberg during the twenty-first century celebration (which in Germany was celebrated over a period of a decade) cannot have failed to notice how the town today is a confection of memorials: from the Luther statue (1821) in the square in front of the Town Hall; to the iron tablet of theses (1858) in the reconstructed Prussian Castle Church; to the *Playmobil* dolls and Luther bears in souvenir shops.

According to Nora, this is not surprising, since it is *change* itself that produces the historical formation of memory. The French revolution, European industrialisation in the nineteenth century, and the World Wars of the twentieth, all had this effect. It is in the experience of an irrevocable break with tradition that collective memory becomes necessary, whether as an antidote to anxiety or an expression of solidarity. In the disappearance of 'a past that is gone for good', a culture experiences a rupture, and in the process, something like a historical consciousness is formed. In a beautiful, elegiac, and counter-intuitive phrase, Nora adds: 'We speak so much of memory because there is so little left'.[20] Identity in such a time and place is reconstructed around what he calls *lieux de mémoire* (or 'sites of memory').[21] A *lieu de mémoire*, Nora says, can be 'any significant entity, whether material or non-material in nature, which by dint of human will or the work of time has become a symbolic element of the memorial heritage of a community'.[22] This phrase has been adopted as the leading metaphor of memory studies in the last generation. It has been particularly popular among historians of material objects, who have found in it a manifesto for a new kind of history, sometimes known as the 'material turn'.[23] The study of material objects at some level recovers the past, in ways that have been occluded by the discourses of history. Objects have taken the place of texts in some studies, as if they speak more directly from the past. This is some-thing of a misreading of Nora himself, however. For Nora, sites of memory come into being precisely as an act of displacement and substitution — in place of the lived experience of a memory that is no longer available. As the products of orga-nised history, they become co-labourers in the strenuous duty to remember, over and against the once effortless, unconscious continuation of invisible and ingrained practice. Memory in Nora works in a complex dialogue between past and present, in ways that require urgent acts of interpretation.

It may be that Nora is recalling here the distinction famously made in Marcel Proust's *À la recherche du temps perdu* (1913–1927), between 'voluntary' memory and *mémoire involontaire*. [24] The autobiographical memories at the heart of his novel — such as the one famously inspired by eating a *madeleine*, possess an authenticity of recollection, without conscious effort.[25] Voluntary memory, by contrast, is char-acterised by a deliberate effort to recall the past. This effort of consciousness, in historical as much as literary writing, is an act of reorganisation and even fabrica-tion, but tends to dominate over the evanescence of lived experiences. Proust suggests that memory is as much about loss as it is about recuperation, about for-getting as much as it is about remembering. His source here may be a nineteenth-century work by his cousin by marriage, the philosopher Henri Bergson. Bergson argued that memory is not single in nature. In 1896 he distinguished between memory as 'motor mechanisms' (the automatic repetition of neural events in the brain) and 'recollection' (the survival of personal memories in the unconscious).[26] Memory in Proust is not only two-sided but also paradoxical. Walter Benjamin explains that Proust's novel describes not life 'as it actually was [*wie es gewesen ist*] but a life as it was remembered by the one who lived it'.[27] Benjamin calls this 'the Penelope work of recollection [*Eingedenken*]'. Just as Penelope in the *Odyssey* weaves a funeral shroud for her father-in-law Laertes by day, and then unravels it again by night, so the woof and warp of remembering and forgetting alternate in the mind. It could even be (Benjamin muses), that the cognitive processing of the daylight hours forgets as much as the dream-work of the night remembers.

Nora's concept of memory, like Proust's, plays freely with concepts of loss, oblivion, denial, fragmentation, appropriation, or invention. Such terms are the inheritance of the early twentieth century, and above all of Sigmund Freud's rewriting of the arts of memory in the wake of psychoanalysis. Written with tragic prescience in 1914, the short essay 'Remembering, Repeating and Working Through' drew on *Studies on Hysteria* (1895) in order to overthrow the very idea of memory as a positive reconstruction of actual experience.[28] Most of the really important memories in a life, he stated with a matter-of-fact counterintuitive daring, can barely be retrieved at all. This is especially true of childhood memory, which is instead subjected to endless rationalisation and interpretation.[29] Freud's patients, and by extension all of us, feel resistance to deep and difficult memories from the past, and reassemble experience into other kinds of pattern, which are nonetheless accepted and absorbed into an individual's narrative life-stream as if they took place in this order originally. Rather than remembering, strictly speaking, a person *repeats* these mental events, with 'everything deriving from the repressed element within himself'.[30] Over time, perhaps with the help of therapy, or perhaps as an act of therapy without any other person present, it may become possible for her to 'work through' the resistance of memory, and 'to overcome it by defying it'.[31] In this way, Adam Phillips suggests that Freud is making out of memory 'the individual's unconscious quest for innovative response'.[32] Unlike his Anglo-Saxon counterparts, Nora seems to have no embarrassment in employing a Freudian frame of reference in his writing. Nora is also highly self-conscious of the powerful national myths by which modern societies operate, myths he calls at once 'hopelessly forgetful' and powerfully organised.[33]

Memory and the Reformation

The Reformation shares all the characteristics of a revolutionary rupture identified in Nora's study of the historical memory of the French Revolution. On the one side it is perceived through a narrative of loss, one most prominent in the English-speaking world in the work of Eamon Duffy. His *Stripping of the Altars* (1992) proposed a revisionist account of the English Reformation, disputing the very notion of a popular Protestant movement, and replacing it with a model of political imposition and suppression, for example in the 'sweeping attack' on the memory of the cult of the saints.[34] Duffy also simultaneously used the resources of historical memory to reassemble a lost world of ritual and prayer, which had been torn asunder by Tudor violence. A primary example of this is the communal memory of the parish, exemplified by the remembering of the names of the dead in the solemn act of worship in the mass.[35] This complex understanding of memory was repeated in Duffy's *The Voices of Morebath* (2001), which moved from a panorama of a whole society to a microhistory of a single village in Devon, as recorded in the parish accounts by Christopher Trychay, the village priest from 1520 to 1574. These 'voices' are the lost identities and memories of the parish. Bringing such voices back to life, Duffy tells the story of how England changed from one of the most vibrantly Catholic countries in Europe to a Protestant nation, a land of whitewashed churches and anti-Catholic propaganda. The village reconstructed its identity again and again, as the religion of late medieval Devon was reformed under Henry VIII and Edward VI, counter-reformed under Mary I, and then revised again under Elizabeth I. In one poignant example, members of the same Devonshire family, the Hurleys, first carry off a Catholic Sarum Missal to be burned in 1549; then buy a new Sarum Missal in 1554 to replace it; then buy a new Protestant Book of Common Prayer to replace that in 1573. At this point, as Duffy puts it, 'a door closes in the memory of Morebath'.[36]

Duffy's brilliant book is a work of mourning as well as of history, and offers an example of Nora's argument at two levels. It contains the sites of memory both *within* the Reformation period, in the vivid description of chalices, misericords, chants, and candles; and *of* the Reformation, as seen from a distance by various forms of modernity. It is the argument of *Remembering the Reformation* that these two forms of memory cannot be separated. The Reformation is still with us. All the great events and characters of history occur twice, observed Hegel; in Karl Marx's famous quip, 'the first time as high tragedy, the second time as low farce'.[37] It is less often noted that Marx made the remark in the context of an analysis of public memory. 'The French', he says, 'so long as they made revolutions, could not rid themselves of the memory of Napoleon'.[38] It is the commonplace of revolutions to conjure up the spirits of the dead, Marx states, while citing the example of Luther 'masquerading as the Apostle Paul'.

One example would be Luther's own tangential effort in autobiography, the preface to the edition of his Latin works that he made in the last year of his life. He recalls his days as a young monk in Erfurt, driving himself mad 'with a violent and disturbed conscience', trying to understand Paul's letter to the Romans — until he made a breakthrough, after which he 'entered as it were the gates of paradise'.[39] Nevertheless, examination of Luther's early writings against his famous account of them thirty years later casts some doubt on the accuracy of private memory.[40] What is not in doubt is Luther's autobiographical imagination of himself in the guise both of Paul and of Augustine, which then entered into the Protestant consciousness as the prototype conversion narrative from Germany to America and beyond.[41]

Collective memory continues to surround the Reformation in further acts of masquerade. In 2017 the 500th anniversary of Luther's Ninety-Five Theses was celebrated by a Protestant movement that now claims something like 900 million believers. The festivities (as Dagmar Freist recounts in the Afterword to this volume) were also conscious, to a degree more obvious than at previous centenaries, of the ironies of bias. Most of all in Germany, which has as good a sense of divided memory as any country in the world, triumphalism gave way to statements about the need for global unity among Christians. Yet the very existence of an anniversary is felt with diametrical difference in the Catholic world, with its 1.3 billion baptised adherents. 'Whose Luther?' the official anniversary asked; but for others the question was more simply, 'Who's Luther?'

It could be said that study of the Reformation, since its earliest days, has suffered alternately from hypermnesia and amnesia. Certainly in the past, histories of early modern religion (Catholic and Protestant alike) tended towards voluminous accumulation of detail, while also displaying an oblivious attitude to the history of the other confession. Friedrich Nietzsche, son of a Lutheran pastor, had something like this in mind in his essay, 'On the uses and disadvantages of history for life' (1874). A culture is capable of having too much historical consciousness. To show this, he analyses the relationship between history as experience, and history as a mode of writing. 'The unhistorical and the historical are necessary in equal measure' for the

health of a culture, he asserts.[42] Often taken as a dismissive rejection of histori-
cism, Nietzsche's essay uncovers a tension between monumental, antiquarian, and
critical uses of history. For a critical mode of history to exist, he claims, it must be
possible at one and the same time to recognise the historicity of human existence,
while also affirming the creative possibility of breaking with the past. In this
complex process, memory plays a variety of roles. Indeed, part of historical consciousness is 'the ability to forget' (p. 62).[43] Such remarks critique the tendency
within Reformation studies to veer between monumentality and antiquarianism.
The spate of recent volumes produced in the lead up to Luther's anniversary
emphasised in turn epochal significance or epic disintegration.[44] Nietzsche provides an antidote to such grandiloquence in a characteristically double-edged
quotation from Luther, to the effect that 'the world only existed through a piece
of forgetful negligence on God's part'.[45] Historical consciousness of the Reformation, on either confessional side, can be an affliction as well as a benefit.
Nietzsche's ironic and troubling view of the past reconfigures the relationship
between memory and rupture, or between imagination and repression, or
between invention and forgetfulness. Memory, by complicating history as a
concept, offers new insight into the Reformation.

The essays in *Remembering the Reformation* are interested both in the way that
the Reformation formulates itself around symbols of collective memory, and how
those acts of collective memory are monumentalised through subsequent history.
By the end of the seventeenth century, the image of the historical Reformation
could be found stamped onto everyday artefacts, such as an extraordinary delftware charger dating from 1692.[46] This object from a Dutch home reflects the
extent to which the sites of memory of the Protestant Reformation had pene-
trated domestic identity. It shows Luther, Calvin, and Beza seated at a table upon
which stands a lighted candle symbolising the Gospel. Opposing them are the
pope, a cardinal, a bishop, and a monk attempting in vain to blow out the flame.
The figures peer out from the luminous blue, distorted in the process of glazing
and by the bevelled shape of the plate, so that the familiar facial features of the
reformers are made uncanny and otherworldly. In turn, the delftware charger is
based on another image of the period, a widely produced engraving. The print,
reproduced as Fig. 1.1, visualises some of the ways in which the drawing together
of different individuals from across time and space could be a powerful statement
of shared identity and purpose.[47] This illustration of 'The Reformation' provides
the opening to the second part of a history of the Church from the birth of
Christ to 'this present age' published in 1682, but it is based upon prints that first
appeared in England in the early seventeenth century.[48]

It portrays a lineage of Protestantism from the fourteenth-century reformer
John Wycliffe to the late sixteenth-century figure of William Perkins. These
key representatives of reform are drawn from across Europe, so that Luther and
Calvin are imagined as seated alongside each other, with Melanchthon and Beza
to either side of them.[49] Men from different Protestant traditions unite here in
opposition to four figures at the bottom of the illustration: the pope, the devil, a

FIGURE 1.1 J[ohn] S[hurley], *Ecclesiastical history epitomiz'd* (London, 1682), title page to part II. Cambridge, University Library, shelf mark: VIII.31.63.
By permission of the Syndics of Cambridge University Library.

monk and a cardinal, all trying but failing to extinguish the light of Reformation. In this depiction, then, the divisions and contradictions of different Reformation movements are visually smoothed over to depict a straightforward narrative of Reformed religion versus the Catholic Church, and of light against dark. It is an act of imagination, willing into being one united entity that can be entitled, as in this print, 'The Reformation'.[50] The Dutch delftware plate modelled on this influential engraved print is a more idiosyncratic object that nonetheless speaks more eloquently of lived experience. It commemorates a personal rite of passage, inscribed on the back with the names of Jan van Dieninge and Jannetie van Wyn Bergen. This may mark the anniversary of their marriage in 1680 or perhaps Jan's election as an officer of his Amsterdam guild. Intertwining remembrance of a private event with remembrance of an international movement that permanently ruptured medieval Christendom, this compelling artefact illustrates the role of material culture in the forging of collective memory of the Reformation at a vital juncture.

As well as exploring monumentality, *Remembering the Reformation* pays attention to fragmentation, loss, and invention. Elsewhere in Holland, Peter Saenredam's haunting painting of the *Interior of St Bavo in Haarlem* (1628) [Fig. 2.1] ambiguously combines memories of medieval stained glass, alongside a powerful rendition of a Protestant aesthetic of divine space, the white walls of a *Deus absconditus*, the hidden God portrayed theologically by both Luther and Calvin. (Saenredam's painting, as a kind of work of mourning, is the subject of James Simpson's essay.) Later, in the nineteenth century, Catholic churches such as the church in Beza's home of Vézelay were remodelled to incorporate this white aesthetic. The eleventh-century Benedictine abbey, sacked by the Huguenots in 1569, neglected in the seventeenth century, and further damaged by the *sans-culottes* in the Revolution, was rescued from total collapse at the behest of Prosper Mérimée (author of *Carmen*), and restored on a massive scale by Eugène Viollet-le-Duc between 1840 and 1861. In a rigorous study of the archive and of architecture, Kevin D. Murphy shows how the church as we know it is a classic example of invented memory (the topic of the fifth section in this book below).[51] This is how modernity wants to see a medieval building: pristine, pure, visibly different from us. In 1845, Viollet-le-Duc moved onto an even grander project: Notre Dame of Paris herself. The façade and other parts of the cathedral had suffered much damage during the Revolution, when statues were beheaded or smashed. In the interior, the choir had been remodelled during the reign of Louis XVI on neo-classical lines; the revolutionaries had subsequently turned it for a while into a secular temple of republican virtue. The bells had been melted down into cannons. By now, the cathedral had become a metaphor for the lost Middle Ages, as in Victor Hugo's nostalgic novel of 1831. While Viollet-le-Duc was in some ways a conservative restorer, he also could not keep himself from reconstructing the pre-revolutionary church according to his invented memory of what Christianity was like before the Reformation and modernity. Many journalists commenting on the catastrophic fire in 2019 failed at first to distinguish between the loss of medieval and nineteenth-century material in Notre Dame, so confused have they become in the modern imagination. The spire which fell to earth was built in 1861. Michael Camille once brilliantly referred to Viollet-le-Duc's fabulous gargoyles (also not medieval) as 'monsters of modernity'.[52] His phrase represents the way that the medieval has come to act as a signifier separating us from the past. The Reformation is a primary metaphor in the transition to modernity, as well as a memorialised event in itself.

Memory and trauma

These different artefacts, from a humble plate to one of the most iconic buildings in the world, provide a short-hand for the variety of sites of memory that are investigated in this volume. Yet as always with the most profound experience of memory, under the surface there is not only separation or division, but also trauma. Trauma, Freud suggests, lies at the heart of tradition, and is his explanation for even the origin of religion itself.[53] Freud's interest in trauma was transformed by his encounters with the victims of shell shock in the First World War. Trauma creates a breach in consciousness, Freud argued, fissuring memory in the process, but making the work of memory in turn crucial in therapy or recuperation. 'Trauma always returns', says Jacqueline Rose in *States of Fantasy* (1996).[54] It is in the recognition of the power of trauma in the formation of memory in response to the Holocaust that twentieth-century memory studies came to its culmination. Lawrence L. Langer in *Admitting the Holocaust* (1995) reveals how traumatic memories of the Holocaust do not progress in chronological fashion. Instead they are subject to 'durational time', a process in which the past disrupts the present, and gets re-experienced in the telling.[55] There could be no more profound challenge to the linearity of history than this. Langer cites Jean-François Lyotard on the definition of the Holocaust past: 'a past located this side of the forgotten, much closer to the present moment than any past, at the same time that it is incapable of being solicited by voluntary and conscious memory'.[56] For Langer, this process is not one of consolation or redemption, as it might be in Dante's use of memory in *Inferno*. On the contrary, memory has the task of disclosing an internal disorder void of consolation. Yet holocaust memory has also been forced to carry out another kind of work, in the fight against that evil twin of repression, denial. Holocaust denial is almost as old as its memorialisation.[57] The historical analysis of memory therein finds powerful justification. Aleida Assmann's moving analysis of memory in relation to the astonishing extremes of violence in the twentieth century shows that, seventy years after the end of the Second World War and the opening of the gates of Auschwitz, the work of memory is still going on.[58]

The Reformation today is not often studied as a site of trauma. Indeed, like the concept of memory, trauma as a concept is often seen as quintessentially modern. It is the hope of this volume that its essays will make a different historical trajectory possible. Estimates of the mortality rate during the European wars of religion have been placed at six million deaths at the low estimate and seventeen million at the other extreme.[59] Among the earliest efforts of Reformation historiography were accounts of the extreme violence of martyrdom. Catholics, Protestants, and Anabaptists recorded their suffering at the hands of one another, whether in France, England, or the Low Countries, perhaps as many as 5000 judicial executions taking place.[60] John Foxe's *Actes and Monuments* (1563 and later editions) is an especially notorious example of its kind, making Protestant suffering both exclusive and exemplary.[61] Triumphalist in tone, a chord that is less frequently noticed in Foxe is his effort at memorial retrieval. Here he shows not only a kind of empathy for the victims of religious persecution, but a desire to memorialise them, combined with a fear of forgetting. 'Remember the blessed Martir Anne Askew in our time, & folow her example of constancy', Foxe writes.[62] It is a multiple layer of memory, since Foxe had found this phrase about Askew, burned at Smithfield in 1546 at the age of 24, in letters written in prison by William Tyms at the King's Bench, some of them using his own blood as ink as he himself waited to die. At the same time the phrase 'remember …' was the standard formula of the medieval chantry. The depiction of cruelty and of evangelical endurance in Foxe's text (and the many woodcut illustrations that accompanied it) shaped generations of English Protestants' understanding of their own past and identity. Foxe spoke to many who had experienced trauma at first hand, and tried to give testimony to it through first-hand reportage of their testimony. That his historical expression of this is biased, and that it was put to such consciously monumental use, does not cancel out his aim of understanding memory through trauma. Almost at the same time, Catholic writers showed the Elizabethan church in a completely different light, as a sponsor of cruelty. One such publication called itself *Ecclesiae Anglicanae Trophaea* ('The trophies of the English Church').[63] Much Reformation historiography has been spent in trading violence, as if either side could be vindicated through sufficient archival endeavour measuring out, on the scales of either confession, unequal experiences of suffering.

Remembering the Reformation

It may be more truthful to acknowledge the whole period as characterised by violence and the shock of memory. In pursuit of a more holistic approach, this volume attends to the ways the Reformation has been remembered as rupture, return, and revolution, as well as a passage into modernity. To do so, *Remembering the Reformation* explores the memory of the Reformation in documents, material artefacts, paintings, urban landscapes, holy sites, poems, festivals, relics, or church graveyards. Examples are taken from across western, central, and eastern Europe, the Spanish Americas, Northeastern America, and Scandinavia, from the sixteenth to the twenty-first centuries. Combining the expertise of historians of early modernity, church history, and late medieval and early modern literature, the collection shows that the Reformation was also a reformation of medieval memory structures.

The collaborative work which lies at the heart of the volume was carried out in the context of the project entitled 'Remembering the Reformation', funded by the UK's Arts and Humanities Research Council, at the Universities of Cambridge and York between 2016 and 2019.[64] All of the essays here began life as contributions to the project's international conference in Cambridge in September 2017, and have benefited from the long-term scholarly conversation that the project allowed. The book is also informed by the results of the digital exhibition, curated by the project team, of over 100 objects and books housed in a number of institutions: principally Cambridge University Library, York Minster Library, and Lambeth

Palace Library, London, but also the British Museum, the Fitzwilliam Museum, Cambridge, and the Victoria & Albert Museum, London. Several of the items in that exhibition feature in the pages that follow.[65]

Many essays reflect on what happens to memory when communities are forced outside of the context in which they first grew, via displacement or migration. Others investigate surviving *lieux de mémoire* that remained behind, involving stubborn resistance to, or else accommodation with, the new makers of memory. In both situations, for those who stayed and those in exile, new strategies were needed to reconnect groups to their pasts and to cope with a sense of loss. In this way, the essays in *Remembering the Reformation* frequently uncover an experience of mourning and anxiety towards historical change. Trauma, and its contradictory effects on history, thus emerges as a primary theme. Suffering and humiliation might generate adaptive and resilient memories in diaspora communities, but could also induce a nation (over generations) to forget, unintentionally or otherwise. If remembering violence and defeat was sometimes an act too painful to repeat, trauma offered powerful reasons not to forget. The fourteen essays are divided into seven sections with titles that are meditative rather than technical. The essays, grouped into pairs, either share and develop a foundational concept in the title or contrast with each other in productive ways. Each section represents one way in which a memorial culture (in either confession) challenged, confronted, or revised the Reformation before, during or after its events.

Section one concerns 'Repressed Memory'. James Simpson's essay argues that the aggressive Reformation project of oblivion ironically produced in its visual culture remembrance of what it wanted to make unremembered. The new memory system severed the dynamic movement between past and present, and enforced a view of the past as still, fixed, and unreproducible. As in its theology, so in its art: by removing and emptying divine presence in Catholic memorial practices, Protestant liturgy generated the empty, melancholic, still-life genre in Calvinist art. He shows how Protestant paintings also recorded silhouettes of forbidden memory, releasing and stimulating remembrance of the medieval world it was supposed to help viewers forget. If Simpson captures something of the unsettled side-effects of Protestant oblivion, Isabel Karremann's essay examines those who actively tried to negotiate, control, and harness it for redemptive ends. In the wake of the Reformation's profound changes to memorial culture that moved the concept of oblivion to centre-stage across the religious divide — through iconoclasm and the abolition of commemorating the dead — she examines how sixteenth- and seventeenth-century antiquarian writers dealt with lost memory. Deeply concerned to remember the pre-Reformation world but aware of new restraints, they developed strategies that could meet Protestant conditions but support their aims by making oblivion part of commemoration.

The second section, 'Divided Memory', centres on conflicts and compromise in Catholic memory inside urban contexts. Carolina Lenarduzzi and Judith Pollmann's piece examines the ways minority Catholic groups in Leiden resisted remembering the Reformation in order to reconnect to their origins in a landscape that had been overtaken by Protestant memory regimes, and to strengthen their ties with Catholics in exile. These counter-memories revived medieval practices with martyrdom stories, physical landscapes, and relics. And yet Catholic memorial culture also promoted their own history and identity by finding common ground, or shared 'mnemonic space', with Protestants. David van der Linden shifts the picture of disagreement to Catholic disharmony in a clearly Catholic context. His essay traces the persistence of two competing memorial cultures about the Holy League in material objects and texts, despite the political edict of oblivion that hoped to erase the ideological civil war that took place between royalists and leaguers after the French Wars of Religion. The essay illuminates a historical example of memory used as a therapeutic tool, and analyses the failures of forced amnesia to heal past wounds and overcome religious differences.

In the third section, Tarald Rasmussen and Natalia Nowakowska survey 'Fragmented Memory' at the national level when 'official' memorial histories split and confuse social memory in cultures that refuse to remember the Reformation because of the religious and political suffering it entailed. Rasmussen surveys the distinctive processes of forgetting and remembering the Reformation in the early modern kingdoms of Norway/Denmark and Sweden, with Norway as a special case of oblivion. Rasmussen shows how and why Norwegian historiography wanted to forget its Reformation heritage, which was associated with Danish political overthrow and cultural loss in 1536, and to remember happier days. By redefining the category of the 'Protestant hero' — turning Lutheran theologians into humanists, and elevating a medieval Catholic saint as a proto-reformer and symbol of national independence — the picture of the Reformation in Norway was fractured and reshuffled. Nowakowska's essay fills a conspicuous gap in contemporary international Reformation histories which have had trouble deciding how to read Poland's legacy in the European Reformation. Through an examination of sixteenth and seventeenth-century Polish Reformation chronicles (from both confessions), her essay challenges the concept that historical forgetting is 'passive'. In Poland, for different reasons and in different ways, oblivion was part of a deliberate and contrived strategy of both ecclesiastical erasure and political toleration that allowed no room for national memory of the Reformation to consolidate.

'Inherited Memory', the subject of the fourth section, recognises the problem and necessity of memory in transition across generations in early modern Protestantism. Phillip Haberkern moves back in time to the Bohemian Reformation, and the need of two sixteenth-century religious communities that emerged from it — the Utraquists and the Unity of Brethren — to position themselves as the rightful successors to the first European anti-Catholic revolution. His essay reveals how the need for identity and the right spiritual ancestry could motivate a religious group's memorial practices, especially in a context where the name Protestant was spreading widely and quickly, but potentially lacking in authority without the right pedigree. The focus on memory across generations provides a transition to Róisín Watson's essay, which observes the diverging aims of earlier and future heirs in the construction of family funeral monuments in Reformation Germany. Although the Reformation could bolster family legacy, future family members who had little connection with the historic past looked to new ways to self-memorialise, thus reshaping ecclesiastical material spaces and altering its memorial message. Together, and more generally, both essays consider which media offer memory the best immunity from time and change.

The essays in Section five, 'Invented Memory', investigate Reformation and Counter-Reformation histories in communities looking for religious continuity and legitimacy in new territories and political circumstances. Katrina B. Olds' essay takes as its central focus the cross of Carabuco, to shed fresh light on the ways that New World chroniclers in the Spanish Latin Americas endorsed a narrative of pre-Hispanic evangelisation to connect the Indies' origin to Apostolic Christianity. It brings into conversation the nature of mixed, fictional memories, when Christian history and local indigenous creation myth blend in cross-fertilisation. Stefano Villani's contribution considers the changing reasons for English Protestantism's powerful attraction to the foundation myths of the Italian Waldensian communities from the sixteenth to the nineteenth centuries. The relationships built around artificial memories assisted both kinds of Protestant confession: the Waldensian church's origin story offered the Church of England links to the apostolic era and provided resources to navigate the modern crisis in church ecclesiology, while prolonged contact with the English helped the Waldensians create a national church.

'Migrating Memory' is the focus of the sixth section, which discusses the role of memory in displaced communities. Kat Hill's essay traces the remarkable survival of Reformation memory in the descendants of sixteenth-century Anabaptism dispersed across North America. Although memory-making was necessary to sustain religious identity across time and space, Hill suggests that a new type of memory emerges after the trauma of dislocation. Diaspora memory is not necessarily marked by a longing for the original homeland, but possesses resilience and creativity that can transcend geographic boundaries and establish the 'trans-local' or 'universal place'. While Hill's essay offers valuable insights about narratives of exile and persecution in forming distinctive diaspora identities, Geert H. Janssen's essay shows how these same stories had the ability to break down denominational differences and trigger long-distance networks of charitable aid. His cross-confessional analysis is thus also a history of emotion, as the 'cult of exile' in post-Reformation Europe stimulated sympathy and solidarity for migrants driven from their countries by religious violence. The paradigm of migrating memory also challenges traditional ways of thinking about the agency of refugees. If memory-on-the-move could provide creative spaces for diaspora groups of the same confession to make sense of their suffering, it also formed space for victims to exchange and circulate memories, and collaborate in religious innovations.

Section seven, 'Extended Memory', presents long perspectives on Reformation memory up to the present day. Andrew Atherstone's essay reflects on the reasons why the Reformation was celebrated in Protestant memorials of the Marian martyrs across Victorian, Edwardian, twentieth, and twenty-first century England and Wales. In analysing the motivations that energised these memorial projects, the essay reveals how shifting attitudes towards the content and expression of religious memory over time are linked to questions about freedom of conscience, civic values, and political legislation. Importantly, it discusses how the ecumenical programme has created a new kind of memory that commemorates sincerity over doctrine to promote the appearance of theological unity. Philip Benedict and Sarah Scholl use memory of the Reformation as a site to explore patterns of continuity and change in Geneva's memory regimes across the early modern and modern divide. Their essay highlights the delicate relationship between political changes and commemorative practices, by illuminating how Genevan Protestants forgot an aspect of Calvinist doctrine in the twentieth century, at a time when public memory was failing to remember its founding theology due to advancing secularism, pluralism, humanitarianism, and ecumenicism.

Finally, the Afterword sets the themes of the seven sections in the context of the recent 500th Reformation anniversaries. In demonstrating the current conflicts within Germany's national, ecclesiastical, and academic memory cultures, Dagmar Freist considers whether placing Reformation memory in a global setting may help us to understand why we are confronted with so many competing images of the development of the Reformation. Viewing the past in a global dimension reveals there is a memory of Protestantism, as old as Protestantism itself, that is still alive in the way we tell (and think we should tell) history. The perception of Protestantism as a disruptive, fracturing force that is messier than its Catholic counterpart, is an old question that is buried like a deep splinter in Reformation memory. Yet as Freist sees it, Protestantism has faced this accusation from the very beginning. It could claim a global narrative because of, and not despite, its permitted diversity across religious practices and perceived memory as something flexible or adaptable. In other words, Protestant memory culture was self-consciously a hybrid, international phenomenon earlier than we might expect.

Indeed Freist's proposal of using 'global memory' to navigate the different understandings of the past in modern Germany's memory cultures can be seen as a new line of response to Aleida Assman's theory of collective memory. Collective memory was helpful for suggesting that nations formed their identities by transferring cultural memories of clear and effective symbols across time. The Reformation complicates this paradigm, for obvious reasons. The theory does not seem to fit the whole story of the Reformation — of the way in which Protestantism burst out of national, geographic, political and religious boundaries and rapidly spread to all corners of the globe, adopting and assimilating to local particularities. Long trails of memories follow, scrambled by contextualisation. As historians turn to study the Reformation in these new locations, it has begun to feel inadequate to read Protestant memory exclusively inside the confines of a nation-state and to look for the old symbols. Rather than squeeze the Reformation to fit back inside the parameters of a theory it has overflowed, global memory offers the Reformation a theory with wider girth. Migration, dislocation, and place are the key words. Global memory pays greater attention to memory practices rather than strong symbols, and to space rather than time. It recognises the need to think about what happens to memory when it has been exported out of its native context. It asks why it sticks and how it mutates in a new environment. These two realms, the original local and future translocal, merge to produce a secondary layer, a kaleidoscopic framework, that requires alternative criteria to analyse travelling memory.

Freist's reflections thus underline two central preoccupations of the volume. First, there is a great deal of European Reformation memory that exists in minds and memories beyond Europe. Three of the essays portray this challenge directly. Second, such a reality seems to demand that sensitivity to location and attention to memory practice itself — over and above historical objects and heroes — become priorities; perhaps even necessities, if we want to make sense of the multiple ways that communities have remembered the Reformation beyond Europe and yet still claimed kinship with Europe's Reformation. Shared symbols cannot account for the way Protestantism has ended up with so many variations but can still identify as essentially Protestant in spirit; and that it has done so without needing to resort to the symbols or founding stories of sixteenth-century Protestantism. The focus on memory practice thus relieves us from giving shared symbols an explanatory role in this history that they are unable to bear.

This is what the new work on global memory promises to give us. But it is also not new. Freist's concluding essay can be read in both directions. It suggests that global memory is a recent paradigm, but at the same time offers us a map that reveals a worn path leading back to Protestant theology in the seventeenth and eighteenth centuries. It is perhaps inevitable that the international status of Protestantism would raise a problem for one theory in memory studies and create an opportunity to return to an older — we could almost say forgotten — approach to memory. Since it exposes how early Protestants used global memory, and considers whether a return to an older theory might help modern memory cultures explain, if not resolve, their tensions, Freist's contribution is an appropriate ending to a book about remembering and forgetting. What we think about memory and how we practice it, is itself a complex process that has emerged from the long and convoluted legacy of the Reformation.

Notes

1 York Minster Library, MS Add. 122, fo. 127v. A facsimile of the page in question can be found in the Arts and Humanities Research Council Digital Exhibition, 'Remembering the Reformation', housed at Cambridge University Digital Exhibitions: https://exhibitions.lib.cam.ac.uk/reformation/artifacts/the-treasurehouse-of-the-mind-memory-in-commonplace-books/.
2 *Rhetorica ad Herennium*, III.xx; ed. and tr. H. Caplan, Loeb Classical Library (Cambridge, MA, 1954), 215. In the Middle Ages and Renaissance this work was usually misattributed to Cicero, adding greatly to its authority as the most widespread treatise on rhetoric from antiquity.

3 Cicero, *De oratore*, II.lxxiv; *On the Orator*, ed. and tr. E. W. Sutton and H. Rackham, 2 vols., Loeb Classical Library (Cambridge, MA, 1996), i, 427.

4 Mary J. Carruthers, *The Book of Memory: A Study of Memory in Medieval Culture* (Cambridge, 1990), 329.

5 Frances A. Yates, *The Art of Memory* (London, 1969), 120.

6 Raphael Samuel, *Island Stories: Unravelling Britain*, Theatres of Memory, 2 (London, 1998), 7.

7 *Island Stories*, 365–6.

8 Paul-F. Geisendorf, *Théodore de Bèze* (Geneva, 1967), 424–5.

9 *Discours de M. Théodore de Bèsze, contenant en bref l'histoire de la vie et mort de Maistre Jean Calvin* (n.p., 1564). See https://exhibitions.lib.cam.ac.uk/reformation/artifacts/jean-calvin-a-life-as-doctrine/.

10 *A discourse written by M. Theodore de Beza, containing the life and death of M. John Caluin* ([London?, 1578?]), sig. A2v.

11 Irena Backus, *Life Writing in Reformation Europe: Lives of Reformers by Friends, Disciples and Foes* (Aldershot, 2008), 127.

12 *Histoire des vies, meurs, actes, doctrine et mort des quatre principaux Heretiques de nostre temps, à scaveir Martin Luther, André Carlostad, Pierre Martyr & Jean Calvin, iadis ministre de Geneve* (Douai, 1580), fo. 82v.

13 *Histoire de la vie, mœurs, doctrine et deportements de Theodore de Bèze* (Paris, 1582), fo. 21r.

14 Mary Douglas, Introduction to Maurice Halbwachs, *The Collective Memory* (New York, 1980), 6.

15 Halbwachs, *On Collective Memory*, ed. and tr. Lewis A. Coser (Chicago, 1992), 182.

16 *Les lieux de mémoire* is the title of his series of collaborative seminars at the École des hautes études en sciences sociales in Paris between 1978 and 1981.

17 Erwin Iserloh, *The Theses Were Not Posted* (Toronto, 1966).

18 Brian Cummings, 'Luther and the Book: the Iconography of the Ninety-Five Theses', *StCH* 38 (2004), 222–32.

19 Scott Berg, '"The Lord Has Done Great Things for Us": The 1817 Reformation Celebrations and the End of the Counter-Reformation in the Habsburg Lands', *Central European History* 49, no. 1 (2016), 69–92.

20 Pierre Nora, 'Between Memory and History', *Representations* 26, special issue: Memory and Counter-Memory (Spring, 1989), 7–24, at 7.

21 The title of his collaborative publication, *Les lieux de mémoire*, 3 vols. (Paris, 1984–92).

22 *Realms of Memory: Rethinking the French Past*, tr. A. Goldhammer (New York, 1996), preface.

23 Harvey Green, 'Cultural History and the Material Turn', *Cultural History* 1, no. 1 (2012), 61–82.

24 The distinction is discussed by Paul Vernière, 'Proust et les deux mémoires', *Revue d'Histoire littéraire de la France* 71, no. 5–6 (Sept. –Dec. 1971), 936–49.

25 The incident with the *petite madeleine* occurs in *Du côté de chez Swann*, ed. Antoine Compagnon (Paris, 1987), 44; text based on the Pléiade Edition of Jean-Yves Tadié.

26 Henri Bergson, *Matter and Memory* (New York, 1971), 77.

27 Walter Benjamin, 'On the Image of Proust', *Illuminations*, ed. Hannah Arendt (London, 1973), 198. Originally published in *Literarische Welt* (1929); German text here from *Schriften* (Frankfurt-am-Main, 1955).

28 *Erinnern, Wiederholen und Durcharbeiten* (1914), in *Gesammelte Werke*, 18 vols., x: 1913–1917 (Frankfurt-am-Main, 1991). On the continuing importance of this text, and its integral part in Freud's writing, see Adam Phillips, 'On Remembering, Repeating and Working Through, Again', *Contemporary Psychoanalysis* 52 (2016), 375–82.

29 'Remembering, Repeating and Working Through', tr. John Reddick, *Beyond the Pleasure Principle and Other Writings*, The New Penguin Freud, ed. Adam Phillips (London, 2003), 35.

30 Freud, 'Remembering, Repeating and Working Through', 37.

31 Freud, 'Remembering, Repeating and Working Through', 41.

32 Phillips, 'On Remembering, Repeating and Working Through, Again', 378.
33 *Realms of Memory*, 8.
34 Eamon Duffy, *The Stripping of the Altars: Traditional Religion in England, 1400–1580*, 2nd ed. (New Haven and London, 2005), 355. Duffy's book followed the revisionist manifesto of *The English Reformation Revised*, ed. Christopher Haigh (Cambridge, 1987).
35 *Stripping of the Altars*, 56.
36 Eamon Duffy, *The Voices of Morebath: Reformation and Rebellion in an English Village* (New Haven and London, 2001), 181.
37 Marx, 'The Eighteenth Brumaire of Louis Bonaparte', *Marx's Eighteenth Brumaire: Postmodern Interpretations*, ed. Mark Cowling and James Martin (London, 2002), 19.
38 Marx, 'The Eighteenth Brumaire of Louis Bonaparte', 21.
39 *Luthers Werke: kritische Gesamtausgabe*, 68 vols. (Weimar, 1883–1999), liv: 180–1.
40 Brian Cummings, *The Literary Culture of the Reformation: Grammar and Grace* (Oxford, 2002), 60–8.
41 Patricia Caldwell, *The Puritan Conversion Narrative: The Beginnings of American Expression* (Cambridge, 1985), 58–9.
42 Nietzsche, *Untimely Meditations*, tr. R. J. Hollingdale, Cambridge Texts in the History of Philosophy (Cambridge, 1997), 63.
43 Nietzsche, *Untimely Meditations*, 62.
44 Among many examples, see Carlos M. N. Eire, *Reformations: The Early Modern World, 1450–1650* (New Haven, 2016); and Brad S. Gregory, *The Unintended Reformation* (Cambridge, MA, 2012).
45 Nietzsche, *Untimely Meditations*, 76.
46 British Museum, Inventory No. 1891, 0224.3. See https://exhibitions.lib.cam.ac.uk/reformation/artifacts/commemorative-tableware-a-dutch-delftware-charger/.
47 See https://exhibitions.lib.cam.ac.uk/reformation/artifacts/an-imagined-reformation-roundtable/.
48 Sheila O'Connell, *The Popular Print in England 1550–1850* (London, 1999), 129–31.
49 Pamela Tudor-Craig, 'Group Portraits of the Protestant Reformers', in *Art Reformed: Reassessing the Impact of the Reformation on the Visual Arts*, ed. Tara Hamling and Richard Williams (Newcastle, 2007), 87–102.
50 Alexandra Walsham, 'History, Memory and the English Reformation', *HistJ* 55 (2012), 899–938 (927–33). See also Alexandra Walsham, 'Domesticating the Reformation: Material Culture, Memory and Confessional Identity in Early Modern England', *RenQ* 69 (2016), 566–616. On the multiple migrations of this print in Continental Europe, see Joke Spaans, 'Faces of the Reformation', *Church History and Religious Culture* 97 (2017), 408–51.
51 Kevin D. Murphy, *Memory and Modernity: Viollet-le-Duc at Vézelay* (University Park, 2000).
52 Michael Camille, *The Gargoyles of Notre-Dame: Medievalism and the Monsters of Modernity* (Chicago, 2008).
53 Freud, *Moses and Monotheism*, ed. James Strachey, Penguin Freud Library, 15 (Harmondsworth, 1986), 293.
54 Jacqueline Rose, *States of Fantasy*, Clarendon Lectures in English (Oxford, 1996), 11.
55 Lawrence L. Langer, *Admitting the Holocaust: Collected Essays* (Oxford and New York, 1995), 19.
56 Jean-François Lyotard, *Heidegger and 'the Jews'*, tr. Andreas Michel and Mark S. Roberts (Minneapolis, 1990), 12.
57 Jeremy Black, *The Holocaust: History and Memory* (Bloomington, 2016), 157.
58 Aleida Assmann, *Shadows of Trauma: Memory and the Politics of Postwar Identity* (New York, 2016).
59 Figures from a variety of summaries by Matthew White in *Necrometrics* (January 2012). These are figures for wars only, which of course have other causes than religion alone.
60 Brad Gregory, *Salvation at Stake: Christian Martyrdom in Early Modern Europe* (Cambridge, MA, 1999), 6.

61 See https://exhibitions.lib.cam.ac.uk/reformation/artifacts/john-foxes-book-of-martyrs-staking-a-claim-to-the-past/.

62 John Foxe, *Actes and monuments of matters most speciall and memorable, happenyng in the Church with an vniuersall history of the same, wherein is set forth at large the whole race and course of the Church, from the primitiue age to these latter tymes of ours, with the bloudy times, horrible troubles, and great persecutions agaynst the true martyrs of Christ* (London, 1583 ed.), sig. 5G3r.

63 *Ecclesiae Anglicanæ trophaea: Siue Sanctor, Martyrum, Qui Pro Christo Catholicæque* (Rome, 1584). See https://exhibitions.lib.cam.ac.uk/reformation/artifacts/catholic-martyrology-trophies-and-inspirations/.

64 https://rememberingthereformation.org.uk/.

65 Digital exhibition: 'Remembering the Reformation', housed at Cambridge University Digital Exhibitions: https://exhibitions.lib.cam.ac.uk/reformation/.

PART I

Repressed memory

2

STILLED LIVES, STILL LIVES

Reformation memorial focus

James Simpson

Cultural historians are predisposed to prize memory, since memory is the very stuff of historiographical tradition. 'Memory' is one of those apple pie words that connote the tradition — the passing on — of a given community. We therefore normally think of 'remembrance' as a nurturing, restorative act.

In this essay, however, I point to the ways in which early English Reformation deployment of the words 'memory' and 'remembrance' packs a dynamically aggressive, non-restorative, *anti*-tradition punch. Tradition moves, from past to present. In early modern evangelical culture, however, the obligation to remember the singularity of the one-off scriptural event, or to repudiate traditions not authorised by Scripture, necessitated stopping tradition dead in its tracks. One-off scriptural events needed to be apprehended in their own, divine terms, and not in any 'traditional', 'human', merely 'imaginative', or mobile terms. In Reformation evangelical culture, that is, 'memory' was a key word, and memory aggressively militated *against* tradition. Tradition is, of necessity, a mobile phenomenon; anti-tradition memory targets that mobility, and insists instead on stillness.

I address this theme by considering an extraordinary image by Pieter Saenredam (1597–1665) [Fig. 2.1], painted in 1628.

No painting like Saenredam's exists in Reformation England, mainly, in my view, because English iconoclasm was so centralised and effective. Despite the very different, much less centralised conditions of the early seventeenth-century Dutch Republic,[1] I nonetheless take the liberty of using a Dutch example to point to English experience because the painting is so profoundly expressive of Reformation predicaments generally. It is one of Saenredam's very first paintings of church interiors.[2] My essential observation with regard to the painting is as follows: that its own centenary remembrance of the Reformation is melancholy and still. The resonant poise of its stillness derives from its capacity to balance two memorial projects. On the one hand, the painting memorialises the triumphalist completeness

FIGURE 2.1 Pieter Saenredam, *Transept of the St Bavokerk, Haarlem, from north to south,* 1628. Panel, 37 x 46 cm.
Malibu, The J. Paul Getty Museum. Public domain.

of a revolutionary project: the Church is restored to its primitive purity; on the other, the painting can memorialise only by signalling tradition that has been unremembered. The memorial project is caught, and almost stilled, between the effort to remember and the pressure to forget. Reflection on the painting will help us understand both Reformation memorialisation, or rather de-memorialisation, and the existential anguish of that de-memorialisation. Those understandings serve as a prelude to a brief attempt to understand our own challenges in remembering the Reformation, the theme of this volume as a whole.

Saenredam's nearly still 1628 St Bavo

Saenredam's painting dates, as I say, from 1628; it is among the first of many paintings by him of the interior of the Church of St Bavo in Haarlem, especially from the period 1628–1636, although he continued to paint Bavo interiors until at least 1660.[3] The church of St Bavo had been rebuilt in the 1470s after a fire destroyed the building in 1470, and had been elevated to the status of cathedral only in 1559.[4] It had escaped the so-called *Beeldenstorm*, or iconoclasm, in the Seventeen Provinces of the Hapsburg Netherlands in 1566, and again in 1573, 'when... Reformed adherents tried to appropriate the cathedral'.[5] The church was, however, soon to suffer its own bout of iconoclasm. Despite the city's final capitulation in brutal siege of Haarlem by Spanish forces under the Duke of Alba in 1573, by 1577 Haarlem's status was determined by the Agreement of Veere. Now under Protestant control, troops of the Prince of Orange attacked the church on Sacrament Day, 29 May 1578, and stripped it of images.[6] Saenredam painted this painting, then, from a Protestant-controlled, Calvinist Haarlem, precisely 50 years after the church had been stripped, and just over 100 years after the beginning of the Reformation.

Before analysis, description. What do we see? A space requiring orientation from its viewer, since the painting is projected from a position askew to the main lines of the building it represents. The painter is placed in the north transept looking across to the south transept, but even within the lines of those transepts, the artist has angled himself off centre, producing only architectural asymmetries. As disoriented viewers we need, therefore, to make sense of, and mentally reconstruct, the entire space of the church as implied from this deliberately awkward angle.

As we do so, we are not much helped by the architecture of what is obviously a late medieval, gothic church, whose west–east lines would take us to the high altar, and beyond that altar to Jerusalem in the east. From another painting by Saenredam of 1630, we are invited to imagine that implied west–east line, from the west, where the statue of the praying bishop looks intently east, unlike anyone else in painting [Fig. 2.2].

Contemporary viewers of this painting from 1630 would have been all the more prompted to imagine the bishop's line of vision and prayer, since the statue of the Catholic bishop is Saenredam's invention: it had never existed in St Bavo.[7] (Despite the fact that Saenredam belonged to a Calvinist family,[8] many of his paintings from the early 1630s 'restore' Calvinist church interiors to pre-Reformation states).[9] Of the 13 paintings by Saenredam of the interior of the Bavokerk, only the last, dated 1660, gives us access to that main line of vision in St Bavo [Fig. 2.3], if again slightly off centre. This is a painting from Saenredam's most stringently aniconic period (1650–1660): as we look toward the high altar from the western end of the choir, our sight line towards the now absent altar is partially blocked by a pulpit.

If the architecture in the 1628 painting refuses to co-operate with our effort to gain spatial bearings, neither does it help us establish temporal bearings. We lack any memory system of images of the kind we find placed strategically in the structure of every late medieval church (e.g. the crucifix of the high altar, mediated historically by the images of saints linking chancel and high altar). We can see such mediation in, for example, a painting by Saenredam of the choir of St Janskerk at 's-Hertogenbosch (1646), where statutes of saints under tabernacles, affixed to columns, lead to the high altar.[10] In this painting, Saenredam once again restores the church to the state it had been in before being taken over by the Dutch States forces in 1629; that visual restoration includes an Adoration of the Shepherds on the high altar, filling the space left by a removed painting, and another imagined bishop, painted as if alive, praying on the north side of the choir.

In the 1628 St Bavo painting, by contrast, we witness an image of a basically imageless, whitewashed space, which cannot help evoke, as itself a spectral image,

FIGURE 2.2 Pieter Saenredam, *View across the choir of St Bavokerk, Haarlem, from north to south, with a fictive bishop's tomb,* 1630. 41 x 37.5 cm.
Paris, Musée du Louvre. Reproduced by permission, Art Resource Inc, NY.

what was there before the saints took their leave. The absence of a saint system is simultaneously the diminution of a memory system. And those joint absences — saints and memory — constitute the absence of any system of mediation and representation (i.e. a tradition): to strip the visual representation of the saints is to mark a further stripping of representation: the saints will no longer represent, or intercede for, individual Christians.

Colour offers no help with orientation. Such chromatic distinctions as are made in this painting consist mainly in the play of shades: principally white shading to grey, as produced by light on the architectural forms. We have no clear, chromatically striking images at all. Of the three windows, one to the left, one slightly to the right

FIGURE 2.3 Pieter Saenredam, *Choir of the St Bavokerk, Haarlem, from west to east,* 1660.
Panel, 70.5 x 54.8 cm.
Worcester, MA, Worcester Art Museum. Reproduced by permission, Bridgeman Images.

of our view, and the other high above us, only the highest one depicting the Virgin
(out of reach of the iconoclast's hammer?),[11] represents a specifically religious image;
the other two record secular donors.[12] Each, in any case, makes only a faint,
bleached, chromatic claim, 'wat'rish, bleak and thin', as George Herbert (1593–1633)
says about uninspiring church windows.[13]

There are in fact only two strong chromatic claims in the entire image: rectan-
gular patches on the columns to our left are darkened. These dark spaces are
devoted not to image but to text, in this case poems (dated to 1580 and 1585)
referring to biblical sources.[14] The writing in the column closest to us as viewers
defends the crafts that produce beautiful, crafted cultic objects. It praises the art of
weaving as practiced by Bezalel and Aholiab. This is a reference to Exodus 31 and
35:35 (texts separated by Moses' commanding the destruction of the Golden Calf
in Exodus 32). Exodus 35:35 praises embroidery especially. Exodus 31 is broader in
the range of artistic skills praised:

[2] Behold, I have called by name Bezalel the son of Uri... [3] Whom I have filled with the Spirit of God, in wisdom, and in understanding, and in knowledge, and in all workmanship: [4] To find out curious works to work in gold, and in silver, and in brass, [5] Also in the art to set stones, and to carve in timber, and to work in all manner of workmanship. [15]

In stripped Bavo, then, we have a textual, biblical defence of the production of beautiful, cultic artefacts precisely when those crafted objects were being ejected from churches and destroyed in Calvinist Europe. Biblical texts defending 'curious works' are written into this very artefact, itself a very 'curious work'.

At this descriptive point, we might already be surprised by an analytic paradox: this is a memorial image of an imageless space, inhabited by anxiety about the divine command against images and likenesses. Such anxiety is written onto one of the columns that one could not help but see along the church's main east-west axis. Only by looking askew to those main lines, from a side angle, can Saenredam make a claim for the object — a likeness — that he himself produces. That product — his own painting — is rebuked by the principal, aniconic, force field of the building his own painting represents. Or perhaps one should make that point in reverse: perhaps the painting, that is, rebukes the represented space. Or, again, perhaps the rebuke is mutual: both space and painting quietly rebuke each other.

Nothing is assured of itself here: the *building* tries to undo its own history, and its own status as a shaped space of special, symbolised charisma, since the evangelical True Church is no longer embodied here, in this material church, but is somewhere else.[16] Saenredam's *image* of the building cannot help but be conscious of the precariousness of its own status as forbidden likeness. This is a beautiful image of a building trying to forget images. The beauty of the painting derives in part from the subdued but unsuccessful effort to forget. As such, it is therefore quietly seditious to the project of the current state of the building it represents.

Above all, everything we see is almost entirely still. There is no sacramental activity happening in this church, no real presence. On the contrary, we enter the church via a peculiar angle, in an off period, when only three humans happen to be there too, and when those figures are themselves examining the church as tourists would, one pointing up to a feature above, another reading a funerary inscription,[17] as if to remember some historical point. The figures are tiny, especially so given the vertically elongated presentation of the church interior. But nothing moves in this spectral space, which as a whole seems so determined not to remember. When we look to the place where the altar on which the Eucharist would have been consecrated before 1578, at the far east end of the choir, as we can in the painting of 1660 by Saenredam mentioned earlier, we are conscious only of a spectral absence. It can be no accident that the 1578 iconoclasm took place on Sacrament Day.

If the church in Saenredam's painting is anything to go by, the Reformation longs to forget. Saenredam's memorial painting, by contrast, longs to remember, but can only do so by registering the spectral absence of the suppressed past. As we remember the Reformation, then, we do so via a period — the 150 traumatic years of the Reformation itself — that has profoundly marked us all, including our own protocols of remembrance, and that longs not to remember. In my description, I said that the interior of the church was entirely still. The painting itself, however, is not quite *entirely* still: it's a work of art, and we can see it at work, remembering what has been unremembered. The beauty of the painting derives, I think, from that hardly perceptible movement: it is beautiful, and suffused with divine presence of a kind, because only *nearly* still, but still moving.

In this essay I want to penetrate the paradox of Saenredam's haunting painting, which subtly remembers, by recording systems of deliberate, not to say traumatic forgetting. I have begun, and will return to, the *aesthetic* feature of memorial stillness as the place to unlock the paradox. In the next section, I articulate the *theological* pressure that underlines early modern evangelical aesthetic stillness, and the personal, existential anguish that must accompany it. In my conclusion, I briefly ask how the Reformation's own forms of forgetting, remembering and stilling shape our current historiographical predicaments.

Theology and stillness

I begin our attempt to penetrate Saenredam's haunting stillness by looking beyond the Reformation to the practice of all revolutions, and in particular to the stilling practices of all successful revolutionary movements. Each revolution claims to usher in the rational, enlightened order, redistributing life- and light-giving animation, and liberating the credulous from mental slavery as it does so. Revolutions, that is, always redistribute accounts of what is allowed to move and what should remain still, what is animate and what isn't. The moving elements are the 'real' drivers of history, and so susceptible of licit animation and personification ('The Gospel', or 'class struggle', for example). Forces that are thought to move the counter-revolutionary, and, more worryingly, move *for* the counter-revolutionary (e.g., in the Reformation period, an image of a saint, or a moving crucifix), are re-described as either phony or diabolically possessed.[18]

The revolution needs to describe, that is, what moves and what must remain still, across the entire revolutionary landscape. In England, sixteenth-century evangelicals accordingly tried to make a chasm between the living and the newly anonymised dead, as in the 1552 Book of Common Prayer, or, in the seventeenth century, more brutally, in the *Directory for Public Worship* of the Westminster Assembly of 1644.[19] Further, no revolution likes moving revenants, even if occasionally a traveller from that bourn seems briefly to return.[20] Reformation theology shares with all revolutionary movements a suspicion of visitors from the *ancien régime* moving illicitly into the present: such movement undoes the non-negotiable claim of the revolution to have started time afresh.

Reformation theologians had, however, a distinctive reason to keep the past still, and to neutralise its force as any kind of ongoing tradition. For all stripes of Reformation theology, past events are past events. The key scriptural events happened once; *that* they happened is decisive, but they have no ongoing, propulsive force in the present. Their occurrence in the past has no figural, determinative spill-over into the futurity of their own moment, and neither can the moment of the past be recreated, or re-presented, in its fullness in the present; the past event is in no way a real presence. The key events themselves turn out, that is, to be still. They don't work in the present. Only bad, erroneous history moves. Only bad, erroneous history creates a tradition.

This insistence on the historical singularity and unicity of biblical events derives from Reformation theology's most profound ecclesiological commitment to Scripture as the only legitimate ground of practice. Any practice without explicit scriptural foundation is to be rejected. For this reason Protestantism is, from the beginning, suspicious of moving tradition in any form, including traditions of its own.[21] Reformation theology is, therefore, in principle temperamentally hostile to the idea of scriptural events being fully available, and reproducible, in the present. Scriptural events are one-off, deserving only of memorialisation. They happened then, not now. They have, as I say, no 'real presence' in the present. They don't move.

Determination to remember that unreproducible moment of the past produces its own powerful impulse to destroy competing forms of memory, and in particular the competing, soul-destroying memory system that was passed on by tradition. The very word 'tradition', indeed — very frequently used in early modern evangelical writing — is *always* pejorative as used by evangelicals, used in phrases such as 'the stinking puddles of men's traditions'.[22] 'Tradition' always signals human invention; it forms part of a lexical set with 'human', 'imagination', and 'invention'. That which is human, invented, the product of imagination, and traditional is, by definition, not grounded in Scripture, and not divinely authorised. Tradition is what moves, and it moves away from a still, scriptural, pre-human, divine beginning, which is always only itself. In consequence, tradition is life-threatening and must be ejected from the still, unchanging, salvific forms of the True Church.

A systematic commitment to strip away tradition therefore produced a fiercely anti-tradition tradition. Anti-traditionalism applied with destructive force to the entire apparatus of the Catholic Church — its iconography, its sacraments, its liturgy, its cult of saints, and its ecclesiastical structures. We shall return to the destruction of images; the principal source of aggression against the ongoing, real presence of scriptural events is directed, however, against the sacramental system of the Catholic Church, and in particular against the Eucharist. Reformation theologians rejected five of the seven sacraments of the Catholic sacramental system (i.e. Confirmation, Penance, Orders, Matrimony, and Extreme Unction) as mere traditions. Only two of the seven Catholic sacraments, the Eucharist and Baptism, survived.[23] But the preserved Eucharist was itself subjected to the logic of anti-traditionalism, a logic that stills the event deep in the past, blocking its power to work through re-presentation in the present. In Zwinglian and Calvinist Europe the Eucharist quickly became a stilled, memorial event, rather than a real and ongoing presence.

Within the larger debate about the sacraments provoked by Luther's *Babylonian Captivity of the Church* (1520),[24] a three-cornered debate erupted concerning the Eucharist, among Catholics, Lutherans, and followers of Ulrich Zwingli (1484–1531). That debate consisted principally of argument about what Christ meant by 'is' in his statement 'ΤΟῦΤΟ ἐστιν τὸ σῶμά μου', or "Hoc est corpus meum", "This is my body" (Matthew 26:26; Mark 14:22; Luke 22:19; and 1 Corinthians 11:22).

There were three distinct positions, Catholic, Lutheran and Zwinglian, each with their nuances and varieties, but clearly distinguishable. The orthodox Catholic view ('transubstantiation') held that Christ meant 'is' literally when he said 'this is my body'; Christ's body is therefore actually present in the Eucharistic host. We can pass over the Lutheran view, not in fact very far from the Catholic position. The Zwinglian view argued, by contrast, that Christ was not using the word 'is' literally when he said 'This is my body': the word 'is' should instead be understood rhetorically. It really means 'signifies'. Christ is, therefore, only in one place when the host is being celebrated, and that place is in heaven. The communicant is not re-experiencing the sacrifice of Christ, but instead remembering it; the host is not generating faith so much as demonstrating that faith publicly.[25]

In England, William Tyndale already adopted the Zwinglian view of memory over presence, of 'signifies' over 'is', in his *Brief Declaration on the Sacraments* (1533–1535). Rightly taught, rightly understood, and rightly remembered, the sacrament is, by Tyndale's account, a form of record. Sacraments serve the same function as stories of memorable events; there is 'no other virtue in them, than to testify… the covenants and promises made in Christ's blood'. The Zwinglian position was instituted by the 1549 edition of the Book of Common Prayer.[26]

It was this view of liturgical memory that had become official policy already within the reign of Henry VIII, a memorial posture with regard to the past that was extended to a wide range of cultic practices. The Second Royal Injunctions of Henry VIII of 1538, for example, order bishops to destroy such images in their dioceses as are used for idolatrous purposes, and to teach their parishioners that such images serve the purposes only of remembrance: the illiterate must only remember, lest 'they abuse for any other intent than for such remembrances', and so 'commit idolatry in the same, for the greater danger of their souls'.[27]

The ostensibly conservative 1539 proclamation, the so-called Six Articles,[28] insists on the same concept of memory: 'Neither holy bread nor holy water, candles, bows, nor ashes hallowed, or creeping and kissing the cross be the workers or works of our salvation, but only be as outward signs and tokens whereby we remember Christ and his doctrine.'[29] The proclamation lists a series of cultic practices, in each of which the word 'remembrance', or 'memory', signals a re-categorisation: no longer do rituals serve as channels through which the past flows into the present, but instead provoke memory. Holy water is sprinkled 'to put us in remembrance of our baptism'; giving of holy bread puts 'us in remembrance of unity'; the bread is made of many grains, 'to put us in remembrance of the housel'; the bearing of candles on Candlemas day is done 'in memory of Christ'; ashes on Ash Wednesday are given to put Christians 'in remembrance of penance'; bearing of palms on Palm Sunday 'reneweth the memory of the receiving of Christ'. Key moments or associations of the past are neutralised, or at least contained, by being described as one-off events, worthy of remembrance but without continuing operations in the present. All these practices will soon themselves be abolished as examples of tradition, but the first move in the anti-tradition campaign is to deny their efficacy in the present; they are non-moving, non-working memorial events.

Theology compacted in still-life painting

As we return, then, to Saenredam's image, we are better placed to understand the function of stillness. The triumphalist stillness of the church of St Bavo answers to the state of the True Church, imagined as imageless, even if the architectural structure of the medieval church itself remains to remind us of the pre-modern commitment to places of especial spiritual charisma. Stillness and whiteness attempt to replicate the integrity of that beginning, and to honour the commitment of memory against tradition.

This triumphalist undoing of tradition comes, however, at existential cost. That anti-tradition memorial effort must whitewash the recent Catholic memory systems. The very form of this painting, in its principal aspects of colour and point of view, represents and analyses the aggressive undoing of tradition in action.

The aggression of that anti-tradition, memorial effort leaves an indelible residue of melancholy in the painting. The effort to honour the integral, tradition-less stillness of the past produces an empty, haunting stillness in the present. It is beautiful, in a new kind of austere, abstract, flat beauty, as Zwingli accurately observed of whitewashed walls: '...die Wänd sind hüpsch wyss'.[30] But it's a melancholy beauty, and it takes a while to attune to it, as suggested by a comment made in 1581, that there 'are very few that can agree to the Genevans' fashion, to have no thing in the church but naked walles'.[31]

The moment recorded by Saenredam's painting, when memory targets tradition with those white walls, in fact marks a moment in the history of the very notion of the work of art. For this is the moment when the category of the aesthetic and the visual gains new traction as an autonomous practice of enquiry and expression in relation to text, community, and history. That moment also heralds a new, specific form of melancholy, not to say personal anguish. We can see Saenredam's commentary on this new discursive formation in this painting of the interior of St Odulphus' Church in Assendelft, painted in 1649 [Fig. 2.4].

The point of view is from the choir looking west. Many of the features of the painting will now be familiar to us from the St Bavo image: the whitewashed, imageless space; the stillness. Unlike St Bavo, this is a populated space, but like St Bavo it's a space dominated by the Word at the expense of the image: the dominant architectural form is the pulpit, from which the Calvinist preacher expounds the biblical text. The almost total absence of images (except for the armorial shields) is belied, however, by two Saenredam contributions: the painting itself, which we are likely not to see as we look through it; and the represented tombstone on the bottom right, which we could easily, and literally, overlook.

The painting is, needless to repeat, by Pieter Saenredam. St Odulphus' Church in Assendelft is the family church of the Saenredams, and the gravestone is that of Saenredam's father, Jan Saenredam, marked as the tomb of 'Iohannis Saenredam, Sculptoris Celeberrimi'. Jan Saenredam had died in 1607, and had been a successful engraver of classical mythological subjects in an Italian style. In this painting, the represented congregation listens in silence and stillness to the distinctively early

FIGURE 2.4 Pieter Saenredam, *Crossing and nave of the St Odulphuskerk, Assendelft, from the right side of the choir*, 1649. Panel, 50 x 76 cm.
Rijksmuseum, Amsterdam (on loan from the City of Amsterdam).

modern culture of the Word and the Word alone. One artistic culture — that of the father — lies entombed in that textual stillness, and another — that of the son — exerts its form and pressure as we imagine ourselves listening. The Word is triumphant, the art is melancholic; both are entirely still.

As a new form of aesthetic autonomy took shape in Northern European painting in the sixteenth century, it is no accident that it should have expressed itself so powerfully through still-life, a term in English we derive from the Dutch *stilleven*. [32] We cannot narrate the history of the genre in England, since the visual artistic tradition was so aggressively stopped there by more than a century of legislated iconoclasm between 1538 and 1643. [33] We can, however, see with especial clarity the possibility of a discursive formation focused on visual stillness in the writings of Calvin (1509–1564).

Calvin was much more explicitly hostile to the idolatry of images than Luther. He located idolatry deep within the human psyche, describing it as 'a factory of idols'. [34] Destroying all images is, however, too tall an order even for Calvin. His solution was to limit the power of images in two ways: one must only paint things that could have been perceptible to the eye, and secondly one must restrict oneself to licit subjects. These are, respectively, histories that teach, and 'images and fashions of bodies, without expressing any of the things done by them'. [35] The second set of licit subjects, by which Calvin seems to designate still-life, is designed only to give pleasure, and has no purpose 'praeter oblectationem' ('beyond pleasure'); it is 'sans aucune signification'. [36] It has no didactic or other function.

We see the future directions in Northern European painting spring into profile with this set of prohibitions and permissions: Calvin's *Institutes* (first published 1536) give, that is, an enormous impulse to portraiture, still-life, and landscape. What we had taken as a new secular culture is in fact in silent dialogue with a repressed culture of the religious image.[37]

We can see these artistic possibilities, and the melancholy they provoke, expressed throughout the extremely well-attested genre of Dutch still-life painting that flourished in the sixteenth and seventeenth centuries. Take, for just one radiant example, the astonishing image by Willem Claesz Heda (1594–1680), another Haarlem painter, from 1651: 'Breakfast still life with ham and wine.'[38] In images such as these we approach an ever receding limit of the stillest moment, always melancholy, and often poised, as here, between the material and the spiritual: the spiritual is registered discreetly (one can note the unmistakable sacramental resonances of chalice, wine, flesh, cloth),[39] but discretion hovers on the edge of irrelevance. The chalice has been overturned. Still-life stands forever under the sentence of abstraction, waiting just behind the still-life image, after the material mess of the *vanitas* has been cleared up. When Bishop Hooper directed the replacement of windows in Gloucester and Worcester in 1551–1552, he determined that 'if they will have anything be painted, that it be either branches, flowers, or posies [texts] taken out of Holy Scripture'.[40] Most of the glass was, of course, replaced with 'white glass', on what was known as a process of 'whiting the church'.[41]

Historiography and stillness

The Reformation, then, produced a theology and aesthetics of stillness and fixity. The demand to remember single, fixed moments in the past imposed a correlative need to repudiate moving tradition. In this final section I turn briefly to the historiographical consequences of that aggressively anti-tradition praxis of memory.

The Reformation, as an ecclesiological revolution that produced a political revolution, shaped, and continues to shape, memory in specific ways.[42] All revolutions do this, and all make remembrance especially difficult. As Alexis de Tocqueville so astutely observed, 'When great revolutions are successful, their causes cease to exist… the very fact of their success has made them incomprehensible'.[43] Successful revolutions all, that is, determine the shapes of memory, and they all aim, with their implausible claim to have started history afresh, to close off the pre-revolutionary past. A given society's cultural investment in its own successful revolutions is so profound that the historical memory has no choice but to confront a dominant narrative of recovery from near death.

The success of the Protestant Reformation has made it especially difficult to remember, if we believe, as I do, that ecclesiological convulsions are, up to the eighteenth century at least, the most powerful and long lasting form of historical convulsion. The seismic effects of an ecclesiological revolution ripple for longer through the culture than those of political revolutions, since the claims of the ecclesiological revolution extend more widely, intimately and lastingly into a culture's every fibre. To recognise ourselves, we have no choice but to negotiate with the forms of recognition and memory promoted by the ecclesiological revolution itself.

The principal historiographical challenge we, as cultural historians of the Reformation, face is, in my view, as follows: the Reformation has bequeathed to us, in secular form, a still-life historiography. As secular historians, we tend to hold an almost religious belief that anachronism is heresy, that one must treat the historical moment wholly in its own terms, free of teleology, free of grand narrative — free, in sum, of ourselves.[44] We must prioritise memory (of single points in time) above tradition. Our historiographical practice is grounded, that is, on the conviction that the synchronic meaning of an event has primacy over the meaning of that event through time. Questions of meaning at precisely defined points *within* past time take priority over meanings *through* time. Such historiography is, therefore, micro in focus and of *courte durée*.

Such strenuously synchronic historiography carefully avoids divagating into any suggestion that the past may prophetically signal the future. As we strive to make the asymptotic approach to the atomic historical moment so as to guarantee our historiographical probity, we continue to repudiate historiography that is attentive to the ways in which an event is both prophetic of the future, and resonant of its own past. We are engaged thereby in an ascetic project of alienating our own place in history from the historiographical project. In sum, we continue to the treat the event most deeply grounded in, and productive of, very long histories as if it had no claim on the future, as if it were, that is, still-life.

There are, to be sure, profound cognitive and ethical reasons why we respect the integrity of the past moment and why we attempt to contain its movement. Above all, we must remain forever vigilant against merely appropriating the past to serve present interest and power. The benefits to be gained from rigorous avoidance of anachronism tend, however, to render history simultaneously true and irrelevant. For we cannot understand our own place in history, or our own way out of history's predicaments, unless we locate ourselves in its ongoing tradition.[45] Traditions bequeath to us the very terms of our impulse to understand history, whether we know it or not.

All I have just said about 'still-life' historiography is, happily, changing in the extraordinary burst of ongoing energy released by Eamon Duffy's *Stripping of the Altars*, published in 1992. Ecclesiastical history has taken its proper place on centre stage over the last twenty five years. In cultural history, however, the histories of (for example) agency, of the image, of secular art, of theatre, of despair, of place, of architecture, of election, and of political liberties all still require *longue durée* cultural historiography.[46]

The historiographical breakthrough Duffy's work enacted has us looking in 2017 at a Saenredam less for what the Calvinist redecorators of St Bavo would have us remember in triumphalist spirit, and more for what they would have us forget. The tone of our memorials of the Reformation are, in 2017, unlike previous Reformation centenaries,[47] more energised by the possibilities of making history whole than by triumphalist celebration of what had been repressed.

How do we realise that energy? How do we break out of still partially paralysed historiographical still-life? All Saenredam's church interior paintings urge us to move beyond synchronic understanding, poised as they all are between competing temporalities. For some final inspiration, let us return to a further image, Saenredam's 1636 *Interior of St Bavo* [Fig. 2.5].

Here we have an image represented *in* the church; it was there all along, immanent in the fabric of the building. Not only that, but it is a joyful image, certainly not at all still, and pointing prophetically to the future. I refer, of course,

FIGURE 2.5 Pieter Saenredam, *View across the choir of the St Bavokerk, Haarlem, from the south ambulatory towards the large and small organs and the Christmas Chapel,* 1636. Panel, 95.6 x 57 cm.
Rijksmuseum, Amsterdam.

to the image of the risen Christ that appears once the organ cabinet has been swung open. As a late medievalist I take inspiration from this glorious image in a variety of ways, but especially because Saenredam seeks to revivify history by making history whole. He does so by reaching back beyond the boundary of the Reformation, and by representing a moving image (and an organ!),[48] in late medieval, fifteenth-century style from the past, as the way of pointing beyond the wounded present and into the future.

Notes

1   For the decentralised political conditions of the Dutch Republic, see Freya Sierhuis, *The Literature of the Arminian Controversy: Religion, Politics and the Stage in the Dutch Republic* (Oxford, 2015), 12–13.
2   Benezit Dictionary of Artists, 'Pieter Saenredam', accessed 31 May 2018, https://www. oxfordartonline.com/benezit.
3   For Saenredam's career, see Gary Schwartz and Marten Jan Bok, *Pieter Saenredam: The Painter and His Time* (London, 1990). For Saenredam's first church interior paintings, including this one (at Fig. 67, p. 63), see chapter 5, 57–76. For the period of especial focus on St Bavo (1634–1636), see Schwartz and Bok, *Pieter Saenredam*, 105–29.
4   Mia M. Mochizuki, *The Netherlandish Image after Iconoclasm, 1566–1672: Material Religion in the Dutch Golden Age* (Aldershot, 2008), 26.
5   Mochizuki, *The Netherlandish Image after Iconoclasm*, 105.
6   Mochizuki, *The Netherlandish Image after Iconoclasm*, 105–6.
7   Schwartz and Bok, *Pieter Saenredam*, Fig. 72, p. 71.
8   Schwartz and Bok, *Pieter Saenredam*, 21.
9   The praying bishop is but one example of Saenredam's deliberately anachronistic insertion of Catholic elements and practices into the Reformed space of St Bavo in the very early 1630s; for the other examples (e.g. a drawing dated 1630, which includes the tomb of a non-existent Catholic bishop, and a 1631 painting representing a Catholic baptism scene that could not have taken place in St Bavo since 1578), see Schwartz and Bok, *Pieter Saenredam*, pp. 67 and 74 respectively. For the scholarship on these deliberate anachronisms, see Almut Pollmer-Schmidt, 'Imagined Spaces: Perspectives on the Study of Church Interiors and Cityscapes', in *The Ashgate Research Companion to Dutch Art of the Seventeenth Century*, ed. Wayne Franits (London, 2016), 129–50 (136–7). See also Angela Vanhaelen, *The Wake of Iconoclasm: Painting the Church in the Dutch Republic* (University Park, PA, 2012), 44–66.
10   Schwartz and Bok, *Pieter Saenredam*, Fig. 215; for detailed analysis and discussion of the deliberately Catholicising restorations, see pp. 204–6. See also Figs. 87 and 89 for 1632 drawings of the same site.
11   Margaret Aston points out the sheer expense of replacing the glass in broken windows; see *Broken Idols of the English Reformation* (Cambridge, 2016), 635–6.
12   Schwartz and Bok, *Pieter Saenredam*, 71.
13   George Herbert, 'The Windows', in *The Complete English Poems*, ed. John Tobin (London, 1991), line 10, p. 61.
14   The texts were ordered by, respectively, the weavers' guild (1580) and the greengrocers' guild (1585). They were 'painted on the columns when the church was transformed from Catholic to Reformed' (Schwartz and Bok, *Pieter Saenredam*, 71), and 'were commissioned by civic guilds whose altars had formerly stood at these sites' (Vanhaelen, *The Wake of Iconoclasm*, 4). These texts are still visible and legible today. The texts are written in poetry, and in alexandrine meter. The first, established by the weavers' guild, praises the art of weaving as having biblical authority: 'In Moyses tijden over menige jaren / Heeft die conste van weeverij al gefloreert / Bezaliel en Ahaliab ghetrouwe dienaren/

Door gods geest gedreuen hebbent self geuseert' ('In the times of Moses over many years did the art of weaving flourish. Bezalel and Aholiab, true servants, themselves practiced it (i.e. the art of weaving)'). I am grateful to my friends Leontine van den Bos and Ad Putter for help with these texts. For the full text and translation, see Mochizuki, *The Netherlandish Image after Iconoclasm*, 338–9.

15 Biblical citation in English from the Geneva Bible, *The Bible and Holy Scriptures conteyned in the Olde and Newe Testament* (Geneva, 1560).

16 The separatist Henry Barrow, for example in keeping with a powerful evangelical repudiation of special places, and a no less powerful evangelical hatred of places that have housed idolatry, recommended in 1590 that evangelicals follow the full logic of both the second commandment, and of the divine mandates as expressed in Deuteronomy 12:2–3, by destroying churches completely. The 'old idolatrous shapes' are 'inseparably inherent unto the whole building'; the only solution is total destruction. See Henry Barrow, *Brief Discoverie of the False Church*, in *The Writings of John Greenwood, 1587–1590: Together with the Joint Writings of Henry Barrow and John Greenwood, 1587–1590*, ed. Leland H. Carlson (London, 1962), 468. Aston, *Broken Idols*, reports that the Rump Parliament, for example, debated three times as to whether or not to demolish 'all cathedral churches' (p. 105). For the evangelical concept of 'place' that underwrites such architectural aggression, see James Simpson, 'Place', in *Cultural Reformations: Medieval and Renaissance in Literary History*, ed. Brian Cummings and James Simpson (Oxford, 2010), 95–112, and further references. See also James P. Walsh, 'Holy Time and Sacred Space in Puritan New England', *American Quarterly* 32, no. 1 (1980), 79–95.

17 Schwartz and Bok, *Pieter Saenredam*, 71.

18 For the destruction of the Rood of Boxley, for example, (which was supposed to move of its own accord), see Aston, *Broken Idols*, 114, 157–8, 724. For rituals by iconoclast soldiers in the 1640s designed to prove that the images are insensate, see Aston, *Broken Idols*, 127. These Civil War tests of the image unknowingly replicate Lollard martyrdoms of the images in the late fourteen century; see Sarah Stanbury, 'The Vivacity of Images: St Katherine, Knighton's Lollards and the Breaking of Idols', in *Images, Idolatry and Iconoclasm in Late Medieval England*, ed. Jeremy Dimmick, James Simpson, and Nicolette Zeeman (Oxford, 2002), 131–50. For the larger presentation of Protestantism as more 'rational', see Alexandra Walsham, 'The Reformation and "The Disenchantment of the World"', *HistJ* 51, no. 2 (2008), 497–528. For the agonising difficulty of fifteenth-century orthodox figures to define the precise degree to which images could or could not move, see James Simpson, 'Orthodoxy's Image Trouble: Images in and After Arundel's Constitutions', in *After Arundel: Religious Writing in Fifteenth-Century England*, ed. Vincent Gillespie and Kantik Ghosh (Turnhout, 2011), 91–113.

19 This is most clearly signalled by changes to the Edwardian Prayer Book. In the first edition (1549), the dead person is addressed by the priest: 'I commend thy soul to God the father almighty, and thy body to the ground'. In the second, revised edition of 1552, the priest addresses not the dead person, but the bystanders around the grave: 'We therefore commit his body to the ground'. See *The Book of Common Prayer: The Texts of 1549, 1559, and 1662*, ed. Brian Cummings (Oxford, 2011), 82, 172 (for the 1559 edition, in this respect identical to 1552). The *Directory*, ratified by the Westminster Assembly in 1645 in order to replace the *Book of Common Prayer*, is much more brutal in its denial of any ceremony for the burial of the dead. The dead shall be buried publically, 'without any Ceremony'. See *A Directory for Publique Worship* (London, 1645), image 22. See also Stephen Greenblatt, *Hamlet in Purgatory* (Princeton, 2001), 310, n. 54.

20 Of course the treatment of ghosts was also extremely sensitive for pre-Reformation culture; for this and the shift to a more draconian boundary between living and dead in the sixteenth century, see Greenblatt, *Hamlet in Purgatory*, chapter 3.

21 For a rich account of this fundamental issue as it applies to Scripture (the key locus for the question of tradition), see George H. Tavard, *Holy Writ or Holy Church?* (London, 1959); see also James Simpson, *Burning to Read: English Fundamentalism and its Reformation Opponents* (Cambridge, MA, 2007), chapter 6 ('History as Error').

22 Cited from 'A Fruitful Exhortation to the Reading and Knowledge of Holy Scripture', in *'Certain Sermons or Homilies' (1547) and 'A Homily against Disobedience and Wilful Rebellion' (1570)*, ed. Ronald B. Bond (Toronto, 1987), 61–7, at 60.

23 The 1536 Henrician *Ten Articles* did not abolish, but did eviscerate, the sacrament of Penance. Penance just survived in those Articles (along with Baptism and the Eucharist), from the seven pre-Reformation sacraments (see *Religion and Society in Early Modern England: A Sourcebook*, ed. David Cressy and Lori Anne Ferrell (London, 1996), 18–20). See also Cummings, *The Book of Common Prayer*, 680 for Article 25 of the Thirty Nine Articles (ratified 1571), specifically limiting the number of sacraments to two (Baptism and the Supper of our Lord).

24 Martin Luther, 'The Babylonian Captivity of the Church', in *Luther's Works*, vol. 36, *Word and Sacrament II*, ed. Abdel Ross Wentz (Philadelphia, 1959), 11–126.

25 For a detailed account of the development of Zwingli's view, see W.P. Stephens, *The Theology of Huldrych Zwingli* (Oxford, 1986), chapter 11, 'The Eucharist'; for the broader picture, see Lee Palmer Wandel, *The Eucharist in the Reformation: Incarnation and Liturgy* (Cambridge, 2006). For the English situation, see James Simpson, 'Tyndale as Promoter of Figural Allegory and Figurative Language: *A Brief Declaration of the Sacraments*', *Archiv für das Studium der Neueren Sprachen und Literaturen* 245 (2008), 37–55. For a succinct summary of all the relevant positions, see Alister E. McGrath, *Reformation Thought*, 3rd ed. (Oxford, 1999), 174–90.

26 See Cummings, *The Book of Common Prayer*, 30: God does 'commaunde us, to celebrate a perpetuall memorye, of that his precious deathe…'.

27 For a conspectus of Henrician and Edwardian legislation against images, see Margaret Aston, *England's Iconoclasts*, vol. 1: *Laws Against Images* (Oxford, 1988), 223–300.

28 For discussion of the environment of these proclamations, see Eamon Duffy, *The Stripping of the Altars: Traditional Religion in England, 1400–1580* (New Haven, 1992), chapters 11 and 12, especially pp. 423–35.

29 P. L. Hughes and J. F. Larkin, eds., *Tudor Royal Proclamations*, 3 vols. (London, 1950–1954) I: no. 188, pp. 278–9. All citations are within these page ranges. For a larger account of the new function of memory in Henrician England, see James Simpson, 'Diachronic History and the Shortcomings of Medieval Studies', in *Reading the Medieval in Early Modern England*, ed. David Matthews and Gordon McMullan (Cambridge, 2007), 17–30.

30 For Zwingli's comment on the beauty of the whitewashed church walls, see Victor Ieronim Stoichita, *L'Instauration du tableau: métapeinture à l'aube des temps modernes* (Paris, 1993), 105. For a specific English example of flattening and making plain, smooth walls from 1571, see Aston, *Broken Idols*, 149: the rood loft (of Winchester Cathedral) is to be 'mured up', 'that the tabernacles of images now standing on the void in the body of the church may be taken away or filled up and the places made plain'.

31 Anthony Gilby, *Pleasaunt Dialogue* (London, 1581), image 13. Cited in Aston, *Broken Idols*, 183.

32 For a survey of scholarship on Dutch still-life painting, see Julie Berger Hochstrasser, 'Still Lively: Recent Scholarship on Still-Life Painting', in *The Ashgate Research Companion to Dutch Art of the Seventeenth Century*, ed. Wayne Franits (Abingdon, 2016), 43–72.

33 Aston, *England's Iconoclasts*, and Aston, *Broken Idols*.

34 John Calvin, *Institutes of the Christian Religion*, ed. John T. McNeill, tr. Ford Lewis Battles (Philadelphia, 1975), 1:11, p. 108. This is an edition of the 1536 edition of Calvin's *Institutio christianae religionis*.

35 The Latin text, from which the Latin phrase is drawn, reads as follows: 'In eo genere partim sunt historiae ac res gestae, partim imagines ac formae corporum, sine ulla rerum gestarum notatione. Priores, usum in docendo vel admonendo aliquem habent; secundae, quid praeter oblectationem afferre prosint non video'. Cited from the 1576 edition of the *Institutio christianae religionis*, 1:11.12, image 36. Calvin, *Institutes*, ed. McNeill, 1:11, p. 112 (though the translation from the Latin is mine, not McNeill's). For discussion see Stoichita, *L'Instauration du tableau*, 107.

36 '...without any signifying power'. Cited from Jean Calvin, *Institution de la religion chrestienne*, ed. Jean-Daniel Benoit, 5 vols. (Paris, 1957), 1:11.12, p. 135.

37 See Stoichita, *L'Instauration du tableau*, 105.

38 Although the painting is in a private collection, it can be viewed online: Willem Claesz Heda, 'Breakfast still life with ham and wine' (1651), *Artstor*, accessed 27 September 2019, https://library.artstor.org/#/assetprint/ARTSTOR_103_41822000696912. Willem Claesz Heda (?1593–?1680–1682) was a Haarlem painter of the Banquet Still Life. For the genre, see Fred G. Meijer, 'Vanitas and Banquet Still Life', in *The Magic of Things: Still-Life Painting, 1500–1800*, ed. Jochen Sander (Ostfilden, 2008), 149–84, especially 153–5.

39 For a vigorous but unpersuasively materialist reading of these banquet paintings (though not of this one in particular), see Simon Schama, *The Embarrassment of Riches: An Interpretation of Dutch Culture in the Golden Age* (London, 1987), 159–63.

40 *Visitation Articles and Injunctions of the Period of the Reformation*, ed. Walter Howard Frere and William McClure Kennedy, 3 vols. (London, 1910), II: 289 (#28).

41 Aston, *Broken Idols*, 629.

42 The abbreviated arguments here are extended in James Simpson, 'Trans-Reformation English Literary History', in *Forms of Time: Temporal Thinking, Periodization, and the Making of Early Modern English History and Literature*, ed. Kristen Poole and Owen Williams (Philadelphia, 2019), 88–101.

43 Alexis de Tocqueville, *The Old Régime and the French Revolution*, tr. Stuart Gilbert (New York, 1955), 5 (first published as *L'ancien régime et la révolution* (Paris, 1856)).

44 See Margreta de Grazia, 'A Story of Anachronism', in Cummings and Simpson, *Cultural Reformations*, 13–32.

45 For which see Hans Georg Gadamer, *Truth and Method*, 2nd ed., tr. Joel Weinsheimer and Donald G. Marshall (London, 1989; first published in German in 1960 as *Wahrheit und Methode*), and the recent, profound reflection on Gadamerian hermeneutics by Thomas Pfau, *Minding the Modern: Human Agency, Intellectual Tradition and Responsible Knowledge* (Notre Dame, 2013), 9–34.

46 See James Simpson, *Permanent Revolution: The Reformation and the Illiberal Roots of Liberalism* (Cambridge, MA, 2019).

47 See, for example, Andrew Atherstone, 'The Stones will Cry Out: Victorian and Edwardian Memorials to the Reformation Martyrs', in this volume.

48 For evangelical determination to undo pre-Reformation musical culture, and the campaign to destroy organs already from the mid-sixteenth century in England, see Aston, *Broken Idols*, 488–542. For an account of Saenredam's 1636 painting as actively intervening in defence of the organ, in a dispute between the city of Haarlem and the Calvinist clergy of St Bavo who wished to silence the organ, see Schwartz and Bok, *Pieter Saenredam*, 124–8.

3

THE INHERITANCE OF LOSS

Post-Reformation memory culture and the limits of antiquarian discourse

Isabel Karremann

In sixteenth- and seventeenth-century Britain, antiquarianism was a key cultural practice for negotiating memories of the Reformation. As scholars from Margaret Aston to Alexandra Walsham have noted, the dissolution of the monasteries and the destruction of saints' images and shrines, stained-glass windows and standing crosses, funeral monuments and bronze inscriptions under the Henrician Reformation created a profound 'sense of literary, cultural and historical loss'.[1] Many antiquaries in the British Isles responded to this experience with what Angus Vine has called a 'resurrective impulse',[2] seeking to salvage from oblivion the remaining traces of the pre-Reformation past. Antiquarian writers often expressed a sense of shame at what was perceived as a fanatic destruction of the country's cultural heritage. John Weever, for instance, called the destroyed monuments 'the shame of our time'[3] and John Stow deemed the iconoclasts 'worthy to be deprived of that memory whereof they have injuriously robbed others'.[4] For others, however, it was the memory of Reformation iconoclasm itself that needed to be preserved, and from this perspective the monastic ruins appeared as signs of God's justice and occasion for grateful remembrance. Well-known examples are the many Dutch engravings showing iconoclastic raids of churches; closer to home, the painting 'An Allegory of the Reformation', features a scene of iconoclasm that Aston has identified as borrowed from Dutch painters. It thus recalls not only a historical event of the Reformation but also an iconographic tradition designed to commemorate it: iconoclasm becomes an iconic sign by which the Reformation is remembered.[5]

These two attitudes toward remembering the Reformation relate to each other as two sides of the same coin, and they illustrate a deep-seated mnemonic anxiety that pervaded antiquarian projects: the antiquaries' aim was either to preserve the traces of the pre-Reformation past, while being constantly reminded by these very traces of how futile any attempt at defying time — or the agents of

Reformation iconoclasm — was; or their antiquarian impulses were compromised by 'their religious beliefs, which convinced them that these were silly superstitions that deserved nothing but contempt'.[6] This paradoxical situation translated into a heightened awareness of the tension between remembering and forgetting that is not only characteristic of antiquarian discourse but also symptomatic of post-Reformation memory culture at large: the collective experience of Reformation iconoclasm necessitated a re-negotiation of attitudes toward memory and oblivion. This resulted in the acknowledgment, often reluctant but sometimes also liberating, that remembering and forgetting functioned as complementary forces in the formation and transformation of memory. The very idea of oblivion was being reformulated: while many persisted in seeing it as mere absence or a threat to memory, oblivion was increasingly recognised as an inherent dimension of memory itself. The inclusion of oblivion changed the deep-structure of cultural memory profoundly.

This becomes particularly manifest in debates which were concerned with ideas and practices of memorialisation. In the controversy over rites of burial and commemoration, for instance, the relationship between remembering and forgetting had to be re-negotiated due to the abolition of traditional practices of commemorating the dead. It would be a mistake, however, to see post-Reformation ritual culture as a mnemonic desert. As the studies by Eamon Duffy and Edward Muir have conclusively demonstrated, the reformed faith itself became the social site at which discarded beliefs could also re-form themselves.[7] More recently, Peter Marshall has argued that changes in ritual practice also affected the ontological and epistemological status of commemorative ritual itself: no longer a habit taken for granted, but a potentially precarious practice that carried with it an awareness of the role that ritual itself might play in forming and deforming memory.[8] This led to a 'markedly heightened sensibility'[9] about the workings of memory in sixteenth- and seventeenth-century Britain, which became particularly manifest with regard to the question of oblivion: when the Catholic exile William Allen noted in 1565 that the Reformation spelled oblivion tout court — 'nowe there is no blessing of mannes memorie at all'[10] — this was a partial and misleading assessment of post-Reformation memory culture. Instead, attitudes toward forgetting ranged across a wide spectrum, from dread and anxiety to indeed even 'a positive advocacy of oblivion'.[11] Whether its connotations were negative or positive, I claim with Marshall that it is this heightened awareness of forgetting, and the development of cultural strategies to come to terms with its spiritual and emotional implications, that became a hallmark of post-Reformation memory culture. This can be observed in many writings concerned with ideas and practices of memorialisation, ranging from theological debates to devotional writings, from epitaphs on funeral monuments to antiquarian texts. In the following, I will explore some of the strategies that antiquarian discourse developed to deal with the inheritance of loss.

Defying oblivion: Camden and Weever

The mnemonic anxieties early antiquarians faced are revealed most clearly in antiquarian texts on the subject of funeral monuments and epitaphs that were
destroyed by Reformation iconoclasm. William Camden's *Britannia* (1586, Engl.
1610), for example, which set the standard for antiquarian endeavours to come,
includes a caveat in the letter from 'The Author to the Reader' that would become
the standard defence for the discussion of Reformation iconoclasm, a difficult topic
under a monarch and a church who had themselves been its main agents:

> There are certaine, as I heare, who take it impatiently that I have mentioned
> some of the most famous Monasteries and their founders. I am sorry to heare
> it, and with their good favour will say thus much, they may take it as impa-
> tiently, and peradventure would have us forget that our ancestours were, as we
> are, of the Christian profession, when as there are not extant any other more
> conspicuous and certaine Monuments of their piety and zealous devotion
> toward God. Neither were there any other seed-gardens from whence Chris-
> tian Religion and good learning were propagated over this isle, howbeit in
> corrupt ages some weeds grew out over-rankly.[12]

While affirming the piety of pre-Reformation believers and insisting on the shared
Christian faith connecting the present with the past, and at the same time admitting
to deplorable excesses, what is above all at stake here is the semantic value of
monuments. Camden decides to read them as signs of 'piety and zealous devotion
toward God' rather than of corruption, and thus defends his own antiquarian project against charges of idolatry.

This defence was repeated almost verbatim twenty years later by John Weever in
the 'Epistle to the Reader' of his *Ancient Funerall Monuments* (1631). Weever
departs from Camden, however, by magnifying the piety of the Catholic past and
the atrocity of iconoclasm respectively. The complete title of Weever's work
announces both the relation to Camden as its model and the author's own creedal
sympathies when it replaces Camden's (or rather, the translator's) neutral formulation *out of the depth of Antiquitie* with a pronounced focus on '*the dissolued Monasteries therein contained; their Founders, and what eminent persons haue beene in the same
interred*'. The introductory letter keeps what the title promises: where Camden
merely 'mention[s]', Weever 'extoll[s]'; Camden's 'piety' becomes 'ardent piety';
'Monasteries' are now specified as 'Abbeys, Priories, and such like sacred Foundations'; Camden's cautious acknowledgement that 'in corrupt ages some weeds grew
out over-rankly' is deleted altogether.[13]

While those few introductory words are pretty much all Camden has to say
about the legacy of Reformation iconoclasm, Weever launches into a lament on
destruction that is indicative of his own, passionately defiant stance as well as of the
changed perspective on sixteenth-century iconoclasm more generally. Under the
high-Anglican Stuart church, and increasingly toward the era of Laud, sympathy

toward the Catholic faith, its relics and rituals, was much more acceptable than during Elizabeth's reign.[14] Looking back from the distance of almost exactly one hundred years, a critique of Henrician iconoclasm becomes the central theme of Weever's 'Epistle to the Reader'. It begins with a comparative account of the monuments, inscriptions and epitaphs to be found on the continent, in order to show by contrast 'how barbarously within these his Maiesties Dominions, they are (to the shame of our time) broken downe, and vtterly almost all ruinated'. The proper reactions to such barbarous acts are grief and, for the antiquarian, the recuperation of the lost past:

> grieuing at this vnsufferable iniurie offered as well to the liuing, as the dead, out of the respect I bore to venerable Antiquity, and the due regard to continue the remembrance of the defunct to future posteritie; I determined with my selfe to collect such memorials of the deceased, as were remaining as yet vndefaced; as also to reuiue the memories of eminent worthy persons entombed or interred, either in Parish, or in Abbey Churches, howsoeuer some of their Sepulchres are at this day no where to be discerned; neither their bones and ashie remaines in any place to be gathered.[15]

Here and in the following, Weever announces his indignation along with his methods of salvaging what has been destroyed: field research (at that time an innovative technique); reliance on oral tradition *in situ* as well as on written church records; reprinting proclamations issued by the government; and correspondence with authorities as well as amateurs, among whom he even enlists the unsuspecting readers, asking them to send him copies of inscriptions and an account of their history (sig. Ar).

In the opening chapter 'Of Monuments in Generall', Weever defines his subject in a way that is indicative of the aims of antiquarian discourse, as well as of its mnemonic limits. 'A monument', he begins,

> is a thing erected, made, or written, for a memoriall of some remarkable action, fit to bee transferred to future posterities. And thus generally taken, all religious Foundations, all sumptuous and magnificent Structures, Cities, Townes, Towers, Castles, Pillars, Pyramides, Crosses, Obeliskes, Amphitheaters, Statues, and the like, as well as Tombes and Sepulchres, are called Monuments. Now aboue all remembrances (by which men have endeauoured, euen in despight of death to give vnto their Fames eternity) for worthinesse and continuance, bookes, or writings, have euer had the preheminence. (1)

What is striking in this passage is Weever's urge to include and salvage everything that can possibly be termed a monument; yet the very comprehensiveness of his definition inspires doubt as to whether such a Sisyphean task can ever be accomplished. In order to cope with this overwhelming range of antiquarian subjects, he introduces a hierarchy of monuments in which the written record has pre-emi-nence: it is more monumental because it is more effective at preserving memory.[16]

In that first chapter Weever self-consciously seeks to contain the oblivional anxiety engendered by the erasure of material monuments through producing a durable written monument. In support, he cites a wide range of classical and con-temporary authors on the immortality of poetry, from Horace, Martial and Ovid to Joachim du Bellay and, most extensively, Edmund Spenser's *The Ruines of Time* (Weever, 4–5). Spenser's poem, however, provides at best ambiguous evidence for Weever's stated belief in the mnemonic superiority of the written, poetic word. As I have shown elsewhere, *The Ruines of Time* challenges the opposition of crumbling monument and permanent poetry. Dedicated to the memory of Sir Philip Sidney, it explores a Protestant poetics of mourning which attempts to come to terms with oblivion as an integral part of commemoration, rather than its opposite. To judge by the epitaph that Weever wrote for Spenser on his death in 1599, he had understood this message quite well.[17] It remains under the surface of *Ancient Funerall Monuments*, however, only to erupt briefly in this first chapter in a short poem attributed to 'a late nameless versifier' but possibly written by Weever him-self, whose condemnation of iconoclasm as a 'barbarous act' it echoes (4). Para-doxically, this poem articulates both his fear of ubiquitous ruin and counteracts his assertion that the written word can provide a stable monument, as this poem 'is in itself a kind of ruin'.[18] Its fragmented form — typical, by the way, of much ruin poetry in post-Reformation England — hints at what Weever seeks to submerge under his exhaustive, learned discourse: the agonising suspicion that the written monument, too, might crumble in the face of ruin.[19] Throughout the rest of his survey, Weever seems to carefully avoid such disruptive moments. Even in chapters 10 and 15, which directly engage with the reformation of religion and the icono-clastic waves under Henry VIII and Edward VI, mercifully stopped by Queen Elizabeth, iconoclasm is not so much condemned as meticulously documented, including the royal orders, proclamations, and commissions that effected the sup-pression (or, under Mary Tudor, the restitution) of religious orders.

Deploying oblivion: Stow

Another treasure-trove of monuments, images and epitaphs destroyed either by time or by iconoclasm is John Stow's *Survey of London* (1598, publ. 1603).[20] This choro-graphical survey of the London wards reconstructs the contemporary cityscape as well as its history. The descriptions of the parish churches constitute a local history of the iconoclastic acts that defaced monuments, erased inscriptions, and turned the sacred spaces of London to secular uses. Typically, Stow coolly records the mere facts and historical circumstances of iconoclasm. A priests' college in Barking parish, Towerstreet ward, for example, 'was suppressed & pulled downe in the yeare 1548, the second of king Edward the sixt, the grounde was imployed as a Garden plot, during the raigns of King Edward, Queene Mary, and parte of Queene Elisabeth, till at length a large strong frame of Timber and bricke was set thereon, and imployed as a store house of Marchantes goodes brought from the sea, by Sir William Winter, &c' (135). Or he states summarily that 'Monumentes of the dead in this Church [were] defaced', adds an apparently complete list (probably drawn from the Church registers) of all people buried in this particular church, and concludes with the regretful remark that since 'their Tombe is pulled downe, no monument remayneth of them' (197). But of course another tomb, a textual tomb, the *Survey* itself, stands in for the destroyed ones and preserves, until today, the memory of those buried in the London churches during the fourteenth to sixteenth centuries. In this sense, Stow's text participates in the compensatory antiquarian project of defying time and restoring the memory of past times to present eyes.

However, Stow was also aware that the project of salvaging the collective memory of London is not always a straightforward process of truthful restoration. The transformation of the material into a textual monument may introduce false memories as well. Giving a survey of 'Candlewicke streete warde', he recounts an almost hilarious instance of misrecognition and misremembering, literally, by the book. Sir William Walworth, the founder of the parish church of S. Michael, was a stockfishmonger, Lord Major of London and, most famously, the captor of the rebel Wat Tyler, for which feat Walworth was knighted by King Richard II. He died in 1385 and

> was there buried in the north Chappell by the Quier: but his monument being amongst other by bad people defaced in the raigne of Edward the sixt and againe since renued by the Fishmongers for lacke of knowledge, what before had beene written in his Epitaph, they followed a fabulous booke, and wrote Iacke Straw, insteade of Wat Tilar, a great error meete to be reformed there, and else where, and therefore haue I the more at large discoursed of this matter. (220)

This passage records a slippage in collective memory, which the recourse to a written account does not so much redress as highlight. The monument of the church founder, Sir William Walworth, which had been destroyed during the Edwardian iconoclastic raids, is restored by members of his guild in commemoration of their illustrious leader; but instead of coupling his name with that which made his own famous, that of Wat Tyler, it is the name of Jack Straw that is erroneously inscribed onto the restored monument. This mistake was an easy one to make, since both Wat Tyler and Jack Straw had been leaders of the 1381 peasants' revolt. It may, however, also have been spurred by the close association with iconoclasm of the substituted name: Jack Straw in particular was notorious for his iconoclastic attitude toward written documents, and thus his name may have more readily suggested itself in connection with acts like that which defaced the original tomb of Walworth. More recently, Straw's rebellion against the social élite as well as the written culture designed to preserve its privileges would have been brought to the collective memory for London theatregoers, including perhaps Stow, by history plays like the anonymous *The Life and Death of Jack Straw* (1591–1592) or

Shakespeare's *Henry VI, Part 2* (1590, rev. 1594–1597), in which Straw is fused with other historical rebels in the figure of Jack Cade. Oblivion, or at least historical error, then, is not always rectified through monumental memory (be it textual or material) but can in fact be produced by it. While Stowe explicitly sees his own textual monument to London as a means of 'reform[ing]' such errors, the passage raises the issue that inscribed monuments, too, can be 'fabulous' rather than factually correct, and that any representation of the past is both informed and potentially deformed by ignorance, imagination, and iconoclastic erasure.

Awareness of the forgotten as a constitutive, if often invisible, part of the antiquarian project manifests itself again and again in the *Survey*. The threatening destruction of London's antiquities, either through former acts of iconoclasm or through contemporary decay and fire, was arguably Stowe's main motivation for transferring perishable material monuments into more durable textual ones. Thus it is perhaps not surprising that Stow's account includes not only epitaphs on famous as well as less-known Londoners, but also an epitaph on images. Describing the London Guild Hall, erected under King Henry VI, Stow notes that the south porch was 'beautified with images of stone' that were pulled down in one of the iconoclastic waves of the previous century. In a gesture typical of the 'imaginative antiquarianism'[21] that Vine has described, Stow crosses the boundaries between history and story, between recollection and imagination. Instead of stating the objective historical facts and measurements of the porch, he offers verses written in the late 1560s by 'William Elderton, at that time an Attorney in the Sheriffes courts there', which commemorate the past act of iconoclasm and, in a performative paradox, counter it at the same time:

> Though most the images be pulled down,
> And none be thought remayne in Towne,
> I am sure there be in London yet,
> Seuen images such, and in such a place,
> As few or none I thinke will hit:
> Yet every day they shew their face,
> And thousands see them euery yeare,
> But few I thinke can tell me where,
> Where Iesu Christ aloft doth stand,
> Law and learning on eyther hand,
> Discipline in the Deuils necke,
> And hard by her are three direct,
> There Iustice, Fortitude and Temperance stand,
> Where find ye the like in all this land? (253)

Instead of explicating the history of the images on the porch, this popular ballad offers a riddle containing a secret map that indicates the location of the seven remaining images in London. Hidden 'in such a place,/ As few or none I thinke will hit', the monumental embodiments of three of the cardinal virtues — justice, fortitude and temperance — are joined by the civic virtues of law, learning and discipline, and presided over by Jesus Christ, providing a moral map for those Londoners who know where to look for them. While an engraving of the post-iconoclasm south porch, produced by Jacob Schnebbelie in 1788,[22] suggests that in fact only the central figure of Jesus Christ had been removed, the verses recreate the entire ensemble in the secret place of the mind where 'thousands see them euery yeare'. The temporal description might either mean 'all the year round', or suggest an annual holiday when these imagined sites are ritually visited and the figures adored. In both cases, the verses poke fun at the efforts of ico-noclasts to entirely erase images from either the cityscape or the popular imagi-nation. Moreover, they raise the haunting possibility of 'many more [images] which still existed, invisible yet undestroyed'.[23] Images and the imaginative habit of moral allegorising cannot be eradicated simply by decree. In this struggle over collective memory is inscribed a struggle between the civic population and an official authority, which is enacted in and emphasised by the genre of the popular ballad inserted into the text of an authoritative antiquarian account. Yet these verses form not so much a counter-discourse as an articulation of antiquarian practice in a different mode: the ballad follows the mnemonic model of both antiquarianism and the ancient *ars memoria* by having the city itself provide the spatial layout for the *loci* where the mind places images of monuments to be recollected. Written down and inserted into the *Survey* some thirty years later, these recollections become a textual monument, consisting not only of the offi-cial text that meets the eye, but also of another, submerged text of hidden mes-sages and obscured memories. The ballad evokes an urban ruin as a double *lieu de mémoire*: the defaced porch is a place that commemorates Reformation icono-clasm and simultaneously evokes the memory of that place as it was before the Reformation. Reading the city of London through an antiquary's eye necessitates a double perspective that takes in both the present and the past, what is there as well as what has been erased.[24] The urban landscape is a result of that double process of remembering and forgetting which is itself the signature of both anti-quarianism and post-Reformation memory culture at large.

Desiring oblivion: Browne

Not everything that is invisible is irretrievably gone, however; and the invisible constitutes an integral part of the archive of the past. Unlike Weever, who understood the destruction of funeral monuments exclusively in terms of erasure and loss, Thomas Browne, writing his *Hydriotaphia, or Urne-Buriall* some sixty years after the *Survey*, would have embraced Stowe's insight that the project of anti-quarianism lies not only in fighting iconoclastic oblivion, but must also take for-getting into account as a force productive of memory. Browne's 'Letter of Dedication' positions the text firmly within the discourse of antiquarianism,[25] even though it is a text that goes beyond its limits. Driven neither by idle curiosity[26] nor, like Weever, by anguished outrage, Browne cites scholarly interest as well as a kind of moral duty as his main motivations: 'We are coldly drawn unto discourses of Antiquities, who have scarce time before us to comprehend new things, or make out learned Novelties. But seeing they [the urns] arose as they lay, almost in silence among us, at least in short account suddenly passed over; we were very unwilling they should die again, and be buried twice among us.'[27] Browne's measured tones here seem to voice confidence in the antiquarian project that is carried out in the first four chapters of the *Hydriotaphia*. However, the same passage already introduces doubts about the feasibility of the antiquarian project, or indeed any attempt at preserving memory. From the perspective of the late-born who 'have scarce time before us' — an apocalyptic view probably inspired less by religious fanaticism than a pragmatic assessment of Civil War England[28] —, it does indeed not make much sense to try and comprehend new things or even to remember the past. When Browne scoffs, 'But who knows the fate of his bones, or how often he is to be buried? who hath the Oracle of his ashes, or whither they are to be scattered?' (509), this differs markedly from the confidence Weever exhibited in his 'Epistle to the Reader', where destruction and oblivion exist only to be overcome by the antiquarian. Exposing the utter folly of desiring posthumous memory in a series of ironic contrasts, Browne articulates a pointed mistrust 'both about the possibility of memorialisation and about the ability of the living to recover true and meaningful messages from the dead'.[29]

But *Hydriotaphia* does not just serve to ridicule and debunk the common errors of his time, as Browne did in *Pseudodoxia Epidemica*.[30] Having indeed exposed the limits of antiquarian discourse as 'posthumous folly' (546), he rather presents in the final chapter a meditation on the conditions of memory in the face of the impermanence of everything on earth, be it human bodies, monuments or ceremonies. In challenging the material and ritual means of preserving memory, he ultimately challenges memory itself. To believe in the permanence of anything created by human hands or minds is, in Browne's words, to succumb to 'a fallacy in duration' (542). Immortality can only be found in Christian transcendence. Interestingly, this transcendence is not set up as an antidote to earthly oblivion, as a kind of superhuman ability of total recall. It is rather itself figured in terms of dissolution and erasure, so that immortality comes to look a lot like oblivion, especially when measured against the attempts at memorialisation surveyed and eventually dismissed in *Urne-Buriall*.

At first sight, *Hydriotaphia* does not overtly engage with the contemporary issue of Reformation iconoclasm. While Browne does write about burial rites — in itself a fraught issue during the protracted process of the Reformation[31] — his text is, unlike Weever's, not a deliberate attempt at salvaging the material traces of funeral monuments destroyed by the iconoclasts. *Hydriotaphia* is instead presented as a piece of occasional writing: 'In a Field of old *Walsingham*, not many moneths past, were digged up between fourty and fifty Urnes, deposited in a dry and sandy soile' (519). The site of this discovery, however, would have rung a bell in contemporary ears: Walsingham Abbey was famously destroyed in the first iconoclastic raids of 1537–8, a traumatic event commemorated later in an anonymous poetic lament on its ruins.[32] By local association at least, the urns are thus connected with the cultural memory of Reformation iconoclasm and the confessional controversy over rites of burial and commemoration. Browne is astonished that the urns, buried as they were a mere 'yard underground, and thin walls of clay', in fact still exist, having 'out-worn all the strong and specious buildings above it; and quietly rested under the drums and trampling of three conquests' (541). This comment, banal as it may seem, enacts a complex feat of forgetting and misremembering. In the telescoping perspective of the antiquarian, these 'three conquests' are likely meant to refer to the Anglo-Saxon, Viking and Norman conquests of Britain; but in recalling only those three, the earlier, *Roman* occupation is cast not as a foreign presence but rather as an imperial genealogy and a worthy national heritage.[33] Browne's language of 'three conquests' may also have evoked the more recent memory of the three waves of Reformation iconoclasm, first under Henry VIII and Edward VI, then again at the beginning of Queen Elizabeth's reign, and most recently the Puritan raids of the early 1640s that sought to destroy, once again, idolatrous monuments as well as rites for commemorating the dead.[34] This association between iconoclasm and foreign invasion is made squarely in a contemporary text, as Walsham reports: 'In 1640, the sight of the ruined chapel of Chertsey Abbey which crowned a Surrey hillside prompted the royalist Sir John Denham to a poetic meditation on the wreckage left by Henry VIII's ruthless pursuit of wealth "varnish[ed] or'e" by the name of devotion: "Who sees these dismall heaps", he wrote with intermingled shame and fear "but would demand / What barbarous Invader sack't the land?"'[35]

Pondering on the reasons for the urns' survival, Browne is quick to point out that they were in fact saved by oblivion: having lain in a grave of obscurity, they remained unmolested while the prominence of richer tombs attracted iconoclastic raids and destruction. The moral Browne draws from this sounds like a conventional articulation of the *sic transit gloria mundi* topos: 'In vain we hope to be known by open and visible conservatories, when to be unknown was the means of their continuation, and obscurity their protection' (541). The contemporary context of confessional conflict turns this into a more specific statement, however: throughout chapter 5, Browne insists on the merits of obscurity and privacy, a value scheme typical of the quietist stance of Royalists during the Interregnum, who indeed withdrew to the obscurity of their private estates or 'lay underground'. As Jonathan F.S. Post has commented, Browne's commendation of retirement is 'not quite a celebration of anonymity but a recollection of the special virtues of anonymity that speak to the disestablished'.[36] While I am not interested in ascertaining Browne's exact political or doctrinal position (as neither, admittedly, is Post), I think that it is important to acknowledge this context in order to appreciate the post-Reformation sensibility toward iconoclasm and commemoration at work in this text. Whether Browne was a Protestant or an Anglican, a supporter of Parliament or a Royalist, is not as important to my argument as the fact that his writing exhibits a heightened awareness of the eventual failure of monumental memory, an awareness produced by the experience of Reformation iconoclasm and the confessional conflicts of the civil war. If the fifth chapter of *Hydriotaphia* is about the experience of Reformation iconoclasm, or the memory thereof, it is much more interested 'in oblivion and its effects than in re-collecting the past from the grave of time'.[37] This foregrounding of oblivion is due to the general post-Reformation sensibility that I have sketched so far; yet what makes Browne's position exceptional is that he is able to see oblivion not as an enemy but as a positive force. This claim necessitates a complex line of argumentation.

In a first step, Browne presents oblivion as an ethical challenge. The experience of forced retirement and obscurity, typically endured by Royalists during the Interregnum,[38] should not lead to an attitude of melancholy and despair. Quite the opposite, Browne praises obscurity as an exercise in living and dying well, for 'Happy are they whom privacy makes innocent, who deal so with men in this world, that they are not afraid to meet them in the next' (546). What he criticises therefore is an excessive desire for this world, which makes a man unfit for a good death: 'the long habit of living indisposeth us for dying [...] But many are too early old, and before the date of age' (542). This does not mean that we should read Browne as an author indifferent to the religio-political controversies of his time; on the contrary, *Hydriotaphia* gives advice on how to live and die well in this faulty, conflicted world so as to achieve eternity. The road to this leads, paradoxically, through oblivion.

How, then, to achieve eternity? This concern becomes explicit in Browne's second argumentative step. While humble bodily relics as those preserved in the Walsingham urns might be more durable than splendid monuments, they cannot guarantee the enduring commemoration of a person either, since they fail to preserve the individual's identity. Not even an antiquarian can turn anonymous bones and ashes into memorials to a person: 'But who were the proprietaries of these bones, or what bodies these ashes made up, were a question above antiquarism' (542). The name a man makes for himself in this world is thus more important and durable than either bones or monuments: 'Had they made as good provision for their names, as they have done for their relics, they had not so grossly erred in the art of perpetuation. But to subsist in bones, and be but Pyramidally extant, is a fallacy in duration' (542). Again, the problem is not a lack of material durability: the bones of the dead can still be found, and the pyramids still stand. But like the pyramids or, to choose an example closer to home, like the monoliths of Stonehenge, the memory that these material monuments embody has become unintelligible to posterity.[39] Such monuments can be no more than 'Emblemes of mortall vanities; antidotes against pride, vain-glory, and madding vices' (542). It is rather the virtuous, honourable life through which a man acquires a good name that works as an antidote against oblivion. Browne immediately dampens the hope that fame might indeed guarantee posthumous memory, however: it is pure folly, given that time itself, and with it, memory is about to end. Whereas 'Pagan vainglories, which thought the world might last forever, had encouragement for ambition [...] in this latter scene of time, we cannot expect such mummies unto our memorie'. 'And therefore', he concludes unmercifully, 'restless unquiet for the diuturnity of our memories unto present considerations seems a vanity almost out of date, and superannuated piece of folly' (542–3). With time running out fast, oblivion, or rather the acceptance of it, becomes a 'necessity'. In the face of such an apocalyptic notion of time, it simply makes no sense to place one's faith for eternity in monuments or, for that matter, in human memory. In fact, it is 'bad faith' in the most literal sense of the word: '[t]o extend our memories by monuments, whose death we daily pray for, and whose duration we cannot hope, without injury to our expectations, were a contradiction in our beliefs' (543). Belief in the coming apocalypse and resurrection in Christ makes nonsense of vain hopes for worldly memory.

Moreover, the crux with fame and name, Browne argues in a third step, is that they are unreliable as well. One reason is that names, be they inscribed in monuments, history books or human memory, are subject to erasure through time: 'There is no antidote against the opium of time, which temporally considereth all things; our fathers find their graves in our short memories, and sadly tell us how we may be buried in our survivors. Gravestones tell truth scarce forty years [...] Old ones being taken up, and other bodies laid under them' (543). The material vehicles of memory — which from a physiological point of view also includes the matter of the human brain[40] — are subject to decay and destruction. And even if they endure, they harbour the possibility of misreadings and misattributions (as the example from Stow's *Survey* illustrates). The problem is now primarily a semiotic one: 'To be read by bare Inscriptions like many in *Gruter*, [41] to hope for eternity by Ænigmaticall epithetes, or first letters of our names, to be studied by Antiquaries, who we were, and have new names given us like many of the mummies, are cold consolations unto the students of perpetuity' (543). To become an object of study and speculation rather than of devout commemoration is cold comfort indeed. The other reason why commemoration by name is unreliable, is that evil men might be remembered while good people are forgotten: 'But the iniquity of oblivion blindly scattereth her poppy, and deals with the memory of men without distinction to merit of perpetuity. Who can but pity the founder of the pyramids? Herostratus lives that burnt the temple of Diana, he is almost lost that built it' (544). Since time and memory are blind to merit, the memory of an iconoclast might be more lasting than that of him who built and believed in a monument.[42] Consequently, the mere fact that a man is remembered does not guarantee his worth.

This observation gives rise to a remarkable meditation on the extent to which the records of history, and by extension cultural memory itself, are indeed circumscribed by oblivion: 'Large are the treasures of oblivion, and heapes of things in a state next to nothing almost numberlesse; much more is buried in silence than is recorded, and the largest volumes are butt epitomes of what hath been'.[43] At this point, oblivion changes from being perceived as an absence or falsification of memory to being credited with constituting an alternative archive, a 'treasure' containing 'heapes of things' forgotten. This advances Browne's argument a further step towards the recognition that human memory and even human life is formed as much by acts of forgetting as by acts of remembering:

we slightly remember out felicities, and the smartest stroaks of affliction leave but short smart upon us. Sense endureth no extremities, and sorrows destroy us or themselves. To weep into stones are fables. Afflictions induce callosities, miseries are slippery, or fall like snow upon us, which notwithstanding is no unhappy stupidity. To be ignorant of evils to come, and forgetfull of evils past, is a mercifull provision in nature, whereby we digest the mixture of our few and evil days, and, our delivered senses not relapsing into cutting remembrances, our sorrows are not kept raw by the edge of repetitions (544–5).

In this series of concise aphorisms, which are quite untypical of Browne's usually more involved baroque style, the physician is speaking. The language of bodily sensation naturalises oblivion as a state of physiological and emotional wellbeing. Forgetting is a necessary part of our lives that allows us to overcome great sorrow, afflictions, and misery. To 'weep into stones', is to succumb to an exaggerated, fabulous degree of mourning that will destroy us.[44] Nothing is more natural, by contrast, than to forget in order to live. Oblivion is a 'mercifull provision in nature' by which our 'senses [are] delivered' from the pain of our worldly existence. In keeping with the pharmaceutical metaphor evoked earlier, the effects of oblivion are like the effects of opium. But in the light of how the argument develops further, oblivion also begins to look like immortality.

   This fifth step in the argument commences with a summary rejection of all human efforts at setting themselves eternal monuments either by 'preservations below the moon' or by 'conceits to perpetuate their names in Heaven' through the art of cosmography (545). The lesson is again that any form of memorialisation undertaken by humans, be it the monuments erected down on earth or up in the sky, is subject to change and decay: 'While we look for incorruption in the heavens, we find they are but like the earth; durable in their main bodies, alterable in their parts' (545). The only immortality one can hope for, then, is one completely independent from human desire or the material and ritual practices discussed so far. Only a Christian vision of the immortality of the soul can make us truly immortal, because it does not aspire to duration but promises durability, not preservation but perpetuity:

> There is nothing strictly immortal, but immortality. Whatever hath no beginning, may be confident of no end (all others have a dependent being and within the reach of destruction); [...] But the sufficiency of Christian immortality frustrates all earthly glory, and the quality of either state after death, makes a folly of posthumous memory. God who can only destroy our souls, and hath assured our resurrection, either of our bodies or names hath directly promised no duration (545–6).

This argument shifts the focus from a foolish concern with the fate of our bodies or names to the fate of our souls. The state of our souls after death 'makes a folly of posthumous memory', for if we are in Paradise, there is nothing to worry about; indeed the soul enters Paradise in a state of blissful forgetfulness, achieved through drinking from the river Lethe, as Dante imagined in his *Divina Commedia*. [45] And should we find ourselves in hell, our commemoration on earth will be the least of our concerns.[46] Moreover, God has 'assured our resurrection' in the soul as clearly as he 'hath directly promised no duration' (546) for either bodies or names.[47] This adds yet another level to our 'fallacy in duration', since in desiring it we obviously disregard God's promise. Does man in his foolishness ever realise this? No, Browne states acerbically: 'But man is a noble animal, splendid in ashes, and pompous in the grave, solemnising nativities and deaths with equal luster, nor omitting ceremonies of bravery in the infamy of his nature' (546). In this passage, human effort at memorialisation becomes the opposite of Christian immortality: 'To subsist in lasting monuments, to live in their productions, to exist in their names and præ-dicament of chimeras', Browne sums up, 'all this is nothing in the metaphysics of true belief'. Being translated into a monument turns us merely into dead stones, while 'To live indeed, is to be again ourselves' (547). This does emphatically not mean to be resurrected exactly as we were before, as individuals identifiable by their 'names, persons, times, and sexes' (542). On the contrary, 'to live indeed' means a dissolution into the indeterminate and for this very reason infinite state of Christian immortality. Faith, for Browne, means to be 'Ready to be anything, in the ecstasy of being ever' (547).

By implication at least, this places immortality and oblivion on an equal level, with oblivion foreshadowing the ecstatic state of immortality. And indeed, the language in which Browne describes immortality curiously echoes the sensual reg-ister he used to describe forgetfulness: 'And if any have been so happy as truly to understand Christian annihilation, ecstasies, exolution, liquefaction, transformation, the kiss of the spouse, gustation of God, and ingression into the divine shadow, they have already had an handsome anticipation of heaven; the glory of the world is surely over, and the earth is ashes unto them' (547). Immortality is rendered here as an experience of ecstatic annihilation which both is and is not a metaphysical state. The material body is not left behind but, at least metaphorically, becomes the very conduit through which we join God. It is a delivery not from the senses, but through them: 'exolution' denotes a state of being loosened or set free, in particular the escape of 'animal spirits' in the act of swooning, not unlike the oblivion-induced delivery of the senses from pain.[48] The Vitruvian 'Circles and right lines [that] limit and close all bodies' (543) dissolve, transforming, and liquefying the body. The blissful merging with God is envisaged in images of physical union, as a marital kiss, and even incorporation: the 'gustation of God' powerfully evokes ingestion and sustenance, prefigured in the Eucharist. Just as the act of eating breaks through bodily boundaries, the ambiguity of the phrase 'gustation', which can be constructed both as the action of tasting and the sensory experience, dis-solves the distinction between God and the soul. As the believer 'tastes' of God, and God tastes of the believer, both are dissolved into and nourished by each other. The powerful metaphor recalls Browne's earlier description of forgetfulness as that 'merciful provision' whereby we 'digest the mixture of our few and evil days', turning oblivion into a foretaste of immortality.

This final vision of the dissolution of personal identity and memory is rarely taken seriously by modern readers of Browne, who find little in it to comment on beyond its obviously mystical tone.[49] Achsah Guibbory, for instance, has read it as a sceptical comment on the 'increased personalisation' evident from seventeenth-century monuments and memorials, and explains Browne's scepticism as an effect of the secularisation process which turned religious into 'civil rites'.[50] Given Browne's deeply religious language, however, this explanation is more in keeping with the Weberian disenchantment-hypothesis than with Browne's oeuvre.[51] Admittedly, Guibbory stops just short of discussing his sensual vision of transcendence. Yet as one can see at first glance, Browne's language here is far from being secular: the discussion is conducted neither in terms of antiquarianism nor of empirical scepticism. Instead, it speaks the language of Christian religious mysticism that validates and indeed courts the notion of a complete dissolution of the individual in the divine.[52] In this discourse, transcendence does not mean a dismissal of the physical, but rather figures as a state that is achieved through bodily sensation and that, at the same time, spells a dissolution of the individual. The spiritual communion with God is metaphorically rendered as an act of corporeal commingling, or of eroticised feeding, or both at the same time. While the rhetoric and imagery recall that of a medieval mystical tradition,[53] they also express an appreciation of oblivion that speaks of a specifically post-Reformation sensibility about the memory of the dead. The Reformation had wrought profound changes in the deep-structure of memory culture, carving out a 'shared discursive space in which poets and preachers, mystics and scientists'[54] explored new ways of becoming eternal.

Against this background, the final chapter of *Urne-Buriall* does not read convincingly as the climax of an essentially modern secularisation process, nor as an 'extravaganza on forgetfulness'[55] but rather as the articulation of a heightened sensibility toward the interplay of remembering and forgetting that resulted from the experience of Reformation iconoclasm and which, ironically perhaps, found a more ready vehicle in the language of religious mysticism. Browne's injunction to give up on the 'folly of posthumous memory' (542) and instead to embrace oblivion as a dissolution of the soul into God, makes oblivion appear as a state of grace.

Conclusion

Faced with the material traces of Reformation iconoclasm, early modern antiquaries had to come to terms not only with the necessity and urgency of their mnemonic project but also with the possibility, even tangible proof, of its ultimate failure. Seeking to remember the pre-Reformation past, antiquaries had to do so under the conditions and constraints determined by the reformed present. Inevitably, these conditions and constraints included a changed attitude toward the workings of memory as such. When asking, therefore, how the Reformation was being remembered by the antiquaries as well as by their contemporaries, we should look not only to the thematic dimension of *what* was remembered of the Reformation, but also acknowledge that the Reformation had wrought profound changes in the very structure of cultural memory. Ideas of *how* memory worked were strongly impacted by the experience of iconoclasm and the widespread abolition or reform of rites of commemoration. Memory became increasingly as much about forgetting as about remembering; and oblivion was a force not just to be feared and defied, but to be strategically deployed or even to be actively desired. The Protestant Reformation was not just a reformation of faith but also, and just as profoundly, a reformation of memory culture.

Notes

1 See Margaret Aston, 'English Ruins and English History: The Dissolution and the Sense of the Past', repr. in *Lollards and Reformers: Images and Literacy in Late Medieval Religion* (London, 1984), 313–37; Alexandra Walsham, *The Reformation of the Landscape* (Oxford, 2011), 273. Angus Vine has recently cautioned that Reformation iconoclasm was not the only influence on the development of antiquarianism in the British Isles, pointing to medieval models like William of Worcester and John Rous, as well as the classical and philological studies of continental scholars; see Angus Vine, *In Defiance of Time: Antiquarian Writing in Early Modern England* (Oxford, 2010), 8–9.

2 Vine, *In Defiance of Time*, 7.

3 John Weever, *Ancient Funerall Monuments, of Great-Britain, Ireland, and the islands adjacent* (London, 1631), sig. Ar.

4 Stow accordingly 'took revenge on the perpetrators by omitting descriptions of their own tombs and epitaphs'; quote and comment in Walsham, *The Reformation of the Landscape*, 275.

5 Margaret Aston, *The King's Bedpost: Reformation and Iconography in a Tudor Group Portrait* (Cambridge, 1993). For further textual examples, see Walsham, *Reformation of the Landscape*, 147–8.

6 Walsham, *The Reformation of the Landscape*, 476.

7 Eamon Duffy, *The Stripping of the Altars: Traditional Religion in England, c. 1400–c. 1580* (New Haven, 1992); Edward Muir, *Ritual in Early Modern Europe* (Cambridge, 1997).

8 Peter Marshall, *Beliefs and the Dead in Reformation England* (Oxford, 2002).

9 Marshall, *Beliefs and the Dead*, 307.

10 Quoted in Marshall, *Beliefs and the Dead*, 265.

11 Marshall, *Beliefs and the Dead*, 302.

12 William Camden, *Britannia, or A chorographicall description of the most flourishing kingdomes, England, Scotland, and Ireland, and the ilands adjoyning, out of the depth of Antiquitie*, tr. Philemon Holland (London, 1610), §7.

13 Camden, *Britannia*; Weever, *Ancient Funerall Monuments*, sig. Ar.

14 On this development, which was brought up short by renewed efforts to remove what was again seen as 'idols' during the wars of the 1640s and 1650s, see Walsham, *The Reformation of the Landscape*, 273–95; esp. on Weever's position, see 277–8.

15 The copy held at the Huntington Library shows no pagination for the first four pages of the 'Epistle', after which it commences with sig. Ar; the quotations can be found on the first two text pages.

16 See also Philip Schwyzer's *Archaeologies of English Renaissance Literature* (Oxford, 2007), 77. In its urge to salvage material monument and to turn them into a written one, this definition of antiquarian practice follows the model set be Francesco Petrarca in his letter to his friend Colonna, which recalls their encounters with ancient ruins on their walks in the city of Rome (Vine, *In Defiance*, 5).

17 See Isabel Karremann 'Edmund Spenser's *The Ruines of Time* as a Protestant Poetics of Mourning and Commemoration', in *Forms of Faith: Literary Form and Religious Conflict in Early Modern England*, ed. Jonathan Baldo and Isabel Karremann (Manchester, 2017), 90–109.

18 Schwyzer, *Archaeologies*, 79.

19 As Jennifer Summit has argued, this increasing doubt concerning the written word is another legacy of Reformation iconoclasm: 'Reading Reformed: Spenser and the Problem of the English Library', in *Forgetting in Early Modern English Literature and Culture: Lethe's Legacies*, ed. Christopher Ivic and Grant Williams (London, 2004), 165–78.

20 John Stow, *A Survey of London* [1603], ed. C. L. Kingsford (Oxford, 1908), 135.

21 Vine, *In Defiance*, 5.

22 Jacob Schnebbelie, 'The old facade of the Guildhall, City of London, 1788', accessed 15 July 2019, http://www.wikigallery.org/wiki/painting_162437/Jacob-Schnebbelie/The-old-faca de-of-the-Guildhall%2C-City-of-London%2C-1788.

23 Margaret Aston, *England's Iconoclasts* (Oxford, 1988), I: 326.

24 On this double perspective as typical of literature on post-Reformation ruins, see Schwyzer, *Archaeologies*, 72–107.

25 *Hydriotaphia* established Browne within the antiquarian community, and he became a sought-after correspondent to many antiquarians. See Graham Parry, 'Thomas Browne and the Uses of Antiquity', in *Sir Thomas Browne: The World Proposed*, ed. Reid Barbour and Claire Preston (Oxford, 2008), 63–79.

26 On curiosity as an important impulse in the development of early modern science, see Brent Nelson, 'The Browne Family's Culture of Curiosity', in Barbour and Preston, *Sir Thomas Browne: The World Proposed*, 80–99, and more generally Lorraine Daston, 'Curiosity on Early Modern Science', *Word & Image: A Journal of Verbal/Visual Enquiry* 11, no. 4 (1995), 391–404.

27 *Thomas Browne: Selected Writings*, ed. Kevin Killeen (Oxford, 2014), 510. All further quotations refer to this edition.

28 Philipp Mayor, '*Urne-Buriall* and the Interregnum Royalist', in '*A man very well studied*': *New Contexts for Thomas Browne*, ed. Kathryn Murphy and Richard Todd (Leiden, 2008), 191–210.

29 Schwyzer, *Archaeologies*, 184.

30 Schwyzer, *Archaeologies*, 181.

31 See Achsah Guibbory, '"A rationall of old Rites": Sir Thomas Browne's "Urn Buriall" and the Conflict over Ceremony', *The Yearbook of English Studies* 21 (1991), 229–41.

32 For a sustained reading of *The Lament of Walshingham*, see Schwyzer, *Archaeologies*, 84–9.

33 Claire Preston, *Thomas Browne and the Writing of Early Modern Science* (Cambridge, 2005), 141.

34 Guibbory, 'A rationall of old Rites', 229–30.

35 Walsham, *Reformation of the Landscape*, 278.

36 Jonathan F. S. Post, *Sir Thomas Browne* (Boston, 1987), 134.

37 Preston, *Thomas Browne and the Writing of Early Modern Science*, 132.

38 See Mayor, '*Urne-Buriall* and the Interregnum Royalist'.

39 Stonehenge exercised the imagination of early modern antiquarians as well as poets considerably, since there were neither inscriptions on the stones themselves nor oral or written records that could account for their origin and purpose. As Vine has shown, antiquarians took refuge in measuring the megaliths as a means of offering at least some objective data, while poets and playwrights seem to have relished the epistemological and mnemonic paradox of Stonehenge as a monument that *fails* to commemorate its builders or origin (Vine, *In Defiance*, 109–38; see also Schwyzer, *Archaeologies*, 81–3). A similar relish for the limits of knowledge and memory places Browne's *Urne-Buriall* within a poetical rather than antiquarian discourse.

40 See the introductory chapter in Garrett A. Sullivan Jr., *Memory and Forgetting in English Renaissance Drama: Shakespeare, Marlowe, Webster* (Cambridge, 2005) and Isabel Karremann, *The Drama of Memory in Shakespeare's History Plays* (Cambridge, 2015), chapter 4.

41 Browne glosses this as *Gruteri inscriptiones antique*, an antiquarian collection of epitaphs and inscriptions on funeral monuments in the Roman world published in 1603 by the Dutch scholar Jan Gruter.

42 Tobias Döring discusses the problem of how to remember Reformation iconoclasts in 'Helden der Auslöschung: Zum Gedenken an Ikonoklasten', in *Heroen und Heroisierungen in der Renaissance*, ed. Achim Aurnhammer and Manfred Pfister (Wiesbaden, 2013), 147–63.

43 Additional passage (London, British Library, Sloane MS 1848, fol. 194), reprinted in *The Works of Sir Thomas Browne*, ed. Geoffrey Keynes (London, 1964), 172.

44 Such a desire is displayed and ridiculed in the lament of Verlame, the female speaker of the first part of Spenser's *The Ruines of Time*; on the debate about acceptable forms of mourning in Spenser's poem specifically, see Carl J. Rasmussen, '"How Weak Be the Passions of Woefulness": Spenser's *Ruines of Time*', *Spenser Studies* 2 (1981), 159–81, and in the early modern period more generally, see Tobias Döring, *Performances of Mourning in Shakespearean Theatre and Early Modern Culture* (Hampshire, 2006).

45 Harald Weinrich, *Lethe: Kunst und Kritik des Vergessens* (München, 1997), 44–5.

46 Purgatory seems to be no alternative here; neither is intercessory prayer, because this would mean that it is indeed important that and how one is being remembered on earth.

47 This refusal of bodily preservation is at odds with Browne's belief in *palingenesis*, the notion of a physical resurrection of the material substance from death, expressed in *Religio medici*: 'This is made good by experience, which can from the ashes of a plant revive the plant, and from its cinders recall it into its stalk and leaves againe. What the art of man can doe in these inferious pieces, what blasphemy is it to affirme the finger of God cannot doe in these more perfect and sensible structures?' Quoted and discussed in Kevin Killeen, '"When all things shall confesse their ashes": Science and Soul in Thomas Browne', in *The Oxford Handbook of English Prose, 1500–1640*, ed. Andrew Hadfield (Oxford, 2014), 669–85 (681).

48 *OED*, s. v. 'exolution'.

49 A recent example being Kevin Killeen's 'Introduction' (xi–xiv) to the Oxford-edition of selected writings of Browne. It begins with G. K. Chesterton's admiring comments on 'Browne's archaeological emotions and mystical clarity' and acknowledges his recognition of Browne as 'a writer in whom, quite singularly, style was the conduit of mysticism' (xi), but has nothing further to say when discussing the end of *Hydriotaphia* (xxi).

50 Guibbory, 'A rationall of old Rites', 239, 241.

51 For an important critique of Weber's hypothesis, see Alexandra Walsham, 'The Reformation and "The Disenchantment of the World" Reassessed', *HistJ* 51, no. 2 (2008), 497–528.

52 Examples of such mysticism in post-Reformation England are the religious poetry of John Donne, George Herbert, Henry and Thomas Vaughan, Thomas Traherne or Richard Crashaw, but also the 'theological materialism' (Killeen, 'Science and Soul in Thomas Browne', 670) of writers who were inspired by hermeticism, alchemy, the cabbala and Rosicrucianism, like Robert Fludd or Sir Kenelm Digby. For recent studies of religious mysticism in seventeenth-century religious poetry see Ryan Netzley, *Reading, Desire and the Eucharist in Early Modern Religious Poetry* (Toronto, 2011) and Kimberley Johnson, *Made Flesh: Sacrament and Poetics in Post-Reformation England* (Philadelphia, 2014); Michael Martin offers a discussion of alchemical and Rosicrucian writings alongside metaphysical poetry in *Literature and the Encounter with God in Post-Reformation England* (Farnham, 2014).

53 Thomas Betteredge has rightly cautioned that 'mysticism as a category cannot easily or unproblematically cross from the medieval to the early modern world': 'Vernacular Theology', in *Cultural Reformations: Medieval and Renaissance in Literary History*, ed. Brian Cummings and James Simpson (Oxford, 2010), 188–205.

54 Martin, *Literature and the Encounter with God*, dust jacket.

55 Preston, *Thomas Browne and the Writing of Early Modern Science*, 154.

PART II

Divided memory

4

BREAD AND STONE

Catholic memory in post-Reformation Leiden

Carolina Lenarduzzi and Judith Pollmann

In medieval Europe, victories, deliverance from enemy attacks and sieges, and the end of epidemics, were widely credited to divine intervention, the help of patron saints or the Virgin. Images, objects and inscriptions associated with such miraculous and providential instances of deliverance were kept in churches and city halls, and memories were kept alive through rituals such as the annual 'general' processions, in which magistrates, clergy and the corporate bodies in the cities processed through urban space. In the course of the sixteenth century Protestants not only abandoned traditional memory practices such as prayers for the dead and the veneration of relics, but also needed to rethink the public commemoration of important events in local or supralocal history. Scholars have highlighted how Protestant regimes invented alternatives such as the celebration of Reformation day, the Accession of Queen Elizabeth, or the foiling of the Gunpowder Plot. Reformed cities also proved inventive in finding new ways of commemorating providential local events; Geneva's *escalade* is one famous example.[1]

Recent research suggests that Catholics, who lived as minorities in Protestant states with such new memory regimes, responded in three distinct ways. The first was to salvage what they could of the Catholic world that had been eradicated, and make sure it would not be completely lost and forgotten.[2] The second was to cultivate 'counter-memories' which centred on suffering in recent history and which could be used to challenge the new memory regimes of the Protestants.[3] The third was to claim a stake for Catholics in new memory regimes.[4] Examples of such strategies have been studied in the British Isles, especially, but mostly at the level of states or translocal networks. In this essay, we want to explore these strategies among a small network of Catholics in an urban setting, the Dutch city of Leiden. This will allow us, first, to study Catholic memory practices in operation in a local network and in urban space, and secondly, in a dynamic with authorities which also developed memory practices for their traditional, civic purposes, to foster the unity of the citizens, as well as assert continuity with urban traditions. By taking a closer look at a set of urban Catholic memory practices, we will see that in the very memory practices that were intended to assert the differences between past and present, we also find peculiar parallels and continuities between the pre- and post-Reformation world. Whether it is hard to establish with any degree of certainty that these were conscious attempts to fit new memories into traditional forms, we will argue that these also allowed individual Catholics room to make their peace with local memory regimes.

Leiden

In 1572 the Holland city of Leiden decided to join a range of Netherlandish cities and Prince William of Orange in their rebellion against the main representative of their overlord, King Philip II of Spain. The decision was taken under the joint pressure of rebel armies, and a part of Leiden's citizens who believed that the city should no longer accept the regime of the King's governor the Duke of Alba. It was always likely that such a decision would involve religious change, and would lead to the acceptance of Protestant worship in the town. Orange had long opposed the anti-heresy policies of King Philip, and many in his armies were Calvinists who had gone into exile to escape Alba's persecutions. What not everyone had foreseen is that a decision to join the rebellion would, within a year, lead to the banning of Catholic worship in the city. Once the Duke of Alba had started a ruthless campaign to eradicate the rebellion, Orange's ideal of religious parity succumbed under the pressure of radicals in his own armies, and of the political leaders who had emerged from Protestant exile circles and now took charge of the rebel cities.[5]

Leiden's elite was deeply divided about the best response to the rebellion. Some local officials decided to support the new regime, while others decided that their oath to the King, or the challenge to their faith, now demanded that they take a stand. For them exile was the only option.[6] In the meantime, it became inevitable that Leiden, like other cities among its Holland neighbours, would at some point be besieged by Habsburg troops. A first siege was soon abandoned, but a second siege, starting in May 1574, was to last for six long months. There was little military action during the siege, but the citizens were cut off from the outside world, and soon food became scarce and disease rampant; between May and October, about 6,000 of the city's 15,000 inhabitants perished. The eventual lifting of the siege on 3 October 1574 was the result of a spectacular rescue operation, which involved the flooding of large parts of the province of Holland to enable a rebel fleet of 400 flat barges and 8,000 soldiers to come to the rescue.[7]

Just as pre-Reformation magistrates had done, Leiden's rebel authorities immediately began to invest in the commemoration of this providential end to their plight. The city commissioned commemorative medals for all major participants in the defence of the city while inscriptions were also placed at various strategic points in the town. On the very day of their liberation, the magistrate decided to institute an annual sermon to give thanks for the relief of the city. This was soon complemented by an annual fair, a parade by the city militia, and public theatrical performances. It commissioned a large tapestry depicting its deliverance, which was put on display in the city hall, and so could be seen by all, since in the early modern period city halls were very public places. Soon, paintings and stained-glass church windows followed.[8] The annual celebration of the relief of Leiden thus became the central feast on the city's calendar, and one with a surprising staying power — it was interrupted only for a decade or two around 1800 and continues to exist to this day.

The public memory culture around the siege focused especially on the famine that the people of Leiden had endured in their struggle for liberty, and it was for this that the siege continued to be remembered. This focus on famine was not as self-evident as we used to think. In 2006 historian Thera Wijsenbeek-Olthuis, concluded that the six thousand casualties of Leiden's siege had died not of famine, but of a range of epidemic diseases that contemporaries identified as 'plague'.[9] Although there were indeed serious food shortages, famine was not the primary cause of death. The city government had actually been quite efficient in sharing out the available rations, and right until the end of the siege there was a ration of horse meat and malt cakes available for all citizens. Even so, from the start, the many histories, plays and poems included graphic descriptions of the suffering caused by the food shortages; people had not only resorted to killing their horses for meat, but also to eating grass and 'gnawing scraps of raw meat from the bones that had been left by dogs', slurping blood from the gutters, and searching dungheaps, while starving infants had in vain sucked the breasts of their dying mothers. Conversely, the most important emblems of the liberation were the loaves of white bread and the herring that the liberators had brought into the city, evoking Christ's feeding of the multitudes at the Sea of Galilee. The 1574 famine in Leiden had ended in a miraculous transformation from famine to plenty, and as such it was publicly remembered. Songs and inscriptions encouraged the citizens to commemorate the end of the famine as evidence of 'God's wondrous work', most notably so on the city hall, where a blue altar stone that had been purged from St Peter's church, was triumphantly redeployed to tell the tale of the city's wondrous deliverance. There is good evidence that famine-associated memories were widely shared among the population and were also quickly appropriated by the many Protestants from Flanders and Brabant who migrated to Leiden in the late sixteenth century.[10]

Bread turned into stone: the Leiden miracle

By foregrounding the hunger which the population had suffered during the siege, Leiden's ruling elite ousted, but in some ways perhaps also echoed and remediated, memories of another famine, and another, much older, Leiden miracle, that had been commemorated in the city's St Peter's church for centuries. Soon after Leiden joined the Dutch Revolt and proceeded to banish

Catholic worship, its churches were sequestered and purged of all objects that made them unsuitable for Reformed worship. One of the objects that had been on display in the church of St Peter, its oldest and most prestigious parish church, was a brown stone, that authenticated a miracle that had occurred in Leiden in 1316, [Fig. 4.1] and that was associated with a famine that raged throughout Western Europe in 1315–1316.[11]

The earliest reference to this miracle is found in a chronicle that was written in the first decades of the fifteenth century by an author known as the Cleric of the Low Countries.[12] The Cleric told how in 1316 'the dearth was such that the poor ate the dirty, stinking raw meat of animal corpses, and ate the grass on the fields […] and children were found suckling their dead mother's breasts and have gnawed or bitten them. Such that this plague only differed from Jeremiah's laments, in that the women did not boil their children so as to cook and eat the meat'.[13] While famine was rife, the Cleric continued, a woman in Leiden saw her neighbour cutting a loaf of bread in half, using the one part to feed her children, and storing the other. The woman asked her if she might buy the stored bread, but her neighbour refused and denied having such a bread in the house at all, saying: 'If there is any bread in my house, God give that it will be turned into stone'. And so, of course, it happened. The Cleric recounted that the stone loaf could be seen in Leiden's church of St Peter, where it was put on display on high feast days by those of the 'Holy Ghost', the municipal officials who were in charge of dispensing charity to the urban poor. In versions of the tale that were included in later chronicles, first in manuscript and later in print, the tale evolved, and became a story about a rich and a poor woman, and eventually a rich and a poor sister.[14] The story of the Leiden miracle was not only remembered through the stone, but also commemorated through the area where the event had happened, 'the land of miracle'. Over time, the fame of the stone came to extend beyond Holland and was retold by chroniclers as far away as Flanders. In the Zeeland city of Middelburg, a painting of the Leiden stone was on display in the local hospital as late as the nineteenth century.[15]

FIGURE 4.1 Picture of the Leiden Miracle Stone.
Museum De Lakenhal, Leiden, inv. nr. 5432.

Despite its fame, or perhaps because of it, the stone was removed during the purging of St Peter's church and its sequestration for Reformed worship. Although Leiden's elites freely talked of a miracle when commemorating their liberation, the formal Reformed position, of course, was that the age of miracles had ended, while display of the stone was also similar enough to that of relics to offend Reformed sensibilities. Yet the reputation of the stone was so significant that local Catholics decided to salvage it. Sometime between 1572 and 1581, the Leiden goldsmith Cornelis van Aecken asked notary Willem van Oudervliet to draft an affidavit in which three men over 75 years of age declared that they were familiar with a piece of stone, of the same texture and colour as half a loaf of rye bread

> which as long as they witnesses can remember was hanging in St Peter's church in Leiden on the pillar in front of the St Nicholas altar and subsequently at the altar of the four crowned martyrs and has always been kept and has been hung up in a reddish casket with iron bars until the year 1574. Of which piece of stone [they] have declared that the aforesaid is the piece of stone that has hung there since before living memory and for very many years as an eternal monument at the north end of the church, so that all would know of the great miracle that had happened in Leiden, that the aforesaid stone had once been bread and was transformed into stone, and they testify that as they were young, they have heard many an old man talk about it.[16]

The notary then read them a passage of Cornelis Aurelius' well-known chronicle of Holland and Zeeland, that had been published in Leiden in 1517, and that recounted the tale of the 1316 miracle, upon which the witnesses confirmed that this was indeed the tale with which they were familiar.[17]

The witnesses whose testimony was recorded had been selected both for age and status; they were Phillips Nachtegael and Jan Barendrecht, both described as 'fiefholders' of the Count of Holland. Nachtegael had been a sheriff of the city, Barendrecht had been an official in the powerful water board of the region. The third was a citizen of Leiden called Ott Cornelisz. The men all lived very close to the church and were probably too frail to walk very far, because the notary visited them at home, together with three men who acted as witnesses to the signing of the affidavit. Two of these were chantry priests. Ott's son Vrank had been a chantry priest in St Peter's church, the other was former chantry priest Jacob Willems of Esselickerwoude, who lived with Vrank and his father. While Vrank had agreed to abjure Philip II, a precondition to receive a pension out of the sequestered possessions of the old Church, Jacob Willems would significantly refuse to do this. The third witness probably clerked for the notary, Willem van Oudervliet.[18]

The goldsmith and innkeeper Cornelis Claesz van Aecken (also known by his Latinised name Cornelis Aquanus), at whose request the affidavit was drawn up, is well-known as a collector of the Roman antiquities that had been found in Leiden earlier in the sixteenth century.[19] Since Van Aecken also kept a collection of naturalia, he may have acquired the stone for that purpose. He has sometimes been seen as a proponent of Protestantism. In November 1567 he was questioned by the sheriff because he had accepted a dare to run through the city's main street in a grey cloak, the hallmark of the noble protesters against King Philip's anti-heresy legislation.[20] Yet we know of many other Catholics who initially supported that protest, and considering the people he involved in drawing up the affidavit it is much more likely that he wanted it for its traditional, Catholic associations. Van Aecken had been deacon of the St Nicholas confraternity, near whose altar the stone had been on display. The move to authenticate the stone's provenance and religious associations, are also quite similar to the efforts to certify the provenance of other relics that orthodox Catholics in the Dutch Republic had in safe-keeping after the Reformation.[21] To protect the sacred remains of their saints from the Protestants, Catholics, both clergy and lay people, had transferred their relics from the custodianship of churches and convents to private houses and to Catholic safe havens abroad. In so far as the chaotic circumstances in the first years after the Reformation allowed, relic-savers recorded in writing the authenticity, place of origin and hiding place of the sacred *materia*, hoping to prevent forgery and theft.[22] It reflected Catholic hope for a better future when their 'kidnapped' relics could return home.

As it happened, the affidavit was not enough for the Leiden bread stone to retain its local significance for the Catholic community. To be sure, the tale of the stone continued to live on. The English traveller William Brereton was told about its history when he visited Leiden in 1634–1635.[23] In the 1670s, travellers were being told that the stone had been 'stolen'.[24] The stone itself only re-emerged, with a copy of the affidavit, in the early nineteenth century, when it belonged to a Catholic noblewoman, Maria Countess Moens, who left most of her worldly goods to the Catholic orphans of Amsterdam.[25] By that time the existence of the miracle stone had been excised almost completely, not only from Leiden's local history, but also from the collective memory of Leiden's Catholic population. The only trace which the miracle had left in Leiden was in the name of *de mirakelsteeg*, an alley located in what had once been the 'land of miracle', but by the nineteenth century this was a slum and no-one knew any longer what this referred to.[26]

The medieval memory practice that the Catholic parties to the notarial deed had tried to save from oblivion, thus did not survive in association with the stone. The miracle of the bread stone had been ousted by that other famine-related 'wonder' that the city was now to publicly celebrate, that of the city's liberation in 1574 and the miraculous feeding of the city's hungry multitudes. Nevertheless, the affidavit points the way to a network of Leiden Catholics, which, as we will see, also found other ways to salvage a place in both Leiden's Catholic and its public memory.

Cornelis Musius, a 'holy house', and a blue stone

As traditional Catholic memory practices disappeared from Leiden's public sphere, a new set of counter-memories that focused on the Catholic victims of the Revolt in Leiden began to make an appearance. Returning Catholic exiles played a pivotal role in this process. In 1576, the so-called Pacification of Ghent, a peace agreement between the rebels and the other Netherlandish provinces, allowed Catholics who had fled the rebel towns in the early years of the Revolt to return to their home-towns. Like most other treaties that concluded early modern civil wars, the Paci-fication included the proviso that all animosities should be 'forgotten'; there was an amnesty for all those who had been deemed traitors by the other side, for instance because they had gone into exile. Private property was to be returned to such families. Yet other losses were less easily repaired. Exiles had been publicly reviled for their desertion of the city in the 1570s, and the amnesty did not cater for a public rehabilitation nor compensation for their suffering. Because most Catholics had been critical of desertion of the local patria, Catholic refugees could not necessarily count on much sympathy from their coreligionists either.[27] This may be why it was returning Catholic exiles who were to prove especially active in the creation of new counter-memory cultures, especially those surrounding local mar-tyrs of the Revolt.

One such exile was former Leiden burgomaster Cornelis van Veen (1520–1591).[28] In 1572 he, his wife and nine of their ten children had fled to the Habsburg Netherlands, leaving their house in the care of no other than notary Willem van Oudervliet, whom we have already met, and who had a long-standing association with the Van Veen family.[29] He had himself trained as a notary with Van Veen, and had at one time been tutor to Van Veen's sons.[30] Yet while Van Oudervliet had looked after the house, he had been unable to prevent its use by the rebels for the torture of the priest Cornelius Musius. Subsequently executed, Musius was one of the clerical victims of the notorious Count Lumey de la Marck (c. 1542–1578), admiral of the so-called 'Sea Beggars' and the representative of rebel leader William of Orange in Holland.

Musius was not a Leiden man. He had lived and worked, lastly as prior of a convent, in Delft, and had been arrested by Lumey's men when he was on his way to The Hague. During the short time he spent in Leiden, Musius was imprisoned in two houses that had been sequestered from exiled Catholics. The first, known as the House Lockhorst, had been given into the use of the rebel nobleman Gijsbert van Duivenvoorde, who himself had spent years in exile under the Duke of Alba.[31] There a mock-trial was set up, in which Musius was forced to engage in a dis-putation with a reformed preacher. When he resisted these quasi-judicial efforts to dissuade him from his religious beliefs, Lumey ordered Musius to be transferred to the neighbouring house to be tortured. This house happened to be the Van Veen family home. Under torture, so the rebels allegedly hoped, the rector would reveal the hiding places of the treasures of his convent. When Musius refused to do so, Lumey had him hanged at Leiden's traditional place of execution, a hexagonal blue stone outside the city hall. It was a slow and painful death: because of a tumour under his chin, the rope did not fit closely round his neck and it took a long time for him to suffocate.[32]

Musius' martyrdom was to be among the most infamous of the Dutch Revolt, because his death triggered a furious row between the Prince of Orange and Lumey, who was, eventually, dismissed. Yet for Leiden's Catholics, Musius' death became the centre of a memory cult for quite different reasons. The violent death of the 72-year-old priest inspired Catholic authors to produce numerous accounts of his life and martyrdom, varying from statements in letters, to poetry to formal martyrologies.[33] Most of these accounts relied heavily on the eyewitness report of the notary Oudervliet and his wife, who had been living in Van Veen's house at the time of Musius' torture. By 1575 Cornelis' house was also home to Susanna van Etten. (c. 1549–1634), a former nun of the Leeuwenhorst Convent near Leiden, who had allegedly persuaded Lumey, whose mother was a family friend, to release the mutilated body of Musius for burial in consecrated soil, and had arranged for his burial under a 'blue tombstone' in St Peter's church.[34] In this way, the house came to play a central role in the local memory culture surrounding Musius' martyrdom.

The association with Musius' martyrdom also rubbed off on Cornelis van Veen himself. The Van Veen family had returned to Leiden in 1577, three years after the end of the Leiden siege. In accordance with the Pacification, Van Veen was guaranteed both an amnesty for his 'treason' during the siege and the return of his old home; in 1577 he swore a new oath of loyalty to the city.[35] Nevertheless, he could not return to political office, and his flight had probably also damaged his social status among Leiden Catholics. By virtue of their house, the Van Veens could quickly rebuild their reputation in Catholic circles, and so restore their position among coreligionists. One of the martyrologists who paid tribute to the Van Veen family home as a *locus sacer* was Petrus Opmeer (1526–1595), a fellow-townsman of the rector and well acquainted with both him and burgomaster Cornelis van Veen.[36] In his well-known history of both pre- and post-Reformation Dutch Catholic martyrs *Historia martyrum Batavicorum*, published posthumously in 1625 and translated into Dutch in 1700, he devoted an entire section to commemorating the martyrdom of Cornelius Musius.[37] In line with the conventions of prose martyr accounts, Opmeer described the priest's impeccable religious credentials, his morally superior character, and his perseverance at the hour of his death. Opmeer did not spare his readers any of the gruesome details of Musius' torments, up to and including his slow and agonising death by hanging. In his martyrology, Opmeer expressly glorified the Van Veen home, referring to it as a 'holy house'. In particular, he commemorated the torture-chamber as an important Catholic *lieu de mémoire*:

> Your household, oh Cornelis Veen, has been sprinkled and thus sanctified by the blood of the great Musius. O, lucky room, that has heard, seen and felt the bitter sufferings of this Blessed Man, and that has deserved to be a fine and worthy witness of his bravery, patience and perseverance.[38]

Opmeer compared the room to a temple, that he hoped to visit one day so that he could kiss the walls that had witnessed Musius' suffering and honour the tools that were used to torture the priest. He prophesied that Catholic poets would celebrate the 'House of Venius' even more than the ancient poets had eulogised the temple of the goddess Diana. Opmeer also praised his friend Cornelis van Veen himself. The former burgomaster had already proven his loyalty to the Old Church by preferring exile abroad over life under a Calvinist regime, but because of the connection between his home and the martyred Musius he was now even more secure of a place in heaven:

> O, thou most fortunate, excellent and worthy Venius, already illustrious and fortunate because of your devout exile and glorious confession of your faith, whose impure hearth has been blessed through the pious blood of the invincible knight of the cross of Christ, at the same time your compatriot and namesake, and who because of this narrow house will in the next world reside in the heavenly courtyard above together with the Glorious Martyr.[39]

In his bulky manuscript *Annales sive historiae de tumultibus Belgicis annis 1566–1615* — a history of the Dutch Revolt cum personal memoir, Catholic polemicist Franciscus Dusseldorpius (1567–1630) also commemorated the life and death of Cornelius Musius. Just as burgomaster van Veen, Dusseldorpius was born and raised in Leiden in an elite family that had for generations supplied the city with magistrates. Similar to the Van Veen family, young Franciscus and his mother had fled the rebels in 1572 and returned to Leiden several years later. Dusseldorpius' hagiography of Musius explicitly incorporated the Van Veen house and its torture-chamber. According to Dusseldorpius he had heard from the notary Oudervliet himself that it had been impossible to wash Musius' blood off the walls of the little room — such was the brutality of the priest's torture.[40]

The room had thus turned into an important *lieu de mémoire*, where Catholics could remember and celebrate the religious heroism of their priest, so strengthening the identity of the Catholic community. Yet, at another level, the focus on the torture room also points to its role in a strategy to restore the social capital of former Catholic exiles. While many Catholics in the 1570s frowned on the decision of coreligionists to go into exile, rather than stick it out in the rebel cities, Geert Janssen has shown that gradually exiles themselves began to articulate and defend their decisions in print.[41] The story of the Holy House suggests they also did so through their involvement in local memory practices. All of those involved in the sanctification of the Holy House had been in exile. Opmeer had gone into exile when the Beggars reached Delft in 1572.[42] He fled first to the Southern Netherlands, and then to royalist Amsterdam. When this city joined the Revolt in 1578, he returned to Delft. During his exile years in Amsterdam Opmeer composed his *Historia*, including the account of Musius' execution.[43] Part of this account was told through a lengthy letter that Opmeer wrote from Amsterdam, 'safe haven for exiles', and that was addressed to another exile, the Delft priest Paulus Taphaeus, who had escaped to Utrecht when the city welcomed the rebels in 1572. Opmeer ends his letter with greetings back and forth from other exiles.[44] Opmeer's eulogy of the Venius' house as a Catholic temple, and his praise of the burgomaster's choice for exile over life under a Calvinist regime, figured in precisely this letter. Exile and an important Catholic *lieu de memoire* were thus linked together. Some members of the Van Veen family appear to have actively exploited the potential of this strategy. Dusseldorpius' side remark in the *Annales* that the table on which Musius had been tortured was still in possession of a daughter of Cornelis van Veen, indicates that she capitalised on the status of their family home as a Catholic urban landmark to wash away the stain of their flight in 1572.[45]

While the reputation of the Holy House seems to have waned once it was left by the family itself in the course of the seventeenth century, the martyrdom of Cornelius Musius nevertheless engendered an enduring legacy both in the collective memory of Leiden Catholics and in urban space. On June 24, 1734 the Feast of St John very exceptionally coincided with Corpus Christi. All through the Dutch Republic, but especially in the provinces of Holland and Friesland, rumours were being spread that on this day the Catholic community would rise up against the Protestants, take back their churches and seize political power.[46] The unsubstantiated stories about an imminent Catholic revolution, fuelled by older prophecies about a Catholic restoration, and the subsequent pamphlets that appeared everywhere, not only caused fear amongst Protestants, but also inspired Catholics. On the night of June 24 these prophesies mobilised Leiden's Catholics into action. In large numbers, they gathered around the Blue Stone where Cornelis Musius was executed in 1572, hoping to see the priest rise from the dead. Although some bystanders later were to claim that they had seen the Blue Stone rise two feet, Catholic hopes for the resurrection of the martyred priest did not materialise.[47] Nevertheless, the 1734 incident shows that Musius' grave and the Blue Stone retained a central place in Leiden's Catholic memory-landscape, and could remain associated with hopes for a restoration.

Feeding the multitudes, bridging the gap

While many of Leiden's Catholics in 1734 hoped for a restoration of power, others argued that 'true Catholics' should reject all revolutionary aspirations; content enough with their position in Dutch society, they thought themselves good patriots.[48] Despite the clear evidence for the existence of counter-memories in Leiden's Catholic community, others adopted a much more accommodating position. There was scope for them to do so. Partly because there was a war to win, the city governments of the newly Reformed Dutch cities did not 'calvinise' all public life; the corporations that formed the backbone of urban culture, like the guilds, the militia companies and literary societies known as 'chambers of rhetoric', remained confessionally mixed. As a consequence city-dwellers could retain many traditional and cross-confessional notions of citizenship, urban harmony, and urban honour that were traditionally celebrated in such corporations.[49]

The emphasis on cross-confessional shared civic values created possibilities of which even committed Catholic families like that of the Van Veens were happy to avail themselves. Van Veen's children had to make their way in a society that allowed only the Reformed to wield political power, and demanded loyalty oaths to the new regime of public officials. As a consequence, much like in England, it was the women in the family who became the guardians of its Catholic character, while most of the men in the family opted for public conformity, and for association with the central myths in the city.[50] While Cornelis van Veen restored his social credit in Catholic circles by the association with the martyrdom of Musius, his sons chose to align themselves with the public memory culture in the city. As early as 1575, the eldest son Simon had been back to serve in the civic militia, and had played a role in the opening ceremonies of the university that William of Orange had granted to Leiden in thanks for its fortitude. Probably not long afterwards, the only son who would never return to live in the city, the painter Otto, dedicated a painting to the liberation of the city by the beggar armies on 3 October 1576, and the feeding of the Leiden multitudes. Despite the fact that he would be a lifelong Catholic and from 1596 a permanent resident of the Habsburg Netherlands, Otto apparently sought to associate himself with the rebel memory culture that emerged in his home town. In 1615 his brother Pieter, a talented amateur-painter, presented the city magistrate of Leiden with a similar painting, based on his brother Otto's earlier work.

Both paintings show how hungry Leideners are wolfing down the bread and herring that are handed out from the beggar ships as they are entering the city. The ships are bearing the rebel flag. Some women are fighting over the food, in the centre a man is eating herring, so hungry that he is ignoring the pleas of a child for its share, while others are on their knees in gratitude. On Pieter's reworking of his brothers' invention we see a severed horse's head and a horse's skull, a reference to the eating of horse meat that had come to epitomise the suffering (perhaps not so much because of a taboo on horse meat as such, but because horses were themselves so costly, thus signifying the sacrifice). Both images have inscriptions that highlight how this sudden gift of food put an end to local suffering.[51]

In their visual representation of the feeding of Leiden's multitudes, [Fig. 4.2 & Fig. 4.3] the Van Veen brothers followed the version of events which the city's new elite had produced. The commemorative stone on the city hall, inscribed by town secretary Jan van Hout, told all comers that: 'After black famine left almost six thousand dead, God took pity upon us and gave us bread again, as much as we could wish for'.[52] It did not say that the stone itself had at one time served as an altar, and had been purged from St Peter's church. It was probably no accident. We know of many similar pre-modern situations in which objects and spaces were consciously redeployed to make political or confessional points.[53] Some Catholic contemporaries may have found that deeply offensive.

Yet in general, the hunger narrative seems to have become essential to a strategy of reconciliation, rather than to rub salt into Catholic wounds. Leiden's population had been deeply divided about both its support for the rebel cause and the ensuing reformation of the city, and the cessation of the siege did not put an end to this. As we have seen the Pacification of Ghent, aiming to facilitate a return to unity, and prescribing oblivion as a tool to achieve this, could not put

FIGURE 4.2 Otto van Veen, *De uitdeling van haring en wittebrood na de opheffing van het beleg van Leiden 3 oktober 1574* [*Distribution of Herring and White Bread after the Relief of the Siege of Leiden, 3 October 1574*], 1574–1629. Rijksmuseum, Amsterdam, inv.nr. SK-A-391.

FIGURE 4.3 Pieter van Veen, *De spijziging van de verloste Leidenaren op 3 oktober 1574* [*The Feeding of the Redeemed Leideners on 3 October 1574*], 1615. Museum De Lakenhal, Leiden, inv.nr. 443.

an end to all bitterness. Yet it opened the door to creating a public version of at least some of the Revolt's events that all parties could agree on. Leiden's hunger narrative emphasised that all had suffered in the famine, rebels and loyalists, rich and poor, Catholics and Protestants, so offering memories of a past on which all might agree.[54] This is what allowed the sons of Cornelis van Veen, who had returned to live in the house where Musius had been murdered by the rebel armies, to also cast those rebel soldiers in the role of liberators, and commemorate them as the bringers of bread and fish.

Conclusion

Some Catholics in Leiden never accepted the new order. Franciscus Dusseldorpius chose to become a pillar of the Dutch Mission, the underground Catholic Church in the Northern Netherlands, rather than pursuing his successful career as a lawyer, which would have forced him to take an oath of loyalty to the Dutch Republic. He was unimpressed by the hunger narrative that Leiden's magistrate and population cultivated. Continuing to deplore the loss of his native city to the Dutch Revolt, he commemorated Musius' martyrdom instead as a defining episode in Leiden's Reformation history. Yet such a hard line was not to everyone's taste. Although the Revolt had forced them into exile, and their father's home had become a centre for Catholic counter-memories, Pieter and Otto van Veen aligned themselves with the memory of collective victimhood that Leiden used to reinvent itself as a united and righteous post-Reformation and post-Revolt community.

That this commemorative strategy proved so inclusive, was probably not least because it offered a remediation of pre-Reformation memories about hunger, bread, and stone. Considering the regular public exposure of the bread stone to raise money for charity, which was presumably accompanied by sermons to encourage them to give, one imagines many Leideners must have been familiar with the gruesome stories about the famine of 1316. This may be one explanation why the famine tales they told after 1574 bore a remarkable resemblance to these stories. Both in 1316 and 1574 people were said to have eaten grass and leaves, gnawed raw meat from bones, picked through dung heaps, and had babies starved on their dying mother's barren breasts. The first historian of Leiden's siege, Jan Fruytiers, may have read Cornelius Aurelius' chronicle about the famine of 1316.[55] Perhaps the descriptions of both famines remediated Flavius Josephus' recounting of the famine during the siege of Jerusalem. But however that may be, memories of famine, and of salvific bread, helped to bridge the gap between the pre- and post-Reformation world. One imagines that parallels between the two famines must have occurred to Cornelis van Aecken, the new owner of the bread stone. During the siege, he had been commissioned with making a house-to-house inventory of what there was left to eat in the city, a delicate and difficult task. And however keen he was to authenticate the bread stone, he was also proud of the city's liberation; he produced a map commemorating the siege of 1574 and composed at least one poem to the same end.[56]

So what have we learned from studying Catholic memory in an urban Protestant context? Firstly, we have seen that all commemorative strategies that earlier scholars identified among Catholic minorities in Protestant states were also in evidence in Leiden. In the affidavit for the bread stone, we have seen how Leiden's Catholics tried to salvage memories of past religious practices. Secondly, the religious watershed of the 1570s also created new 'underground' memory cultures in Leiden's Catholic community. Such was the case with the torture and execution of the priest Cornelius Musius in 1572 by the hands of the Beggars, which also usefully served to reconnect exiles with the fortunes of the Catholics who had chosen to remain in the city. Both the house where the priest had been tortured and the Blue Stone where he had been executed became landmarks in the Catholic urban memory landscape, also emphasising the importance of physical locality in memory practices.

Thirdly, we saw how the post-Reformation memory culture in Leiden, allowed Catholics some room to align themselves with urban memory practices. This was not just owing to the relative confessional neutrality of Leiden's memory practices, but also because these remediated local pre-Reformation themes, in which hunger, bread, and stone continued to play a pivotal role. While it is evident that it was at a local level that the religious break with the past presented itself most starkly to the people of Reformation Europe, urban memory practices, with their emphasis on civic values, internal harmony, and local virtue, also offered opportunities and incentives to bridge the gap between past and present.

Notes

1 Judith Pollmann, *Memory in Early Modern Europe, 1500–1800* (Oxford, 2017), 96–102; David Cressy, *National Memory and the Protestant Calendar in Elizabethan and Stuart England* (London, 1989).

2 E.g. Alison Shell, *Oral Culture and Catholicism in Early Modern England* (Cambridge, 2007); Alexandra Walsham, *The Reformation of the Landscape: Religion, Identity and Memory in Early Modern Britain and Ireland* (Oxford, 2011); Liesbeth Corens, 'Dislocation and Record-Keeping: The Counter-Archives of the Catholic Diaspora', in *The Social History of the Archive. Record-keeping in Early Modern Europe*, ed. Liesbeth Corens, Kate Peters, and Alexandra Walsham, *P&P* issue supplement 11 (2016), 269–87; Carolina Lenarduzzi, *Katholiek in de Republiek: Subcultuur en tegencultuur in Nederland, 1570–1750* (PhD thesis, Universiteit Leiden, 2018), 122–72.

3 Anne Dillon, *The Construction of Martyrdom in the English Catholic Community, 1535–1603* (London and New York, 2016); Clodagh Tait, 'Catholic Martyrdom in Early Modern Ireland', *History Compass* 2, no. 1 (2004), 1–5.

4 Christopher Highley, *Catholics Writing the Nation in Early Modern Britain and Ireland* (Oxford, 2008); P. P. V. van Moorsel, 'De devotie tot Sint Willebrord van ong. 1580 tot ong. 1750', *Ons Geestelijk Erf* 31 (1957), 337–69; Willem Frijhoff, 'The Function of the Miracle in a Catholic Minority: The United Provinces in the Seventeenth Century', in Willem Frijhoff, *Embodied Belief: Ten Essays on Religious Culture in Dutch History* (Hilversum, 2002), 137–52.

5 S. Groenveld, 'Leiden in de eerste Jaren van de Nederlandse Opstand, 1566–1574', in *Leiden: De geschiedenis van een Hollandse stad*, ed. R. C. J. van Maanen and J. W. Marsilje, 4 vols. (Leiden 2002-2004), I: 201–11.

6 W. A. Fasel, 'De Leidse glippers', *Leids Jaarboekje* 48 (1956), 68–86; Louis Sicking, *Geuzen en glippers: Goed en fout tijdens het beleg van Leiden*, 3 Oktoberlezing (Leiden, 2003).

7 Robert Fruin, *Het beleg en ontzet der stad Leiden* (The Hague, 1874); Henk den Heijer, *Holland onder water: De logistiek achter het ontzet van Leiden* (Leiden, 2010).

8 R. C. J. van Maanen, *Hutspot, haring en wittebrood: Tien eeuwen Leiden, Leienaars en hun feesten* (Leiden, 1981); I. W. L. Moerman and R. C. J. van Maanen, *Leiden, eeuwig feest* (Leiden, 1986); Jori Zijlmans, *Leidens ontzet, vrijheidsstrijd en volksfeest* (Leiden, 2011).

9 Thera Wijsenbeek-Olthuis, *Honger*, 3 Oktoberlezing (Leiden, 2006).

10 Judith Pollmann, *Herdenken, herinneren, vergeten: Het beleg en ontzet van Leiden in de Gouden Eeuw*, 3 Oktoberlezing (Leiden, 2008); Pollmann, *Memory in Early Modern Europe*, 105–16.

11 Elizabeth den Hartog and John Veerman, *De Pieterskerk in Leiden: Bouwgeschiedenis, inrichting en gedenktekens* (Zwolle, 2011), 183–4.

12 [Anonymous], *Clerc uten lagen landen bi der zee*, c. 1409–1417 (The Hague, Koninklijke Bibliotheek, National Library of the Netherlands, inv.nr. D 71 F 30). See about the clerk: 'Kroniek van Holland', *Narrative Sources*, accessed 23 September 2019, http://www.narrative-sources.be/naso_link_nl.php?link=227.

13 Cornelis Aurelius, *Divisiekroniek*, XII, viii. The transcript is available online, accessed 23 September 2019, https://web.archive.org/web/20110724160354/http://www.karintilmans.nl/pdf/dk1-29.pdf.

14 See for variants to this tale the website of the *Nederlandse Volksverhalenbank*, accessed 23 September 2019, http://www.verhalenbank.nl/items/show/7904; [Frenay], 'Het Leidsche broodwonder', IV. See bibliographic information below.

15 [Frenay], 'Het Leidsche broodwonder', III: 40, citing G. N. de Stoppelaar, *Catalogus der oud- en zeldzaamheden, schilderijen, teekeningen en portretten, aanwezig in de Oudheidskamer ten Raadhuize van Middelburg* (Middelburg, 1876), 42.

16 Leiden, Bibliotheek Erfgoed Leiden, Ms 501, [(J. D. Frenay), 'Het Leidsche brood-wonder', 4 vols. plus 2 vols. of appendixes A and B]. Although the title page suggests this account was written by B. de Bont, the actual author was the Leiden priest and medical doctor J. D. Frenay (1816–1895), who had been asked by De Bont to research the local provenance of the stone. His results were summarised in H. van Rooijen, 'Het Mirakel van Leiden', *Leidsch Jaarboekje* 35 (1943), 108–30.

17 One of them added that his father (sic!) had been well-acquainted with these sisters. The text that was read to them was [Cornelis Aurelius], *Die cronycke van Hollandt, Zeelandt ende Vrieslant, beghinnende van Adams tiden tot die geboerte ons heren Jhesu: voertgaende tot den jare 1517: met die cronike der biscoppen van Utrecht* (Leiden 1517).

18 Van Rooijen, 'Het Mirakel van Leiden', summarises the information on the witnesses that had been collected by Frenay, who discussed it in great detail in 'Het Leidsche broodwonder', vols. I–II in extenso, and referenced it in Appendix B with extracts from the urban records.

19 Van Rooijen, 'Het Mirakel van Leiden', esp. 118–20. See also Jan Fruytiers, *Corte beschrijvinghe van de strenghe belegheringhe ende wonderbaerlijcke verlossinghe der Stadt Leyden in Hollandt* (Delft, 1577), fol. 4, who explicitly refers to Cornelis van Aecken as the owner of a large collection of antiquities found in and around Leiden.

20 [Frenay], 'Het Leidsche broodwonder', III: 3, citing *De Navorscher* 12 (1862), 359.

21 Van Rooijen, 'Het Mirakel van Leiden', 119.

22 See for the transportation and authentication of relics in the Dutch Republic e.g. A. C. de Kruijf, *Miraculeus bewaard: middeleeuwse Utrechtse relieken op reis: de schat van de oud-katholieke Gertrudiskathedraal* (Zutphen 2011); Lenarduzzi, *Katholiek in de Republiek*, chapter 4.

23 William Brereton, *Travels in Holland, the United Provinces, England, Scotland, and Ireland, MDCXXXIV-MDCXXXV*, ed. Edward Hawkins (London, 1844) I: 47–8.

24 Jean Nicolas de Perival, *Les délices de la Hollande, contenant une description de son pais, de ses villes, & de la condition des habitans, avec un racourci de ce qui s'est passé depuis le temps qu'ils se sont mis en liberté, jusqu'à l'annee 1669: nouvellemtent revues, corrigez & augmentés d'une*

histoire de la derniere guerre contre le roy de France & ses alliez, continuée jusqu'au mariage de Guillaume Henry III, prince d'Orange: avec les villes et forts en taille douce (Amsterdam, 1678). According to [Frenay], 'Het Leidsche Broodwonder', IV: 95 it was only recorded in this edition.

25 Probably because it had no material value it was not included in the inventory of her possessions (Amsterdam, Stadsarchief Amsterdam, Archief van de familie Moens en aan-verwante families, toegang 192, inv.nrs. 110–9, esp. 114). The heir of the stone, whose grandson Henricus Bouvy was to leave it to the Museum Amstelkring, was the executor of Moens' will.

26 In Frenay's days it was thought to relate to the miraculous escape of a local criminal from police hands. See 'Het Leidsche broodwonder', I: 4–5.

27 Judith Pollmann, *Catholic Identity and the Revolt of the Netherlands, 1520–1635* (Oxford, 2011), 131–4; Geert H. Janssen, *The Dutch Revolt and Catholic Exile in Reformation Europe* (Cambridge, 2014).

28 G. Eschauzier, 'Het Leidse geslacht Van Veen', in *Genealogische en Heraldische Bladen* 3 (1908), 360–80; R. E. O. Ekkart, 'Het gezin van Cornelis van Veen', in *Leids Jaarboekje* 66 (1974), 95–105.; Sicking, *Geuzen en glippers*, 9, 27.

29 Petrus Opmeer, *Historia Martyrum Batavicorum, sive Defectionis a fide maiorum Hollandiae initia: duas in decades distribute/auctore Petro Opmeero* (Cologne, 1625). For this essay we have used the Dutch translation: *Martelaars-boek, ofte historie der Hollandse martelaren, welke om de Christen Catholijke gods-dienst, soo ten tijden van de woeste heidenen, als der Hervormde nieugesinden seer wreed sijn omgebragt:/beschreven door Petrus Opmeer* (Antwerp, 1700). The notary is mentioned on p. 161, as is his wife, who was said to have protested against the torture of Musius, arguing (and rightly so) that from a legal point of view the nearby city jail was the only appropriate place to inflict judicial violence.

30 [Frenay], 'Het Leidse broodwonder', appendix A, 12–13, citing Leiden's *Gerechtsdagboek*, 4 March 1569.

31 H. F. K. van Nierop, *Van ridders tot regenten. De Hollandse adel in de zestiende en eerste helft van de zeventiende eeuw* (Amsterdam, 1990), 21; Fasel, 'De Leidse glippers', 84.

32 Opmeer, *Martelaars-boek*, 142–3. The story of his slow death because of a tumour in: *Annales sive historiae de tumultibus Belgicis annis 1566–1615 Francisci Dusseldorpii*, 2 vols. (Cologne, 1615–1616), Utrecht, University Library Utrecht, coll. hss. 775, vol. 1, fol. 312. Chronicler Franciscus Dusseldorpius had obtained this piece of information from a friend who lived close to the Blue Stone and who had heard the priest's sighs all night through his open windows.

33 B. A. Vermaseren, 'De bronnen voor onze kennis van het leven van Corn. Musius', *Archief voor de Geschiedenis van de Katholieke Kerk in Nederland* 2 (1960), 93–108.

34 P. C. Boeren, 'Susanna Vanetten, weldoenster van Cornelius Musius', *Leids Jaarboekje* 64 (1972), 77–82, at 77–8; Els Kloek, ed., *1001 Vrouwen uit de Nederlandse geschiedenis* (Nijmegen, 2013), 189–90.

35 Leiden, Erfgoed Leiden en Omstreken, Stadsarchief Leiden (SA II), 1574–1816, toe-gangs NL-LdnRAL-0501A, inv.nr. 1369, Register van teruggekeerde ballingen. Zie ook Sicking, *Geuzen en glippers*, 27, and Fasel, 'De Leidse glippers', 68–86.

36 B. J. M. de Bont, 'Het katholieke Amsterdamsche patriciaat der XVIIe en XVIIIe eeuw: Petrus van Opmeer, Amsterdammer, en zijne Historia Martyrum Batavicorum', in *De Katholiek. Godsdienstig, Geschied- en Letterkundig Maandschrift* 117 (1900), 197–210, esp. 204–5.

37 Opmeer, *Martelaars-boek*, 112–68. See also note 29.

38 Opmeer, *Martelaars-boek*, 141.

39 Opmeer, *Martelaars-boek*, 141–2.

40 *Annales*, vol. 1, fol. 312.

41 On the changing views of exile among Catholics, see Janssen, *The Dutch Revolt and Catholic Exile*, 35–79.

42 Although having been an exile himself, he nevertheless disinherited in 1593 his two sons living in the Habsburg Netherlands because they had rejected their 'fatherland'. See

Janssen, *The Dutch Revolt and Catholic Exile*, 156–7. This might be another explanation as to why he felt it necessary to try and restore the social status of Cornelis van Veen, who was after all a close friend.

43 See Opmeer's preface in the Latin edition of the *Martelaars-boek*, the *Historia*.

44 For the purpose of the posthumous publication of the *Historia* in 1625, Opmeer's original letter was probably edited and supplemented by an anonymous author. It is puzzling that the anonymous editor tried to give the impression that the letter was not written by Opmeer himself, but by someone else. See P. Noordeloos, 'De brief aan de heer P. Taphaeus over de marteldood van Musius', in *Haarlemse Bijdragen, Bijdragen voor de Geschiedenis van het Bisdom Haarlem* 64 (1957), 165–90.

45 *Annales*, vol. 1, fol. 312.

46 For the relation between these prophecies and the June panic of 1734, see Willem Frijhoff, 'Prophecies in Society: The Panic of June 1734', in Frijhoff, *Embodied Belief*, 181–213.

47 Frijhoff, 'Prophecies in Society', 207.

48 E.g. [Justus van Effen], *Hollandsche Spectator*, vol. 10, nr. 276, June 18, 1734.

49 Gabrielle Dorren, *Eenheid en verscheidenheid: De burgers van Haarlem in de Gouden Eeuw* (Amsterdam, 2002).

50 John Bossy, *The English Catholic Community, 1570–1850* (London, 1975) 150–60; Lenarduzzi, *Katholiek in de Republiek*, 94–110.

51 Otto van Veen, *De uitdeling van haring en wittebrood na de opheffing van het beleg van Leiden 3 oktober 1574*, 1574–1629, Amsterdam, Rijksmuseum Amsterdam, inv.nr. SK-A-391; Pieter van Veen, *De spijziging van de verloste Leidenaren op 3 oktober 1574*, 1615, Leiden, Museum Lakenhal Leiden, inv.nr. 443.

52 Den Hartog and Veerman, *De Pieterskerk in Leiden*, 183–4.

53 Pollmann, *Memory in Early Modern Europe*, 145.

54 Pollmann, *Herdenken, herinneren, vergeten*.

55 Jan Fruytiers, *Corte beschryuinghe vande strenghe belegheringhe ende wonderbaerlicke verlossinghe der stadt Leyden* (Delft 1574, and many reprints).

56 E. Pelinck, 'Cornelis van Aecken en de gedenksteenen in de St. Jeroensbrug', in *Leids Jaarboekje* 35 (1943), 180–5, esp. 183–4. Van Aken was also in possession of poems by Jan van Hout that were inscribed in the commemorative stone at the city hall, and a similar commemorative stone under one of Leiden's bridges.

5

REMEMBERING THE HOLY LEAGUE

Material memories in early modern France

David van der Linden

Remembering the Reformation in early modern France was always contentious. The movement for religious renewal had led to a series of civil wars between Catholics and Protestants, known as the French Wars of Religion (1562–1598). Although the 1598 Edict of Nantes ultimately installed religious coexistence between the two confessions, the monarchy was well aware that recalling past divisions risked undermining the hard-won peace. King Henry IV therefore ordered the wars to be forgotten, decreeing that 'the memory of all things that have happened on either side, since the beginning of the month of March 1585 until our coronation, and during the preceding troubles, shall remain extinguished and suppressed, as if they have never taken place'. The king hoped that by leaving the past behind, former enemies would be able to 'live peacefully together as brothers, friends, and fellow citizens'.[1]

Yet the policy of forgetting was not just aimed at burying the conflict between Protestant and Catholics; it was also an attempt to cover up the rifts that had opened up between Catholics. It is significant that the edict singled out the period between March 1585 and Henry's coronation on 27 February 1594 as worthy of particular forgetting, as these dates marked the rise and fall of the so-called Holy League. This alliance of Catholic noblemen, clergy, officeholders, and devout laymen had vowed to eradicate Protestantism and had disputed Henry's accession to the throne, because he had been born and raised as the Protestant prince of Navarre. By 1588 the League controlled most major cities in France, including Paris and Lyon, leaving Henry IV with the arduous task of regaining his kingdom through a series of battles and sieges, supported by both Protestants and moderate Catholics.[2]

Because Henry ultimately succeeded in defeating the League, the movement was best consigned to oblivion, scholars have argued. The king was indeed keen to wipe the slate clean, pardoning his Leaguer opponents and offering them prominent places in government to ensure their loyalty.[3] Former Leaguers often agreed that the less said about their rebellious past, the better. In his otherwise exhaustive history of Lyon, the former Leaguer councillor Claude Rubys skipped the five years in which the League had held sway over the city, writing that 'I will not give a specific account, not only so as not to violate the amnesty, which has been ordered by the edicts of His Majesty, but also because it would not be fitting for me, given that even I howled with the dogs'.[4]

This essay argues, however, that edicts and official histories are poor guides for understanding how the League survived in historical consciousness in early modern France. For despite the rhetoric of forgiving and forgetting the troubles of the League were actively remembered, especially in material form. Post-war France witnessed a proliferation of purpose-made objects that memorialised the troubles of the League, including triumphal arches, monuments, statues, gifts, and paintings. That memories of the troubles were codified in tangible objects is not surprising. At a time when the vast majority of the French population was illiterate, objects — especially those displayed in public — could communicate the past far more effectively than written texts. And because objects could survive for decades, they also offered the possibility to transmit memories to future generations. Images of the infamous Procession of the League, for example, perpetuated the memory of the League far beyond 1598.[5] Material memories of the League proved to be contested ground, however, as post-war France witnessed the emergence of two competing narratives of the troubles. On the one hand, the monarchy and turncoat Leaguers propagated a royalist memory of the League, presenting it as a dangerous rebellion that had undermined a legitimate monarch with the aid of Habsburg Spain. Committed Leaguers, on the other hand, held on to their experience of opposition and developed a proud counter-memory that resisted official narratives about the recent past.

Forgetting the League

That the Holy League should be remembered in post-war France was not self-evident. As a growing number of Leaguer governors and cities surrendered to Henry IV from 1594 onwards, the king actually promised his former enemies to forget the troubles of the League. Between January 1594 and March 1598 Henry IV issued over 70 capitulation treaties, assuring Leaguer partisans they would not be prosecuted for rebelling against his rule, and prohibiting discussion of events that had occurred during the League.[6] Lyon, the second Leaguer city to side with Henry IV in February 1594, was granted an edict in which the king promised 'to forget everything that may have happened on the authority of the city council against our authority & service, since the beginning of the last troubles until the return to our obedience', and forbade anyone from seeking redress in court.[7] Subsequent treaties would repeat this injunction to forget the League. Upon entering Paris in March 1594, the king even had a tract handed out in the streets, informing citizens that 'His Majesty […] wants & intends that all the things that have happened & occurred during the troubles will be forgotten'.[8]

The king had compelling reasons to issue such oblivion clauses. Legal scholars had theorised the necessity of granting amnesty in order to transition France from civil war to durable peace and concord. Foremost among them was Antoine Loisel, a lawyer in the Parlement de Paris (the most important court of appeal in France), who, quoting the ancient author Lucian, argued that 'the best defence against civil war is oblivion'.[9] Remembering past injustices only helped to 'embitter and renew old wounds', Loisel argued, which could provoke a new cycle of violence. The only remedy was 'to efface everything as quickly as possible, to ensure that nothing remains in the minds of the people on either side, and to never speak or think of it again'.[10]

Yet Loisel's passionate defence of expunging the past does not explain how Henry IV expected people to forget about the League. After all, the monarchy could not police the minds of those who had experienced the wars. Yet scholars have argued that the aim of these oblivion clauses was not to impose forgetfulness, but to control public discourse about the past. Both the Edict of Nantes and the preceding capitulation treaties issued a moratorium on evoking or investigating the troubles of the League, which was not quite the same as ordering complete forgetfulness. Past injustices were not pardoned; rather, by pretending they had never occurred, the monarchy prevented people from acting upon their knowledge of the past, in particular in court. In essence, oblivion was a form of legal amnesia to prevent future conflict.[11] Antoine Loisel confirmed this crucial distinction between forgiving and forgetting in his opening speech to the court of Guyenne. The pardoning of past crimes was unwise in the wake of civil war, he observed, because neither party would admit to its guilt, while people would surely feel wronged if their suffering was not acknowledged. Oblivion, on the other hand, had the virtue of avoiding the thorny question of assigning blame: it did not deny past crimes, but only suspended their prosecution.[12] The monarchy hoped that as long as Frenchmen conformed to the public fiction that the League had never existed, it was possible that its private memory would slowly be forgotten, too.

Yet despite Henry's repeated injunctions to bury the memory of the League, its memory survived across France, in particular as material representations, appearing in monuments, paintings, statues, and even gifts to the monarch himself. This may seem surprising, since recalling an episode that was likely to embarrass ex-Leaguers seemed at odds with the king's attempts to leave the past behind and co-opt the support of his former opponents. But as Judith Pollmann has suggested, precisely because oblivion clauses forbade citizens to evoke past events, they also created an opportunity to formulate new historical narratives, preferably ones that superseded former divisions.[13] Indeed, royalists quickly realised that the memory of the League could help to overcome past conflict, by portraying the civil wars not as a religious struggle between Protestants and Catholics, but between Frenchmen who had been loyal to the monarchy, irrespective of their faith, and those who had colluded with Spain to overthrow it. The antithetical memory of the League thus deflected attention from the religious struggles, uniting the nation around the monarch as the restorer of order.

The League in Lyon

As the second city to fall into royalist hands in February 1594, Lyon functioned as a key laboratory for the forging of this new memory of the League: royalists and turn-coat Leaguers both began to propagate a mythical story of Lyon as a loyal city, which they claimed had voluntarily broken the shackles of Leaguer domination to acknowl-edge Henry IV as France's legitimate ruler. The city had joined the Leaguer rebellion in 1589, after King Henry III, fearful of the growing influence of the nominal leaders of the League, the Duke and Cardinal de Guise, had ordered their assassination. Yet Henry's attempt to regain his authority backfired spectacularly: Catholics throughout France rallied to the League, including in Lyon. On 2 March 1589 the town council renounced the king's authority, instead proclaiming loyalty to the Parisian League, and swore a solemn oath to defend the Catholic religion at all cost. In addition, a separate *conseil d'état* was set up, headed by the Duke of Nemours and Archbishop Pierre d'Épinac. Yet dwindling trade and the wars of the League soon saddled the city with a financial deficit, while the Duke of Nemours alienated the city council by trying to create a personal fiefdom in the region, with Lyon as its capital. In order to end the duke's authoritarian rule, in 1593 the council imprisoned Nemours in the citadel of Pierre-Scize. The city still refused to acknowledge Henry IV, until on 7 February 1594 royalists inside Lyon proclaimed their support for the king and opened the city gates to Alphonse d'Ornano, the royal governor of Dauphiny.[14]

Following the royalist take-over of Lyon, the city council was purged of League supporters and replaced with men loyal to Henry IV. The new council arrested 65 prominent Leaguers, putting 6 under house arrest and banishing the others.[15] The council also moved to destroy all material evidence recalling the city's prior adherence to the League. Black and red sashes — symbols of the League and Spain — were burnt throughout the city, along with the coats of arms of King Philip II, the Duke of Savoy, and the Duke of Nemours. The city executioner also burnt an effigy of the League, painted in the form of a sorceress to symbolise the enthralling power the League had held over people's minds. On 16 February, finally, children constructed a pyramid hung with war trophies on the Place du Change, which was set ablaze to celebrate the demise of the League [Fig. 5.1].[16]

Having cleansed Lyon of all apparent vestiges recalling the League, royalists and former Leaguers began supplanting its memory with a new material narrative. The first indication that this royalist memory centred around objects idolising the king's triumph over the League came during the take-over of Lyon in February 1594. On the morning of 7 February, one of the city councillors suspended a painted portrait of the king from a town hall window, telling the assembled crowd: 'Here's the portrait of our King, he wants to preserve us in the Catholic, Apostolic & Roman Religion. Let us obey him, let us pray God for his prosperity, health, & long life, & let us all cry out *Vive le Roi!*' The portrait played a pivotal role in persuading the population to acknowledge Henry IV, as it was subsequently paraded through town and displayed at the Place du Change for another week, where inhabitants flocked to salute their king with more shouts of *Vive le Roi!* [17]

FIGURE 5.1 The capitulation of Lyon in February 1594: *Warhafftige Zeitung aus der Statt Lyon wass sich fur freyden haben zugetragen nach dem sie sich dem Konig von Navarra ergeben den 7. tag February des 94 Jars* (Nuremberg: Georg Lang, 1594).

Paris, Bibliothèque nationale de France, QB-201(11).

Royalist memories

The royalist memory of the League that spread across France in the next decade found its expression in a recurring visual narrative. On the one hand, allegorical images regularly depicted Henry IV as Hercules slaying the Hydra of Lerna, the ancient monster that now symbolised the rebellious League, while historical images showed the king triumphing over his Leaguer opponents in a series of epic battles and sieges. Both representations found their origins in the abundant print culture of civil war France, in particular the visual propaganda produced by royalists to defame the League.[18] Many of these engravings and newsprints were preserved by the diarist Pierre de l'Estoile, who collected them in order to expose 'the abuses, impostures, vanities and furies of this great monster of the League'. Indeed, several of the anti-Leaguer prints in his collection depict the League as the Lernean Hydra slain by Henry IV.[19] Likewise, representations of Henry's battlefield victories may well have been inspired by a series of newsprints produced in the workshop of Frans Hogenberg, who memorialised the troubles of the League from 1587 onwards.[20]

In Lyon, both expressions of this royalist memory of the League — allegorical as well as historical — came together in the ceremonial entry of Henry IV in September 1595. Royal entries were an enduring feature of Renaissance France, as monarchs relied on this ritual to affirm their often precarious authority in the face of powerful urban elites.[21] Henry likewise used his entry into Lyon and other Leaguer cities to consolidate his authority and reconcile formerly rebellious communities with the monarchy.[22] Chancellor Pomponne de Bellièvre, who had arrived in Lyon in June 1594 to ensure the city's smooth transition to Bourbon rule, had repeatedly insisted that a royal entry was crucial in securing popular support, since the city still counted many disgruntled Leaguers keen to undo the royalist coup. In July 1594 he assured the king that 'your presence, Sire, will reassure all those who have a French heart, and dispel and confound the malice of your enemies'.[23]

When Henry made his way to Lyon in the late summer of 1595, the town council hired two local artists, Jean Maignan and Jean Perrissin, to paint a series of triumphal arches, statues, and columns that would line the king's entry on 4 September. Perrissin was well-suited for this task, as he had previously worked on the Quarante Tableaux, a series of engravings documenting the first three religious wars. The design of the monuments was entrusted to Pierre Matthieu, a playwright and lawyer who had served as secretary to the Leaguer *conseil d'état* in Lyon, but had since managed to convince Bellièvre of his loyalty to Henry IV — it was the chancellor who persuaded the town council to hire Matthieu as artistic director.[24]

The elaborate iconography Matthieu developed in consultation with Bellièvre focused on Lyon's submission to Henry IV, who was praised for ending civil discord by defeating the League. Matthieu designed a series of arches that celebrated the virtues of a just ruler: piety, clemency, force, and courage [Fig. 5.2].

FIGURE 5.2 Royal entry of Henry IV in Lyon on 4 September 1595. Anonymous
      engraving, in Pierre Matthieu, *L'Entree de tres-grand, tres-chrestien, tres-mag-*
      nanime, et victorieux prince Henry IIII. Roy de France & de Navarre, en sa bonne
      ville de Lyon (Lyon: Pierre Michel, 1595).
Paris, Bibliothèque nationale de France, QB-201 (12).

The second arch, dedicated to Henry's clemency, showed a lion strangling the
Hydra of the League, along with an appropriate verse: 'This generous ire dashes
forwards/ by means of fire and the sword/ to plunge into Hell/ the Hydra that
ravaged France'. The arch was topped with a lion offering his prey to Hercules, an
allegorical image that evoked Lyon's surrender to Henry IV.[25] The third and most
spectacular arch praised the 'victories & triumphs of the King'. It focused entirely
on the troubles of the League, showcasing three battle scenes: Henry's victory
against the Duke of Mayenne at the Battle at Arques in September 1589, the Battle
of Ivry on 14 March 1590, and the defeat of a combined army of Leaguer and
Spanish soldiers at Fontaine-Françoise, near Dijon, on 5 June 1595.[26]

Towards the end of his procession the king also encountered a commemorative column, modelled after Emperor Trajan's column in Rome, which
was painted with 'the most remarkable events of these last troubles', and crowned
with a statue of Atlas shouldering the world — another reminder of Henry's
herculean struggle against the League. A melange of historical as well as allegorical images, the ten scenes lining the column included Henry's ascension to the
throne in 1589, the siege of Paris in 1590, an allegorical image of piety to symbolise Henry's conversion to Catholicism in 1593, the surrender of Leaguer cities
from 1594 onwards, and the figure of Leaguer rebellion falling into an abyss.[27]

This visual decalogue of Henry's recent life once again recalled his triumph over the League as well as his conversion to the Church of Rome, an important turning-point in his struggle with the League.

Henry's entry into Lyon and other Leaguer towns offered communities a form of closure, as they could distance themselves from a disgraced past by touting their loyalty to Henry IV. Yet in doing so, cities were paradoxically forced to recall the troubles of the League, if only as an abhorrent counter-example. These visual memories, painted on arches, columns, and other monuments, were as much an attempt to leave the troubles of the League behind as an effort to preserve its memory in post-war France. In the preface to his published description of Henry's ceremonial entry, Pierre Matthieu even advised his readers to 'keep this book as a Medal of happiness of this great French Alexander' and to 'use it as a rich tapestry of the history of these last troubles'.[28] Long after the makeshift arches and columns had disappeared, the book was to serve as a material reminder of the League and its ultimate defeat. It even contained a fold-out engraving of the entire procession, not unlike a tapestry, which was probably designed by Jean Perrissin, who had also been hired to produce plates of the event.[29]

Reciprocal memory-making

It is worth underlining that this royalist memory of the League was not imposed top-down, but was the result of a reciprocal process of peace-making between the king and former Leaguers. Although Henry IV carefully choreographed his entries into Paris and Rouen, most other Leaguer cities, including Lyon, Cambrai, Abbé-ville, and Moulins, planned and designed the entry themselves.[30] The city of Lyon even entrusted the project to a former Leaguer, Pierre Matthieu. This reciprocal process was further encoded in precious gifts to the king, as Leaguer cities aimed to restore their fragile patron-client relationship with the Bourbon monarchy.[31] Following Henry's entry, the Lyon town councillors offered him a small golden statue produced by two local goldsmiths, which showed the king extinguishing the fire of rebellion with one hand, while in the other he presented an olive branch and pomegranate — the tokens of peace and concord — to a kneeling lion, which had freed itself from the shackles of the League to offer Henry a crown.[32]

That Leaguer cities actively participated in the creation of a royalist memory of the League is also evident from another example of gift-giving: in December 1600 the city of Paris offered Henry IV a rapier and companion dagger to celebrate the king's marriage with Marie de' Medici. These were not only precious objects, the rapier was also a material memory, depicting in both visual and textual narrative the troubles of the League [Fig. 5.3]. Rapiers had originally developed in Renaissance Europe as weapons of self-defence, meant to be worn not into battle but with everyday clothing. They gained in popularity around 1600, as the wearing of armour declined and noblemen sought to retain their warrior status by wearing ornamented and flamboyant rapiers.[33]

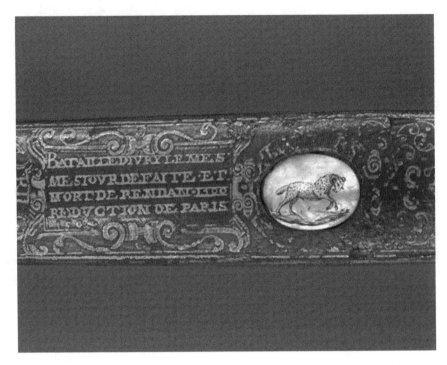

FIGURE 5.3 Anonymous artists, Blade detail of the rapier gifted by the city of Paris to Henry IV, 1600. The medallion of Aries corresponds to a cartouche recalling the battle of Ivry (March 1590) and the capture of Paris (March 1594). Paris, Musée de l'Armée. © RMN-Grand Palais/Pascal Segrette.

Because rapiers were mostly worn sheathed, owners would usually have the visible pommel and hilt decorated, but the rapier gifted to Henry also sported an embellished blade, offering further evidence that it was intended for ostentatious display. The blade was encased with twelve mother-of-pearl medallions representing the signs of the zodiac, interspersed with golden cartouches that contained brief texts commemorating the troubles of the League. Covering the period from 1587 until 1598, the blade memorialised Henry's battles at Coutras, Arques, and Ivry; the submission of Leaguer towns, including Lyon, Paris, Rouen, Le Havre, Orléans, Bourges, and Amiens; and key events from the king's life, such as his reconciliation with Henry III and subsequent ascension to the throne in 1589, Henry's coronation at Chartres in 1594, his reconciliation in 1595 with the Leaguer chiefs, the Duke of Mayenne and the Duke of Nemours, and the Peace of Vervins concluded with Spain in 1598.[34] Besides the incongruous 1587 battle at Coutras, where Henry had led a Huguenot army to victory against King Henry III, all the other cartouches focused on his victorious campaign against the League and the reconciliation with his former enemies. The rapier, then, sought to expunge the shameful memory of Leaguer rebellion, initiated by the city of Paris in 1588, replacing it with a triumphant royalist narrative that depicted the king as the restorer of order and a clement ruler pardoning his rebellious subjects.

FIGURE 5.4 Antoine Schanaert, *The Capture of Grenoble, c. 1615.* Grenoble, Bibliothèque municipale de Grenoble.
Courtesy of the Musée dauphinois, Grenoble.

The royalist memory of the League also appeared in another form of material memory: picture galleries decorating the chateaux of the monarchy, nobility, and office-holders. In the wake of the wars Henry IV undertook a vast campaign of architectural renewal of his palaces, including the creation of galleries that were often decorated with scenes recalling his victories against the League. The Galerie de Diane he constructed at the palace of Fontainebleau, for example, contained ten canvases depicting King Henry's victories, including the battles at Coutras, Arques, Ivry, Fontaine-Françoise, and Honfleur, and the surrender of Mantes and Vernon-sur-Seine, the inhabitants kneeling down to hand Henry the city keys.[35]

Historical picture galleries commemorating Henry IV's victories quickly spread to aristocratic galleries across France. In the aftermath of the wars several royal clients created similar galleries in their chateaux, showcasing the same royalist victories against the League that Henry IV had chosen at Fontainebleau, alongside wartime events that had marked their own lives. A striking example was the gallery of the Duke of Lesdiguières, a royalist commander from Dauphiny, who in 1614 installed seventeen tableaux depicting events from the wars, in his castle at Vizille. Nine of these paintings narrated Henry IV's well-known triumphs: the battles of Coutras, Arques, Ivry and Fontaine-Française, the capture of Rouen, Amiens, La Fère, and Montmélian, and the king's entry into Paris in 1594. The eight paintings on the opposite side, however, traced Lesdiguières' personal military triumphs in Dauphiny, beginning with his capture of the Leaguer stronghold of Grenoble in 1590 [Fig. 5.4].[36]

Similarly, in 1632 the Catholic nobleman Matthieu Sève, who had served as town councillor and prévôt des marchands of Lyon, had the Italian artist Pietro

Ricchi paint a series of mural frescos in his chateau at Fléchères, several of which evoked the troubles of the League. In the so-called Chambre de la Parade, Ricchi depicted soldiers parading in full gear to evoke the participation of the Sève family in opening the city to royalist troops in 1594 and preparing the king's royal entry of 1595. In the nearby antechamber, Hercules can be seen wrestling with the Hydra, a familiar reference to Henry's triumph over the League [Fig. 5.5].[37]

Just like the city councillors of Paris and Lyon, then, Lesdiguières and Sève buried the memory of Leaguer rebellion in favour of a royalist memory that celebrated Henry's supremacy. This royalist memory of the League, which graced monuments, commemorative objects, and picture galleries throughout France, helped to remember the wars without descending into partisan conflict again — the defeat of Leaguer rebels by the Bourbon monarchy became a shared visual and material topos that transcended the memory of religious opposition.

FIGURE 5.5 Pietro Ricchi, Hercules wrestling with the Hydra, 1632. Fareins, Chateau de Fléchères.
Courtesey of the Chateau de Fléchères.

Leaguer counter-memories

Despite the rapid spread of a royalist memory that condemned the League to perpetual ignominy, not all Catholics embraced this narrative. In the privacy of their homes and convents, committed Leaguers continued to cherish memories of resistance, long after they had ostensibly rallied to the Bourbon regime and sworn to bury the past. Michel Foucault has coined the term 'counter-history' to describe this process, defining it as a narrative that resists official versions of historical truth.[38] Counter-histories are born out of oppression, opposing the powers that be by remembering a past that is deliberately being obscured or twisted. The aim of counter-history, Foucault writes, is 'to disinter something that has been hidden, and which has been hidden not only because it was neglected, but because it has been carefully, deliberately, and wickedly misrepresented'.[39] Counter-histories thus focus on experiences that have not been heard and integrated in official histories; they are a form of remembering against the grain, by people whose memories do not fit the dominant historical narrative. As such, the memories of French Catholics who refused to accept the narrative of the League as a misguided movement are a poignant example of counter-memory, a form of resistance against royalist attempts to rewrite the recent past.

This counter-memory was especially resilient among the French mendicant orders, who had been ardent supporters of the League. Franciscan preachers in particular had condoned regicide in their sermons and had created lay confraternities across France in defence of the Catholic faith.[40] The Franciscan order eventually accepted Henry IV's authority after the defeat of the League, but the Capuchins continued to oppose the king, their repugnance bolstered by the issuing of the Edict of Nantes in 1598. The friars not only preached against the edict, they also organised public prayer sessions and processions in Paris, asking God to prevent the implementation of the edict. In response the king had the most vocal Capuchin preacher, Jean Brulart, banned from the capital in 1599.[41]

Crucially, these residual Leaguer sympathies were fuelled by memories of past resistance against the monarchy, which proved to have a reactivating power even after Henry IV had conquered Paris. On 27 December 1594 the king narrowly escaped an assassination attempt by Jean Chastel, the son of a Parisian merchant draper, who attacked him with a knife. During his interrogation Chastel claimed to have acted alone, but the authorities discovered that his Jesuit tutors at the Collège de Clermont — a known Leaguer hotbed — had exercised a powerful influence on the boy's conviction that it was lawful to assassinate a heretical ruler. When officers raided the college they found the Jesuit father Jean Guignard in possession of various sermons and manuscripts, written in his own hand, that eulogised Jacques Clément, the Dominican friar who had murdered King Henry III in 1589, and that condemned Henry IV as a tyrant who should be executed.[42] It is noteworthy that the Parlement of Paris subsequently accused Guignard not only of composing seditious writings, but of keeping alive these memories of Leaguer resistance in flagrant contravention of the oblivion edict issued in 1594.[43]

Both Guignard and Chastel were swiftly executed for lese-majesty, while the Parlement used the botched assassination attempt to expel the Jesuits from its jurisdiction. The court also ordered the creation of yet another material memory of

FIGURE 5.6 Jacob de Weert, *Portrait de la pyramide dressée devant la porte du Palais*, 1597. Rijksmuseum, Amsterdam.

the League: the house of the Chastel family, located on the Île de la Cité just opposite the Parlement, was raised to the ground, and a pyramid erected in its place to memorialise Chastel's crime and the expulsion of the Jesuits; the sentence of the Parlement was even etched in marble on the monument [Fig. 5.6].[44] The Chastel pyramid, then, was another attempt at keeping a lid on Leaguer memories, by supplanting them with a royalist memory of the troubles.

News of Chastel's assassination attempt soon reached Lyon, where a Te Deum was sung, followed by a general procession to thank God for preserving Henry's life. Yet memories of the League still cast a dark shadow over the city: unrest had been growing since July 1594, when the Duke of Nemours had escaped from the citadel of Pierre-Scize disguised as his own valet, and now threatened to raise 8,000 troops to retake Lyon for the League.[45] Bellièvre also reported that clerical opposition to the king was rife, despite the submission of Archbishop d'Épinac and the clergy of Lyon. The chancellor worried in particular about the monastic orders that clung to their Leaguer past, writing to the king that 'in some monasteries that are partial to those of the League they say among themselves that Your Majesty cannot avoid an attempt on his life'.[46] Bellièvre saw his worst fears confirmed in July 1595, when he discovered a plot to assassinate the king on his imminent visit to Lyon, orchestrated by a group of Capuchin friars loyal to the League. Founded in Italy in 1525, the Capuchin order had settled in France as part of the Counter-Reformation campaign to halt the Protestant tide, opening a first convent in Paris in 1574. A second convent opened in Lyon in 1575, funded by wealthy Italian merchants, three of whom would become important League financiers — a past for which they would suffer banishment in 1594. Lyon's Capuchins played an important role in stimulating popular devotion during the League: in 1593 the friars exposed the Host for forty hours at the church of Sainte Croix, where it became the focus of communal veneration, followed by a moving sermon and a procession attended by the Duke of Nemours.[47] The Capuchins continued to support the League after Lyon had surrendered to Henry IV. They were the only monastic order that boycotted a 1594 procession celebrating the royalist take-over of Lyon, just as they refused to hold a Te Deum service after Chastel's failed assassination attempt in 1595.[48]

Bellièvre uncovered the Capuchin plot by chance: on 24 July 1595 his officers intercepted a letter written by the head of the Capuchin order, who instructed his abbot in Lyon not to let friar Cherubin talk to anyone. When Bellièvre had the friar interrogated, Cherubin claimed that five of his Capuchin brothers were planning to assassinate Henry IV, and that several others were prepared to travel from Italy 'to suffer martyrdom'.[49] Material counter-memories played a crucial role in keeping alive this Leaguer resistance. Cherubin singled out two friars as especially dangerous because they owned Leaguer relics that proclaimed their true allegiance. Father Anastase was so devoted to Philip II, Cherubin explained, that he owned a portrait of the Spanish king.[50] He also disclosed that father François had stabbed an effigy of Henry IV with his knife, 'believing that this would cause harm as he has seen happen by those who use evil spells'.[51] Lyon's Capuchins thus ascribed objects both supernatural and mnemonic powers, which helped them to keep alive a counter-memory of Leaguer resistance.

The persistence of Leaguer images among devout Catholics was far from unique. Parisian post-mortem inventories reveal that some people owned portraits of prominent Leaguers long after 1594. When the notary Nicolas Nourry passed away in 1608, an image of the Duke of Mayenne was found in his home, and as late as 1633 the wine merchant Pierre Sotty owned five portraits depicting the Guise brothers.[52] Perhaps these pictures were simply an unwanted inheritance, difficult to offload on the art market after the oblivion clauses had banned the League from public view. Yet the picture gallery of

Sébastien Zamet, a former Italian financier of the League, suggests that some Catholics did preserve portraits to memorialise the League with a sense of pride. Although Zamet had joined the royalist cause in 1593, he never forgot his Leaguer past, commemorating the troubles in a picture gallery he had constructed in his Parisian townhouse in 1598. The gallery included nineteen portraits that stressed the links between France and the Spanish Habsburgs, in particular their support for the League. Zamet owned portraits of Philips II and his French wife, Elisabeth of Valois, as well as of his successor Philip III and his consort, Margaret of Austria. The gallery also contained a portrait of the Duke of Parma, who had invaded France in 1590 to relieve Paris from the besieging troops of Henry IV, and portraits of the archdukes Albrecht and Isabella, who had captured Calais and Amiens in 1596–1597. The gallery thus showcased a visual pantheon of figures who had supported the League in its attempt to depose Henry IV, a counter-memory that sat uneasily with Zamet's support for the new Bourbon regime.[53]

Conclusion

In the aftermath of the French Wars of Religion, Catholics and Protestants faced the difficult task of reconciling competing memories about the conflict, but this was especially true for Catholics, who had also been divided between supporters of the Holy League and royalists who had backed King Henry IV. Although royal edicts ordered them to bury the Leaguer rebellion, its memory nonetheless survived in cities, convents, and chateaux across France, especially in material form, ranging from ceremonial gifts and commemorative pyramids to royal entries and picture galleries. The communicative power of material memories, which were accessible to illiterate audiences and could be transmitted across generations, explains why both royalists and proud Leaguers disregarded the injunction to forget the past: royalists sought to control public discourse about the troubles of the League, while unrepentant Leaguers wished to strengthen their identity as uncompromising Catholics.

In doing so, royalists and turncoat Leaguers cast the movement as an abhorrent example of the dangers of rebellion and touted their loyalty to the Bourbon regime by celebrating Henry IV's triumphs over the League. Purged city councils in the wake of Leaguer capitulation propagated a historical narrative that bridged the divisions between citizens, not unlike the attempts of confessionally mixed cities elsewhere in Europe. In Leiden, for instance, the confiscation of Catholic property and expulsion of clerics by Dutch Calvinists was superseded by a new narrative of collective suffering during the 1574 siege by Spanish troops. The citizens' bravery and subsequent lifting of the siege became a topos in urban memory culture that bonded Protestants and Catholics together, irrespective of their faith.[54] Lyon likewise used the painful episode of Leaguer rebellion to claim the city had been led astray by Spain, until it had voluntarily broken the shackles of foreign domination to acknowledge Henry IV. Rather than portraying the League for what it really was — a radical Catholic movement that had opposed the Protestants and Henry IV — the memory of the troubles was used to unite former Leaguers, royalists, and Protestants around the monarchy as the restorer of order. A minority of committed Catholics, on the other hand, continued to eulogise the League, formulating a proud memory of resistance against the dominant royalist narrative of the League. This counter-memory was especially popular among the mendicant orders, who had been instrumental in garnering public support for the League, and who found it difficult to accept Henry IV and his policy of religious pluralism.

These competing memories are reminiscent of a solution that was crucial in managing religious pluralism in early modern Europe more generally. As Benjamin Kaplan has shown, authorities often allowed religious dissenters to worship in the privacy of their homes and house chapels, as long as their meetings remained invisible and did not disturb the fiction of religious uniformity in the public realm.[55] It appears that French magistrates pursued a similar course of action in handling the troubles of the League. The monarchy's main purpose of decreeing oblivion was to put an end to the conflict and control public narratives about the past, but it could do very little to police the private memories of those who had adhered to the League. The amnesty offered by Henry IV was above all a pragmatic quid pro quo to help end the wars, not a move to extinguish all memories of the League. Indeed, the existence of Zamet's gallery suggests that Leaguer counter-memories were tolerated as long as they did not become visible and threaten the public peace. Hidden from view in picture galleries, monastic cells, and jealously guarded manuscripts, these counter-memories only emerged in the open when they inspired renewed resistance or even regicide, as in the case of Chastel and the Lyon Capuchins, which prompted authorities to invade these private spaces and police the boundaries of admissible memory. This battle over the memory of the League was ultimately won by the French monarchy: as the royalist memory of the troubles came to dominate the historical narrative, it profoundly shaped the negative image historians have long conjured up of the Holy League.

Notes

* Research for this essay was funded by the Dutch Research Council (NWO). I am grateful to Tom Hamilton and the editors for their insightful comments.

1 Edict of Nantes, articles 1 and 2, in 'L'édit de Nantes et ses antécédents', ed. Bernard Barbiche, accessed 3 June 2019, http://elec.enc.sorbonne.fr/editsdepacification/edit_12.
2 Mack Holt, *The French Wars of Religion, 1562–1629*, 2nd ed. (Cambridge, 2005), 123–55; Jean-Marie Constant, *La Ligue* (Paris, 1996).
3 Philip Benedict, 'Shaping the Memory of the French Wars of Religion: The First Centuries', in *Memory before Modernity: Practices of Memory in Early Modern Europe*, ed. Erika Kuijpers, Judith Pollmann, Johannes Müller, and Jasper Van der Steen (Leiden, 2013), 111–25 (122–4); S. Annette Finley-Croswhite, *Henry IV and the Towns: The Pursuit of Legitimacy in French Urban Society, 1589–1610* (Cambridge, 1999); Michel De Waele, *Réconcilier les Français: Henri IV et la fin des Troubles de Religion, 1589–1598* (Quebec, 2010).
4 Claude de Rubys, *Histoire veritable de la ville de Lyon* (Lyon, 1604), 446. On Rubys, see François-Zénon Collombet, *Études sur les historiens du Lyonnais* (Lyon, 1839), 50–68.
5 Tom Hamilton, 'The Procession of the League: Remembering the Wars of Religion in Visual and Literary Satire', *French History* 30, no. 1 (2016), 1–30.
6 De Waele, *Réconcilier les Français*, 274–84; Michel Cassan, 'La réduction des villes ligueuses à l'obéissance', *Nouvelle Revue du XVIe Siècle* 22, no. 1 (2004), 159–74.
7 *Edict et declaration du Roy, sur la reduction de la ville de Lyon, soubs son obeyssance* (Lyon: Guichard Jullieron and Thibaud Ancelin, 1594), 13.

8　Déclaration du Roy, 20 March 1594, Paris, Archives nationales, Y 19, fol. 1r; De Waele, *Réconcilier les Français*, 1.

9　Jotham Parsons, 'The Political Vision of Antoine Loisel', *SCJ* 27, no. 2 (1996), 453–76; Mark Greengrass, 'Amnistie et "oubliance"': Un discours politique autour des édits de pacification pendant les guerres de religion', in *Paix des armes, paix des âmes* (Paris, 2000), 113–23.

10　Antoine Loisel, *Amnestie ou de l'oubliance des maux faicts et receus pendant les troubles & à l'occasion d'iceux* (Paris: Abel l'Angelier, 1595), 29.

11　Paul-Alexis Mellet and Jérémie Foa, 'Une "politique de l'oubliance"? Mémoire et oubli pendant les guerres de religion (1550–1600)', *Astérion* 15 (2016), accessed 14 August 2018, https://journals.openedition.org/asterion/2829; Judith Pollmann, *Memory in Early Modern Europe, 1500–1800* (Oxford, 2017), 140–54.

12　Loisel, *Amnestie ou de l'oubliance*, 28–30.

13　Pollmann, *Memory in Early Modern Europe*, 151–4.

14　Pierre-Jean Souriac, 'Entre capitale protestante et citadelle catholique: Lyon de 1563 à 1594', in *Lyon 1562, capitale protestante: Une histoire Religieuse de Lyon à la Renaissance*, ed. Yves Krumenacker (Lyon, 2009), 221–71; Yann Lignereux, *Lyon et le roi: De la bonne ville à l'absolutisme municipal, 1594–1654* (Seyssel, 2003), 26–8; Pierre Richard, *La Papauté et la Ligue française: Pierre d'Épinac, Archevêque de Lyon, 1573–1599* (Paris, 1901), esp. 440–69, 531–66.

15　Lignereux, *Lyon et le roi*, 170–6; Estier-Freisseix Delphine, 'La fin des Ligueurs', in *Henri IV et Lyon: La ville du XVIIe Siècle*, ed. Françoise Bayard et al. (Lyon, 2010), 119–20. On the banishment of Leaguers from Paris, see Robert Descimon and José Javier Ruiz Ibáñez, *Les Ligueurs de l'exil: Le refuge catholique français après 1594* (Seyssel, 2005).

16　Lignereux, *Lyon et le roi*, 48; Antoine du Verdier, *Discours sur la reduction de la ville de Lyon à l'obéissance du Roy* (Lyon: Thomas Soubron, 1594), 36.

17　Du Verdier, *Discours sur la reduction*, 30–1; Lignereux, *Lyon et le roi*, 51–2.

18　Martial Martin, 'Images de propagande? Les représentations de la Ligue et l'élaboration de l'image du roi Henri IV', in *Henri IV: Art et pouvoir*, ed. Colette Nativel (Tours and Rennes, 2016), 91–104; Corrado Vivanti, 'Henry IV, the Gallic Hercules', *Journal of the Warburg and Courtauld Institutes* 30 (1967), 176–97.

19　Tom Hamilton, *Pierre de l'Estoile and his World in the Wars of Religion* (Oxford, 2017), 160–4; Hamilton, 'Recording the Wars of Religion: The "Drolleries of the League" from Ephemeral Print to Scrapbook History', in *The Social History of the Archive: Record-Keeping in Early Modern Europe*, ed. Liesbeth Corens, Kate Peters, and Alexandra Walsham, *P&P* issue suppl. 11 (2016), 288–310.

20　Alexandra Schäfer, 'Les guerres de Religion en France dans les imprimés de l'atelier colonais d'Hogenberg', in *Médialité et interprétation contemporaine des premières guerres de Religion*, ed. Gabriele Haug-Moritz and Lothar Schilling (Berlin, 2014), 98–120.

21　Neil Murphy, *Ceremonial Entries, Municipal Liberties and the Negotiation of Power in Valois France, 1328–1589* (Leiden, 2016); Nicolas Russel and Hélène Visentin, eds., *French Ceremonial Entries in the Sixteenth Century* (Toronto, 2007).

22　Finley-Croswhite, *Henry IV and the Towns*, 47–62; Margaret McGowan, 'Les stratégies politiques dans la fabrication de l'image du roi: Entrées royales en 1595 (Lyon), 1600 (Avignon), 1610 (Paris)', in *Henri IV: Art et pouvoir*, ed. Colette Nativel (Tours, 2016), 179–86.

23　Bellièvre to Henry IV, Lyon, 22 July 1594, Paris, Bibliothèque nationale de France (hereafter BnF), MS Dupuy 64, fol. 14r. On Bellièvre's mission to Lyon: Olivier Poncet, *Pomponne de Bellièvre (1529–1607): Un homme d'État au temps des guerres de religion* (Paris, 1998), 189–94; Raymond F. Kierstead, *Pomponne de Bellièvre: A Study of the King's Men in the Age of Henry IV* (Evanston, IL, 1968), 75–89.

24　Lignereux, *Lyon et le roi*, 60. On Perrissin and Matthieu, see Philip Benedict, *Graphic History: The 'Wars, Massacres and Troubles' of Tortorel and Perrissin* (Geneva, 2007), 54–61; Gilbert Schrenck, 'Livres du pouvoir et pouvoirs du livre: L'historiographie royale et la conversion d'Henri IV', *Revue française d'histoire du livre* 50 (1986), 153–80; Louis Lobbes, 'P. Matthieu dramaturge phénix', *Revue d'histoire du théâtre* 3 (1998), 207–36.

25 Pierre Matthieu, *L'Entree de tres-grand, tres-chrestien, tres-magnanime, et victorieux prince Henry IIII. Roy de France & de Navarre, en sa bonne ville de Lyon, le IIII. Septembre l'an MDXCV* (Lyon: Pierre Michel, 1595), 39–40.

26 Matthieu, *L'entree de tres-grand prince Henry IIII*, 43–55.

27 Matthieu, *L'entree de tres-grand prince Henry IIII*, 89–91.

28 Matthieu, *L'entree de tres-grand prince Henry IIII*, 'Aux lecteurs', sig. †3.

29 Benedict, *Graphic History*, 60–1.

30 Margaret McGowan, 'Henri IV as Architect and Restorer of the State: His Entry into Rouen, 16 October 1596', in *Ceremonial Entries in Early Modern Europe: The Iconography of Power*, ed. J. R. Mulryne (Farham, 2015), 53–75 (53–4).

31 On gift-giving in France, see Natalie Zemon Davis, *The Gift in Sixteenth-Century France* (Madison, 2000); Sharon Kettering, 'Gift-Giving and Patronage in Early Modern France', *French History* 2, no. 2 (1988), 131–51.

32 Lignereux, *Lyon et le roi*, 115–6; Matthieu, *L'entree de tres-grand prince Henry IIII*, 96.

33 Angus Patterson, *Fashion and Armour in Renaissance Europe: Proud Lookes and Brave Attire* (London, 2009), 58–67; Tobias Capwell, *The Noble Art of the Sword: Fashion and Fencing in Renaissance Europe* (London, 2012).

34 Luisa Berretti, 'Épée d'Henri IV', in *'Paris vaut bien une messe!' 1610: Hommage des Médicis à Henri IV, Roi de France et de Navarre*, ed. Monica Bietti, Francesca Fiorelli Malesci, and Paul Mironneau (Paris, 2010), 243–4.

35 David van der Linden, 'Memorializing the Wars of Religion in Early Seventeenth-Century French Picture Galleries: Protestants and Catholics Painting the Contested Past', *RenQ* 70, no. 1 (2017), 132–78 (149–53).

36 Van der Linden, 'Memorializing the Wars of Religion', 161.

37 Sébastien Vasseur, 'Le château de Fléchères: État des connaissances actuelles sur un fleuron du patrimoine', *Dix-septième siècle* 228, no. 3 (2005), 547–62; Jean-Christophe Stuccilli, 'Pietro Ricchi à Lyon: Les fresques du château de Fléchères', *Revue de l'art* 138 (2002), 63–70.

38 Michel Foucault, *Society Must Be Defended: Lectures at the Collège de France, 1975–76*, tr. David Macey (London, 2004), 70.

39 Foucault, *Society Must Be Defended*, 72.

40 Megan Armstrong, *The Politics of Piety: Franciscan Preachers During the French Wars of Religion, 1560–1600* (Rochester, NY, 2004); Robert Harding, 'The Mobilization of Confraternities Against the Reformation in France', *SCJ* 11, no. 2 (1980), 85–107.

41 Megan Armstrong, 'Adjusting to Peace: The Observant Franciscans of Paris and the Reign of Henri IV', in *Politics and Religion in Early Bourbon France*, ed. Alison Forrestal and Eric Nelson (Basingstoke, 2009), 42–62; Frederic J. Baumgartner, 'The Catholic Opposition to the Edict of Nantes, 1598–1599', *Bibliothèque d'Humanisme et Renaissance* 40, no. 3 (1978), 525–36.

42 Robert Descimon, 'Chastel's Attempted Regicide (27 December 1594) and its Subsequent Transformation into an Affair', in ed. Forrestal and Nelson, *Politics and Religion in Early Bourbon France*, 86–104; Roland Mousnier, *L'Assassinat d'Henri IV, 14 mai 1610* (Paris, 1964), 201–8.

43 'Extrait des livres couvert de parchemin sur lequel est escripte Dormi Secué, lequel a esté escript et composé par Jehan Guignard Jesuite', BnF, MS Français 15588, fol. 167v.

44 Pierre Wachenheim, 'La Pyramide du Palais ou Henri IV représenté malgré lui: Un épisode de la genèse de l'image du roi à l'aube du XVII Siècle', in *L'Image du Roi de François Ier à Louis XIV*, ed. Thomas W. Gaehtgens and Nicole Hochner (Paris, 2006), 57–76.

45 Bellièvre to Henry IV, Lyon, 29 July 1594, BnF, MS Dupuy 64, fols 18r–19r; Kierstead, *Pomponne de Bellièvre*, 80–1.

46 Bellièvre to Henry IV, Lyon, 2 January 1595, BnF, MS Dupuy 64, fol. 59r–v.

47 Bernard Dompnier, *Enquête au pays des frères des anges: Les Capucins de la province de Lyon aux XVIIe et XVIIIe siècles* (Saint-Étienne, 1993), 26–31; Michelange de Chalon, *Annales Capitulaires des freres Mineurs Capucins de la Province de Lyon*, vol. 1, Dijon, 1633, Paris, Bibliothèque Franciscaine des Capucins, fols. 45–46.

48 Henri Hours, 'Les aventures d'un capucin royaliste après la Ligue: Étienne Le Maingre de Boussicaud', *Bulletin de la Société historique, archéologique et littéraire de Lyon* 18 (1952), 55–78 (68–9).

49 Bellièvre to Henry IV, Lyon, 30 July 1595, BnF, MS Dupuy 64, fols 72r–74r. See also Hours, 'Les aventures d'un capucin'.

50 Deposition by Cherubin, 29 July 1595, BnF, MS Dupuy 64, fol. 73v.

51 Deposition by Cherubin, 29 July 1595, BnF, MS Français 15893. fol. 280r.

52 Georges Wildenstein, 'Le goût pour la peinture dans la bourgeoisie Parisienne entre 1550 et 1610', *Gazette des Beaux-Arts* 38a, no. 3 (1951), 11–343 (45, 228); Wildenstein, 'Le goût pour la peinture dans la bourgeoisie parisienne au début du règne de Louis XIII,' *Gazette des Beaux-Arts* 37a, no. 2 (1950), 153–274 (205).

53 Van der Linden, 'Painting the Past', 145–8.

54 Pollmann, *Memory in Early Modern Europe*, 105–16, 153–4.

55 Benjamin Kaplan, 'Fictions of Privacy: House Chapels and the Spatial Accommodation of Religious Dissent in Early Modern Europe', *The American Historical Review* 107, no. 4 (2002), 1031–64.

PART III

Fragmented memory

6

REMEMBERING THE PAST IN THE NORDIC REFORMATIONS

Tarald Rasmussen

The Reformation movements tended to present themselves as a new start, with a radically critical attitude to the medieval church. Nevertheless, both Lutheran and Calvinist Reformation movements had important cultural and intellectual roots in medieval traditions, and they also looked back upon and tried to connect to medieval history in order to promote their own profile of a new start. This took place in many different ways, both on a local and on a more central level: on behalf a city or local community or on behalf of an entire kingdom.

This contribution will concentrate on ways of remembering and using — but also about forgetting — the medieval past in the Nordic Reformations. Reformation research throughout the last 40 years has strongly enhanced our insight into a number of ways in which the Reformation was rooted in and indebted to late medieval culture and late medieval theology.[1] Many of these (re-)discovered links and connections between the Reformation and the late Middle Ages had been neglected and forgotten by former generations eager to stress the new start of the sixteenth century reformers.

But asking about remembering or forgetting the past is a different kind of question from the question of being influenced by the past. It is totally possible for instance — as recent research has demonstrated — for a Reformation movement (e.g. in Wittenberg or in Copenhagen) to be highly influenced by the late medieval past as it tries to neglect this and forget about it. Or the other way around: it is totally possible for a country (like Norway) to be culturally and religiously deeply reshaped by the Reformation, and at the same time try to neglect and forget about this and instead give priority to remembering the good times prior to the Protestant era. And then again: one could, as was the case in Sweden, both be strongly influenced by and also actively remember the medieval roots of the Reformation.

These different ways of remembering and forgetting are not only relevant for understanding ways of *using* the past by different Reformation movements. They can also contribute to our historical understanding of these Reformations themselves.

In the early modern period, the Nordic region primarily comprised two kingdoms: Denmark/Norway on the one hand and Sweden on the other. In recent attempts to discuss Reformation history in a broader European perspective, Scandinavia or 'the North' is often dealt with as one region — comprising both of the Nordic early modern kingdoms.[2] Several observations may support this kind of approach: this Nordic region, separated from Continental Europe by the Baltic Sea, emerged as a permanent stronghold of Lutheranism, less affected by confessional controversies than many parts of Central Europe, and ruled by royal dynasties which (with some exceptions) were devoted to the Lutheran confession. In the late Middle Ages they had constituted a political union (The Calmar Union), which lasted for more than 120 years. In the nineteenth and early twentieth centuries, the idea of a closer Nordic political and cultural cooperation was revitalised in different contexts.

On the other hand: precisely in the Reformation era, in the period of consolidation of the two strong Protestant kingdoms in the North in the sixteenth and seventeenth centuries, it is equally obvious that these two kingdoms are different. Their ways of introducing and strengthening Lutheran religion are significantly different, their international political and confessional networks are different, and their roles within a broader European confessional context are different.

These initial observations may be taken as an adequate point of departure for a (not frequently applied) Nordic comparative approach: within the framework of 'Early Modern Nordic Lutheranism' as a *tertium comparationis*, this essay shall concentrate on a comparison between the case of Denmark (including Norway) and the case of Sweden: how did the Reformation in these new Lutheran countries relate to the past? How did the Nordic Reformations remember their middle ages? And how does the answer to this question contribute to identifying important differences between the Nordic Reformations?

The first two parts of the essay have a focus on holy places: on different ways of re-using, remembering, and forgetting major medieval Nordic sites of sanctity. Comparing Danish and Swedish strategies will be the primary objective. In a third part, the special case of Norway is taken into closer consideration. Here, the history of the Reformation was in a particularly radical way a history of loss and political humiliation. How did the country deal with this quite difficult point of departure: on the one hand wanting to confirm a Lutheran identity, on the other hand looking at the Reformation as a political and cultural disaster?

Medieval religious centres of the Nordic countries

Sweden

Sweden had a martyr king — Erik. He had been killed by his enemies, and was buried in the cathedral of Old Uppsala, a few kilometres away from the present Uppsala. Old Uppsala was an archbishopric since 1164, but also one of the most famous cult cites of Old Norse religion, a place of sacrificing animals as well as

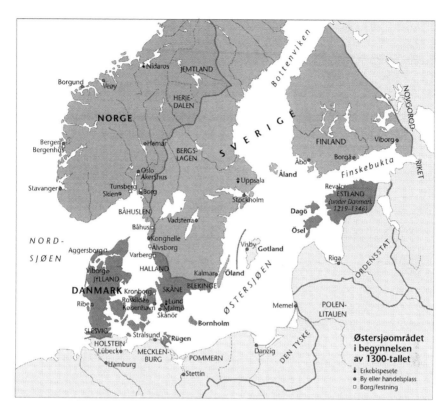

FIGURE 6.1 Map of the Nordic region in the late Middle Ages.
Produced by Author.

human beings, and a place explicitly described in Adam of Bremen Chronicles. The huge cathedral of Old Uppsala — the first church of the archbishop — was built in the early thirteenth century, and was located very close to the sites of pre Christian sacrifice.[3] So, it was a holy place of cult continuity, reorganised for new purposes within a Christian context.

This cathedral burnt down in 1245, and after the fire, it was not rebuilt in the same place. In spite of popular opposition in Old Uppsala, the church of the archbishop was rebuilt in the 1260s and 1270s in the city, which we now know as Uppsala (old name: *Östra Aros*). The reason given for the change of location was primarily practical. But the new location, too, was closely connected to the life of the martyr king: it was the site where he had celebrated his last mass, and it was close to the site where he had died as a martyr. Among the first things to be moved over to the new location were the relics of Erik (1273). In his new resting place, his legend was also written down, and liturgies for his feast days were composed.

Also, the contact to the old resting place of Erik was liturgically maintained through an annual procession on Erik's feast day. Previously, in the time of the Old Uppsala Cathedral, this procession passed with the relics of the saint from Old Uppsala to the place of the Martyr's death in Östra Aros and back again. After the translation, the direction was reversed. Now, every year on St Erik's feast day the relics were brought home to their original resting place and then back again to the high altar in the new cathedral.[4]

In addition to the Uppsala-traditions of St Erik and the archbishop, Sweden had, since the fourteenth century, fostered the traditions associated with the internationally highly appreciated mystic St Bridget. Her revelations were read throughout Europa. And even though she lived in Rome for more than 20 years and had died there, her bones were shortly after her death brought back to Vadstena and were venerated there.[5]

Denmark

Denmark had the archbishopric of Lund (Danish territory until 1658) since 1104, which was from the beginning responsible for all the Nordic countries. Lund was originally established by the Papacy as an administrative centre of the North, and the holiness of the place was most of all attributed to the dignity of the office of the archbishop who resided there. It was not an important pilgrimage site, there were no relics with any kind of national importance connected to them.

Denmark's royal saint, Knut, had never been buried in the cathedral in Lund. He had been put to rest in Odense, on the Funen, the church where he died as a martyr in 1086. He was canonised by the pope in 1102, and was venerated as an important saint in Denmark, but rarely outside it.

For Danish political purposes, the cathedral of Roskilde emerged in the late Middle Ages as a religious centre of greater national importance than both Lund and Odense. This was most of all because Roskilde had in the early fifteenth century been established as the burial place of the Danish kings — starting with the illustrious Queen Margrete I who had ruled over the whole Kalmar union. After her death in 1415, the quire in Roskilde had even been rebuilt in order to give enough space to a fitting grave monument for the great queen.[6] But Roskilde was not an archbishopric, and within a late medieval context not really a religious centre in its own right. Nevertheless, it was the cathedral located closest to Denmark's new political centre, Copenhagen.

Norway

The third mid-twelfth century archbishopric (next to Lund and Uppsala) in the North was that of Nidaros in Norway, confirmed by the pope in 1152. This new ecclesiastical centre was not primarily connected to the centres of royal power in medieval Norway (as was the case with Uppsala in Sweden). But there are other similarities to the creation of Uppsala as an archbishopric in Sweden taking place 12 years later: Nidaros, too, was the burial place of a holy king, a king who was since the eleventh century the National saint of Norway, and who was celebrated as the most outstanding Martyr King of Northern Europe. King Olaf's reputation of sanctity by far overruled that of Erik in Uppsala (who was more of a local saint).

Chapels and churches consecrated to Olaf were erected not only in Norway, but in great numbers also in Sweden, Denmark, England, Northern Germany and the Baltic region, the Netherlands (e.g. in Amsterdam), France, and even Bethlehem. The Olaf iconography (the martyr king with the axe in one hand, often also with his foot on a dragon representing the heathendom which he had put down in the battle of Stiklestad in 1030) was spread throughout northern Europe, as was also the Olaf liturgy. And the position of Nidaros as a holy centre in the North was continually supported and strengthened throughout the high and late Middle Ages by the pilgrimages to Nidaros, to the shrine of Olaf.[7]

FIGURE 6.2 Saint Olaf from a mural painting by the Isejord Master in Tuse Church, Denmark, c. 1460–1480.

Photograph: Enlightenment Production/www.kalkmalerier.dk

This story of Olaf's extraordinary sanctity was the most important fundament of the new religious centre in Norway, and it also remained the core of the Nidaros tradition throughout the late Middle Ages — even though Nidaros in this period was gradually strengthened as an administrative ecclesiastical centre as well: as a centre for a part of Northern Europe which had so far not been very well included in papal jurisdiction; namely the overseas areas of Iceland, Shetland, Hebrides, and Orkneys. Nidaros in this way reached out to the west, and did its best to confirm ecclesiastical power in these old parts of Norwegian dominion.[8]

The traditions pertaining to the medieval kings were also supported by the Old Norse literature, where Norway together with Iceland had a particularly rich heritage. The Sagas were a kind of semi-secular legends of saints, mostly dealing with royals, one of them also being a real saint. Together with the liturgical texts supporting the liturgies of St Olaf in Nidaros, these Old Norse Saga texts were an essential part of the 'hegemonic' medieval tradition of Norway.

Reformation uses of the past

How did the Nordic Reformations deal with these most important holy places and most precious parts of medieval Christianity, in a spectrum reaching from *rejecting/ forgetting* through *negotiating* to active *taking over* and *re-using*? The point of departure for the argument is once again that even though we are talking about three countries with evident similarities (old Christian kingdoms, each with a royal saint, each with a medieval archbishopric), the Reformation strategies for dealing with these parts of the medieval heritage are strikingly different.

Denmark: a new start

Roskilde and Our Lady in Copenhagen

The most radical solution takes place in Denmark, ruled by an uncompromising Lutheran king (Christian III, king from 1536 to 1559) with close links to the leaders of the Wittenberg Reformation. Here, the new Lutheran elite, to a great extent, went for a new start. Linking this new start to the old archbishopric in Lund was hardly an option. Lund had in the first place a too inconvenient location, across the Øresund. Neither was it important for dynastic legitimation, as the church of a holy martyr king (like Nidaros or Uppsala). Consequently, remembering the former ecclesiastical dignity of the Lund traditions had no priority to the Danish Reformation kings. In 1552 Niels Palladius was installed here as superintendent. But he is better known as author of Lutheran treatises than as guardian of the medieval traditions of Lund.

Instead, the new Protestant kings — to a certain degree — made use of the late medieval traditions in Roskilde by choosing the cathedral of Roskilde as their burial place. In this way, they could demonstrate a political continuity between the most glorious queen of the Kalmar union Margrete and the new strong Lutheran kings and queens of Denmark, all belonging to the emerging Oldenburg dynasty.[9]

The holy city of Copenhagen

But the re-uses of the Roskilde traditions were not comprehensive. The new Lutheran Bishop of Seeland Peder Palladius[10] — the primas of the Danish church and most influential first generation Lutheran church leader in Denmark — did not take Roskilde as his residence. His residence was Copenhagen, close to the king and to the university. Here Our Lady in Copenhagen, since the high Middle Ages a collegiate church of the cathedral of Roskilde, soon emerged as the main church of the new Lutheran rulers. The status of this church had grown during the fifteenth century, and King Christian I had been crowned here in 1449.

In this church Bugenhagen installed the new Lutheran bishops in 1539. Furthermore, Our Lady church was frequently used for university purposes. And high-ranking members of the new Lutheran elite were buried here. Peder Palladius himself was put to rest in Our Lady, and his successor Hans Poulsen Resen (professor and Bishop of Seeland) insisted on being buried next to his predecessor Peder Palladius. Peder Palladius and Hans Poulsen Resen could certainly not be compared to Luther and Melanchthon in Wittenberg, but as the early spiritual leaders of the Danish Lutheran church they were remembered in this church, redesigned for the purposes of the new confession. So, Our Lady church was staged not only for the close cooperation with the university, but also in order to serve as a place of memory (*Erinnerungsort*) of Danish Lutheranism.[11]

In this way the Reformation king Christian III created his own tradition and established Copenhagen not only as a political, but to a certain degree also as a religious centre. A university renewed and strengthened in the spirit of Protestantism, a new ecclesiastical hierarchy closely tied to the king by oath, and new religious buildings close to the royal court in Copenhagen, were important factors in Christian III's and his successor Frederic II's (1559–1588) new construction of Copenhagen as a holy city.

Christian III had close connections to and a deep respect and reverence for Wittenberg. He regarded it as a holy city: the concept is picked up from the letters of Christian III to Georg Major in Wittenberg. According to the king, Wittenberg was holy because Luther had rediscovered the Gospel there, and because it was the place 'from which the right and firmly rooted divine truth, and the true justification through Christ´s work, in which we take part by faith alone, for the first time found its expression and was came forth'.[12] Wittenberg was the fountain of the newborn Christian truth, and for that reason, according to the king, it deserved to be called a holy place, a holy town. And the king added that the truth of this fountain was preserved and taken care of by the church and the university of Wittenberg.

For this reason, he urged his own theologians and also other civil servants to go to Wittenberg, the fountain of the new discovered truth of Christianity, and stay there for a while before they came home in order to serve their own country. But the inner disagreements in Wittenberg from the 1560s on changed this situation and destroyed something of Wittenberg's reputation. Christian was deeply disappointed by what he heard from Saxony. And it was precisely in this period that Copenhagen gained its reputation as a new Lutheran centre in the North.[13]

Copenhagen stood forth as a centre of a new kind of holiness, not built on relics and old cathedrals, but on the attempt to make real a Christian community on the conditions defined by Protestant theology. In the 1560s Denmark was honoured by Philipp Melanchthon as the ideal Protestant kingdom of the North. In 1560, he wrote a preface to the poetical-humanistic work *Bucolica* written by the Danish Humanist and Theologian Erasmus Laetus (Danish: Glad) and printed in Wittenberg. Here, Melanchthon praised Denmark as the resort of the true church in the world, due to the two last kings of this country, Christian III and Frederik II, who followed in the footsteps of the Old Testament kings David, Josaphat, Ezechias, Josias and Cyrus and also in the footsteps of the Roman emperors Constantine and Theodosius, supporting true religion and high learning in close combination with each other.[14]

In this period, Copenhagen emerged as the most effective and most influential Protestant centre in Scandinavia, overruling not only Nidaros, but also Uppsala and Stockholm. It was the centre of a new start: of a university reordered according to new statutes, of a redefined church with new structures of authority closely linked to the king, with a strong anti-Catholic attitude and no strategies of remembering and re-using medieval ecclesiastical traditions.

Sweden: Re-uses of the past

Gustav Vasa and Stockholm

The new cathedral in Uppsala was finished shortly before the Reformation. It was consecrated as late as 1435. In 1477 the ecclesiastical centre of Uppsala was strengthened through the foundation of a university, confirmed through a bull issued by Sixtus IV. Along with these pre-Reformation efforts to establish New Uppsala as the supreme ecclesiastical centre of Sweden, the city of Stockholm, to the south of Uppsala, also strengthened its position throughout the fifteenth century. Supported by favourable trade agreements with the city of Lübeck and with the Hanseatic League as well as by a letter of privilege from the Swedish 'Riksråd' (National Council) from 1436, Stockholm grew rapidly and established itself as Sweden's wealthiest city and also as the city with the largest population (c. 7,000 by 1500).[15]

With the Lutheran Reformation, Stockholm gradually also took over the position of a main religious centre of Sweden. Sweden's Reformation king, Gustav Vasa, ruled from 1523 to 1560, and he systematically supported Protestant preachers and Protestant religion. The Reformation in Sweden went along with an opposition to Danish dominance in the country during the later years of the Kalmar Union. Denmark had emerged as the strongest partner in this union. In Sweden, the defenders of the Reformation also were the defenders of Swedish independence from Denmark.

The turning point was the so-called Blood Bath in Stockholm. Here, a considerable part of the Swedish high nobility was murdered through an initiative of the Danish king Christian II. These dramatic actions took place in early November 1520. They marked the starting point of Gustav Vasa's way to royal power, and the end of the Kalmar Union. In 1523 Gustav Vasa was elected King of Sweden. One of his most important strategies during his first years of reign was to neutralise the bishops who had supported the old regime, including the Archbishop of Uppsala. Their properties and castles were taken over by the king through a political action called '*Reduktion*'. Protestant ideas could support such actions. And defenders of the new Lutheran faith were chosen as the king's men in religious matters.

The most important of these men was Olaus Petri (1493–1552), who is often looked upon as the *Reformer of Sweden*. He had studied in Leipzig and in Wittenberg from 1516 to 1518, and had started preaching Reformation ideas in the cathedral of Strängnes in 1520. In 1524 he was transferred to Stockholm, the new capital of Sweden, and he was ordered to report directly to the king. His new obligation was to be the preacher of the main church of the adherents of the new faith, *Storkyrkan*.

In the mid-1520s, there were already quite a number of Lutherans in Stockholm, due to the close contacts to Lübeck, Rostock, and the Hanseatic League. *Storkyrkan* had been used as the church for all Germans in Stockholm since the fifteenth century, and now it became the first main church of the Protestants. Through the following years Olaus Petri came to play a key role as preacher, author, administrator and advisor — and sometimes also critic — of the king. When he died in 1552, he was buried before the altar of *Storkyrkan* in the middle of Stockholm.[16]

Stockholm and Uppsala

But what happened to Uppsala? How did the king deal with the challenges connected with this old ecclesiastical centre? Uppsala represented a heritage that was most important to the national cause, defended by Gustav Vasa. At the same time, Uppsala was the city of Gustav Vasa's powerful opponent, the Archbishop Gustav Trolle. The strategy of the king was a gradual take-over of Uppasla, without cutting the connections to Uppsala's medieval traditions. His 'Protestantisation' of the cathedral of Uppsala started with a solemn crowning ceremony in the cathedral in 1528. On this occasion, Olaus Petri offered a famous 'Crowning sermon' to the king, underlining Protestant virtues important to a Lutheran king.

The next action was to choose a new Lutheran archbishop. It is remarkable that the title and position of an archbishop was preserved, quite opposite to what happened in Lund in Denmark or in Nidaros in Norway. The new Protestant archbishop was Laurentius Petri (1499–1573), the brother of Olaus Petri. He, too, had studied in Wittenberg, and was consecrated to his new position on September 22 1531. Laurentius Petri was archbishop in Uppsala for 42 years. When he died in 1573, he was buried right in front of the High Altar, according to old tradition. But the liturgical context is different, and the text on the slab has been 'Protestantised'. On his rather simple grave slab is written:

> Here lies the body of the honourable Father, Master Laurentius Petri Nericius, Archbishop of Uppsala, who – since the darkness of false teaching had been driven away by the pure Word of God – with God's help has faithfully served and nourished this church and this diocese for more than 40 years. During these years he has, with piety and sincerity, written and organised much, in order for the purity of the heavenly teaching to remain strong in this realm. After having lived for 74 years, he died silently on October 26th in the year of Christ 1573.[17]

Laurentius Petri followed a late medieval tradition when he chose to be buried in the quire of his cathedral. Several of his predecessors had been buried here. In the text on the slab, there is no prayer for the soul to be saved (*miserere mei*), as one can frequently read on similar pre-Reformation slabs: the inscriptions on earlier grave slabs often connected to the prayers and masses needed in order to secure eternal salvation. An example is Archbishop Jakob Ulvsson (1469–1515), who was buried right behind the high altar of the cathedral. On his slab is written: 'O Jesus Christ. For the sake of your five wounds, let all those who are buried here and everywhere else always enjoy the eternal rest' (*requiem sine fine*), alluding to the Catholic requiem liturgy.[18]

Laurentius Petri's slab is different. At the bottom of the slab, he himself is talking to the reader of the inscriptions with words from the Book of Psalms, demonstrating a typical Lutheran conviction that he is going to see the goodness of the Lord in the land of the resurrected. (*Credo me visurum bonum Domini in terra viventium*, Psalm 27) ('I believe that I shall see the goodness of the Lord in the land of the living', Psalm 27:13).[19]

The burial of the kings

In his testament, Gustav Vasa had made a decision of great importance for the construction of Uppsala cathedral as a new religious centre for Swedish Protestantism. He had been married twice, and both his wives died before him. They had both been buried in the main Protestant church of Stockholm, the *Storkyrkan*, together with Olaus Petri. Before the king died in 1560, he had decided that he himself, together with his two wives, should have their resting place in the cathedral in Uppsala. The bright and beautiful chapel of Our Lady, right behind the high altar, was prepared for this purpose, and in 1560 the king and his two wives were taken in a procession from Stockholm to Uppsala. There, the funeral ceremony was celebrated on December 21. A huge funerary monument, made in the Netherlands, was completed in the early 1570s.[20]

After Gustav Vasa, the Swedish kings and queens up to Gustav II Adolf, the Lutheran Hero of the Thirty Years' War, were buried in Uppsala. Of particular interest in this connection is the funeral monument of Katherina Jagellonica (1526–1583), the first wife of Johann III.[21] She had taken responsibility for renewing the casket of the martyr saint of Sweden, Erik. When she died, she was buried in the chapter room of the cathedral, which gradually received the name 'The Jagellonica Quire'.

Katherina was a Catholic, and in the Jagellonica Quire an altar was left for reading Catholic masses for her soul. At the same time, the inscriptions on her beautiful tomb definitely sound as if they could have been in memory of a Protestant, underlining the certainty of faith facing death: *Securus moritur qui scit se morte renasci. Mors ea nec dici sed nova vita potest.* ('The one who knows that she will be born again when she dies, dies with confidence. Here, death is not supposed to be called death, but rather a new life.')[22]

FIGURE 6.3 The tomb of Gustav Vasa and his wives in Uppsala Cathedral, made by Willem Boy, finished c. 1571.
Photograph: Håkan Svensson (Xauxa), taken 20 May 2004.

Bridget and the Vadstena traditions

In Uppsala, the new Protestant kingdom of the Vasa-dynasty was firmly linked to the late medieval traditions of Swedish Catholicism. What happened to the traditions of St Bridget in Vadstena? Her memory was very much alive in many parts of Catholic Europe through the sixteenth and seventeenth centuries. Her European reputation was most of all linked to her writings, especially to her *Heavenly Revelations*, and less to a particularly holy place — be it Vadstena or one of the places where she had been active in Rome.

In Sweden, Vadstena was protected from the most severe consequences of the Reformation until the end of the sixteenth century. In the early years of the Reformation the sister of King Gustav Vasa was a nun here, and in the 1560s Katherina Jagellonica guarded Vadstena as one of the remaining Catholic strongholds in Sweden. The last nuns were allowed to live there at least until 1595, and the casket with the bones of St Bridget was kept in the Abbey church after that time.[23] Even if the convent was secularised and used for other purposes since the early seventeenth century, the Lutheran authorities in Sweden felt no need for more radical actions in order to have the people forget about Bridget.

Comparison: Stockholm/Uppsala vs. Copenhagen/Roskilde

The Reformation definitely contributed to making Stockholm a much more important religious centre in Sweden. The city had no bishop and no university, and this did not change with the Reformation. But the Protestant preaching had from the 1520s its most important stronghold in the city, mainly due to Olaus Petri and his activities in *Storkyrkan*. The central royal castle, renewed by Gustav Vasa, was also in Stockholm, and the king was the main supporter of the Protestant church. So, Stockholm was the centre of church politics and of legislation pertaining to religious matters.[24] Also, the first Protestant printing press was set up in the city, and used for printing Protestant books not least written by Olaus Pertri, and for printing the first Swedish Bible translation in 1541 (the 'Gustav Vasa Bible'), decisively promoted by Laurentius Petri.

At the same time, an interesting and indispensable interaction was built up between Stockholm and Uppsala. Even though universities and places of learning were generally of great significance for constituting Protestant centres in Europe, the university of Uppsala played no important role in sixteenth century Sweden. In Denmark the University of Copenhagen, reformed according to Wittenberg ideals, had a crucial role in promoting the Reformation. In Sweden the Uppsala University (also a late fifteenth century institution like the one in Copenhagen), had no significant role in the Reformation process.

Much more important was the Uppsala Cathedral. It did not only serve as a new burial place for the Reformation kings and queens (as did Roskilde Cathedral in Denmark since Christian III was transferred there some years after his death in 1559). Just as important was the 'Protestantisation' of the role of the archbishop, with Laurentius Petri as the first to fill this new Lutheran position. In Denmark, the Bishop of Roskilde left this city after the Reformation and the new bishop resided instead in Copenhagen as the Bishop of Seeland (even if Roskilde was still his cathedral). In Sweden, the archbishop continued to be the Archbishop of Uppsala with his residence in Uppsala.

The Bishop of Seeland in Copenhagen could enhance his importance by profiting from a close cooperation with the Copenhagen University. In Sweden, the Uppsala archbishop profited instead from the somewhat un-Lutheran ecclesiastical dignity of his position as an archbishop, and also from the likewise un-Lutheran dignity of the martyr king tradition of St Erik. At the same time, he was a key person promoting Lutheran theology and Lutheran Church Law.[25]

Conclusion

In Sweden, priority was given to a strategy of negotiation. A central part in these negotiations was played by Uppsala. Not only through the traditions of the martyr King Erik, but also through the continuity back to the diverse traditions of Old Uppsala, this city was of special importance in the emerging Kingdom of Sweden. The Reformation ideals of Gustav Vasa were quite different from the ideals of the Danish kings. Gustav Vasa had no intention of building up a new Wittenberg in Sweden. Rather, he gradually took steps in order to 'Protestantise' the Uppsala tradition without letting go of or forgetting about its medieval heritage.

Even though Gustav Vasa strengthened Stockholm as the political centre of Sweden, and even though he supported *Storkyrkan* in Stockholm as the main church of the Lutherans there, it seems to have been an even more important part of his Reformation strategy to maintain and confirm strong links to essential parts of Sweden's Medieval Christian heritage. Here, remembering and connecting the new Lutheran regime to the diverse medieval traditions represented by the Uppsala Cathedral seems to have been a major concern.

Remembering the Reformation in Norway

The fall of Nidaros

Norway did not succeed in opposing Danish take over in the 1520s and 1530s. So, the country lost its sovereignty. In 1537 the troops of the Danish King Christian III took over control, and Norway was degraded from being a partner kingdom within a political union to being an integrated part of Denmark on a similar basis as the duchy of Southern Jutland. Along with this political take-over, the Lutheran Reformation was introduced in Denmark as well as in Norway, and every important decision concerning politics and religion in the new and expanded kingdom of Denmark-Norway was taken in Copenhagen.

In Nidaros, the cathedral had been damaged by fire just before the Reformation. On April 1 1537 Archbishop Olav Engelbrektsson fled the country. St Olaf's shrine was removed and hidden. Due to the Reformation, the proudest part of Norway's medieval heritage lay in ruins. If Norway had been ruled according to the strategy of Gustav Vasa, the changes might have been less radical. But the new king was Christian III, and he wanted Norway to have a new start with Copenhagen as the new political and religious centre. So, Nidaros was radically degraded from being the proudest place of religious memory in the Nordic countries to being the administrative centre of one of the many new Superintendents appointed by the king in Copenhagen.

Nevertheless, even if Nidaros as a place of pilgrimage and as an archbishopric was gone, the new Protestant Norway continued to remember its medieval past, in spite of the efforts of the king and his officials to efface it. One example: on a popular level, people in Trøndelag — the part of Norway where Nidaros is situated — continued to use the name Olaf (after the saint as well as the archbishop) as one of the most popular names long after the Reformation.[26]

The missing Reformation heroes

There is hardly any other Protestant dominated country in Europe which has a similarly unhappy point of departure for remembering the Reformation. Denmark and Sweden both had their Reformation kings Christian III and Gustav I Vasa. In both cases, the Reformation went along with a process of consolidating new and influential early modern states.[27] And in both cases, popular and venerated Reformation heroes entered the scene, most of them having studied in Wittenberg and having met personally with Luther and Melanchthon. They could promote the memory of the Reformation and be remembered as Reformation heroes.

First of all, Sweden had the Petri brothers: Olaus and Laurentius Petri as they called themselves in humanist manner, after returning from Wittenberg. Originally their names were Olaus and Lars Pettersson, the sons of a blacksmith from Örebro. Thus, there were even heroes emerging from the ordinary people, the first one rising to become 'Sweden's reformer', the second to the position of Uppsala's first Lutheran archbishop.

Denmark, too, had their hero-theologians: the first one was Hans Tausen, an early Lutheran reformer in Viborg. Then we have once again two most influential brothers: Peder and Niels Palladius. The former, Peder Palladius, had not only studied in Wittenberg; he had even received his doctoral degree there in 1537, after having defended theses on justification in the Schloßkirche in Wittenberg in front of both Luther and Melanchthon. After having received his degree, he was sent right back to Copenhagen and was installed there as the first bishop or superintendent of Seeland, and for practical purposes also as a kind of archbishop of Denmark and Norway.[28] In addition to these theologians, there were also more secular Lutheran heroes, like the naval commander and founder of Herlufsholm school Herluf Trolle, who was not only a man of war, but also a devout Lutheran after having studied in Wittenberg under Melanchthon.[29]

Even Finland, which in the sixteenth century was not a country at all, has its own Reformation hero, coming right back from Wittenberg to the Swedish diocese of Åbo with the new tools of Protestant-humanist education. There, he translated the New Testament and the Psalms of David into Finnish and also published a grammar book in order to support the education of the youth in their own native language. His name was Michael Agricola, and even today he is remembered and celebrated every year on April 9 in Finland as the Father of the Finnish language, directly inspired by the humanist ideals of the Reformation. He is also present in the neo-classical centre of Helsinki in the Cathedral from 1852, designed by Carl Ludvig Engel. Here he stands as a Protestant hero equal to Luther and Melanchthon guarding the inside of the church.[30]

Humanism and the medieval roots of Norway

Norway did not have Lutheran heroes who could match any of these people. Admittedly, some young talented men from Norway were sent to Copenhagen or even to Wittenberg to take part in the religious and cultural renewals which had their sources at these universities. One example is Absalon Pederson Beyer from Aurdal in Western Norway.[31] He was sent from Bergen to Copenhagen where he studied for five years under Peder Palladius (who was not only Bishop of Seeland, but also professor at the university). Later Pederson Beyer was sent to Wittenberg and had the opportunity to study under Melanchthon. Back in Bergen, he spent his life there as an influential teacher of theology at the Latin school and as an author. Another example is Jens Nilssøn from Oslo, who had also studied in Copenhagen under Palladius before he became superintendent in his hometown. The two of them were leading figures in two humanist circles in Norway, labelled after the two main cities Oslo and Bergen (the Oslo-humanists and the Bergen-humanists). These circles were definitely inspired by early Protestant humanists, and most of the leading humanist figures in Norway had studied theology in Copenhagen (and a few also in Germany).[32]

However, the main interest of the prominent Norwegian humanists was not so much Protestant theology, writing Protestant treatises, or translating biblical texts into the native language, as was very often the case with their colleagues belonging to the Protestant elite in Sweden and Denmark. Rather, they preferred working with medieval Norwegian history, including the Sagas. In the spirit of Protestant humanism, they also learnt the Old Norse language in order to read these old texts. The best known example is Jens Nilssøn's transcription of *Jofarskinna*, a Saga manuscript that was later lost, but which we know due to him.

St Olaf as substitute

In Norwegian historiography, the Reformation is not looked upon as a recovery from or a reaction to the 'dark' Middle Ages. Rather, the dark period *starts* with the Reformation and with the Danish take-over of political and ecclesiastical power in 1536–1537. This makes it easier to understand why history writing in Norway tends to neglect the Reformation period, and instead deals with the more glorious periods of the country's past, like the Middle Ages and the nineteenth century. For such reasons, the Norwegian case is not so much a story about remembering the Reformation or more specifically about a Reformation remembering its medieval past. It is rather a story of a Lutheran country trying to forget about the Reformation and striving to replace it with a 'Protestantised' version of Norwegian medieval history. In this perspective, two heroes emerge: the Archbishop Olav Engelbrektsson and the royal Saint Olaf.

When taking up the Reformation period for a closer look, Norwegian historians first of all like to remember the last proud effort to defend Norwegian independence, represented by Olav Engelbrektsson.[33] He was a Norwegian by birth, he was well educated at European universities, and he was in possession not only of ecclesiastical, but also of political power, since he was the leader of the National Council of Norway — an institution which also came to an end with the Reformation. This man, a Catholic archbishop, is the only genuine Reformation hero of Norway. He had to flee the country early in 1537, and died as a kind of a national martyr in the Flemish city of Lier one year later.[34]

In addition to the archbishop, Norway also had another and even more important replacement of real Reformation heroes, namely Saint Olaf, who contributed to Norway's reputation in the good times — the high Middle Ages. Admittedly, we know little about who he really was. He emerged as a symbolic figure, a martyr king venerated all over Northern Europe — with an interesting potential for being 'Protestantised' in order to fit into the framework of a Protestant hero. Due to him, Norway was rewarded with the see of an archbishop who also defended the cause of Norwegian sovereignty at the time of the Reformation. Neither was Olaf too closely connected to Rome and to Roman Catholicism, which would appear disturbing to some. Rather, he had little to do with Rome. Instead, he went other places, to France, to England, and to the Black Sea.

But most important is his national role. He is looked upon as the founder of Norway's national church, and he supported the use of the Old Norwegian language in a religious context. In this respect, he may appear as a kind of a *proto-reformer*, who can to a certain extent replace both Luther and Melanchthon. He was a religious hero who conquered idolatry and false (Old Norse) religion, just like the Lutheran reformers did 500 years later. He also promoted a national interpretation of Christianity by favouring Old Norse language, and he fought against the Danes: in both cases typical achievements which one would have expected from a true Norwegian Lutheran hero. So, Norway tended to prefer remembering St Olaf to remembering the Reformation and the loss of sovereignty when the archbishop left the country in 1537.[35]

Remembering and forgetting Anno 2017

In 2017 the 500th anniversary of the Reformation was taking place in many parts of Europe and in the USA. In all Nordic countries the Reformation was remembered, but in quite different ways. Denmark was definitely in a leading position, with several national celebrations in the presence of the queen, a large number of books and articles were published and a lot of smaller conferences, workshops, and special lectures were organised.[36] In Sweden, the most important contribution was an ecumenical mass in the cathedral of Lund (31 October 2016), right before the start of the anniversary, with the pope and the Archbishop of Uppsala taking part. In Norway, there was an official celebration in the Nidaros Cathedral in the presence of the king, and also some commemorations within the Lutheran church. But both within the church and in addressing a broader public, preparing for the 2030 millennium of the martyrdom of St Olaf is definitely more important than remembering the Reformation.

Notes

1 A few examples of scholars and books who have contributed to a better understanding of the medieval roots of the Lutheran Reformation during the last two generations: Heiko A. Oberman, *Werden und Wertung der Reformation: Vom Wegestreit zum Glaubenskampf* (Tübingen, 1979); Berndt Hamm, *Frömmigkeitstheologie am Anfang des 16. Jahrhunderts: Studien zu Johannes von Paltz und seinem Umkreis* (Tübingen, 1982) and more recently *Ablaß und Reformation: Erstaunliche Konvergenzen* (Tübingen, 2017); and finally Volker Leppin, *Martin Luther* (Darmstadt, 2006).

2 A recent example is James Larson, *Reforming the North* (Cambridge, 2014).

3 Cf. Herman Bengtsson, 'Kyrkan', in *Kyrkan i Gamla Uppsala: Från Katedral til Församlingsksyrka*, ed. Gunnar Granberg (Karlstad, 2014), 33–54.

4 More on the cult of Saint Erik in Christian Lovén, 'Erik den Helige och Gamla Uppsala', in Granberg, *Kyrkan i Gamle Uppsala*, 79–98.

5 See Sven-Erik Pernler, 'Det Började i Visby: Om Upptakten till Birgittas Helgonförklaring', in *Birgitta av Vadstena: pilgrim och profet, 1303–1337*, ed. Per Beskow and Annette Landen (Stockholm, 2003), 177–88.

6 See Poul Grinder-Hansen, 'Margrete 1 og Håkon', in *Danske Kongegrave*, ed. Karin Kryger, vol. II, (København, 2014), 99–132.

7 See Anne Lidén, *Olav den helige i medeltida bildkonst: Legendmotiv och atribut* (Stockholm, 1999).

8 A comprehensive history of the archbishopric can be found in the volume *Ecclesia Nidarosisensis, 1153–1537: Søkelys på Nidaroskirkens og Nidarosprovinsens historie*, ed. Steinar Imsen (Trondheim, 2003).

9 On the history of the Roskilde cathedral, see Ulla Kjær, *Roskilde Domkirke: Kunst og Historie* (København, 2013). A detailed investigation of the funerary monument of Margrete I in the cathedral can be found in Grinder-Hansen, 'Margrete 1. og Håkon' (fn. 6).

10 Cf. Martin Schwarz Lausten, *Peder Palladius: Sjællands første lutherske biskop* (København, 2006).

11 A detailed analysis of Vor Frue in Copenhagen is available online: 'Vor Frue Kirke', *Nationalmuseet*, accessed 26 September 2019, http://danmarkskirker.natmus.dk/koebenhavn-by/vor-frue-kirke/.

12 Martin Schwarz Lausten, *Den hellige Stad Wittenberg* (København, 2002), 195. (German translation: *Die Heilige Stadt Wittenberg* (Leipzig, 2010), 197.

13 More on this in Martin Schwarz Lausten, *Den hellige Stad Wittenberg*.

14 Minna Skafte Jensen, 'Melanchthon, the Muses and Denmark', in *Renaissance Culture in Context: Theory and Practice*, ed. J. R. Brink and W. F. Glentrup (Aldershot, 1999), 136–44. See also Philipp Melanchthon, in Erasmus Laetus, *Bucolica cum dedicatoria Philippi Melanchthonis Praefatione* (Wittenberg, 1560).

15 See Helena Friedman and Göran Söderström, *Stockholm: En Historia i Kartor och Bilder* (Stockholm, 2008), 28–9.

16 A short overview of early Swedish Reformation history with a bibliography can be found in Tarald Rasmussen, 'Stockholm: Gustav I. Vasa und Olaus Petri', in *Europa Reformata, 1517–2017. Reformationsstädte Europas und ihre Reformatoren*, ed. Michael Welker, Michael Beintker, and Albert de Lange (Leipzig, 2016), 385–94.

17 HIC IACET CORPUS REVERENDI PATRIS DOMINI. MAGISTRI. LAURENTII PETRI NERCII/ARCHIEPISCOPI VPSALENSIS/ QUI ADIVVANTE DEO/ DEPULSIS DOCTRINÆ TENEBRIS/ PVRO VERBO DEI HANC/ ECCLESIAM ET DIOCESIN / FIDELITER PAVIT ET /REXIT SUPRA ANNOS LX/ QVO TEMPORE / PRO RETINENDA IN HOC REGNO / PURITATE DOCTRINÆ CELESTIS / MVLTA PIE ET GRAVITER / SCRIPSIT ET ORDINAVIT AC CUM VIXISSET ANNOS LXXIIII./ PLACIDE OBIIT DIE XXVI. OCTOBRIS ANNO CHRIISTI MDLXXIII. Cf. Herman Bengtsson, *Uppsala Domkyrka VI. Gravminnen* (Uppsala, 2010), 297.

18 Bengtsson, *Uppsala Domkyrka*, 293.

19 Bengtsson, *Uppsala Domkyrka*, 297.

20 A detailed description of the 'Vasa Quire' can be found in Bengtsson, *Uppsala Domkyrka*, 23–36 (fn. 17).

21 Bengtsson, *Uppsala Domkyrka*, 55–62.

22 Bengtsson, *Uppsala Domkyrka*, 56.

23 A skull supposedly belonging to St Bridget was stolen by a French Catholic visiting Sweden in 1645, and it was never returned to Vadstena. It was handed over to a church in Burgundy, but is now (since 1959) kept in the Bridgettine convent in Uden in the Netherlands.

24 See Friedman and Söderström, *Stockholm*, 38–47 (fn. 15).

25 See Sven Kjøllerstrøm, ed., *Den Svenska Kyrkoordningen 1571: jämte studier kring tillkomst, innehåll och användning* (Lund, 1971).

26 Henning Laugerud has recently published a study focusing on Norwegian strategies of keeping the memory of the old times alive after the Danish take-over with the Reformation: Henning Laugerud, *Reformasjon uten Folk* (Oslo, 2019).

27 On the political strategies of consolidating new confessional monarchies in the north, see Susan Richter, *Wissensaustausch und Innerdynastische Verrechtlichung von Konfession in Schweden und Dänemark mittels Deutscher Fürstentestamente* (Heidelberg, 2015), 15–32.

28 On Palladius see Schwarz Lausten, *Peder Palladius* (fn. 10).

29 On Herluf Trolle as Danish Lutheran hero, see Sebastian Olden-Jørgensen, *Herluf Trolle* (København, 2016).

30 More on Agricola in Simo Heininen, *Mikael Agrikola: Liv och Verk* (Helsinki, 2018).

31 See Anders Bjarne Fossen, 'Absalon Pedersson Beyer', *Norsk Biografisk Leksikon*, accessed 26 September 2019, https://nbl.snl.no/Absalon_Pedersson_Beyer.

32 On the Oslo humanist circles after the Reformation, see Inger Ekrem, 'Jens Nielssøn (Johannes Nicolai) 1538–1600', in *A History of Nordic Neo-Latin Literature*, ed. Minna Skafte Jensen (Odense, 1995), 219–28.

33 See Tarald Rasmussen, 'Report on Norway', 189–204 in the PDF *The 'Long Reformation' in Nordic Historical Research*, ed. Per Ingesman (2014), accessed 26 September 2019, http://reformatoriskteologi.au.dk/fileadmin/Reformatorisk_Teologi/Joensuu_report__vs1_.pdf.

34 Right after the Second World War the leading national historian Halfdan Koht published his book *Olav Engelbriktsson og sjølvstende-tapet 1537* (Oslo, 1951). Here, the Catholic archbishop is celebrated as a national hero fighting against foreign take-over. For a more recent publication discussing the role of the archbishop, see Steinar

Supphellen, ed., *Nytt søkelys på Olav Englebrektsson: Skrifter* (Det Kongelige Norske Videnskabers Selskab), 2/2004a.

35 More on this in Tarald Rasmussen, 'Erkjennelse og interesse – middelalderen i norsk ksirkehistorieskriving', in *Den Kirkehistoriske Utfordring*, ed. Steinar Imsen (Trondheim, 2005), 27–34.

36 See Niels Henrik Gregersen, Carsten Bach-Nielsen, and Niels Kærgaard, *Hvorfor holder vi reformationsjubileum? Om reformationen og erindringen* (København, 2018).

7

RIOTING BLACKSMITHS AND JEWISH WOMEN

Pillarised Reformation memory in early modern Poland

Natalia Nowakowska

In 1539, the Polish monarchy witnessed its only sixteenth-century burning for heresy, when Catherine, widow of the Kraków councillor Melchior Weigel, was executed in the city's market square for the crime of converting to Judaism. The case was already a decade old. Catherine had received her first episcopal warning to stop consorting with Jews in 1529, and in 1530 she was briefly jailed, before publically abjuring on her knees 'all the heresies, superstitions and errors of the sect and rite of the Jews into which she had fallen', as the court record has it. Bishop Samuel Maciejowski found her guilty of a fatal relapse in 1539, and she was sentenced to death.[1] On the face of it, Catherine's case has little to do with the Reformation. However, it forms a rare common thread which, twisting and turning, runs through early modern historical accounts of the Polish Reformation written by Catholics and Protestants alike. This essay explores how sixteenth- and seventeenth-century Polish chronicles 'remembered' the Reformation as both a local and international event and how, by failing to produce a shared social memory which commanded widespread support, they in effect collectively failed to remember it — suggesting that profoundly, persistently fragmented memories, or historical narratives, might produce similar outcomes to outright forgetting. To borrow a phrase originally developed by social scientists to describe the con-fessionally-based parallel societies of the twentieth-century Low Countries, what we find in early modern Poland is in effect a *pillarisation* of Reformation memory: where each of the kingdom's many churches honed their own different versions of events.[2]

The Polish monarchy offers a good case study for early modern memory of the Reformation, because chronicles produced in this kingdom — the would-be master-narratives of their own times — present us with a number of problems, or riddles. Many of these books barely talk about or acknowledge the Reformation at all. Where they do, their narratives differ so wildly from one another, that there is no consensus among them as to what the key events of the Polish or European Reformation were. The chronicles' accounts also differ significantly from the story of the European Reformation which scholars tell today, their narratives striking us as alien and not immediately intelligible. Furthermore, these texts' heterogeneous accounts of the Reformation differ sharply from the rich Polish archival record itself, most of which never entered chronicle memory at all. The circa 60 trials for Lutheran heresy pre-1540 found in Polish diocesan archives, the scores of royal and episcopal letters lamenting the influx of Lutheranism and Anabaptists, the steady flow of students from the Polish monarchy to Wittenberg, the avalanche of anti-Trinitarian literature in the later sixteenth century — virtually none of this, painstaking pieced together in the archives by modern scholars from Wincenty Zakrzewski (1844–1918) onwards, is to be found in contemporary chronicles.[3] Early modern Polish chroniclers, then, have given us a story, or memory, in many pieces.

This essay will examine a selection of six chronicles of Polish history printed between 1521 and 1695, to trace how early modern memory of an early modern event (the Reformation) unfolded in its first stages of narration, interpretation, and memorialisation. Certain noted Polish chronicles of the early modern period — such as Martin Kromer's *De origine et rebus gestis Polonorum* (Basel, 1555) — are not included here, because they narrated only Poland's pre-Reformation past, stopping their accounts well before the 1520s. Our six chronicles showcase the contrasting mnemonic strategies of different groups or confessions, and thus illustrate the fragmentation of early modern Polish Reformation memory. They include the late medieval *Chronica Polonorum* by the Kraków cathedral canon Maciej of Miechów, or Miechowita (Kraków, 1521); the Renaissance humanist chronicle by the diplomat Bernard Wapowski (manuscript, *ante* 1535); the kingdom's first vernacular chronicle, *Kronika Polska*, by the layman Marcin Bielski (Kraków, 1597); the *Libri Quatuor Slavoniae Reformatae* by the Calvinist minister Andrzej Węgierski (Amsterdam, 1679); the *Historia Reformationis Polonicae* written by the exiled anti-Trinitarian Stanisław Lubieniecki (Freistadt, 1685), and a Polish Counter/Catholic Reformation history, *Roczne dzieje kościelne*, by the Jesuit Jan Kwiatkiewicz (Kalisz, 1695). 'Chronicles' is a term here used broadly to include 'secular' chronicles of the Polish *regnum* as a legal-political community focused on the king, as well as chronicles of the universal church, and also hybrids of these two, i.e. histories of a people/realm and its church. By 1517, the national chronicle was a well-established genre across the kingdoms of Northern Europe. In Poland, its master-text was the voluminous *Annales seu chronicae incliti Regni Poloniae* written by the Kraków cleric Jan Długosz (d.1480). What renders this kingdom's early modern chronicles unusual in a European context is their sheer number. Norbert Kerksen, for example, has counted some 14 new surveys of national history composed in sixteenth-century Poland, compared to a European norm of just four to five.[4]

Early modern chronicles — *chronica, annales, historia*, or the vernacular *dzieje* — have been analysed in modern scholarship principally as works of history, rather than as deliberate mnemonic acts.[5] Polish research, for example, continues to analyse their textual motifs or construct more fully their author's biographies.[6] International scholarship on Reformation and Counter/Catholic Reformation *historia sacra*, meanwhile, has tended to focus on the intellectual models, social functions, and polemical strategies of such works.[7] Clearly, early modern chronicles were produced within the highly self-conscious and long-standing genre of history-writing. Yet if we examine the prefaces and dedicatory letters of Polish authors, we can see that sixteenth- and seventeenth-century historians also explicitly invoked, and appealed to, *memoria*. Setting out their motives for writing history, for example, our Polish authors routinely listed truth-telling, patriotism, didacticism, and the preservation of memory. Miechowita thus declared (1521) that he wrote his Polish chronicle to correct errors made by *inexpertos*, and because without histories 'we cannot know, or remember forever' the origins, growth, and deeds of the kingdom.[8] Bielski (1597) sought, he claimed, to pass on Poland's deeds to future ages, so that 'they did not fade into forgetting', but lived forever on earth.[9] The Jesuit Kwiatkiewicz asserted that the great events of his own age needed recording, 'because they deserve to be known by future generations'.[10] And the editor of Węgierski's Calvinist history opened his preface in more general terms by paraphrasing Cicero: 'History, which bears witness to the passing of the ages, gives life to memory…'.[11] An explicit discourse of memory did thus exist within the standard early modern rhetorics, and even topoi, of history-writing.

This essay opens with something the Polish chronicles themselves cannot, or will not, supply: a bird's-eye narrative overview of the Reformation in this kingdom. We then consider the chronicles in turn, setting out the evolution and splintering of Reformation memory from the 1520s to the 1690s, before analysing its key features. The overriding characteristic of Polish chronicle-memory is that in lieu of a loosely agreed national narrative of Reformation events, each confession (Lutheran, Calvinist, anti-Trinitarian, pre- and post-Tridentine Catholic) produced its own version of local religious history, which did not and could not cohere with each other. This reflected realities on the ground, in a kingdom where a delicate balance of power long endured between many different churches.[12] These chronicles, with their memories-in-parallel, suggest that in the Polish kingdom the experience of early modern religious pluralism generated a silo-like, deeply fragmented and ultimately 'pillarised' memory culture — at least at the level of formal written histories. A second notable feature of these chronicles is how, for all their radical ideological differences, they nonetheless share a certain preoccupation with Judaism, talking to and about one another indirectly through the figure of the local Jew, as we shall see. In particular, several chronicles focus on the figure of the Jewish woman, a puzzle which invites some analysis. Finally, these Polish chronicles speak to the wider field of memory theory, which tends to construct 'remembering' as active and 'forgetting' as more passive and one-dimensional. In their chronicles, each of these Polish confessions forgot in their own way, with cumulative and curious long-term effects.

The Polish monarchy and its Reformations (c.1518–1658)

The *regnum Poloniae* was a classic sixteenth-century composite state, which consisted of five principal territories — western Poland (*Wielkopolska*) and southern Poland *(Małopolska)*; the Orthodox areas of Rus-Podolia, today mostly in Ukraine; the appanage duchy of Mazovia with its capital of Warsaw; and Royal Prussia, a German-speaking Baltic province dominated by the Hanseatic towns of Danzig, Elbing, and Thorn. The monarchy existed in dynastic union with the Grand Duchy of Lithuania, with the two states later fully fusing into a legal whole, or Commonwealth (1569).[13]

In the reign of King Sigismund I (r.1506–1548), a precocious influx of Lutheran books into the monarchy's Prussian ports led to full-scale, pro-Reformation revolts in Danzig and Elbing in 1525, headed by radical preachers, blacksmiths, and sailors. These briefly established radical reforming regimes, which the king overthrew in person in a military intervention of 1526. Yet at the same time, Sigismund I oversaw the dissolution and secularisation of the Teutonic Order in Prussia, accepting Grand Master Albert of Brandenburg as his lay vassal, converting the monastic state into a fief of the Polish Crown, and permitting Duke Albert to create Europe's first officially Lutheran polity. The 1520s saw a major peasant Reformation revolt in Ducal Prussia, an eastern extension of the ruinous German Peasants' War. Throughout King Sigismund's reign, Lutheran preaching was reported in Kraków, Poznań and many smaller towns, and top magnates such as Lukasz Górka openly favoured Wittenberg.[14]

The aged king was succeeded by his son Sigismund Augustus (r.1548–1572) who, although Catholic, turned a blind eye both to the first Calvinist synods held in southern Poland, and the arrival of radical Italian exiles such as Francesco Stancaro of Mantua. The Polish reformer Jan Łaski (John a Lasco) returned to his home country in 1556, in the (thwarted) hope of guiding a Crown-sponsored Reformation. In 1570, the major Protestant groups signed the Sandomierz Consensus, seeking to forge a united front. When Sigismund Augustus died without an heir in 1572, the Polish territories and nobles were split into three roughly equal camps — Catholic, Lutheran, Calvinist. The kingdom also contained some of the most theologically radical communities found in sixteenth-century Europe, in the form of the thriving anti-Trinitarians (also known as Arians, Socinians, or Polish Brethren), in centres such as the town/commune of Raków.[15] In the chaotic interregnum of 1572–1575, the nobility drew up the Warsaw Confederation, a guarantee of toleration for those 'dissident in religion'. This was probably the high-water mark of the Polish Reformation.

The tide started to turn from the 1580s, when the Vasa royal family of Sweden established themselves as the Jagiellonian dynasty's heirs and successors in the Commonwealth. King Sigismund III Vasa (r.1587–1632) supported Counter-Reformation preachers such as Piotr Skarga, urban violence occurred against Protestant churches in the 1590s, and non-Catholics increasingly found royal offices barred to them. The establishment of highly successful Jesuit colleges across Poland

and Lithuania, from the 1580s, attracting pupils of all confessions, precipitated a major shift back towards Catholicism among the nobility.[16] A devastating invasion of the Commonwealth (the Deluge, 1655–1660) by the Vasa's Swedish Lutheran cousins sharpened confessional identities and conflicts. King John Casimir (r.1648–1668) accused the anti-Trinitarians of plotting with Protestant Swedes to defeat the Commonwealth, and in 1658 a parliamentary decree ordered this community to convert or leave.[17] The dates of the Polish Reformation can thus tentatively be sketched as 1518–1658. How this story has been recalled in the modern era, particularly in the nineteenth and twentieth centuries, is a drama in its own right, but this essay will limit itself to the question of early modern memory.[18]

Six chronicles, six stories

Let us turn to our first chronicle, by the geographical theorist, medical professor, university rector, cathedral canon, and polymath Maciej of Miechów (1457–1523). His *Chronica Polonorum* — recalled and censored in 1519, and reprinted in 1521 — was the first printed chronicle of Poland.[19] It narrates the affairs of the kingdom only up to the year 1506, but it was completed during the Luther affair (1517–1521). Miechowita's work provides us with an important benchmark for how an essentially late medieval writer, on the very cusp of the Reformation, might handle religious affairs within a chronicle of kings. The *Chronica Polonorum* thus offers a kind of control, or baseline point of departure, for later Reformation-era histories of the monarchy, many of which incorporated chunks of this work wholesale. While much of the chronicle simply repeated Długosz's earlier *Annales*, the account covering the years 1480 to 1506 was Miechowita's own. In keeping with the conventions of the form, the chief subject matter of this portion of the *Chronica* is the deeds of kings — royal succession, military campaigns against the Turks, Tartars and Muscovites — spiced up with a fair share of omens, comets, and monstrous births.

Within this framework, there is room for plenty of religious events, both normative and transgressive. Normative religious developments, reported by Miechowita with approval, included ecclesiastical patronage by the Polish royal family: pious gifts to Kraków cathedral by Queen-Mother Elizabeth (d.1505), the founding of new benefices by King Alexander (d.1506), or financial support of the university by King John Albert (d.1501) out of love for 'the divine cult'.[20] Miechowita also diligently reported appointments to Polish bishoprics, and papal acts such as the issuing of the 1500 Jubilee Year indulgence.[21] Transgressive religious events, by contrast, included bad decisions by the royal family, such as an attempt to marry Princess Elizabeth (d.1517) to an Orthodox Moldavian prince of a different rite, or the nepotistic ecclesiastical career of Cardinal-prince Frederick.[22] Transgressions likewise included acts of physical and metaphysical religious disorder, such as looting of diocesan lands by royal soldiers returning from the eastern front.[23] Bad religion might also involve charlatans, outsiders, and outcasts. Miechowita recounted the expulsion of Kraków's Jews into the neighbouring town of

Kazimierz in the 1490s in the wake of a major fire, the birth of a monstrous child to a Jewish mother, and secret activity by alchemists in the royal capital.[24] He was particularly exercised by the case of 'the prophet Baliński', a Greek-speaking soothsayer, allegedly quack doctor and fraud who extorted money from the poor and tricked courtiers.[25] Miechowita's ire fell too on corrupt, religiously insincere laypeople, such as the woman (named as 'the wife of Albert', a Wawel castle servant) whom he claimed had contracted French disease on pilgrimage in Rome, and was responsible for bringing the new malady to Kraków.[26] To this late medieval catholic clerical chronicler, then, bad religion essentially consisted of scandals — and this motif of the religious scandal would later morph into something quite different in early modern Reformation historiography, used to different ends.

Our second chronicle dates from the following decade, also from a learned Kraków milieu. It was the work of Miechowita's fellow cathedral canon Bernard Wapowski (1450–1535), a diplomat, doctor of canon law, cartographer, and author of panegyric Latin orations for the royal court, who today enjoys the distinction of having a crater on the moon named after him.[27] Wapowski's untitled chronicle, which circulated widely in manuscript in the sixteenth century, is a far more purist, consciously humanist, classical, Renaissance work than Miechowita's gossipy tale. Wapowski's focus is upon the grand affairs of diplomacy and war, with ecclesiastical matters scarcely touched upon. His chronicle has virtually nothing to say about the Reformation. The canon was extremely well informed about general European affairs: he describes, for example, Charles V's meeting with Henry VIII in Dover (or 'Dobra') in 1522, the fall of Rhodes, the internal politics of the kingdom of Naples, and events in Milan, Genoa, Constantinople and Crimea, in a tale covering a vast geographical panorama.[28] Yet the European Reformation does not make it into his survey of European history from 1480 to 1535. Wapowski reported German high political events, such as the death of the Emperor Maximilian, but anybody looking for references to the Luther affair, *Exsurge domine*, the Diet of Worms, or the 1530 Augsburg Diet in his work will come away disappointed — even though we know from contemporary correspondence that the latter gathering was avidly followed in Poland.[29]

When writing of the Polish monarchy itself, his story's centre of gravity, Wapowski did pay some lip-service to the Reformation, but only where it directly impinged on his preferred themes of geopolitics and war. He notes, for example, that Danzigers had succumbed to 'the nepharious impiety of the Lutheran heresy', provoking fear that the city would spark a wider Baltic war.[30] King Sigismund's 1526 pacification of Danzig is the only aspect of the Reformation domestically covered by Wapowski in any detail — as a tale of a king, his army, and a military campaign. The execution of 12 rebel leaders and the 'religious' elements of the Danzig crisis merit only two passing lines, before Wapowski returns to the bigger military landmarks of 1526–1529, the Battle of Mohács in Hungary, the capture of Rome by imperial troops, and the Ottoman siege of Vienna.[31] Lutheranism in King Sigismund's monarchy functions as a mere subplot in the bigger drama of Polish royal power in the Baltic. In Wapowski's humanist text, history is a chessboard-like stage, on which kings, princes, emperors, and armies make moves. Heretics are not an acknowledged or legitimate actor on his board. Thus, in this learned Latin work we see the mould-breaking events of 1517–1535 awkwardly squashed into a rigid, prestigious, classical framework of history writing. In part, the genre itself limits what should, or with dignity could, be said. By 1535, therefore, no Polish chronicle had fully addressed, described, or acknowledged the Reformation at home or abroad head on.

The first vernacular history of the kingdom was the *Kronika Polska* (1597), a family effort begun by the lay nobleman Marcin Bielski and finished by his son Joachim (d.1599). Bielski junior had been educated in Lutheran Silesia, but converted to Catholicism, taking up a place at the Vasa royal court.[32] The *Kronika* offered some coverage of the European Reformation, albeit idiosyncratically so: Bielski's dedicatory letter to King Sigismund III stated that history is the foundation of Christian faith because it transmits knowledge of the Bible and Christ, yet all he offers us on the European Reformation in over 800 pages is a short paragraph on the German Peasants' War (1524–1525), and a papal letter to Kraków condemning the 'unChristian' behaviour of Henry VIII of England (1535).[33] There is still no Luther Affair, Worms, or Augsburg. Regarding Reformation events in Poland itself, Bielski repeated Wapowski's account of the Danzig crisis, embellishing the trial and sentencing of the Lutheran leader Johannes Scholz with dramatic dialogue.[34]

Yet as a chronicler Bielski, in common with Miechowita eighty years earlier, is most animated by religious transgressions or boundary-crossing — by scandals which, in this case, have seemingly nothing to do with the Reformation or Protestantism, but with Jews. In contrast to its indifference towards Protestantism, the *Kronika* contains two lengthy anecdotes about Christian-Jewish relations. It tells the story, for example, of the nobleman Stanisław Radwankowski, who having disgraced himself in war in the 1520s fled to Lwów, where 'out of desperation' he stole a consecrated Host and sold it to the Jews. For this, the parliament condemned him to death, and twelve of Radwankowski's noble companions had to swear they had known nothing of his intentions.[35] Bielski's only mention of the Reformation as a general crisis in Christendom, meanwhile, comes when he reports, for the year 1540, that many Poles were converting to Judaism:

> At this time, the Jews saw that people were in disagreement about the Christian faith and seemingly in doubt about it. Not a few Christians here converted and were accepted into the Jewish faith, and so that these were not punished, the Jews sent them through Hungary to Turkey… And in this way Satan did his work.[36]

In this passage, Protestantism and confessional conflict are not broached head on, but presented obliquely via the phenomenon of local Judaism. This would become an increasingly important feature of Polish chronicles as they entered the seventeenth century.

By 1600, total surveys of Polish history published in the large, prestigious *folio* format and graced with fine woodcuts, such as Miechowita's magnum opus or Bielski's *Kronika*, were dying out, giving way to accounts of recent military campaigns, or biographies of living kings.[37] If in the sixteenth century 'chronicles of Poland' had been the vehicle for talking about the Reformation (or not), the seventeenth century saw a major shift towards writing the histories of individual churches instead. Here, we see an explicitly Protestant Polish historiography in action for the first time and, by the century's end, an explicitly Counter/Catholic Reformation church history as well. Such confessional chronicles, in Poland printed in smaller *quarto* or *octavo* formats, were a new enterprise. As Roger Mason puts it, Protestant responses to Catholic critics 'perforce took a historical form', and they 'quickly saw the necessity of rewriting ecclesiastical history'.[38] Paul Knoll too has noted how one effect of the Reformation was 'the enhancement of historical writing as a tool used by advocates to determine and argue the validity of their religious tradition'.[39]

The first Protestant history of the Reformation in Poland was written by Andrzej Węgierski (1600–1649), a man rooted in Poland's Calvinist community. He was a minister in eastern Poland (as were all his brothers), who saw his parish and library burnt in the Chmielniecki Cossack rising of 1648.[40] Węgierski's *Libri Quatuor Slavoniae Reformatae* was published posthumously in 1652, with a new edition of the text printed in 1679.[41] As Euan Cameron has written, 'Protestant history was always ecclesiastical history, the history of the ecclesia, the congregation, the community living its religious life'.[42] The *Libri Quatuor* marks a departure from late medieval and humanist chronicles — its scope is not the Polish kingdom but the wider Slav lands, and its subject not a *regnum* but a true church. The *Libri Quatuor* is an ambitious, ground-breaking but anarchic text. It consists of three books which tell the history of Polish and Slav religion in three parallel narratives: a history of the true churches, of persecutions, and of local 'theologians and pastors'. The text often takes the form of simple lists of names, and much material is repeated across the three books. Węgierski, in keeping with by then well-established impulses within Protestant historiography, sought to prove the antiquity and existence of a true church in the Slav lands. He first told the story of medieval dissent in central Europe, of Waldensians, Hussites and Bohemian Brethren, the theologically adventurous Polish priest Biernat of Lublin (c.1500), and early martyr Adam of Kujawy, burnt for Hussitism. Węgierski went on to list the 'evangelical doctors' who had then preached the Reformation in Poland in its early decades.[43] Thereafter, the Calvinist synods held in Poland from the 1550s are enumerated in vast, rich historical and biographical detail, up to the 1620s.

This effect of this grand new narrative of the Reformation was two-fold. Firstly, it presents, or imagines, the Polish Reformation as chiefly a Calvinist affair. Not only did Węgierski flatten out all differences between his highly heterogeneous collection of late medieval martyrs, presenting them as uniformly Protestant in intent. He also effectively wrote out the Lutheran first generation of Reformation activity in Poland: Węgierski does this by omitting Prussia entirely from his story, and by including minimal information (three pages) on Polish Protestantism before 1550, followed by hundreds of pages outlining Calvinist activity. This creates the impression that nothing much had happened in the Polish monarchy by way of religious change before Calvinist preachers arrived, and in effect shifts the start date of Poland's Reformation movement to thirty years later than it really was. Many of his chapter-titles start explicitly in 1550, or 1551.[44] The dramatic Prussian events of the 1520s', so gripping to sixteenth-century chroniclers, have all but vanished.

And for Węgierski too, Judaism is important if uncomfortable. He repurposes as authentic Calvinist history not only a ragbag of late medieval figures, but also the kingdom's most famous convert to Judaism. Catherine of Kraków, executed in 1539, plays a central role in his Polish martyrology, and thus in his historical vision of the church in Poland — as a woman killed, as Węgierski has it, for denying the transubstantiated presence of Christ in the Eucharist, as Calvinists themselves adamantly did. Here, the Jew helpfully becomes a sacramentarian. Węgierski did not however wish to imply that Polish Jewry, in its totality, formed the kingdom's original, native Calvinist community, by virtue of not believing in the Real Presence. He thus reinvents the widow Catherine as a reformed Christian, and not at all a Jew:

> Katherine Zalassowska, wife of the senator of Cracow Melchior, for denying the divinity of Christ present in the bread of the Eucharist, as the Roman Church believes, was condemned by the Bishop of Kraków... and burnt rejoicing in the city square. But it is a calumny spread by the malicious, from pure hatred, to say that she had repudiated Christian doctrine and embraced the delirium of Judaism.[45]

Clearly, an actual Polish Jew could not serve as the archetypal Polish Calvinist martyr, but Catherine can play this part in Węgierski's history because she is a Christian — by belief, he asserts, though we might also note by name and blood. It is these which apparently make her safe, just about, as the protomartyr for reformed Protestantism in this account. Węgierski's later Dutch editor Gisbertus Voetius also saw Catherine's story as particularly significant, because his 1679 version of the text boasted, on its very frontispiece, that it included 'the history of Catherine Zalassovia'.[46] She is a conspicuously lone female figure in Węgierski's account of the origins of the Polish Reformation.

Our fifth chronicle is the *Historia Reformationis Polonicae* by the anti-Trinitarian Stanisław Lubieniecki (1623–1675), published posthumously in Freistadt in 1685. Lubieniecki's life story epitomises the dying days of the Polish Reformation. He was born into the celebrated Anti-Trinitarian community of Raków, educated at Saumur in France, and ended his life in exile in Hamburg following the expulsion decree of 1658.[47] Paul Knoll has described this work as the 'first history of European Unitarianism and a major monument of Polish historiography'.[48] The *Historia Reformationis* is an anti-Trinitarian mirror image of Węgierski's Calvinist chronicle, equating the Polish Reformation almost entirely with anti-Trinitarians, as its subtitle shows: 'in which is told the origin and progress of anti-Trinitarians in Poland and surrounding provinces'. Lubieniecki too reduces the Reformation in Poland before 1548 to just three chaotic pages, mentioning for example the 1525 Danzig rebels and Jan Łaski the younger. He explicitly labels this as still a pre-Reformation period, giving this chapter the title: 'How preparations for the Reformation began... in Poland from 1546 to 1550'.[49] With book two — which starts with an account of 'How the seeds of divine truth came from Italy to Poland with Socinius in 1551' — Lubieniecki reaches his true subject, the story of Polish anti-Trinitarians, to which he devotes over 250 pages. In this chronicle, then, both Lutherans and Calvinists alike are rhetorically manoeuvred out of the picture, and a different story of the true church offered.

Yet Lubieniecki too finds a special place for the story of Catherine of Kraków, who is a key figure in his very brief account of Polish reform under King Sigismund I. In the *Historia Reformationis*, Catherine is again Poland's first martyr of the true faith — executed here not as a Jew, or sacramentarian, but as an anti-Trinitarian, because she had insisted on the indivisible nature of the one God. He wrote that there was much 'terror in the kingdom at the sad case of Catherine wife of Melchior Vogel a consul of Kraków,' who had regarded the Roman church's adoration of the Host as 'idolatry'.[50] 'She was suspected', Lubieniecki wrote, 'of being a Jew, because she denied that the Son of God could be eternally begotten of the essence of the Father'.[51] Lubieniecki noted that she was executed in the very same year that Faustus Socinius was born in Italy. Anti-Trinitarians, who denied the divinity of Christ and saw veneration of the Trinity as potential idol-worship, were often denounced by their early modern critics simply as outright converts to Judaism. In spite of this, Lubieniecki is willing to make the risky rhetorical move of claiming Catherine as one of his own community, in Polish anti-Trinitarianism's quest for origins, history, and an authentic local past. This 1539 Christian-Jewish affair in the Kraków diocese, of the type which Miechowita or Bielski had found bemusing and scandalous, thus in the seventeenth century becomes the main narrative hinge for Protestant history writing in Poland. Catherine, the aged burgher's widow who consorted with local Jews, becomes the historic, legitimising, female point of origin of the Polish Reformation.

As it happens, it was these two Protestant histories, by the Calvinist Węgierski and anti-Trinitarian Lubieniecki, which would later form the bedrock of the first history of the Polish Reformation composed in English. In 1838, the Polish count Walerian Krasiński was in London, drumming up British support for the Polish national cause and armed struggle during the Partitions. To win sympathy from a British-American Protestant public, Krasiński published his *Historical Sketch of the Rise, Progress and Decline of the Reformation in Poland*. Depicting Poland as a historically Protestant state, his work was based closely on the narratives of Lubieniecki and Węgierski — one lost cause (the Polish Reformation) here invoked in the service of another (Polish nineteenth-century independence).[52] Writing two centuries after Lubieniecki, Krasiński was intrigued, if disconcerted, by the case of Catherine of Kraków. Gingerly, he chose to locate the episode outside his main heroic narrative, making it the subject of an extended footnote instead, in which he noted the 'remarkable story' of the 'deluded woman' Catherine, executed in 1539.[53]

In the face of the new, weighty, bold, and influential Protestant histories of the seventeenth-century, how did the Catholic Church in the Polish monarchy respond? Counter/Catholic Reformation clergy in Poland chose as their vehicle not national chronicles, but panoramic histories of the universal Catholic Church. Janusz Tazbir has showed how intensely Poland's high clergy followed and supported the labours of Cardinal Cesare Baronio (1538–1607) in Rome, author of the monumental, 12-volume *Annales Ecclesiastici*, a defining, erudite Catholic history for the confessional age.[54] The Polish court preacher Piotr Skarga organised production of an abridged Polish translation of the *Annales* in 1603, for example, and it was a Polish Dominican, Abraham Bzowski (d.1637), who was appointed by Pius V to continue Baronius' magnum opus after his death (the venerable cardinal's account having reached only the year 1193).

Our final chronicle, part of this constellation of Polish scholarly activity inspired by Baronius, is thus the *Roczne dzieje kościelne od roku pańskiego 1198 aż do lat naszych* ('The Annals of the Church from the Year of Our Lord 1198 to our own day'), produced by the Polish Jesuit Jan Kwiatkiewicz in 1695. While Baronius and Bzowski had written on the medieval church only, Kwiatkiewicz with a leap synthesised numerous national chronicles and church histories in order to narrate a universal Catholic history of the sixteenth century, in the Polish vernacular. Rejecting those who 'contented themselves with writing about their own kingdoms, kings, or bishops', Kwiatkiewicz's was a one-volume history of the church across the world, albeit with a strong Polish twist.[55] For each year of his annals, Kwiatkiewicz runs in turn through events in western Europe, Poland and Hungary, and the global missions. However, whereas divisive Reformation events in Germany, the Netherlands, Low Countries and especially England are dealt with blow by blow from 1517 onwards, Poland's sixteenth-century religious history is (through silence) made to appear entirely pacific. The Polish events Kwiatkiewicz includes are chiefly high political in nature: royal marriages, successions, and deaths. In his lengthy work, the Jesuit has very little to say about religious affairs in his native kingdom — just a few lines on legislation against Orthodox Christians, on the Danzig revolt, or on the preaching of Utraquism in Vilnius in 1557.[56] Only when it reaches the 1590s does his story acquire hints of a sharper edge, describing Sigismund III's crackdown on Lutheranism in Prussian cities, and Skarga's conversion of a prominent Protestant senator, Prokop of Granowo.[57] Thus Kwiatkiewicz's 1695 work, within the grander framework of a Eusebian-style church history, also offered a local vision of a Poland essentially unruffled by the Reformation, which by the 1590s in the capable hands of Sigismund III Vasa was securely, loyally Roman Catholic. We are a world away from Bielski's oblique anecdotes about Jews and Christians in sixteenth-century Poland, from Węgierski's Calvinist tome, and Lubieniecki's Raków.

Conclusions: Reformation without memory?

Under the Jagiellonian and Vasa kings, the Polish monarchy produced no equivalent of Andras Farkas' *Chronicle on the Introduction of the Scythians into Hungary and Jews out of Israel* (1538), Foxe's English *Actes and Monuments* (1563) or John Knox's (d.1572) *History of the Reformation of Religion within the Realm of Scotland*, and no state-led Reformation sponsored a new national history-writing project.[58] No early modern Polish historian fused national history, as those texts did, with that of Protestantism to offer a master-narrative of a covenanted people which commanded official or widespread support; nor did a Catholic version of such a vision clearly arise in chronicle form.[59] On the one hand, the European Reformation was a complex, epochal, slow-burn event, its outcomes not visible or legible to contemporaries for many decades, and perhaps the chaos of Polish chronicles reflects simply this. Norbert Kerksen reminds us, too, that early modern history was, as a genre, surprisingly heterogeneous.[60] Perhaps it is anachronistic to bring to this body of writing the expectation of a crisp, single, national master-narrative of the Reformation. We should consider how far the desire to find, or tell, a single national-confessional story was reinforced by nineteenth-century nationalist scholarship, which was so keen to write normalising, homogenous national stories.

The early modern Polish kingdom was, nonetheless, especially unpromising territory for an agreed memory of the Reformation to emerge within. As we have seen, our six chronicles tell completely variant stories of early modern Polish religion, with individual or pillarised Lutheran, Catholic, Calvinist, and Anti-Trinitarian memories and narratives. Taken together, this clutch of chronicles would seem to limit the potential for the emergence of any shared, functional, widely legible, social, or 'cultural' memory of the Polish Reformation in the early modern period — what one scholar calls 'a socially acceptable reference text of national history'.[61] The thriving coexistence of Catholics, Lutherans (from 1518), Calvinists (from 1540s) and Anti-Trinitarians (from 1550s) in the kingdom, cemented in the 1573 Warsaw Confederation, only formally ended in the 1650s, when the mid-seventeenth-century crisis of the Commonwealth precipitated mass expulsions of radical Protestants. If in political-historical terms Polish Protestantism was ultimately a failed project, it was perhaps the variety and longevity of Poland's Protestant churches, with their avid historians, which prevented the emergence of a coherent collective memory of the country's Reformation, by repeatedly splitting memory. In other words, the political reality of Christian pluralism had a profound impact on how early modern historians in this monarchy remembered the Reformation; and on why that society was, in the long-term, in some sense unable to do so. In Poland, the narrative chaos of early modern chronicles regarding the Reformation is arguably a reflection of unresolved memories, and indeed unresolved history.

The strange progression of Catherine of Kraków in these chronicles, from juicy scandal, to Calvinist witness, to the anti-Trinitarian martyr whose death lit up Faustus Socinius' birth, well illustrates how historians from different confessions used exactly the same Polish materials or events to radically different ideological ends. The plasticity of Catherine's Jewish story fits with the findings of Magda Teter, who shows how in Poland from the 1550s onwards Jews were used rhetorically and physically to perform Reformation conflict — in a slew of executions of Jews for Host-sacrilege, and in printed Protestant-Catholic theological polemics about these trials. This was not the only kingdom where Jews got caught up in the events or literature of the European Reformation.[62] Our chronicles show, however, that Jews, Catholics and Protestants were deeply entangled not just in early modern Polish social, legal and theological conflict, but also in the kingdom's written Reformation memories, where followers of Judaism (whether acknowledged as such or not) often act as a pivotal narrative device.

Here, we might pause to consider the interaction between Catherine of Kraków's gender, and the alternative religious identities eagerly ascribed to her (lapsed Catholic, Jew, Calvinist, anti-Trinitarian). In late medieval Polish chronicles, the image of a badly-behaved Jewish (or quasi-Jewish) woman had specific textual functions; functions which seventeenth-century Protestant writers inherited and inverted. Miechowita's 1521 *Chronica Polonorum*, for example, featured two types of women: virtuous royal women, and scandalous non-elite women. The latter include Albert's syphilitic wife, and the Catholic and Jewish women who birthed 'monsters'.[63] Female-ness and Jewishness were thus both key signifiers of potential scandal in the late medieval chronicle tradition, especially where they occurred in combination. The 1539 documented trial and execution of Catherine of Kraków, once it was narrated as history, therefore fitted this late medieval scandal 'topos' very well. Thus, when seventeenth-century Polish Protestant chroniclers came to place Catherine's trial so prominently within their texts, they were borrowing and echoing the gendered textual motifs of the local late medieval chronicle, consciously or not. Reformation writers, of course, presented Catherine and her death in a positive way, turning the story upside down — transforming defiance of bishops into Protestant dissent, and 'scandal' into 'witness'. However, this move was not unproblematic, and Catherine's female identity rendered her a profoundly anomalous figure, no more than an isolated symbol in Polish Protestant narrative. Certainly, by the nineteenth century Walerian Krasiński found this awkward origin-story entirely unusable, as we have seen, physically removing it from his main account and placing it in the cordon sanitaire of a footnote in small font. There is, then, an ongoing gender paradox in these Polish Protestant memories of the Reformation.

The early modern cacophony of Polish Reformation chronicle memories we have explored here had a profound long-term impact on knowledge, research, and cultural remembering. When nineteenth-century enthusiasts took up their pens to write histories of the Polish Reformation, for example, they would find no ready-made, baseline chronicle narrative to adopt, repeat, or build upon. Pioneers such as Teodor Wotschke (d.1939) or Julian Bukowski (d.1904) ended up simply amplifying the early modern Babel of Reformation stories, as factors in the modern world further mitigated against the emergence of a consensus-commanding narrative (or memory) — factors such as the Partitions of Poland, which locked the scholars and archives of the former Commonwealth into three different modern empires; the growth of nationalist historiography, which divided the lands of the former monarchy into ethnic nations such as Poland and Germany, writing their Reformation stories separately; and ongoing confessional competition, with Wotschke, for example, a polemicising Lutheran pastor, and Bukowski a polemicising Catholic priest.[64] The ideological imperatives of the early modern period, which split memory, met the ideological imperative of later eras, such as ethnic nationalism, which split it further. The absence of a clear story from Poland, in early modern chronicles or in subsequent periods, has had an impact on the kingdom's presence in modern international, especially Anglophone, histories (and memories) of the European Reformation — try as they might, leading historians struggle to find firm narratives of Polish events to hold onto in their own syntheses. The gap in modern international Reformation studies where Europe's largest sixteenth-century polity might be is not caused primarily by the Cold War, or by language barriers; it is deeper, and at heart has sixteenth-century roots.

Although this essay has focused on early modern mnemonics, it is worth glancing at one twentieth-century curiosity in the light of the chronicles considered here. Here we can return one last time to Catherine of Kraków. The original account of her trials was recorded by the notaries of Kraków's episcopal court in a special manuscript, reserved by the bishop's staff for recording misdemeanours such as clerical misbehaviour and heresy. This manuscript, held for centuries in the episcopal archive in Kraków, went missing in the 1970s or shortly thereafter — the only volume lost from an otherwise complete set of twelve sixteenth-century court books, as Magda Teter has also noted. Today, we know the text of Catherine's trial only because it was copied out by the nineteenth-century scholar Żegota Pauli, and survives among his papers.[65] Here, early modern half-remembering has persisted as literal misplacing of the Reformation past.

These early modern Polish chronicles perform for us a complex dance of forgetting. Theoretical literature on cultural memory tends to portray 'remembering' as active, and 'forgetting' as passive. Leaders in the field use active vocabulary to define cultural memory: the 'reconstruction' of the past (Halbwachs), 'the past created and recreated' (Erll), 'a complex process of cultural production' (Kansteiner).[66] Fiendt et al. have stressed the active way in which memory is remediated, performed again and again.[67] This instinct is most explicit, and likely partially originates in, Assmann's famous division of social memory into 'functional' (what is actively remembered), and 'latent' or 'storage' memory (what is recorded, but not currently used). For her, stored/forgotten material is by definition passive, because it is not in active cultural use: it is non-usable, deep-frozen.[68] In these ways, historic forgetting is implicitly presented by theorists as a non-dynamic, static process, like something (accidentally?) dropped down the back of the sofa and left to moulder there for centuries.[69] However, Polish Reformation chronicles remind us that forgetting was an active, complex, and iterative process in the early modern period. These texts forget both individually (deliberately omitting key events), and collectively (inadvertently, they together render the story so incoherent, that it cannot function as a story). The chronicles keep (re)forgetting what the archives might testify to, for different reasons, and in different ways. Wapowski would only include events befitting of Renaissance humanist conventions for reasons of literary prestige; Bielski practised ecumenical discretion; Węgierski forgot Lutherans; Lubieniecki forget Lutherans and Calvinists; the Jesuit Kwiatkiewicz contrived to forget or refuse stage-space to them all. The widow Catherine passes like a spinning top through these stories. These sixteenth and seventeenth-century Polish books show us that there are many different ways to forget, or to fail to tell (which might amount to the same thing) across confessions.

Ultimately, these six chronicles paint a picture of a monarchy which, in its self-memorialisation, practised an early modern form of confessional pillarisation — and where the price to pay for religious coexistence was, seemingly, Reformation without a coherent national memory. To paraphrase the political scientist David Ricci, this is not so much 'politics without stories', as toleration without narrative.[70]

Notes

1 Kraków, Biblioteka Jagiellońska, MS 5357 [papers of Żegota Pauli], vol. 9, fols. 72–73 (fol. 73): 'omnemque haeresim, superstitiosam sectam, ritus, erroresque Judeaorum in quam inciderat…'. For debates about religious violence in early modern Poland, see Janusz Tazbir, *A State Without Stakes: Polish Religious Toleration in the Sixteenth and Seventeenth Centuries* (New York, 1973); Magda Teter, *Sinners on Trial: Sacrilege After the Reformation* (Cambridge, MA, 2011); Natalia Nowakowska, *King Sigismund of Poland and Martin Luther: The Reformation Before Confessionalization* (Oxford, 2018).
2 *OED*, 'Pillarisation': 'Division or organization of society into parallel groups, each with their own hierarchy, on the basis of religious or ideological difference, esp. in the Netherlands and Belgium'.
3 Wincenty Zakrzewski, *Powstanie i Wzrost Reformacyi w Polsce, 1520–1572* (Leipzig, 1870).
4 Nobert Kerksen, 'Reformation and the Writing of National History in East-Central and Northern Europe', in *The Reformation in Eastern and Central Europe*, ed. Karin Maag (Aldershot, 1997), 50–71. See also Andrzej Grabski, *Zarys Historii Historiografii Polskiej* (Poznań, 2000).
5 See however Piotr Węcowski, *Początki Polski w Pamięci Historycznej Późnego Średniowiecza* (Kraków, 2014).
6 For recent scholarship, see Dariusz Śnieżko, *Kronika Wszystkiego Świata Marcina Bielskiego: Pograniczne Dyskursów* (Szczecin, 2004); Andrzej Borowski, *Iter Polono-Belgo-Ollandicum. Cultural and Literary Relationships between the Commonwealth of Poland and the Netherlands in the 16th and 17th Centuries* (Kraków, 2007); Wacław Urban, 'Andrzej Węgierski jako kaznodzieja włodawski i jego związki z Czechami', *Odrodzenie i Reformacja w Polsce*, 47 (2003), 173–5.
7 Katherine Van Liere, Simon Ditchfield, and Howard Louthan, eds., *Sacred History: Uses of the Christian Past in the Renaissance World* (Oxford, 2012).
8 Miechowita, *Chronica Polonorum* (Kraków, 1521), prefatory letter *ad lectorem*: 'non possunt sciri, nec imperpetuum rememorari'.
9 Marcin Bielski, *Kronika Polska* (Kraków, 1597), prefatory letter, n.p.: 'jakoby w niepamięc z laty nieszły'.

10 Jan Kwiatkiewicz, *Roczne dzieje kościelne od roku pańskiego 1198. Aż do lat naszych* (Kalisz, 1695), prefatory letter, n.p.: 'o ktorych nie mniey należało wiekom potomnym wiedzieć'.

11 Andrzej Węgierski, *Libri Quatuor Slavoniae Reformatae* (Amsterdam, 1679), preface by Gisbertus Voetius, 2: 'Historiam testem temporum, vitam memoriae…'.

12 This point is made also by Kerksen, 'Reformation', 62.

13 See Robert Frost, *The Oxford History of Poland-Lithuania*, vol. 1 (Oxford, 2015).

14 For a fuller narrative, see Nowakowska, *King Sigismund*, chapter 1.

15 See Mihály Balázs, 'Antitrinitarianism', in *A Companion to the Reformation in Central Europe*, ed. Howard Louthan and Graeme Murdock (Leiden, 2015), 171–94.

16 See also Piotr Stolarski, *Friars on the Frontier: Catholic Renewal and the Dominican Order in Southwestern Poland, 1595–1648* (Farnham, 2010).

17 George H. Williams, *The Polish Brethren: Documentation of the History and Thought of Unitarianism in the Polish-Lithuanian Commonwealth and in the Diaspora, 1601–1685* (Missoula, MT, 1980).

18 For modern memory, see Natalia Nowakowska, 'Forgetting Lutheranism: The Historiography of the Early Reformation in Poland', *Church History and Religious Culture* 92, no. 2–3 (2012), 281–303.

19 See Henryk Barycz, ed., *Maciej z Miechowa, 1457–1523: Historyk, Geograf, Lekarz, Organizator Naukowy* (Wrocław & Warsaw, 1960).

20 Miechowita, *Chronica Polonorum* (Kraków, 1521), 359, 376, 378.

21 Miechowita, *Chronica*, 360.

22 Miechowita, *Chronica*, 368, 373.

23 Miechowita, *Chronica*, 364.

24 Miechowita, *Chronica*, 349, 360.

25 Miechowita, *Chronica*, 368.

26 Miechowita, *Chronia*, 357; her identity is spelt out only in the censored 1519 version of the chronicle.

27 Bernard Wapowski, *Kroniki Bernarda Wapowskiego: Część Ostania*, ed. Józef Szujski (Kraków, 1874); 'Wapowski', Gazeteer of Plantary Nomenclature, accessed 3 August 2018, https://planetarynames.wr.usgs.gov/Feature/14541.

28 Wapowski, *Kroniki*, 159, 187, 192, 197.

29 For Poland and the Augsburg diet, see *Acta Tomiciana*, vol. 12 (Poznań, 1906).

30 Wapowski, *Kroniki*, 200–1,'nepharia impietate Lutheranam haeresim suscepit'.

31 Wapowski, *Kroniki*, 209–11.

32 Henryk Barycz, 'Joachim Bielski', in *Polski Słownik Biograficzny* 2 (1936), 61–4.

33 Bielski, *Kronika*, 555, 573.

34 Bielski, *Kronika*, 556.

35 Bielski, *Kronika*, 549.

36 Bielski, *Kronika*, 580–1: 'Żydowie tego czasu widzac iz sie ludzie ieli o wierze swey Chrześcianskiey gadac y swarzyc iakoby watpiac o niey niemało Chrześcian u nas na Zydowska wiarę zwiedli y onych pobrzewoali: a żeby sie tego nie kaiali z korony ie do Wegier a potym do Turek wysyłali… Tak był niele począł Szatan swe proporze rościagnac'.

37 See Grabski, *Zarys Historii*, 50–3.

38 Roger A. Mason, 'Useable Pasts: History and Identity in Reformation Scotland', *Scottish Historical Review* 76, no. 201 (1997), 54–68 (56).

39 Paul Knoll, review of 'History of the Polish Reformation and Nine Related Documents', by Stanislas Lubieniecki and George Huntston Williams, *SCJ* 28, no. 2 (1997), 567–70.

40 Janusz Tazbir, 'Praefatio' in Andrzej Węgierski, *Libri Quatuor Slavoniae Reformatae* (Warsaw, 1973), v–xxv.

41 Andrzej Węgierski, *Andreae Wengerscii Libri quatuor Slavoniae reformatae* (Amsterdam, 1679). First published as *Systema Historico-Chronologicvm, Ecclesiarum Slavonicarum per*

Provincias varias, Præcipue, Poloniæ, Bohemiæ, Litvaniæ, Rvssiæ, Prvssiæ, Moraviæ, etc. Distinctarum (Utrecht, 1652).

42 Euan Cameron, 'Primitivism, Patristics and Polemic in Protestant Visions of Early Christianity', in *Sacred History: Uses of the Christian Past in the Renaissance World*, ed. Katherine Van Liere, Simon Ditchfield, and Howard Louthan (Oxford, 2012), 27–51 (29).

43 Węgierski, *Libri quatuor*, 71–4.

44 Węgierski, *Libri quatuor*, for example, 218, 227.

45 Węgierski, *Libri quatuor*, 207: 'Catharina, Melchioris Zalassovii, Senatoris Cracoviensis uxor, ob religionem, quod de divinitate Christi in hostia panis Eucharistici, secundum fidem Romanae Ecclesiae, nihil crederet, ab Episcopo Cracoviensi Petro Gamrato ad rogum damnatur… inque medio fori Cracoviensis laetabunda ignibus exusta est. Quod vero fertur, eam repudiam Christianae doctrinae misisse, & Judaica deliria amplexam fuisse, malevolorum est calumnia, ex puro puto odio, per audax mendacium… '.

46 Węgierski, *Libri quatuor*: an appendix at 527–8 gave further details of the case, taken from Łukasz Górnicki's unpublished account.

47 Janusz Tazbir, 'Stanisław Lubieniecki młodszy', *Polski Słownik Biograficzny* 17 (1972), 603–7.

48 Knoll, review of 'History of the Reformation', 568.

49 Stanisław Lubieniecki, *Historia Reformationis Polonicae* (Freistadt: Johannes Aconius, 1658), 14.

50 Lubieniecki, *Historia*, 17: 'Injecerat enim multis in regno terrorem triste Catharinae Melchioris Vogelii Consulis Cracoviensis uxoris…'.

51 Lubieniecki, *Historia*, 17: 'suspectam eam Judaismi fuisse, quod Filium Dei, credo, ex essentia Patris ab aeterno genitum, negarit'.

52 Walerian Krasiński, *Historical Sketch of the Rise, Progress and Decline of the Reformation in Poland*, 2 vols. (London, 1838, 1840).

53 Krasiński, *Historical Sketch*, 131–2.

54 Janusz Tazbir, 'Baronius a Skarga', *Odrodzenie i Reformacja w Polsce* 26 (1981), 19–33.

55 Kwiatkiewicz, *Roczne dzieje*, dedicatory letter: 'się kontentowali, abo opisaniem swoich Krolestw i Krolow, abo też Biskupów'.

56 Kwiatkiewicz, *Roczne dzieje*, 631, 641, 694.

57 Kwiatkiewicz, *Roczne dzieje*, 796–7.

58 On Farkas' *Cronica de introduction Scyttarum in Ungariam*, see Graeme Murdock, 'Magyar Judah: Constructing a New Canaan in Eastern Europe', in *StCh*,36, ed. Robert Swanson, (Woodbridge, 2000), 263–74; see also Kerksen, 'Reformation', 62.

59 See Mason, 'Usable Pasts'.

60 Kerksen, 'Reformation', 71.

61 Kerksen, 'Reformation', 68.

62 Teter, *Sinners on Trial*. See also Debra Kaplan and Magda Teter, 'Out of the (Historiographic) Ghetto: European Jews and Reformation Narratives', *SCJ* 40, no. 2 (2009), 365–94 (386).

63 Miechowita, *Chronica*, 357–8, 360.

64 See Nowakowska, 'Forgetting Lutheranism'.

65 Biblioteka Jagiellońska, Kraków, MS 5357.

66 Maurice Halbwachs, *On Collective Memory*, tr. and ed. L. A. Coser, (Chicago, 1992), 40; Astrid Erll, 'Regional Integration and (Trans)cultural Memory', *Asia Europe Journal* 8, no. 3 (2010), 305–15 (305–6); Wulf Kansteiner, 'Finding Meaning in Memory: A Methodological Critique of Collective Memory Studies', *History and Theory* 41, no. 2 (2002), 179–97 (179).

67 Gregor Feindt et al., 'Entangled Memory: Towards a Third Wave in Memory Studies', *History and Theory* 53, no. 1 (2014), 24–44. See also Natalia Nowakowska 'Introduction: Time, Space and Dynasty', in *Remembering the Jagiellonians*, ed. Natalia Nowakowska (Abingdon, 2019), 1–27.

68 Aleida Assman, *Cultural Memory & Western Civilisation: Functions, Media, Archives* (Cambridge, 2011). See also Merike Lang, 'Cultural Memory in the Museum and its Dialogue with Collective and Individual Memory', *Nordisk Museologi* 2, no. 2 (2007), 62–75.

69 With the exception of theories of cultural traumatic amnesia: see the discussion by Uilleam Blacker, 'The Wood Comes to Dunsinane Hill: Representations of the Katyń Massacre in Polish literature', *Central Europe* 10, no. 2 (2012), 108–23.

70 David Ricci, *Politics Without Stories: The Liberal Predicament* (Cambridge, 2016).

PART IV

Inherited memory

8

THE FIRST AMONG THE MANY

Early modern cultural memory and the Hussites

Phillip Haberkern

By the time that Martin Luther published his theses against indulgences in late 1517, one kingdom in Europe had already undergone over a century of Reformation. What began as a preaching campaign promoting sacramental piety and moral regeneration in the Bohemian capital of Prague around the middle of the fourteenth century had, by the 1410s, evolved into a mass movement for the reform of ecclesiastical abuses with a decidedly subversive edge.[1] When the leader of this movement, the popular preacher and professor Jan Hus, was executed at the Council of Constance for Eucharistic heresy and his failure to submit to ecclesiastical authorities on July 6, 1415, the Czech lands exploded into revolution. Led by a coalition of noblemen committed to reform and the masters of Prague's university, the 'Hussites' venerated the martyr Hus and his companion Jerome of Prague as authentic saints, promoted the reception of communion in both kinds by the laity, and mobilised an army of holy warriors to defend their religious practices and uphold the law of God.[2]

Over the course of the 1420s, the Czech 'warriors of God' defeated five crusades that were called against them and secured a hearing for their religious teachings at the Council of Basel. Arriving there in early 1433, the Hussites debated with Catholic masters for months over their Four Articles, which represented the core of their ideology and asserted the necessity of: 1) communion in both kinds for the laity; 2) free preaching by all priests; 3) secular authorities' punishing manifest sin; and 4) the disendowment of Church leaders and poverty of the clergy.[3] The council fathers at Basel refused to countenance the last three of these articles, but they did eventually allow that the Czechs' Eucharistic practice was licit. This concession was enshrined in a treaty called the *Compactata* that recognised the legitimacy of the Bohemians' Utraquist church, so-called for is practice of administering the sacrament '*sub utraque specie*', and forbade the prosecution of future holy wars against the former Czech heretics.[4]

The foundation and formal recognition of this church did not, however, mean that a new religious uniformity prevailed in the Czech lands. There remained a substantial minority that was faithful to the Roman church; the remnants of radical groups who had established a utopian, mountaintop community at Tábor and formed the backbone of the Hussite military forces; and idiosyncratic thinkers like Petr Chelčický, who argued for the complete dissolution of ties between the Church and worldly authority.[5] The persistence of these groups meant that sustained debate and negotiation were central to the maintenance of a religious *modus vivendi* across the fifteenth century, so that the Czechs were necessarily precocious in crafting frameworks of religious tolerance and coexistence for themselves. The most notable example of these was the Peace of Kutná Hora, a decree issued by the Catholic King Vladislav Jagellonský in 1485 that made Bohemia the first legally bi-confessional kingdom in Europe, and went considerably beyond 1555's Peace of Augsburg in affirming individuals' right to choose their religious affiliation.[6]

Although the Peace of Kutná Hora was progressive for its time, it did not include all religious communities in the Czech lands. Specifically, it excluded the Unity of Brethren, a pacifist, voluntaristic group that emerged in the 1450s.[7] The Unity represented a unique blend of Tábor's communitarian impulses and Chelčický's vernacular theology, a sectarian movement that withdrew from society to create small communities living within the bonds of strict religious discipline. Unlike the Utraquist church, which maintained the principle of apostolic succession and had their priests ordained by Catholic bishops, the Unity established their own ranks of ministers; its first pastors and bishop were selected by lot in 1467, and after that its clergy trained through a system of apprenticeship. The Unity initially eschewed political involvement and military service, but an increasing number of nobles and burghers were attracted by their piety and morals. Thus, even though the Unity was excluded from the Peace of Kutná Hora and subject to periodic persecution by the crown, it grew steadily and slowly became more integrated into the cultural and intellectual mainstream of Czech society.[8]

The fact that the Unity and Utraquists had already experienced the tribulations of founding, growing, and defending churches that had separated themselves from Catholic ecclesiastical institutions marked them as unique among European religious dissidents in the sixteenth century. Whereas the Protestant movements that arose in Wittenberg, Zürich, Geneva, and points in between sought to forge historical lineages and genealogies of dissent for themselves that mined the past in order to justify their present demands for reform, the Czech churches already had such a history.[9] As such, their priority was to determine the best way to both preserve the cultural memory of their own founding and to establish communication and potential alliances with their newly reformed neighbours, rather than merely invent a new tradition for themselves.[10]

In 1517, the Czechs had been politically isolated for a century due to their religious deviation from the traditional Church. With the widespread outbreak of reform in the Holy Roman Empire, however, that history of dissent became newly attractive to Protestant leaders who sought to establish a link between themselves to these potential predecessors. Both the Unity and Utraquists initially sought to explore connections with foreign reformers, but at the same time they needed to affirm their status as the rightful heirs of the fifteenth-century Hussite revolution. The founders of that revolution (and especially Jan Hus) became some of the most prominent figures claimed by early modern Protestants as forerunners, so sixteenth-century Czech reformers could not merely assume that they would be recognised as such.[11] It was therefore through the propagation of distinctive forms of memory that the Czech churches asserted ownership of their native Reformation's past in dialogue with international Protestantism.

In order to understand how commemoration worked for the Unity of Brethren and Utraquists as they sought to carve out a niche for themselves among European evangelicals, it is well worth considering the concepts of 'communicative' and 'cultural' memory developed by Jan and Aleida Assmann.[12] For these scholars, communicative memory is primarily oral, decentralised, and dynamic. It comprises the recollections of eye-witnesses to certain events whose testimonies are passed down over several generations and reify a given moment as emblematic of a social group's defining characteristics. After eighty or a hundred years, however, this type of social memorialisation inevitably changes. Paintings are commissioned, holidays are instituted, books are written, and political leaders appropriate an event or individual and promote a certain interpretation of its significance. This process of 'canonisation' elevates specific events and people to a higher status in the cultural memory of a group in order to provide it with a ground for unity. Conversely, this process also relegates other people, places, and events to a cultural 'archive' that may be preserved, but is only rarely, actively remembered, thus creating 'a narrative that is emotionally charged and conveys a clear and invigorating message' anchored in public spaces or monuments, rituals, and calendars.[13] Despite their official marginalisation, archived cultural memories always maintain a latent power that can be activated by groups that want to push back at the hegemonic propagation of a given historical narrative.[14] Heretics and rebels can always be transformed into martyrs and freedom fighters, and the efforts of Protestant scholars in the sixteenth century to transform medieval dissidents into the champions of an oppressed, true Christianity provide ample evidence for how powerful this type of activation could be.[15]

Cultural memory is, in a word, plastic: able to be shaped and moulded to fit a variety of cultural purposes. Certainly the commemoration of the Bohemian Reformation's foundation played multiple roles in the sixteenth century. On the one hand, it served as a basis for the Utraquists' and Unity of Brethren's unique identities and prerogatives, and these churches invoked their fidelity to the Hussites' founding *kerygma* as a legitimising principle for their current institutions and practices. On the other hand, however, the memory of the Hussites could be invoked as a resource for establishing common ground among religious groups that were opposed to Rome — a sort of pre-confessional wellspring of teaching on reform and resistance upon which all groups could agree.[16] These calls for co-operation occurred in both international and domestic contexts, and they intensified as Czech and international Protestants sought to secure legal recognition for themselves in response to the rising tide of Habsburg confessional absolutism.[17] The preservation of cultural memory thus had significant practical consequences for the churches of the Bohemian Reformation, and the success (or failure) of those who sought to shape that memory played an essential role in determining the confessional landscape of the early modern Czech lands.

The Hussites among the nations

The Bohemian Reformation's international reputation underwent a stunning reversal around the year 1520. Whereas the Hussites had previously been seen as religious bogeymen who posed the greatest military and cultural threat to Christendom beside the Turks, now there was a growing minority within the Holy Roman Empire who saw them as champions of divine truth. This change in perception effectively began in 1519, when Martin Luther argued during the Leipzig Debate with Johannes Eck that some of Jan Hus's teachings condemned at Constance had actually been orthodox.[18] Luther's defence of Hus only intensified after that disputation, and a number of his most important treatises from 1519 and 1520, most notably the *Address to the German Nobility*, urged his readers to 'take up earnestly and truthfully the cause of the Bohemians and unite them with ourselves'.[19] In these texts, Luther asserted that Hus and Jerome of Prague had been unjustly executed, and he further presented their deaths as evidence that church councils could err and that the institutional Church had been subverted by the agents of the Antichrist. Luther also promoted his personal connection to Hus both publicly and privately, claiming that 'without knowing it, we are all Hussites'.[20] Certainly Luther moderated his praise of Hus by saying that the Bohemian martyr's critique of the papacy had been too limited, as it was concerned with morality rather than the office's fundamental legitimacy. This qualification should not, however, obscure Luther's public embrace of the Hussites, and especially their eponymous founder, in the earliest years of his campaign against the papacy.[21]

Luther's support resulted in the widespread dissemination of Hussite texts and a subsequent increase in familiarity with their practices. Luther again played a leading role in this process, as he issued a call for the laity to receive communion in both kinds in late 1519 and shepherded two editions of Hus's *De Ecclesia* through the press in 1520.[22] The Bohemians' Eucharistic practice had, of course, long been recognised as a disturbing deviation from Christian norms, but Luther was joined by other authors in his re-appraisal of the Hussites' heterodoxy. The early 1520s witnessed the publication of editions of the Hussites' *Four Articles* and the Czech nobility's defence of Hus's orthodoxy from 1415, both of which emphasised that the Bohemian Reformation provided a precedent for the local political oversight of religious reform. Multiple editions of the humanist Poggio Bracciolini's sympathetic account of Jerome of Prague's execution also appeared at this time, which showed that prominent humanists had admired the Hussite reformers.[23] Their continued appeal to intellectuals was demonstrated by individuals such as the Strasbourg reformer Wolfgang Capito, who wrote a pamphlet in 1524 that lauded the Bohemians for their establishment of a successful alliance between religious reformers and pious noblemen that had effectively resisted papal intervention. The message from this history was clear to the humanist Capito: 'Nothing could be a greater consolation to us, than if our leaders became like this.'[24]

In all of these publications, sixteenth-century German authors appropriated Hussite history in order to substantiate their contemporary theological and political arguments. These texts recast Hussite history in a positive light and broadcast it to a wider audience than it had previously reached, but the image of the Bohemian Reformation's origins that they propagated was geared towards legitimising the nascent German Reformation. The wave of publications about the Hussites produced in the first half of the 1520s was not, however, a one-sided affair. Indeed, the leaders of the Utraquist church and the Unity of Brethren actively inserted themselves into the expanding discussion of the Hussites' relevance for sixteenth-century reform, even as they sought to learn more about the new religious movements emerging in Saxony and the Swiss lands. Evidence of the Czechs' interest in these reformist currents can be found in the vast number of treatises by figures like Luther and Erasmus that appeared in Czech translation at this time.[25] This textual knowledge was augmented by the increasing number of individuals sent by the Czech churches to Wittenberg and other centres of reform. The Unity of Brethren sent five delegations to Luther's university by 1525, including both students and leaders of the church sent to observe the morality of the Wittenbergers. The Utraquists also sent representatives to Luther, and these personal contacts foregrounded extended exchanges of letters and treatises that allowed living, rather than just historical, 'Hussites' to shape the public perception of their churches' teachings.[26]

The Czechs' dialogue with Swiss and German reformers initially focused on two topics: the nature of the priesthood and the presence of Christ in the Eucharist. And it must be pointed out that their differences on these topics were far from trivial. Regarding sacramental theology, the Utraquists maintained the traditional Catholic doctrine of transubstantiation and viewed the Mass as a sacrifice. The Unity, conversely, had adopted a memorial view of the sacrament that was close to the position taken by Ulrich Zwingli. In terms of priests' role in the church, the Utraquists had long defended the principle of apostolic succession, despite the difficulty of securing these ordinations over time. The Unity, of course, had rejected apostolic succession, but it still promoted clerical celibacy because it better enabled their priests to face the risk of persecution and suffering, a position that distinguished them from most Protestant groups.[27]

Both the Utraquists and the Unity of Brethren had refined their positions on these issues through intensive debate with each other and Catholics for over fifty years, and their convictions had been tested by legal oppression and war. As such, neither group was inclined to meekly surrender their sacramental theology or understanding of the priesthood in the face of Lutheran or Reformed arguments. They did, however, prove willing to debate Protestants on both issues, and both the Unity and Utraquists employed a wide spectrum of genres to communicate their stances on these crucial issues, including those that would become most characteristic of Protestant polemics. The Unity of Brethren, for instance, reprinted an *Apology* they had first published in 1511 to explain their stance on the Eucharist to Luther, and they issued a German edition of an earlier catechism for children to clarify the *Apology*'s somewhat opaque language.[28] The Unity subsequently published a German translation of one of their hymnals at the end of the decade, which was then edited by Katharina Schütz Zell in Strasbourg. Her versions of the Unity's songs were later incorporated into other Protestant hymnals, meaning that the Unity's practices that lay 'on the boundary between liturgy and popular piety', to use Elsie McKee's helpful categories, also became widely known across the sixteenth-century confessional spectrum.[29]

Along with these publications, both the Utraquists and Unity maintained strong networks of correspondence with reformers across the continent. Luther, Erasmus, Philipp Melanchthon, Martin Bucer, and eventually John Calvin all received letters from, and sent them to, the leaders of the Czech churches. The Unity in particular preserved this correspondence, printing the letters they received as evidence of their acceptance by the leaders of international Protestantism.[30] Exemplary of this trend was a letter written by Bucer to the Brethren after he had spent forty-two(!) days in conversation with a delegation they had sent to meet with him. According to this letter, the Unity had instilled 'pure, useful, and salutary discipline' in their communities, so that Bucer was ashamed to compare the Unity's achievements to his community's 'mediocre' progress. Bucer did wonder at the Unity's continued adherence to clerical celibacy, but he distinguished their custom from the Catholics' diabolical 'cult of virginity'. In the conclusion to his letter, he recognised the Unity as evangelical fellow travellers, and he offered up the hope that Christendom might be restored through their 'mutual consolations and admonitions'.[31]

These epistolary exchanges acknowledged the differences that existed between the various programmes for reform emerging in the sixteenth century and those that had arisen during the Bohemian Reformation. Letters also complemented the outward facing texts produced by Czech authors during the 1520s that sought to establish their churches' evangelical bona fides as the earliest exponents of the renewed gospel vis-à-vis Rome. And while the variety of genres employed and topics addressed in this campaign can seem bewildering, as it encompassed new editions of older Hussite texts, learned treatises, hymns, catechetical texts, letters, and sermons, that diversity is crucial. It demonstrates that during the formative years of the European Reformations, the Utraquists and Unity established themselves as equals to the Protestant reformers by leveraging their history to offer insight into evolving debates about the sacraments, the nature of the church and its leadership, and the structuring of the Christian community.

The mobilisation of memory

In the decades after the outbreak of the German and Swiss Reformations, the Utraquists and Unity were fundamentally changed by their contact with the burgeoning world of international Protestantism. The channels that had opened up in the 1520s allowed new challenges to old orthodoxies to flow into Bohemia, even as they enabled the Czechs to broadcast their own theological traditions and agendas. This influx of external ideas about Christian belief and practice met with resistance, especially among the Utraquists. Their privileged legal position in the Czech lands and veneration for the early leaders and history of their church led them to push back against Protestant claims to represent the heirs of the heroic Hussites. One early instance of this contested view of the past occurred in 1524, when a Utraquist synod assembled to give answer to Luther's critique of their maintenance of apostolic succession. Responding specifically to Luther's claim that the Utraquists had betrayed the memory of Jan Hus and their other martyrs by preserving a Roman conception of the priesthood, the Utraquist leadership promulgated a list of twenty articles reaffirming their church's traditional teachings on the clergy, the sacraments, the cult of the saints, and other 'Catholic' religious practices.[32] This synod framed its decrees with references to a foundational Hussite synod in 1421 that had laid out the liturgical and devotional guidelines that Utraquists would continue to follow for the next century, while also citing the Four Articles, the preaching of Hus and other early Hussite masters, and the example of 'Master Jan Hus and the other Czech martyrs' as authorities underwriting their positions.[33]

These 1524 decrees marshalled the memory of seminal moments and ideas from the Hussite era to contest Luther's claims that contemporary Utraquists had misinterpreted or forgotten their founding charters. In the two decades after this first volley, Utraquist authors continued to produce texts that employed Hussite sources and authors to address specific issues on which they diverged from Luther and other Protestant groups. These texts were typically written in Czech, and they were saturated with references to, and citations of, earlier authors from the Bohemian Reformation.[34] These texts specifically highlighted the pedigree of the Utraquists' teachings on the devotional role of sacred art, the celebration of certain saints' feast days, the administration of communion to infants, and the preservation of the traditional liturgy and all seven sacraments. The maintenance of these ritual practices differentiated the Utraquists from Protestants, even as certain aspects of their theology brought them closer to Wittenberg.

The clearest sign of theological convergence lay in the incorporation of Lutheran ideas about justification into both the Czech churches' theology. The Unity and Utraquists produced confessions in the 1530s to summarise their beliefs, and these texts adopted (and adapted) the structure and language of the Lutheran Augsburg Confession to highlight the ideological common ground that existed among central European Protestants. Eventually, both of the Czech churches accepted the validity of clerical marriage, and the Unity reduced the number of sacraments it observed to two.[35] The accumulation of changes such as these has led many scholars to conclude that the churches of the Bohemian Reformation were essentially assimilated by the Lutheran and Reformed traditions over the course of the sixteenth century, and that whatever remained of the Unity and Utraquists represented ossified institutions that had surrendered the religious dynamism of the previous century.[36]

Such a conclusion ignores, however, the complementary preservation of early Hussite ideology within these confessional documents. Take, for instance, the confession of faith prepared by the Unity of Brethren in 1535.[37] This document had multiple purposes; its primary aim was to present the Unity's beliefs to King Ferdinand I of Bohemia as entirely unobjectionable so he might recognise the legality of their church in the Czech lands. Secondarily, the confession was meant to garner a positive response from foreign Protestants (mainly Luther and his followers) as an expression of the Unity's evangelical Eucharistic beliefs and stance on good works as necessary for salvation. Interestingly, this text followed close on the heels of a confession published by the Unity in 1533 that had been written for the Margrave of Brandenburg, and the two texts were theologically very similar.[38] The latter confession, however, mimicked the structure of the Lutheran *Augustana* and was submitted to Luther and Melanchthon for their review prior to its publication. These steps suggested that the Unity was trying to put its best foot forward with this confession, and the positive preface that Luther contributed for its 1538 publication attested to the Unity's success. Indeed, Luther affirmed in his prologue that his previous disagreements with the Brethren were due to merely linguistic differences and praised the Unity as performing the 'miracle' of turning away from human traditions and 'meditating on the Law of the Lord day and night'.[39]

Alongside Luther's preface, however, the 1535 confession featured another, longer introduction. This second text was composed by the Unity's ministers, and it showed their commitment to presenting themselves to their king and an international Protestant audience as rooted in the original vision of the Bohemian Reformation. They offered this vision as perfectly aligned with orthodox, catholic tradition, representing the Unity as the true heirs of both the apostolic and early Hussite communities. This text was also clear that the Unity supported neither theological innovations nor social disturbances. Rather, it was a church devoted to upholding the word of God and retaining the practices of the apostolic Church — especially with regards to the Eucharist and preaching — that had been revived in the Czech lands during the previous century. This text was explicit about the individuals who authored that revival, listing the fourteenth-century scholar Matěj of Janov, Jan Hus ('a man whom no succession of ages might cause to be forgotten'), Jakoubek of Stříbro, and Jan Rokycana as teachers of this divine truth.[40] The preface also singled out Petr Chelčický, whose works had been massively influential on the founders of the Unity.[41] Beyond names, the preface appealed specifically to letters written by Hus in Constance and the early writings of Matěj on the Antichrist, as these sources predicted that 'a new people' would arise who were shaped by God, provided with holy ministers, and set in opposition to all 'avarice and the glory of this life, and zealous for heavenly conduct'.[42]

The recollection of these founding figures was complemented in the preface by a more general exhortation for people to remember their cultural heritage. Reflecting on the origins of the Bohemian Reformation in the re-introduction of communion in both kinds, a practice 'in which we were born, raised, and educated', this text called for its adherents to remember 'our forebears, the old Czechs, and to understand ecclesial and religious matters much more with them, than with more recent people'. To do this would mean that 'we are made to be subject in all things and ruled by the Word of God', so that the Unity would 'become equal inheritors of eternal life'.[43] This appeal to the ancient underpinnings of true faith incorporated both the early teachings of the Bohemian Reformation and those of the primitive church. Throughout this preface, the Unity described itself as receiving, accepting, and restoring the oldest practices of the Christian community; such appeals were meant both to demonstrate the pedigree of the Unity's decision to choose a new clergy for themselves and to contradict any accusations that they were Anabaptists or embraced illicit theological novelties.[44] In short, the Unity presented their confession of faith in 1535 as a contemporary expression of beliefs and practices that had been initially practiced by the Church, subsequently forgotten, and then restored at the outset of the Bohemian Reformation. According to the Unity, they alone had ensured the survival of these founding principles and had withstood persecution for their faithful stewardship. As such, they sought recognition as 'true and faithful Christians, not heretics, who are embraced as such in the name of our salvation by the entire Church of our age'.[45]

A thematically similar, if ultimately contradictory claim to represent the original spirit of the Bohemian Reformation was made by the Utraquist scholar Bohuslav Bílejovský, who published a history of religious reform in the Czech lands in 1537. His *Church Chronicle* offered up the Utraquists as the sole group that had preserved authentic sacramental practices and maintained proper church governance in recent times.[46] According to Bílejovský, the Unity (whom he derisively called 'Pikarts') had imported false Eucharistic beliefs from abroad and sought to undermine the community of 'faithful Czechs', but had heretofore been resisted by the Utraquist leadership and pious nobles of Bohemia and Moravia.[47] For Bílejovský, the keys to the Bohemian Reformation were its restoration of communion in both kinds, its administration of the sacrament to infants, and its preservation of the vernacular liturgy. And while Bílejovský had to engage in some torturous, oft inaccurate historical argumentation to show the near continuity of these practices in the Czech lands, his main point was clearly articulated throughout his *Chronicle*: that the Utraquist church preserved rituals that had come into the Czech lands in the ninth century and would have been practiced continually, but for the interference of foreign popes and the persecution of the Utraquists.[48]

Bílejovský's history of Christianity in the Czech lands was distinguished by its constant efforts to ground its narrative of events in the development and preservation of certain ritual practices. His *Chronicle* was concerned less with the most dramatic events of the Bohemian Reformation, such as the martyrdom of Hus or the violence of the Hussite Wars, and more committed to preserving the memory of how communion in both kinds was initially introduced and later revived among the Czechs. Indeed, much of Bílejovský's narrative sketched a history of Czech Eucharistic practice, and the text's more polemical sections were devoted equally to Catholic 'enemies of the chalice' who forbade the laity from receiving the cup and Pikarts who did not honour the presence of Christ in the sacrament. In between these two poles of false teaching stood Bílejovský's Utraquist church, which had persisted in its defence of authentic Christian practice through a series of conflicts with the popes and church councils, Tábor, and the Unity. The Utraquists in the sixteenth century could therefore claim 'credit with the Lord God and honor among Christians', because they were 'an example of righteousness to other nations, and expeditiously bringing them back to the truth'.[49]

The Utraquists' insistence on their status as the sole heirs of the Bohemian Reformation's founders could make for strange bedfellows. Thus, in the 1530s they shared fifteenth-century texts with the Catholic polemicist Johannes Cochlaeus and the Bishop of Vienna, Johannes Fabri, so they could bring new editions of them to press.[50] Both Cochlaeus and Fabri used these sources to argue that the Utraquists were closer to Rome in their ecclesiology and sacramental theology than they were to any Protestant group, so they should seek full reunion with the Church; from a Catholic perspective, such a union could help offset the loss of German territories. Granted, Fabri's and Cochlaeus's arguments fell on deaf ears (and Fabri had to go into hiding when mobs in Prague threatened his safety), and the Utraquists resisted their blandishments for a rapprochement with Rome. Their publishing efforts did, however, demonstrate the perceived power that lay in the invocation of early Hussite authorities as binding models on the contemporary Czech churches and the range of confessional goals towards which these authorities could be directed.

Conclusion

In writing about cultural memory and collective identity, Jan Assmann memorably employed an immunological metaphor to describe the rituals and texts that served as anchors for a religious group's identity as a cultural 'immune system' that circulated antibodies throughout the social body of the group.[51] These antibodies comprised memories and the values associated with them that were essential to the group's identity, and Assmann argued that their rehearsal built up a group's resistance to outside influences. A social process of commemorative 'inculturation' therefore promoted a stronger sense of identity by raising up certain people and moments as embodiments of the group's core values and laying exclusive claim to those cultural signifiers.[52] In the first decades after the outbreak of the German and Swiss Reformations, the leaders of the Czech Utraquists and Unity of Brethren undertook such a process of inculturation. Both groups created a canon of texts and celebrated historical figures that together reified a particular cultural memory of the Bohemian Reformation. They did this for both a burgeoning international Protestant community and variegated domestic audiences, with the intention of publicising their inheritance from the Hussite movement and thereby claiming a special status as the first people to throw off the papacy's shackles.

The two churches had different motivations in establishing their ties to Jan Hus and his revolutionary successors. The Unity of Brethren sought to parlay their acknowledgement abroad as Protestant fellow travellers into the recognition of their legitimacy (and legality) in their own country; the Utraquists, conversely, wanted to affirm their historical status as the sole legitimate non-Catholic church in the Czech lands while establishing cultural and political alliances that might limit the power of their Habsburg king. Despite their divergent aims, both churches propagated the memory of many of the same events and people. Their canons were not identical, but overlapped substantially, and their shared memory of figures like Jan Hus or events like the Hussite Wars established a narrative of suffering and perseverance that resonated deeply with sixteenth-century audiences. This narrative was elaborated in many forms, as early modern Czech authors took full advantage of print technology to disseminate songs, sermons, theological statements, pedagogical texts, and Hussite primary sources for their contemporaries. With these textual building blocks, early modern authors across the European continent constructed histories of the Bohemian Reformation that helped to underwrite their various political and religious agendas. But only Czech authors could go beyond the writing of history to revivify the memory of the Bohemian Reformation's origins and thus sustain their collective identities as its heirs.

Notes

1 On the origins of the reform movement in Prague, see Olivier Marin, *L'Archevêque, le Maître, et le Dévot: Genèses du Mouvement Réformateur Pragois: Années 1360–1419* (Paris, 2005); and Vilém Herold, 'The Spiritual Background of the Czech Reformation: Precursors to Jan Hus', in *A Companion to Jan Hus*, ed. František Šmahel (Boston, 2015), 69–95.

2 The authoritative analysis of the Hussite revolution remains: František Šmahel, *Die Hussitische Revolution*, tr. Thomas Krzenck, 3 vols. (Hannover, 2002). See also the nuanced theological analysis in: Howard Kaminsky, *A History of the Hussite Revolution* (Berkeley, 1967); and the treatment of these three particular ideological tenets of the early revolution in: Thomas Fudge, *The Magnificent Ride: The First Reformation in Hussite Bohemia* (Aldershot, 1998), 124ff.

3 On the centrality of the Four Articles as a binding agent among the disparate groups in the Hussite revolution, see the classic work by František Bartoš, *Do čtyř Pražských Artikulů: Z Myšlenkových a Ústavních Zápasů let 1415–1420* (Prague, 1940). Cf. Kaminsky, A History of the Hussite Revolution, 361–83.

4 A separate agreement between the Bohemians and King Sigismund of Hungary (also known as the *Compactata*) recognised his claim to the throne of the Czech lands. On these debates and their diplomatic resolution: E. F. Jacob, 'The Bohemians at the Council of Basel', in *Prague Essays*, ed. R. W. Seton-Watson (Oxford, 1949), 81–123; and William Cook, 'Negotiations between the Hussites, the Holy Roman Emperor, and the Roman Church, 1427–1436', *East Central Europe* 5 (1978), 90–104.

5 On the origins of Tábor, see Šmahel, *Die Hussitische Revolution*, 1032–157. On Chelčický: Murray Wagner, *Petr Chelčický: A Radical Separatist in Hussite Bohemia* (Scottsdale, PA, 1983).

6 These developments are analysed in: Jarold Zeman, 'The Rise of Religious Liberty in the Czech Reformation', *Central European History* 6, no. 2 (1973), 128–47; Winfried Eberhard, 'Der Weg zur Koexistenz: Kaiser Sigmund und das Ende der Hussitischen Revolution', *Bohemia* 33 (1992), 1–43; and František Šmahel, 'Pax Externa et Interna: Vom Heiligen Krieg zur Erzwungenen Toleranz im Hussitischen Böhmen', in *Toleranz im Mittelalter*, ed. Alexander Patschovsky and Harald Zimmerman (Sigmaringen, 1998), 211–73.

7 On the Unity's founding, see Otakar Odložilík, 'A Church in a Hostile State: The Unity of Czech Brethren', *Central European History* 6, no. 2 (1973), 111–27; and David Holeton, 'Church or Sect? The Jednota Brtarská and the Growth of Dissent from Mainline Utraquism', *Communio Viatorum* 38 (1996), 5–35.

8 For a thorough analysis of the Unity's development in the late fifteenth century, see Craig Atwood, *The Theology of the Czech Brethren from Hus to Comenius* (University Park, PA, 2009).

9 On the importance of historical memory and historiography among Protestant communities, see Bruce Gordon, ed., *Protestant History and Identity in Sixteenth-Century Europe* (Brookfield, VT, 1996); Irena Backus, *Historical Method and Confessional Identity in the Era of the Reformation (1378–1615)* (Boston, 2003); Matthias Pohlig, *Zwischen Gelehrsamkeit und Konfessioneller Identitätsstiftung: Lutherische Kirchen- und Universalgeschichtsschreibung, 1546–1617* (Tübingen, 2007); and the essays collected in the 2010 *ARG* 'Themenschwerpunkt: The Protestant Reformation and the Middle Ages'.

10 This language is taken from Eric Hobsbawm's classic introductory essay in: Eric Hobsbawm and Terence Ranger, eds., *The Invention of Tradition* (New York, 1983), 1–14.

11 On the problematics of this terminology and its ubiquity in scholarship on the Protestant Reformations, see Heiko Oberman, *Forerunners of the Reformation: The Shape of Late Medieval Thought* (New York, 1966), esp. 1–50; and Theodor Mahlmann, '"Vorreformatoren", "vorreformatorisch", "Vorreformation": Beobachtungen zur Geschichte eines Sprauchgebrauchs', in *Reformer als Ketzer: Heterodoxe Bewegungen von Vorreformatoren*, ed. Günter Frank and Friedrich Niewöhner (Stuttgart-Bad Cannstatt, 2004), 13–55.

12 The fundamental work in this body of scholarship is: Jan Assmann, *Das Kulturelle Gedächtnis: Schrift, Erinnerung und Politische Identität in Frühen Hochkulturen* (Munich, 1992). See also the essays in Jan Assmann and Tonio Hölscher, eds., *Kultur und Gedächtnis* (Frankfurt am Main, 1988); and the work of Aleida Assmann, especially *Erinnerungsräume: Formen und Wandlungen des Kulturellen Gedächtnisses* (Munich, 1999); and *Der lange Schatten der Vergangenheit: Erinnerungskultur und Geschichtspolitik* (Munich, 2006).

13 Writing is the main, but not exclusive, vehicle for the preservation of such archives. See Aleida Assmann, 'Re-framing Memory: Between Individual and Collective Forms of Constructing the Past', in *Performing the Past: Memory, History, and Identity in Modern Europe*, ed. Karin Tilmans et al. (Amsterdam, 2010), 35–50 (43). Cf. Jan. Assmann, *Das Kulturelle Gedächtnis*, 48–56.

14 Aleida Assmann, *Cultural Memory and Western Civilization: Functions, Media, Archives* (New York, 2011), esp. 127–30.

15 For an analysis of the Lutheran construction of a 'counter-history' of the church, see the work of Thomas Fuchs, particularly: 'Protestantische Heiligen-Memoria im 16. Jahrhundert', *Historische Zeitschrift* 267, no. 1 (1998), 587–614; and 'Reformation, Tradition, und Geschichte', in *Protestantische Identität und Erinnerung*, ed. Joachim Eibach and Marcus Sandl (Göttingen, 2003), 71–89. See also: Euan Cameron, 'Medieval Heretics as Protestant Martyrs', in *Martyrs and Martyrologies*, ed. Diana Wood, *StCH* 30 (Cambridge, MA, 1993), 185–207.

16 The notion of a more fluid religious outlook in the sixteenth century as 'pre-confessional' is adapted from Natalia Nowakowska, *King Sigismund of Poland and Martin Luther: The Reformation before Confessionalization* (Oxford, 2018), esp. 13–21.

17 On the Habsburg's use of religion to further their dynastic power, see Karin MacHardy, 'The Rise of Absolutism and Noble Rebellion in Early Modern Habsburg Austria,

1570–1620', *Comparative Studies in Society and History*, 34:3 (1992), 407–38; and James Palmintessa, 'The Prague Uprising of 1611: Property, Politics, and Catholic Renewal in the Early Years of Habsburg Rule', *Central European History* 31, no. 4 (1998), 299–328.

18 The scholarly literature on Martin Luther's evolving appreciation for Jan Hus is substantial. For an overview of earlier scholarship and insightful analysis of the role played by Hus in Luther's developing self-conception as a reformer, see the recent work of Thomas Kaufmann: 'Jan Hus und die Frühe Reformation', in *Biblische Theologie und Historisches Denken*, ed. Martin Kessler and Martin Wallraff (Basel, 2008), 62–109; and *Der Anfang der Reformation: Studien zur Kontextualität der Theologie, Publizistik, und Inszenierung Luthers und der Reformatischen Bewegung* (Tübingen, 2012), 30–67.

19 Martin Luther, *An den christlichen Adel deutscher Nation von des Christlichen Standes Besserung*, in *D. Martin Luthers Werke, Kritische Gesamtausgabe: Schriften*, ed. J. K. F. Knaake et al., 66 vols. (Weimar, 1883–) 6: 381–469 (454). (Abv. *WA*).

20 This explicit formulation occurred in a letter from Luther to Georg Spalatin (February 1520) in which Luther commented on his response to reading Hus's *De Ecclesia*. The letter has been published in: *D. Martin Luthers Werke, Kritische Gesamtausgabe: Briefwechsel*, ed. J. K. F. Knaake et al., 18 vols. (Weimar, 1930–1985) 2: 40–2.

21 A critical analysis of Luther's claim to be a Hussite can be found in Scott Hendrix, '"We Are All Hussites"? Hus and Luther Revisited', *Archiv für Reformationsgeschichte* 65 (1974), 134–61; cf. the more positive conclusions about their substantive similarities in Heiko Oberman, 'Hus and Luther: Prophets of a Radical Reformation', in *The Contentious Triangle: Church, State, and University*, ed. Rodney Petersen and Calvin Pater (Kirksville, MO, 1999), 135–66.

22 Jan Hus, *De Causa Bohemica* (Hagenau, 1520) appeared in the spring of 1520, with references made to it by Zwingli in May; the second edition, entitled *Liber Egregius de unitate Ecclesiae, Cuius autor periit in concilio Constantiensi* (Basel: Adam Petri, 1520), was published in the summer. Luther's appeal for the sacrament of communion to be received in both kinds by the laity was published in: Martin Luther, *Eyn Sermon von dem Hochwirdigen Sacrament des Heyligen Waren Leychnams Christi Und von den Bruderschaften*, in *WA* 2: 738–58.

23 On these pamphlets, see Siegfried Hoyer, 'Jan Hus und der Hussitismus in den Flugschriften des Ersten Jahrzehnts der Reformation', in *Flugschriften als Massenmedium der Reformationszeit*, ed. Hans-Joachim Köhler (Stuttgart, 1981), 291–307.

24 Wolfgang Capito, *Antwurt B. Wolffgang Fab. Capitons auff Brüder Conradts Augustiner ordens Provincials vermanung* (Strasbourg, 1524). On this text's place within the corpus of polemics that politicised Hussite history on behalf of German evangelicals, see Phillip Haberkern, *Patron Saint and Prophet: Jan Hus in the Bohemian and German Reformations* (New York, 2016), 170–4.

25 On the translation of Luther's writings in the Czech lands, see Rudolf Říčan, 'Tschechische Übersetzungen von Luthers Schriften bis zum Schmalkaldischen Krieg', in *Vierhundertfünfzig Jahre lutherische Reformation 1517–1967*, ed. Franz Lau (Göttingen: 1967), 282–301; and the more expansive, recent work of Petr Voit, 'Česká a Německá Reformace v Ilustraci České Knihy První Poloviny 16. Století', in *In Puncto Religionis: Konfesní Dimenze Předbělohorské Kultury Čech a Moravy*, ed. Kateřina Horníčková and Michal Šroněk (Prague, 2013), 137–62.

26 On the impact of these contacts on Czech religious developments, see Winfried Eberhard, *Konfessionsbildung und Stände in Böhmen, 1478–1530* (Munich, 1981), 139–81; and Amedeo Molnár, 'Luthers Beziehungen zu den Böhmischen Brüdern', in *Leben und Werk Martin Luthers von 1526 bis 1546*, ed. Helmar Junghans, 2 vols. (Göttingen: 1983) I: 627–39.

27 For a summary of the development of these positions, see Zdeněk V. David, *Finding the Middle Way: The Utraquists' Liberal Challenge to Rome and Luther* (Baltimore, 2003), 106–7 and 143–5; and Atwood, *The Theology of the Czech Brethren*, 167–72.

28 The *Apology* was written by the Unity's senior bishop, Lukáš of Prague and published as *Apologia Sacre Scripturae* (Nuremberg, 1511). Regarding the Unity's catechism,

commonly known as the *Kinderfragen*, the Czech original went through twelve editions by 1515, and the German translation went through a dozen editions by 1525. For an overview of the book's publication history, see the modern edition printed as Alexander Kästner, ed., *Die Kinderfragen: Der erste Deutsche Katechismus* (Leipzig: 1902), 1–14. The best overview of the Unity's publishing efforts with an international Protestant audience in mind remains: Joseph Theodore Müller, *Die Geschischte der Böhmischen Brüder*, vol. 1 (Herrnhut, 1922), 389–417.

29 Elsie Ann McKee, *Reforming Popular Piety in Sixteenth-Century Strasbourg: Katharina Schütz Zell and her Hymnbook* (Princeton, 1994), 13. The original text was published as: Michael Weisse, *Ein new Geseng Buchlen* (Mladá Boleslav, 1531). On this text, see Ute Evers, 'Deutsch-Tsechischer Melodienaustausch in Gesangbüchern des 16. Jahrhünderts', *Lied und Populäre Kultur* 55 (2010), 169–82.

30 By the end of the sixteenth century, the Unity published samples from this correspondence in their confessional and historical texts as a sign that they had been accepted as legitimate by other Protestants. See, e.g.: *Confessio Fidei et Religionis Christianae* (Wittenberg, 1573), 216–21; and the more substantial collection included in a 1599 history later published as: Jan Łasicki, *Historiae de Origine et Rebus Gestis Fratrum Bohemicorum Liber Octavus*, ed. J. A. Comenius (1649), 213–59.

31 This letter was printed in Łasicki, *Historiae de Origine*, 236–7 (237).

32 These articles are included in the contemporary chronicle of Bartoš Písař, a Utraquist artisan from Prague. His narrative has been printed as: Bartoš Písař, *Kronika*, in *Fontes rerum Bohemicarum: Prameny Dějin Českých*, ed. Josef V. Šimák, vol. 6 (Prague: 1907), 1–296. The articles are printed on pp. 21–5. On the 1524 synod, see David, *Finding the Middle Way*, 64–9; and Eberhard, *Konfessionsbildung*, 150ff.

33 The 1421 synod remained a touchstone for sixteenth-century Utraquists. For an overview of the discussions at the original synod, see Kaminsky, *A History of the Hussite Revolution*, 451–5.

34 For a detailed bibliography of these Utraquist texts, see David, *Finding the Middle Way*, 115–27; and Voit, 'Ceská a Německá Reformace', 137–62, esp. 148–50.

35 Zdeněk David has analysed Utraquist confessions in his 'Utraquists, Lutherans, and the Bohemian Confession of 1575', *Church History* 68 (1999), 294–336. For a detailed analysis of the Brethren's confessions, see Milos Strupl, 'Confessional Theology of the Unitas Fratrum', *Church History* 33, no. 3 (1964), 279–93. On the broader drift in the Unity's theology towards sixteenth-century Protestant norms, see Atwood, *Theology of the Czech Brethren*, 273–94.

36 The classical expression of this critique came in the work of Ferdinand Hrejsa. See, e.g., his 'Luterství, Kalvinismus a Podobojí na Moravě před Bílou Horou', *Český Časopis Historický* 44 (1938), 296–326 and 474–85. For a more recent iteration of this argument, see Jaroslav Pánek, 'The Question of Tolerance in Bohemia and Moravia in the Age of the Reformation', in *Tolerance and Intolerance in the European Reformation*, ed. Ole Peter Grell and Bob Scribner (New York, 1996), 231–48.

37 *Confessio Fidei ac Religionis Baronum ac Nobilium Regni Bohoemiae, Serenissimo ac Invictissimo Romanorum, Bohoemiae etc. Regi, Viennae Austriae, sub anno Domini 1535 oblata* (Wittenberg, 1538). This text was written in 1535 and published in Czech in 1536; the Latin edition was published only after two priests from the Unity consulted with Luther on the text's discussion of deathbed absolution and clerical celibacy.

38 This text was published with a preface by Luther as: *Rechenschafft des glaubens, der dienst und Ceremonien, der Bruder in Behemen und Mehrern, welch von etlichen Pickarten, und von etlichen Waldenser genant warden* (Wittenberg, 1533).

39 Luther's preface is included in the *Confessio Fidei ac Religionis* on pp. A2r.-A3v (A3r).

40 The latter two figures were leaders of the Utraquist church from the time of Hus's death until the 1470s. On them, see Paul de Vooght, *Jacobellus de Stříbro, 1429: Premier Théologien du Hussitisme* (Louvain, 1972); and Frederick Heymann, 'John Rokycana: Church Reformer between Hus and Luther', *Church History* 28, no. 3 (1959), 240–80.

41 The ministers' text is included in the *Confessio Fidei ac Religionis* on pp. B1r-D3v (B3r).

42 *Confessio Fidei ac Religionis*, B4v.
43 *Confessio Fidei ac Religionis*, B3r.
44 On the origins of the Unity's clergy, see *Confessio Fidei ac Religionis*, C1r–C1v. On the accusations of Anabaptism against the Brethren, see *Confessio Fidei ac Religionis*, C4v–D1v.
45 This closing statement is taken from a brief preface written by the noble patrons of the Unity and included in the confession after the ministers' preface. See *Confessio Fidei ac Religionis*, D3v–D4v (D4v).
46 This text has been published in a modern edition as Bohuslav Bílejovský, *Kronyka Cýrkewni*, ed. J. Skalický (Prague, 1816). On the *Chronicle's* overall composition and contents, see David, *Finding the Middle Way*, 83–106.
47 Bílejovský appended second and third sections to his main narrative of Utraquist history that tracked the origins of the 'Pikarts' from French refugees in the late 1410s. He thus linked the contemporary Unity to a foreign party characterised by moral depravity and sacramental error. Cf. Bílejovský, *Kronyka Cýrkewni*, 50–60.
48 The middle portion of the Chronicle tracked the history of the vernacular liturgy and the administration of the chalice to the laity in the Czech lands. See Bílejovský, *Kronyka Cýrkewni*, 14–26.
49 Bílejovský, *Kronyka Cýrkewni*, 40.
50 Cochlaeus published these texts in his *Historiae Hussitarum Libri Duodecim* (Mainz, 1549). Although published at this late date, the work was largely completed by 1534. On the publication history of this work, see Ralph Keen, 'Johannes Cochlaeus: An Introduction to his Life and Work', in *Luther's Lives: Two Contemporary Accounts of Martin Luther*, ed. and tr. Elizabeth Vandiver, Ralph Keen, and Thomas D. Frazel (New York: 2002), 40–52. Fabri published his Utraquist sources in, *Confutatio Gravissimi Erroris Asserentis in Sacramento Altaris* (Leipzig, 1537). In this text, he referred explicitly to the works of Hus, Příbram, and Rokycana, while also citing the *Compactata* and decrees from multiple Hussite synods. On this work, see Leo Helbling, *Dr. Johann Fabri, Generalvikar von Konstanz und Bischof von View (1478–1541)* (Münster: 1941), 112–26. Regarding Fabri's collaboration with the Utraquists, see David, *Finding the Middle Way*, 139.
51 Jan Assmann, 'Der Zweidimensionale Mensch: Das Fest als Medium des Kollektiven Gedächtnisses', in *Das Fest und das Heilige: Religiöse Kontrapunkte zur Alltagswelt*, ed. Jan Assmann (Gütersloh, 1991), 13–30, esp. 18–25. Cf. Assman, *Das Kulturelle Gedächtnis*, 143.
52 This language is taken from Paul Post, 'Introduction and Application: Feast as a Key Concept in a Liturgical Studies Research Design', in *Christian Feast and Festival: The Dynamics of Western Liturgy and Culture*, ed. Paulus Post et al. (Leuven, 2001), 47–77 (61).

9

REMEMBERING AND FORGETTING THE DEAD IN THE CHURCHES OF REFORMATION GERMANY

Róisín Watson

In 1535 a doctor in the free imperial city of Ulm, Wolfgang Reichart, wrote to the confessor at the convent of the Poor Clares in Söflingen to complain that the Lutherans in the city had forbidden him from erecting an epitaph to his son in the city's church. He wrote that they had 'destroyed almost every memory of the dead by removing sarcophaguses, tombs, and gravestones along with their epitaphs'. Hitherto Reichart had followed Martin Luther's progress enthusiastically, at one stage labelling him the 'new Apollo', but this encounter with iconoclasm, and what he perceived as a Lutheran disrespect for the dead, saw the doctor distance himself from the evangelical movement. In his letter, Reichart praised 'the sculpting of coats of arms, insignia, and epitaphs' as a means of 'reviving the memory' of the dead.[1] Although the act of iconoclasm was most likely not the work of Lutherans but of evangelicals influenced by Zwinglian theology, it is clear from Reichart's comments that, during this early period of religious upheaval, contemporaries made a connection between Lutheranism, iconoclasm, and the erasure of the memory of the dead. These associations make clear the importance that sixteenth-century communities placed upon physical memorials to their dead. The doctor equated the removal of monuments with the removal of memory. As a substitute for a stone monument for his son, Reichart sent an image of his family coat of arms to his colleagues, instructing them to deposit the image among their papers, so that when they filed through them they might see it and remember his family. His desire to visualise memory was typical of the time, and was one that did not abate among Lutheran converts.[2] Lutherans continued to use the church as a site to enact and preserve the memory of the dead, but who was remembered and how had to be reconfigured to reflect the memorial priorities of a confession that placed Christ's sacrifice at its centre and that no longer saw a link between remembering the dead and salvation.

Epitaphs and other funerary monuments returned to the Ulm Minster in the 1550s. It was often in the second half of the sixteenth century that Lutherans across the Holy Roman Empire, noble families in particular, sought to establish their dynastic and confessional legacies through the foundation of burial grounds within churches. Families erected epitaphs and monuments to display their dynastic lineage and to weave their narratives of ancestral homogeneity into the history of the Reformation and into Christian salvation itself.[3] But as well as being sites of remembering, burial grounds were also sites of forgetting. The distillation of a family history into one monument, or the crystallisation of this history around an individual, required a prioritisation of memory. These sites have frequently been presented as monolithic, but the memories housed within them were not impervious to new meanings. The initial memorial impulses behind a monument could be superseded as further monuments were added to the church space or as burial grounds receded from use. This esssay considers the long-term dynamics of material commemoration beyond the initial founding of Lutheran burial grounds within churches. First, it explores the ways in which the commemoration of the dead reflected the broader role that memory played in the new confession. Secondly, it considers how Lutherans might balance memories of dynastic longevity and homogeneity that bridged religious rupture with memories of the Reformation and the maintenance of Lutheranism within the same space. Finally, the essay considers how the church as a site of commemoration changed as the memory of confessional struggle receded and burial sites transitioned from being a component in the active construction of dynastic memory to an emblem of a territory's heritage.

The plethora of Lutheran funerary monuments demonstrates the importance of place in the construction of confessional memory. Early modern memory is often characterised by its mediality, fragmented into a broad range of objects and texts and communicated to a broad range of people.[4] The Lutheran funeral monument does not deny this trend. Its meanings were communicated in funeral sermons, chronicles, and antiquarian collections of inscriptions. But in all their iterations, the monument's effectiveness as a vehicle for memory was its association with a physical space and its continued visual presence for those that used the space. These objects, and those that commissioned them, had to contend with the preexisting layers of memories within these churches, as well as the ways in which changes to ecclesiastical space could bring new meanings to old monuments. While burial grounds might be seen as repositories of official memory, these memories might shift over time.

The burial grounds in the Duchy of Württemberg in south-west Germany are the primary focus here, especially those of the Dukes of Württemberg. Duke Ulrich von Württemberg implemented evangelical reform in the duchy when he returned from exile in 1534. The early Reformation adopted elements from both Lutheran and Zwinglian strands of reform, but by the second half of the sixteenth century the territory was among the leading Lutheran forces of the Holy Roman Empire.[5] The collegiate church in Stuttgart had been the burial ground of the Counts of Württemberg since the fourteenth century, but from 1537 the choir of St George's church in Tübingen became the dynasty's burial ground.[6] While the focus here often falls upon noble memorialisation, it is clear that the commemorative impulses and concerns that drove dynastic memory were shared by non-noble groups.

The German Reformation and material memory

The place of memory and commemorative practice within Lutheranism was central to the dynamics of reform.[7] Alongside the question of the best pathway to attain salvation, a fundamental concern of Protestant movements was how Christians should best commemorate Christ's sacrifice on the cross. This produced a new schema of remembrance that determined who was remembered and how that memory might be expressed. Participation in these new memorial practices became an important tool for the creation of confessional bonds that nurtured nascent confessional cultures. Lutheran ceremony and ritual were to prompt remembrance of the holy story rather than be an enactment of it, as Catholic practice had done. Saints were to be commemorated for their Christian virtue, rather than worshipped in their own right. Here, the act of commemoration created distance between Lutheran congregations and their saints, placing the latter firmly in the past and removing from them the role of intercession. The Reformation necessitated a reconsideration of how the church defined the relationship between its past and its present, since it was both an institution with a history and one that existed outside of chronological time.[8] Legitimacy for the new faith came from the expansion of its history to give the church a sense of permanence. Remembrance of the early Christian church bound the new confession to a form of Christianity uncorrupted by the Catholic Church, and shielded Lutherans from the accusation of innovation. While this required an expansion of historical memory, spiritual remembering often required the collapsing of multiple temporal and spiritual memoryscapes into one. Conflating memories of the past church with those of the holy story and the events of the Reformation gave legitimacy to the new confession that could present their battle as concurrent with spiritual events.[9] In creating a Lutheran past, the topography of remembrance also transformed. Confessional histories were reimagined and maps redrawn so that the commemorative geography of Lutheran Germany turned away from the centres of Catholic power and myth, and converged upon those places associated with the lives of Martin Luther and his colleagues.[10]

The question of how to remember in the new confession became entangled in debates on the role of the ecclesiastical image within the Protestant Church. A common Lutheran defence of images was that they were kept more easily in the memory than the written or spoken word — visualisation was a key part of the process of remembering.[11] Early modern memory interacted with images and objects in numerous ways. First, the presence or absence of objects provoked remembrance. Secondly, objects themselves were records of memory.

Monuments made the deeds of past communities visible for successive generations, but this was not a simple transmission from one generation to the next. They reflected a retrospective recognition of historical change and a contemporary evaluation of what was worthy of remembrance. Finally, objects were themselves things that were remembered, forming 'mental debris' within individual memoryscapes.[12] The Reformation was remembered not only through its protagonists, but through the objects that had been lost as a consequence of religious upheaval or those that were generated through confessional change. As reformers sought to concentrate religious memory within institutions that they could control, the space of the church became a primary location for the construction of confessional memory. Susan Boettcher's characterisation of Lutheranism as a 'community of memory' saw this memory constituted within the space of the church through the Word of God, the performance of ritual, and through the material and visual fabric of the building.[13]

Above all, the church was a memorial space because it was here that a community's dead were commemorated and sometimes buried. It is well known that Lutheran theology had separated the dead from the living. The dead were no longer called upon to intercede on the behalves of the living and the prayers of the living had no effect on the fate of the dead.[14] The act of remembering was separated from the theology of salvation. But Lutherans encountered the dead on a regular basis through the memorials, whether epitaphs or monuments, that adorned local churches. Martin Luther only briefly considered physical memorials to the dead, arguing in 1542 that 'if we wanted to honour graves in some way, it would be more fitting to paint or write on walls good epitaphs or passages from the Bible, so that they should be seen by those going to tombs or to the cemetery'.[15] Early Lutheran church ordinances rarely regulated the material commemoration of the dead. They were more often concerned with the protection of the body from livestock once buried.[16] In fact, Luther had disapproved of burial within the church, but this was frequently overlooked by later Lutheran communities. Epitaphs, gravestones, and sculpted funerary monuments became the staple decoration for many parish churches. For those in Württemberg, these memorials were often the only form of ecclesiastical decoration.[17]

Burial grounds within Lutheran churches reshaped the spatial dynamics of confessional commemoration. Lutheran nobles were frequently buried in the choir of their local church, which had been the sacred heart of the pre-Reformation building. Here the high altar had sat, which had contained saintly relics and was where Christ's body had been made real in the ritual of the Mass. The space remained a focus for Lutherans as the site of communion. But as the number of memorials to individual Lutherans and their families within the space grew, the choir became one that memorialised the Lutheran community's participation in communion too. Luther had placed the congregation at the centre of the ritual. Its efficacy was dependent on their presence. The placement of memorials at the site of communion tied the memory of these Lutherans to the ritual act. It reminded the living of the successive generations who had perpetuated true faith through participating in the distribution of the Eucharist.[18] Their presence also replaced the secondary function of the choir as a place for the worship of the saints. Physical memorials presented the human models that were to guide the congregation, rather than the saintly figures that had led Catholic congregations to idolatry. This was most evident in epitaph-altars, where those objects dedicated to saints in the pre-Reformation church were now dedicated to the memory of those individuals who perpetuated Lutheranism through the protection of ritual.[19] Through memorials, congregants might replace saints as the commemorative focus of the space.

Explicit discussion of the iconography of the funerary monument or epitaph was often absent from discussion on the role of images in the Lutheran church. This contrasted with debates in England, where funeral monuments were connected to the origins of idolatry.[20] But certain iconoclastic strands of Protestantism sought to protect personal memorials from obliteration. In Zürich, the city council stipulated in June 1524 that memorial images could be returned to the families that had commissioned them.[21] Authorities in the free imperial cities of Reutlingen, Ulm, and Memmingen in south-west Germany also allowed families to collect their epitaphs before all images from the church were removed.[22] The portability of such memorials most likely determined whether they were collected or left to iconoclastic authorities. Targeted attacks on funerary monuments were not necessarily attacks on the act of remembering, but ensued when evangelical protest fused with a strong opposition to political power. In the French Wars of Religion, monuments to the dead transformed into symbols of political regimes and iconoclasts attacked not only idolatrous imagery, but the effigies of the dead.[23] Elsewhere, the desecration of the memory of the dead could become a powerful form of religious protest. In Augsburg in 1524 a cobbler smeared epitaphs in the cathedral in Augsburg with cow's blood to show his disapproval of traditional religion.[24]

But more often these objects were caught in the crossfire rather than being the focus of religious violence. In Esslingen in southwest Germany, Konrad von Schwabach complained to the city council that his wife's gravestone had been damaged during the removal of the Dionysius altar from the church.[25] We have little record of the monuments that were removed from Württemberg churches during the iconoclasm in the territory in the 1530s. But we might deduce from later complaints and pre-Reformation survivals that their removal was due to their iconography rather than because they were vehicles for the memory of Catholic individuals.[26] Post-Reformation monuments sometimes recognised the potential idolatry they might invoke. The monument for Magdalena zur Lippe (d.1587) and husband, the Landgrave Georg I. von Hessen-Darmstadt (d.1596), disassociated itself from any possible idolatry and defended itself against future iconoclasts in its inscription, which reminded the viewer that 'this crucifix does not imply idolatrous worship / verily otherwise he who breaks this [crucifix] does not profit'.[27]

The Lutheran funeral monument bound individuals to their localities, but it also bound them to a Lutheran community that extended beyond their immediate environment. Monuments acted as a prompt to the memory of the individual. Inscriptions detailed their achievements and exemplary Lutheran lives that were to be models for the living congregation. In painted epitaphs individuals would often appear alongside their families, cementing the dynastic networks in which they operated. The sculptures and paintings of the dead were to depict the dead faithfully so that they could be recognised by the living. Remembrance required visual verisimilitude to be most effective, stirring the appropriate degree of grief for a believer assured in Christ's sacrifice.[28] The memorial was also a prompt to the memory of a body of religious knowledge that bound Lutheran congregations to each other across space and time. These monuments developed standard iconographies that centred on the Crucifixion and its Old Testament foreshadowing to reinforce the theological message of the object — salvation by faith alone made possible by Christ's sacrifice.[29]

Remembering a Catholic past and remembering the Reformation

Wolfgang Reichart's disapproval of iconoclasm in Ulm stemmed from a perceived break with the past that the destruction of epitaphs symbolised. The physical manifestations of the memories of the dead anchored early modern societies in their past iterations and frequently became the basis for establishing the hierarchies of the living. The medieval practice of creating retrospective tombs to demonstrate ecclesiastical rights demonstrates the extent to which monuments might substantiate written legal documents.[30] Therefore the removal of funerary monuments reflected more than an aesthetic shift. It had the potential to change social hierarchies and reimagine the foundation of social and political authority. Unlike Reichart's experience, Lutherans sought not to challenge the position of memory in the creation of authority, but to integrate memories of a Catholic past into a Lutheran memoryscape. Within the physical church, this involved what, at first sight, might be seen as contradictory aims of remembering a Catholic past, while celebrating the advent of evangelical religion. This was particularly the case for the Lutheran nobility, whose authority would always be rooted in their ancestral origin.[31] Noble rulers had a responsibility to remember their forebearers. In 1537 Joachim Camerarius the Elder praised Duke Ulrich von Württemberg for his 'eagerness [...] in celebrating our ancestral custom'.[32] The Württemberg burial ground demonstrates how the impulse to remember Catholic ancestors and to celebrate a Lutheran dynasty could coexist within the same memorial space and how official memory over time might integrate Catholic memory into a Lutheran narrative.

Location was essential for sanitising the memories associated with pre-Reformation monuments. Catholic monuments might be integrated into a Lutheran history by being placed in spaces where their commemorative meanings could be controlled. Noble Lutheran families frequently translated the bodies of their Catholic ancestors to the new theological and political centres of the Reformation. In 1537 Duke Ulrich von Württemberg brought the body of Duke Eberhard im Bart from St Peter zu Einsiedel to the choir of St George's in Tübingen. His son, Christoph, followed his father's example in 1554, bringing the remains of Eberhard im Bart's parents, Count Ludwig von Württemberg-Urach (d.1450) and Mechthild von der Pfalz (d.1482), and his sister, Anna (d.1530), to Tübingen. Elsewhere in the Holy Roman Empire, the Counts of Mansfeld moved the gravestones of their pre-Reformation ancestors from the Cistercian convent in Helfta to the church in Eisleben, the site where Luther delivered his final sermons.[33] Moving bodies and monuments from monastic foundations realigned the memories of the deceased. It placed them within a dynastic network that focused on evangelical centres of power rather than crystallising their posthumous memory around acts of monastic patronage. The choice of Tübingen for the burial of Eberhart im Bart had multiple motivations. The selection reflected a wish to emphasise the family's ducal title, separating the Dukes of Württemberg from the counts who were buried in Stuttgart. It also reflected Eberhart im Bart's own legacy, since he had founded the university in Tübingen in 1477. But the burial site was also connected to the duchy's Reformation. The church's choir had been the site of the university's theology faculty since 1534. The connection between the church and the Reformation only grew over the century as it furnished the Württemberg church, and churches elsewhere, with Lutheran pastors, and as the painted epitaphs to the leading Lutherans of the duchy were increasingly displayed in the church.[34]

The meaning of the monument stemmed not only from location, but from use. The translation of Catholic ancestors severed their memory from the theologically-tainted associations of their original resting places, but also saved them from obsolescence as monastic sites were abandoned. Memory of the dead could not be effectively perpetuated by a physical monument if it remained in an unused space.[35] Duke Ulrich III von Mecklenburg became concerned about the monuments of his Catholic ancestors in the Cistercian chapel in Doberan since the space was no longer used following the monastery's dissolution in 1552. As well as instigating an extensive programme of renovation, the duke reinstituted a liturgical service at the church in 1553.[36] Implicit in this act was the belief that these vehicles of Catholic memory might be sanitised when viewed in the presence of the Lutheran faith, binding the memories of the deceased to the remembrance of Christ and his promise of salvation.

But integration of Catholic ancestors into Lutheran burial grounds also required material adaptation. When Duke Christoph von Württemberg brought Mechthild von der Pfalz to Tübingen he remade her stone monument, depicting the noblewoman in repose, so that it no longer contained references to the old faith. The new monument had removed the saints that had adorned the base of the original sculpted by Hans Multscher. The first monument of Christoph's sister had depicted her clutching rosary beads, but these were removed by Jakob Woller when he was commissioned to remake it [Fig. 9.1].[37]

This iconographical adaptation was not only undertaken by nobles, but Lutheran congregations, too, wishing to maintain the memories of their Catholic ancestors and circumvent Lutheran authorities prefering to remove the memory of those associated with idolatry. Tübingen Professor Martin Crusius noted in 1596 a

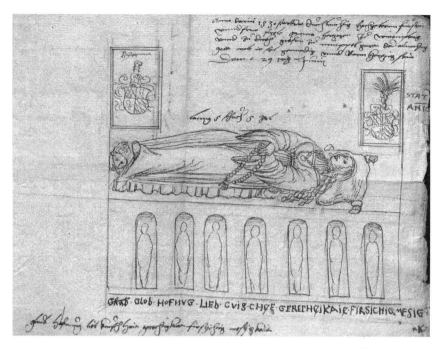

FIGURE 9.1 Sketch of Anna von Württemberg's original funeral monument in Guterstein (c.1554).
© Hauptstaatsarchiv Stuttgart (G47 Bü 24).

Catholic epitaph in the Württemberg town of Brackenheim that had evangelical sayings perhaps added to assure its survival after the Reformation.[38] In Marbach the church choir contained a painting of two knights who had died in 1460 during the Palatinate War, Caspar Speth and Conrad von Heinrieth; they knelt in front of the Virgin Mary. In 1565, as Duke Christoph sought to root out idolatrous images, a crucifix was painted over the Virgin, while the knights remained untouched. Accompanying texts were painted that drew parallels between the sacrifice the knights had made for their homeland and the sacrifice Christ had made for humankind [Fig. 9.2].[39]

This moment of re-framing the memorial with Lutheran text spoke to a means of redirecting a Catholic memory of past heroism, but also to historicising the image's iconography. The newly painted text would have stood out in contrast to the fifteenth century image. Drawing a historical distance between viewer and image had the potential to place the practice of idolatry in the past. The distance could also create a sense of permanence and durability of memory. This was the case in Tübingen. When Duke Christoph commissioned the figural monument for Count Ludwig von Württemberg-Urach in the 1550s the sculptor retained the fifteenth century armour of the count's original tomb. Ludwig's wife's fifteenth-century monument was reused and also depicted her in contemporary dress. As

FIGURE 9.2 Wall painting of Caspar Speth and Conrad von Heinrieth kneeling before the Virgin Mary/Crucifix, Marbach *Stadtkirche* (c. 1460/1565).
Photograph: Author.

monuments to the Württemberg family were added in the sixteenth century, the passage of time was increasingly visualised through the changing style of dress. This imparted a sense of durability to a dynasty that had ruled only intermittently in the first half of the sixteenth century.

The extent to which the events of the Reformation became a focal point for the memorialisation of the dead varied according to local circumstance. The establishment of noble burial grounds in the second half of the sixteenth century certainly coincided with a growing recognition of the Reformation as a moment of historical change. Although the Reformation may have elicited this flurry of memorial activity, it did not follow that the events of the Reformation were central to commemoration itself. In Saxony altarpieces depicting rulers alongside Martin Luther and Philipp Melanchthon crystallised posthumous memory around their proximity to evangelical reformers. These depictions also acted as polemical tools as the struggles between Lutheran factions after Luther's death sought dominance. But depictions of Martin Luther in the ecclesiastical art of Württemberg were limited.[40]

In Württemberg, non-noble epitaphs might seek to align themselves with the Reformation in order to establish their Lutheran credentials. In the Herrenberg collegiate church the Neuffer family placed their painted epitaph in the church c.

1610, most likely on the occasion of jurist Christoph Besold's funeral oration for legal scholar Johannes Valentin Neuffer.[41] However the epitaph did not depict the subject of the oration, but his uncle Johannes Neuffer (d.1581). The decision to crystallise the Neuffer family memory around Johannes was certainly based on his status as one of the earliest converts to Lutheranism and his position as the first Protestant steward of the Herrenberg church. Although among the first evangelicals, his epitaph was a late addition to a church interior that contained a number of painted epitaphs. The family utilised his proximity to the Reformation to establish themselves at the apex of a Lutheran hierarchy in Herrenberg. They were among the last to place an epitaph commemorating a sixteenth-century burgher in the church, but used the image of Paul's conversion on the road to Damascus to emphasise Neuffer's own monument of conversion and the legacy he established for his family.

The Württemberg dukes had difficulties aligning themselves with the Lutheran Reformation. Its early reform had vacillated between evangelical centres in Zürich, Strasbourg, and Wittenberg. Luther had never visited the duchy and had opposed Duke Ulrich's restitution in 1534, afraid of the connections contemporaries might make between Ulrich's violent toppling of Habsburg power and the implementation of evangelical reform. As Ulrich and Christoph developed the burial ground in Tübingen, their mind was on remembering their ducal status and forgetting the intermittent periods of powerlessness experienced by the noble house, first Ulrich's exile from 1519 until 1534 and then the direct imposition of Habsburg rule during the Augsburg Interim from 1548 until 1550. Centring dynastic memory on Eberhard im Bart the first Württemberg duke, was a key part of this emphasis on the ducal title. Only as Eberhard im Bart's own memory shifted, did the Württemberg alignment with their first duke come to be about the beginnings of Protestantism.[42]

Monuments to Eberhard im Bart and Ulrich von Württemberg were commissioned by Duke Christoph in 1550. The two graves were to mirror each other. A sketch of the choir in Tübingen by Jacob Woller in 1556 depicts the two figures lying side by side, both monuments the same size, supported by eight deer, and both men dressed in armour [Fig. 9.3]. A textual epitaph hung behind the two monuments. Its Latin text made clear the parallels between Dukes Eberhard and Ulrich:

'Reader, in this stone you can consider
   that for a human nothing is not perishable,
   since it covers the bones of two heroes,
   Dukes Eberhard and Ulrich.
   Out of these one was to be loved by the good,
   out of these the other was to be feared by the bad
   and each of the two was truly beloved to Christ.
   Here however each, with their corrupted flesh
   put down in death, rests at the same time.'[43]

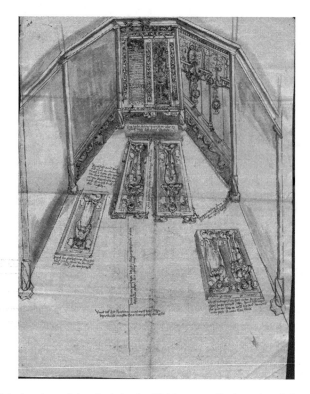

FIGURE 9.3 Ink drawing of the choir in the Tübingen collegiate church by Jacob Woller (1556).

© Hauptstaatsarchiv Stuttgart (G47 Bü 24).

The comparison was fitting in some respects — Eberhard had reunited the divide territory in 1492 and Ulrich had returned the territory to its ancestral rulers in 1534. But the epitaph erased the stark differences between Eberhard and Ulrich, reconfiguring popular memories of the two men. Johannes Agricola, in his 1529 volume of German proverbs, wrote of Eberhard that 'if God were not God then who else could be God other than our Lord from Württemberg?'[44] In contrast, Ulrich was remembered for his terrorising of the free imperial cities in southern Germany. One popular song used the structure of the Lord's Prayer to record Ulrich's misdemeanours.[45] The placing of the two men together was a political strategy that sought to rehabilitate Ulrich's memory by binding it to the princely ideal of his Catholic ancestor. It contradicted a living memory of the deceased perpetuated in contemporary popular culture.

The focus of this comparison of these two men focused on their rulership, rather than their religion. Eberhard im Bart's Catholicism was problematic, hence the monuments themselves made little reference to the confessional allegiances of both men. A separate inscription for Ulrich referred to his restoration of the gospel of Christ, but in the context of his restitution this could be read as a reference to the corruption of Habsburg rule. On the occasion of Eberhard's translation in 1537 Johann Camerarius presented Eberhard's faith as a product of his time, inherited from his ancestors.[46] But sixteenth-century understanding of the duke's piety began to change in the second half of the century. In 1552 Phillip Melanchthon told of Eberhard's trip to Rome in 1482 where the Württemberg duke witnessed the murder of a Cardinal in St Peters. The event, Melanchthon argued, highlighted to Eberhard the corruption of morals of the Catholic Church and acted as a catalyst for theological reform in the duchy.[47] Writing in 1593, Martin Crusius emphatically presented Eberhard as the beginning of the Württemberg Reformation. He excused the duke's pilgrimage to the Holy Land since it was focused on Christ rather than a saint, noted Eberhard's support of monastic reform and his opposition to the corruption of the Catholic Church, and praised Eberhard's founding of the Tübingen university as an institution destined to spread the true Lutheran faith.[48]

While in 1537 Eberhard's faith played an insignificant role in shaping the legacy of both himself and Ulrich, by the end of the century it had become a crucial element in reconciling the two. The extent to which religion had become a way for the Württemberg dukes to define their posthumous memory becomes clear when considering the monument of Duke Ludwig III (d.1593). Crusius' reconsideration of Eberhard appeared five months before Ludwig's death. The religious iconography of Ludwig's monument, produced by sculptor Christoph Jelin, distinguishes it from its counterparts. Below the horizontal sculpture of the duke were a series of reliefs that decorated the tomb's base depicting Old Testament heroes: Gideon and his army gathering to fight the Midianites, Samson slaying the Philistines, David and Goliath, the Israelites' conflict with the Amalekites, and Sennacherib's defeat. These images drew parallels between triumphant biblical figures fighting heresy and Ludwig's own battles against unorthodoxy in the name of Lutheranism.[49] The reliefs put the viewer in mind of Ludwig's own achievements. He had furthered Lutheranism not only in Württemberg, but further afield, sending his most eminent theologian, Jacob Andreae, to compose the Book of Concord, published in 1580, and to oversee the dispute with Calvinists at the Colloquy of Mömpelgard in 1586. The religious iconography of the monument allowed Ludwig to memorialise his individual achievements while also associating himself with the cornerstone of the dynasty's memorial programme — Eberhard im Bart, whose rule was now understood as the beginnings of the Württemberg Reformation. While the monument of Ludwig's ancestor had not physically changed, the memories it embodied had fundamentally altered by the end of the sixteenth century. A static monument did not result in static meaning.

Monuments to the dead beyond the Reformation

Martin Crusius ended his chronicle of Swabian history in 1596 with a description of the Tübingen choir. Here, he relayed to his reader the inscriptions on the tombs and epitaphs of Württemberg's sixteenth-century dukes. His history had begun almost four thousand years before the birth of Christ and had seen Crusius travel, both literally and metaphorically, across Swabia, Europe, and beyond. But, in contrast, his monumental work concluded in a very specific time and place. Crusius compared himself to a ship that had travelled through Swabia's past and come to rest in a harbour of the present day, anchoring itself within the memorial space dedicated to the Dukes of Württemberg.[50] Concluding his work in this way reflected the importance that the Tübingen burial ground had for him as a site memorialising the duchy's history. The dukes embodied the territory's past. But Crusius wrote at a moment when the choir's own position was in flux. Duke Ludwig's monument was the last dedicated to a ruling duke. Ludwig's successor, Friedrich I, was buried in the crypt of the Stuttgart collegiate church in 1608, which was to become the resting place for Württemberg's dukes in the seventeenth century.

It was the fate of a burial ground to be superseded, as, in the words of Peter Sherlock, 'the triumph of one generation is materially exceeded by the next'.[51] In his publication, Crusius fixed for posterity the memorial texts that decorated the Tübingen choir at a moment when the space would transition from its role as an active component in the construction of memory to an emblem of the duchy's collective heritage. To what extent did this space continue to echo the meanings that the sixteenth-century Dukes of Württemberg had carefully constructed? How did successive generations read and use these monuments? Crusius hinted at the popularity of the Tübingen site for visitors in 1596.[52] Court archivist Andreas Rüttel had also recorded in 1573 damage to the monuments as a result of frequent viewings.[53] Guides to dynastic burial grounds appeared from the seventeenth century onwards as these sites became tourist destinations for the European traveller desirous of inhabiting those spaces where great men had once stood. English antiquarian John Weever wrote in 1631 that visits to those places 'wee [sic.] know to have been frequented or inhabited by men, whose memory is esteemed, or mentioned in stories, doth move and stirre us up as much, or more, than the hearing of their noble deeds, or reading of their compositions'.[54] Guides to burial grounds were popular. In Tübingen, Johann Baumhauer published a guide to the funeral inscriptions within the church in 1619, with further editions in 1624 and 1627.[55] Melchior Hoffman supported a third edition of Michael Hempel's guide to the burial chapel of the Saxon Dukes in Freiberg in 1619 since 'many important people, but especially foreigners, who had visited this delightful burial ground' had asked after it.[56] These texts demonstrate the allure of place when consuming memory. While curious travellers could read about the exploits of those buried in Tübingen and Freiberg, it was the site where their bodies lay that 'stirre[d] [them] up [...] more'.

These publications provide insight into the resonances that funeral monuments might have for those unconnected with their production. Many of these works were written by pastors, a position that held particular significance for the maintenance of confessional memory. Stefan Dornheim has labelled Lutheran pastors as 'specialists in remembrance', since they were charged with embodying and preserving parochial memory through the celebration of Lutheran anniversaries, the maintenance of church books, and the commemoration of the dead.[57] Their everyday interaction with the church space meant that they witnessed the deterioration of burial sites and the vulnerability of material memory, setting down in print the inscriptions of monuments they feared might be lost. This had been Johann Baumhauer's motivation and demonstrated the responsibility he felt for preserving the memory of past congregations.[58] Pastors also produced these guides as a response to the wishes of their congregation, who sought to entrench their status through the more portable printed record. Gottlieb Oettrich provided a catalogue of monuments in 1709 arranged chronologically for the noble families with ancestors buried in the church of St Sophie in Dresden.[59] It allowed relatives to trace their historical presence within the space, from which they could bolster their own social authority.

These instances of collecting inscriptions were not simply driven by an antiquarian desire. They were often inflected with confessional meaning. In 1640 the pastor of St Leonhard's in Stuttgart, Johann Schmid, produced a manuscript record of all monuments in his church and in the town's collegiate church.[60] Schmid drew up his collection during the Thirty Years' War, when the Jesuits had reintroduced Catholic services to the city's collegiate church and had removed from it the body of Johannes Brenz, an architect of the Württemberg Reformation.[61] While the Jesuits reclaimed a Lutheran space by removing human remains, Schmid embedded the Lutheran ownership of ecclesiastical space through cataloguing the community's monuments to the dead, giving a sense of stability to a community under threat.[62] Burial sites continued to act as confessional markers for pastors well into the seventeenth century. In Halle, Saxony in 1674, Pastor Johann Gottfried Olearius published a description of 'the most noble tombs and their most-notable inscriptions' that he introduced as a text that would teach the Lutherans that they '[were] only pilgrims and guests in this world' and the faith in Christ's sacrifice they required to die in the true faith, distinguishing Lutherans from their confessional opponents.[63] Although not explicitly stated, Olearius' guide, brimming with biblical quotations and maxims, could easily be read as a devotional manual, directing the reader (or visitor) in the best way to prepare for their own death.

Olearius recorded in his catalogue 'an ancient papist image of a Franciscan', which was the central image of a memorial to the Von Diskau family erected in the fifteenth century. In 1665 Lutherans added an inscription that highlighted to viewers how 'the merits of Christ were destroyed during the papacy'.[64] Unlike the examples of early Lutherans already encountered sanitising the memory of their Catholic ancestors in order to integrate them into a Lutheran schema of memory, the Lutherans of the seventeenth century here did not make the memory of their Catholic ancestors confessionally palatable. Instead, they highlighted the memory of heresy embedded in the painted epitaph. Retaining such an image had polemical value. Crusius noted that it was necessary to maintain memories of the heretical so that Lutherans remained grateful to God 'that he illuminated his church with the light of truth'.[65] Württemberg Pastor Johannes Schuler used the surviving Catholic images in his church during a series of sermons from 1608 as a tool to remind his congregation of the heretical practices of Catholicism and foster a sense of gratitude within them.[66] Similarly, Olearius recounted in his introduction the location of the burial chapel where Johannes Tetzel had infamously sold indulgences that excused the crime of raping the Virgin Mary.[67] Maintaining this memory reminded contemporary Lutherans in the late seventeenth century of the heretical history of their confessional opponent and the necessity to protect Lutheranism. Thus showing that memory of a Catholic past did not always have to be sanitised or reimagined as Duke Christoph had done for his ancestors in Tübingen.

Conclusion

Lutheran funeral monuments could contain multiple memories — the memory of individual achievement, the memory of the beginnings of evangelical religion, the memory of the successive congregations sustaining Lutheranism through the performance of ritual, even the memory of a heretical Catholic past. To what degree these memories were emphasised within the object was determined not only by those who designed and commissioned them, but by the spaces they inhabited and the activity that took place within them. The church interior's function as a site for commemorating the dead saw it become a space with the capacity to bridge past and present and to create a sense of community that traversed confessional change, but also a site in which confessional difference might be emphasised and reinvigorated. The maintenance of monuments or their removal required successive generations of Lutherans to interrogate actively the purpose of remembering the dead. This essay has outlined three aspects of this discussion — What should they do with pre-Reformation monuments? How might they best memorialise the Reformation? How should they interact with the monuments of past Lutheran generations and the elements of the Catholic past they had chosen to preserve? The space of the church captured these memorial tensions for future generations who in turn brought their own meanings to these commemorative spaces.

The material appearance of many of the funeral monuments discussed here, especially the large and imposing stone tombs of the Dukes of Württemberg, give the modern viewer the impression of their stability and permanence. But successive monuments, while appearing similar, were often designed with differing memorial intentions in mind, as successive generations were required to insert their memories into an already established commemorative framework. In the case of the Württemberg family, they turned from emphasising their noble title to memorialising their faith. The physically stationary monument did not equate to an immutable memory. Their material meanings were not isolated from other vehicles of memory, such as print, but interacted with these networks to create new memorial resonances.

Remembering the dead presents us with a mode of early modern memory that was fundamentally tied to a notion of place and space. Their presence within the space of the church emphasised a new topography of confessional memory where remembrance was concentrated and controlled in those ecclesiastical institutions answerable to Lutheran authorities and where the rituals of Lutheranism were enacted. Memories of the dead provided the living congregation with new models of piety that distanced them from the idolatrous worship of saints. Luther's theology saw the church as being made manifest through the participation of a congregation in ritual, and we might see the multiplication of portraits of the dead as a visualisation of this belief. Remembering the dead gave a sense of permanence to the church space that was not only important in the early years of reform, but also in moments of confessional tension, which saw pastors return to cataloguing the monuments of the dead as a means to emphasise ownership and control of the space. The right to remember reflected confessional authority. But the relationship between space and memory was not one way. Memories of the dead also gained meaning from the spaces they inhabited. As certain church spaces became more closely aligned with centres of Lutheran power, so too did those commemorated within them.

Wolfgang Reichart wrote in 1535 that his 'efforts to forget, in fact, brought about a revival of the memory'. The more he tried to forget his son the greater his memory of him became.[68] Here he highlights that the act of forgetting was never completely possible. Forcing communities to ignore elements of their past could lead to the strengthening of that which authorities wished them to forget. But within the space of the church, memories of the dead could be adapted to fit the commemorative aims of the present. These, in turn, would be modified too. It was the fate of such sites to be continually reconfigured so that over time a form of forgetting might take place.

Notes

* My thanks to the editors and reviewers, as well as Bridget Heal, for their helpful comments on this essay.
1 Walther Ludwig, 'Der Ulmer Humanist Rychardus und sein Totes Kind: Humanismus und Luthertum im Konflikt', *Daphnis* 24 (1995), 263–99 (273–4, 284).
2 Ludwig, 'Der Ulmer Humanist Rychardus und sein Totes Kind', 289; Philip Hahn, 'Sinnespraktiken: Ein neues Werkzeug für die Sinnesgeschichte? Wahrnehmungen eines Arztes, eines Schuhmachers, eines Geistlichen und eines Architekten aus Ulm', in *Praktiken der Frühen Neuzeit: Akteure – Handlungen – Artefakte*, ed. Arndt Brendecke (Cologne, 2015), 462.
3 For studies of noble Lutheran burial see Oliver Meys, *Memoria und Bekenntnis: Die Grabdenkmäler evangelischer Landesherren im Heiligen Römischen Reich Deutscher Nation im Zeitalter der Konfessionalisierung* (Regensburg, 2009); Inga Brinkmann, *Grabdenkmäler, Grablegen und Begräbniswesen des lutherischen Adels: Adelige Funeralrepräsentation im Spannungsfeld von Kontinuität und Wandel im 16. und beginnenden 17. Jahrhundert* (Berlin, 2010). On non-noble monuments see Doreen Zerbe, *Reformation der Memoria: Denkmale in der Stadtkirche Wittenberg als Zeugnisse lutherischer Memorialkultur im 16. Jahrhundert* (Leipzig, 2013); Jan Harasimowicz, *Kunst als Glaubensbekenntnis: Beiträge zur Kunst- und Kulturgeschichte der Reformationszeit* (Baden-Baden, 1996), 97–143.
4 On the mediality of early modern memory see Judith Pollmann and Erika Kuipers, 'Introduction: On the Early Modernity of Modern Memory', in *Memory before Modernity: Practices of Memory in Early Modern Europe*, ed. Erika Kuijpers and Judith Pollmann (Leiden, 2013), 11–4.

5 On the Württemberg Reformation see Martin Brecht and Herman Ehmer, *Südwest-deutsche Reformationsgeschichte: Zur Einführung der Reformation im Herzogtum Württemberg 1534* (Stuttgart, 1984).

6 On the Württemberg burial grounds see Harald Schukraft, *Die Grablegen des Hauses Württemberg* (Stuttgart, 1989); Theodor Demmler, *Die Grabdenkmäler des Württembergischen Fürstenhauses und ihre Meister im 16. Jahrhundert* (Strasbourg, 1910).

7 Alexandra Walsham, 'History, Memory, and the English Reformation', *HistJ* 55, no. 4 (2012), 899–938.

8 Maurice Halbwachs, *On Collective Memory*, tr. Lewis A. Coser (Chicago, 1992), 88.

9 Susanne Wegmann, *Der Sichtbare Glaube: Das Bild in den lutherischen Kirchen des 16. Jahrhunderts* (Tübingen, 2016), 52–6.

10 Kat Hill, 'Mapping the Memory of Luther: Place and Confessional Identity in the Later Reformation', *German History*, available at: https://academic.oup.com/gh/advance-article-abstract/doi/10.1093/gerhis/ghz098/5722287.

11 Sergiusz Michalski, *The Reformation and the Visual Arts: The Protestant Image Question in Western and Eastern Europe* (London, 1993), 1–42.

12 See this division in Marius Kwint, 'Introduction: The Physical Past', in *Material Memories: Design and Evocation*, ed. Marius Kwint, Christopher Breward, and Jeremy Aynsley (Oxford and New York, 1999), 2.

13 Susan R. Boettcher, 'Late Sixteenth-Century Lutherans: A Community of Memory?', in *Defining Community in Early Modern Europe*, ed. Michael J. Halvorson and Karen E. Spierling (Aldershot, 2008), 121–41.

14 Craig Koslofsky, *The Reformation of the Dead: Death and Ritual in Early Modern Germany, 1450–1700* (London, 2000); Peter Marshall, 'After Purgatory: Death and Remembrance in the Reformation World', in *Preparing for Death, Remembering the Dead*, ed. Jon Ø. Flaeten and Tarald Rasmussen (Göttingen, 2015), 25–42.

15 Quoted in Michalski, *The Reformation and the Visual Arts*, 41.

16 *Die Evangelischen Kirchenordnungen des XVI. Jahrhunderts*, ed. Emil Sehling, vol. I (Leipzig, 1902), 317.

17 On the image question in the Duchy of Württemberg see Róisín Watson, 'Lutheran Piety and Visual Culture in the Duchy of Württemberg, 1534–c. 1700' (PhD thesis, University of St Andrews, 2015).

18 Maria Deiters, 'Epitaphs in Dialogue with Sacred Space: Post Reformation Furnishings in the Parish Churches of St. Nikolai and St. Marien in Berlin', in *Lutheran Churches in Early Modern Europe*, ed. Andrew Spicer (Farnham, 2012), 75–9.

19 Wegmann, *Der Sichtbare Glaube*, 134–50.

20 Margaret Aston, 'Art and Idolatry: Reformed Funeral Monuments', in *Art Re-formed: Re-Assessing the Impact of the Reformation on the Visual Arts*, ed. Tara Hamling and Richard L. Williams (Newcastle, 2007), 244.

21 Lee Palmer Wandel, *Voracious Idols and Violent Hands: Iconoclasm in Reformation Zurich, Strasbourg, and Basel* (Cambridge, 1995), 94–5.

22 Gudrun Litz, *Die reformatorische Bilderfrage in den schwäbischen Reichsstädten* (Tübingen, 2007), 82, 146.

23 Rebecca Constabel, 'Faith and Fury: Funerary Monuments in Reformation France', in *Dying, Death, Burial and Commemoration in Reformation Europe*, ed. Elizabeth Tingle and Jonathan Willis (Farnham, 2015), 142–5.

24 Pia F. Cuneo, *Art and Politics in Early Modern Germany: Jörg Breu the Elder and the Fashioning of Political Identity, ca. 1475–1536* (Leiden, 1998), 45–6.

25 Litz, *Die reformatorische Bilderfrage*, 194–5. For destruction of monuments elsewhere in Germany see Zerbe, *Reformation der Memoria*, 157–60.

26 Stuttgart, Landeskirchliches Archiv Stuttgart, A1 1588 II. 'Synodusprotokolle I (Visitationsberichte)' (1588), fol. 132r-v.

27 Brinkmann, *Grabdenkmäler, Grablegen und Begräbniswesen*, 327.

28 On funeral monuments and grief see Bridget Heal, *A Magnificent Faith: Art and Identity in Lutheran Germany* (Oxford, 2017), 163–88.

29 Harasimowicz, *Kunst als Glaubensbekenntnis*, 97–143.
30 Christopher S. Wood, *Forgery, Replica, Fiction: Temporalities of German Renaissance Art* (Chicago, 2008), 118–28.
31 Otto Gerhard Oexle, 'Soziale Gruppen in der Ständegesellschaft: Lebensformen des Mittelalters und ihre historischen Wirkungen', in *Die Repräsentation der Gruppen: Texte – Bilder – Objekte*, ed. Otto Gerhard Oexle and Andrea von Hülsen-Esch (Göttingen, 1998), 21.
32 Joachim Camerarius, *Oratio Funebris dicta a Ioachimo Camerario de illustrissimo Principe Eberhardo Duce Vuirtembergensi, &c.* (Tübingen, 1537), n.p.
33 Brinkmann, *Grabdenkmäler, Grabelegen und Begräbniswesen*, 359–62.
34 Stefanie Knöll, *Die Grabmonumente der Stiftskirche in Tübingen* (Stuttgart, 2007).
35 On the relationship between memory and activity/use see Alexandra Walsham, 'Domesticating the Reformation: Material Culture, Memory, and Confessional Identity in Early Modern England', *RenQ* 69, no. 2 (2016), 566–616; Sasha Handley, 'Objects, Emotions and an Early Modern Bed-Sheet', *History Workshop Journal* 85 (2018), 169–94.
36 Brinkmann, *Grabdenkmäler, Grabelegen und Begräbniswesen*, 118–9.
37 Schukraft, *Die Grablegen des Hauses Württemberg*, 39–42.
38 Martin Crusius, *Schwäbische Chronick: worinnen zu finden ist was sich von Erschaffung der Welt an biss auf das Jahr 1596 in Schwaben*, vol. 2, tr. Johann Jacob Moser (1733), 215.
39 *Die Inschriften des Landkreises Ludwigsburg*, ed. Anneliese Seeliger-Zeiss and Hans Ulrich Schäfer (Wiesbaden, 1986), 60–1.
40 Reinhard Lieske, *Protestantische Frömmigkeit im Spiegel der kirchlichen Kunst des Herzogtums Württemberg* (Munich, 1973), 119–24.
41 Roman Janssen, 'Das Epitaph Neuffer in der Herrenberger Stiftskirche: Rekonstruktion und Deutung eines außergewöhnlichen Zeugnisses der Württembergischen Reformationsgeschichte', in *'Der Sinn ist funden': Neue Entdeckungen und Darstellungen zur Herrenberger Geschichte*, ed. Roman Janssen (Sigmaringen, 1997), 77.
42 This argument is fully explored in Dieter Mertens, 'Eberhard im Bart als politische Leitfigur im Frühneuzeitlichen Herzogtum Württemberg', *Zeitschrift für Württembergische Landesgeschichte* 59 (2000), 43–56.
43 Johann F. Baumhauer, *Inscriptiones monumentorum, quae sunt Tubingae in conditorio illustrissimorum Wurtembergicae principum: in templo divi Georgii et divi Jacobi in coemeterio intra extra urbem* (Tübingen, 1627), 2.
44 Quoted in Mertens, 'Eberhard im Bart als politische Leitfigur', 43.
45 *Historische Volkslieder der Deutschen vom 13. bis 16. Jahrhundert*, vol. III, ed. Rochus von Liliencron (Leipzig, 1867), 237–40.
46 Camerarius, *Oratio Funebris*, n.p.; Mertens, 'Eberhard im Bart als politische Leitfigur', 52.
47 Mertens, 'Eberhard im Bart als politische Leitfigur', 52–3.
48 Martin Crusius, *Oratio de Illustriss. Principe Eberhardo Barbato, primo Wirtembergensi Duce* (Tübingen, 1593), 11, 15–6, 22–4.
49 Schukraft, *Die Grablegen des Hauses Württemberg*, 50–4; Stefanie Knöll, 'The Ducal Burial Place at Tübingen, Germany, 1537–93', *Church Monuments* 20 (2005), 98–100.
50 Crusius, *Schwäbische Chronick*, II: 392–94.
51 Peter Sherlock, 'The Art of Making Memory: Epitaphs, Tables and Adages at Westminster Abbey', in *Religion, the Supernatural and Visual Culture in Early Modern Europe: An Album Amicorum for Charles Zika*, ed. Jennifer Spinks and Dagmar Eichberger (Leiden, 2015), 356.
52 Crusius, *Schwäbische Chronick*, II: 392.
53 August von Wintterlin, 'Die Grabdenkmale Herzog Christophs, seines Sohnes Eberhard und seiner Gemahlin Anna Maria in der Stiftskirche Tübingen', in *Festschrift zur vierten Säcular-Feier der Eberhard-Karls-Universität zu Tübingen dargebracht von der königlichen öffentlichen Bibliothek zu Stuttgart*, ed. Württembergische Landesbibliothek et al. (Stuttgart, 1877), 46–8.
54 John Weever, *Ancient funerall monuments within the united monarchie of Great Britaine, Ireland, and the islands adiacent, with the dissolued monasteries therein contained: their founders, and*

what eminent persons haue beene in the same interred (London, 1631), 40–1. On the phenomenon of tomb tourism see Frits Scholten, *Sumptuous Memories: Studies in Seventeenth-Century Dutch Tomb Sculpture* (Zwolle, 2003), 211–31.

55 Baumhauer, *Inscriptiones monumentorum*.

56 Michael Hempel, *Conditorium Saxonicum de novo Tabulis Aeneis incisum,et luculenta descriptione latina & Germanica illustratum* (Freiberg, 1619), n.p.

57 Stefan Dornheim, *Der Pfarrer als Arbeiter am Gedächtnis: Lutherische Erinnerungskultur in der Frühen Neuzeit zwischen Religion und sozialer Kohäsion* (Leipzig, 2013).

58 Róisín Watson, 'Funeral Monuments, Ritual and Print: Strategies of Memorialization at the Württemberg Court', in *Cultures of Lutheranism: Reformation Repertoires in Early Modern Germany*, ed. Kat Hill, *P&P* 234, issue suppl. 12 (2017), 139–64 (154–7).

59 Dornheim, *Der Pfarrer als Arbeiter am Gedächtnis*, 63.

60 Johann Schmid, 'Inscriptiones Monumentorum, cuae sunt Stutgardiae in Conditorio Illustrissimorum Württembergiae Prinicipum in Temple S. Crucis vel Cathedrali' (1640), Stuttgart, Württembergische Landesbibliothek, Cod. Hist. 80 18.

61 Schmid, 'Inscriptiones Monumentorum', 112–3.

62 Dornheim has explored a similar phenomenon in Saxony. Dornheim, *Der Pfarrer als Arbeiter am Gedächtnis*, 62–4.

63 Johann Gottfried Olearius, *Coemiterium Saxo-Hallense Das ist, Des wohlerbauten Gottes-Ackers der löblichen Stadt Hall in Sachsen Beschreibung* (Wittenberg, 1674), n.p.

64 Olearius, *Coemiterium Saxo-Hallense*, 180–1.

65 Crusius, *Schwäbische Chronick*, I: 4.

66 Johannes Schuler, *Etliche Chritliche Predigen/Darinnen angezeigt wirdt/ wie hoch Gott das Hertzogthumb Würtemberg/und under anderm auch die Statt Kircheim under Teck erhaben/beedes leiblich und geistlich begnadet/und uber alle massen gesegnet hab* (Stuttgart, 1612), 173, 33, 66, 82, 87.

67 Olearius, *Coemiterium Saxo-Hallense*, n.p.

68 Ludwig, 'Der Ulmer Humanist Rychardus und sein Totes Kind', 289.

PART V

Invented memory

10

THE MATERIAL OF MEMORY IN THE SEVENTEENTH-CENTURY ANDES

The Cross of Carabuco and local history

Katrina B. Olds

Spanish chroniclers helped reshape memory in the early modern Catholic world while also negotiating between local contexts and universal concerns. They achieved this work not through anti-Protestant polemics — as in so many sermons, theological treatises, and pamphlets of the sixteenth and seventeenth centuries — but rather when they wrote sacred history.[1] Recent studies have detailed how cleric-antiquaries documented and shaped historical memory in the core and peripheries of post-Reformation Spain; and how, in the effort, they strained mightily to wrestle the heterogeneous elements of Spanish history — such as the long Islamic presence — into the Procrustean bed of an unchanging and eternal Catholicism.[2]

To date, parallel efforts in the Spanish Americas have received far less attention. As this essay will suggest, chroniclers in the Spanish Americas shared with their European counterparts an interest in the *longue durée* of local history, as well as a hopeful hermeneutic that would put their home regions at the centre of Catholic history. New World chroniclers kept their ears to the ground as they excavated objects and legends that, they hoped, might recover lost memories of a Christian past. Like sacred historians elsewhere, they confronted the formidable challenge of tracing deep continuities across radically disruptive epochs. Their especially formidable hurdle was to establish that the Americas — like most of the known world — had been introduced to Christianity during the first century after Christ, possibly by one of his apostles.

In support of the hypothesis of a primeval evangelisation of the Indies, chroniclers made note of objects, local memories, and natural phenomena that seemed to confirm that an apostle had preached the Gospel in the New World. In one particularly well-documented instance, an actual wooden cross was discovered in Carabuco, an indigenous community on the shores of Lake Titicaca in the Andean highlands of colonial Peru, at the turn of the seventeenth century. This cross, portions of which are still enshrined today in the Bolivian locales of Carabuco and Sucre, was purported by oral traditions to have been carried thence upon the back of an apostle, whose evangelical itinerary had taken him from the Holy Land to India, then to Brazil, next up the river valleys of the Southern Cone, and finally into the Andean highlands. There he preached the Gospel to the ancestors of the very same Aymara-speaking peoples whom the apostle's spiritual descendants — Spanish Jesuit, Augustinian, and secular clergy — were trying to Christianise during the colonial era.

In focusing on the story of the Cross of Carabuco, this essay brings the history of the theory of the pre-Hispanic evangelisation into conversation with scholarship on the history of memory and of the Counter-Reformation.[3] Most analyses have instead focused on the place of this myth in European intellectual history: as one strand in a variety of attempts to assimilate the New World and its inhabitants (not to mention its animal life, flora, and fauna) into the universal framework of biblical and Christian history, to address questions about the ultimate genealogical origin of the Indians, and to argue for their inherent capacity for Christianisation.[4] In this vein, speculation about the possibility of a pre-Hispanic evangelisation of the Indies is usually described as an eccentric feature in the tapestry of European responses to the ongoing epistemological and historiographical challenge posed by the realisation on the part of Europeans that this was truly a New World.[5] Yet attempts to make sense of the new world order went both ways of course, and scholars have also pointed, quite rightly, to the fact that stories of a primeval apostolate to the Americas were generated through the cross-fertilisation of indigenous creation myths with Christian legends of apostolic sojourns.[6] For example, a similar complex of Spanish, indigenous, and creole myths arose regarding the apostle St Thomas, who was also understood to have been the Mexica deity Quetzacoatl.[7]

So, too, in the Andes, was the material of memory fungible and shapeshifting. As early modern devotees narrated various versions of the tale of the Cross of Carabuco, the theory of an early Christian visit intertwined with existing Andean iconography and oral histories in a reformation of social memory that also reflected shifting realities for native Andeans. While the tale of an apostle to the Andes seems to have been overlaid upon the pre-existing story of a figure named Tunupa who would return someday, the Cross of Carabuco was not only created by native Andeans.[8] In analysing the narratives, material objects, and artistic representations of the apostle and his cross, we shall see how various social and political agents negotiated the reformation of memory by creating and circulating narratives about origins. This oscillation between the past and present resembles the reformation(s) of memory elsewhere in the Spanish Americas, as well as in post-Reformation Europe.

The apostles in the world

The history of the Cross of Carabuco might seem impossible: as we know, there was no memory of Christianity in the Americas, since the Gospel did not arrive until sixteenth-century Europeans did. Yet for many missionaries, the notion that half of the world would have been left out of the history of salvation for well-nigh a millennium and a half seemed not only unlikely but unjust. Although the question of the Native Americans' origins would remain unsettled for at least two hundred more years, early modern Spanish writers agreed that they, like all humans, descended from the common parents of humanity.[9] Yet when and how the Americans had arrived from the Old World, and exactly *who* they were, remained far from clear. In his 1590 *Natural and Moral History of the Indies*, the Jesuit José de Acosta carefully considered, and rejected, each of the prevailing theories in turn, including that the Indians descended from the lost ten tribes of Israel, migrated from the lost island of Atlantis, or resided in the biblical territories of Ophir. Nor did the prominent Spanish Jesuit consider it possible that inhabitants of the Western Hemisphere had been exposed to the Gospel, since there was no evidence of ancient knowledge of this part of the world. Finally, Acosta also denied that the natives possessed an implicit monotheism; any seeming similarities between Christian and indigenous American rites were due to diabolical mimicry, not a primeval evangelisation or *prisca theologia*. [10]

Modern scholars often infer that Acosta's reasonable and measured voice on this matter was the prevailing opinion. To the contrary: at the time, Acosta's was certainly not the last word in this debate, nor was it necessarily heeded by many of his fellow Jesuits. A few clues suggest that the pre-Hispanic evangelisation already had traction among missionaries in the trenches, as it were. For example, in a letter to Spain from the last decades of the sixteenth century, a diocesan cleric named Martín González reported from South America that, in the provinces of Paraguay and the River La Plata, the natives practiced a rudimentary monotheism transmitted via their ancestors, who had been instructed by St Thomas. González also took note of several locations which preserved miraculous imprints of the apostle's footprints.[11] One of Acosta's contemporaries, the Lima-born Jesuit Antonio Ruiz de Montoya, also drew on his own missionary experience — in the Jesuit strongholds of Paraguay — as well as biblical exegesis to argue for an apostolic history. As he reasoned in his 1639 *Spiritual Conquest Accomplished by the Religious of the Society of Jesus*, it would be absurd to presume that when Christ enjoined the apostles to 'Go into all the world, and preach the gospel to every creature' (Mark 16:15) that he would have excluded the Americas, which constituted 'nearly a third of the earth'. Rather, the apostles would have conscientiously undertaken their duty to 'circulate throughout the entire world with their preaching'. Otherwise, 'how is it thinkable that they should have left all America in darkness, deprived of the light of the gospel?'[12]

Here Ruiz de Montoya echoed several centuries of post-biblical legend, which extended apostolic itineraries to the very edges of the earth. The apostle St Bartholomew was believed to have reached Armenia and India, and St Thomas, China and India, where he had converted the famous 'St. Thomas Christians' of Kerala.[13] Early modern explorers and missionaries to India duly sought — and found — traces of Thomas' itinerary, including footprints impressed in stone, as well as his very body. Jesuit missionaries continued to discover and publicise additional relics in the sixteenth and seventeenth centuries, in the hopes of giving new life to the legend and reawakening local Christianity, whose historic traces were, as Ines Županov explains, 'imprinted in the landscape, but remained only superficially present in human consciousness'.[14]

Indeed, almost ever since Columbus beheld islands he reckoned to be off the coast of India, Europeans had been discovering traces of what seemed to them distorted and poorly remembered Christian doctrines and practices. At a time when the precise western boundaries of the New World were still unclear to Europeans, the possibility that Thomas or Bartholomew might have continued in an easterly direction from Asia to reach the Americas did not seem unlikely at all.[15] Thus, when the anonymous author of the 'New Gazette from the Land of Brasil' (c.1515) wrote about a territory that, by his estimation, was not far from India, it was logical that he would find evidence that the people in lower Brazil possessed an all–but–forgotten 'memory' of St Thomas, confirmed by the mute testimony of nearby footprints.[16] This report was elaborated significantly in subsequent retellings, most influentially in a vivid and influential 1549 letter from the Jesuit Manuel da Nóbrega about the expedition of the first Portuguese Governor-General Tomé de Sousa to Brazil, where Nóbrega claimed to have collected oral testimony from the Tupinambá people regarding the visit of an apostle:

> They say that Saint Thomas, who they call Zomé, came this way. This was reported to them by their ancestors. And that his footprints are marked next to a river, which I went to see for greater certainty about the truth. I saw with my own eyes four very distinct foot- and toe-prints, which are sometimes covered by the river when it swells. They also say that when he left these footprints he was fleeing the Indians who wanted to shoot him with arrows, and when he arrived at this spot the river opened up for him, and he passed right through the middle of it to the other side without getting wet. And from there he set off for India. They also tell that when the Indians tried to shoot him with arrows, the arrows turned around and headed toward them, and the reeds parted for the arrows to pass. Others tell this as if with derision. They also say that he promised that he would return again to see them; that he sees them from heaven; and that he is their intercessor before God, so that they can come to know Him, and receive the holy faith, as we desire.[17]

Nóbrega's account circulated widely: in manuscript among Jesuits worldwide, in a printed Spanish translation in 1551, and throughout the sixteenth century in Italian, German, and Latin editions.[18] Thus, certain elements of his narrative would recur in nearly every subsequent account of an apostolic visit to the Americas: the visitor from afar chased out of town in fear for his life; a miraculous escape through the water; the impressions left by his feet upon a nearby rock or flood plain; and the sense that the tale had been passed down for several generations.

The story thereafter travelled with Spanish and Portuguese clerics to the Southern Cone, from Brazil to Paraguay and the Andes, where, in the hands of seventeenth-century chroniclers, it was to receive its most enthusiastic and prolific treatment. Since most of the existing evidence for these beliefs is from non-native written sources, it is tempting to dismiss the notion of a pre-Hispanic evangelisation as a European invention, and the product of wishful thinking. As we shall see, several elements within these and other stories do suggest European mis-readings of indigenous etiological myths as actual memories of a thaumaturgical and itinerant apostle. Yet if we look more closely at the case of Carabuco, which is attested in a relatively variegated body of primary sources from disparate perspectives, we discern a much more complex and dynamic situation. Here the memory of an apostolic mission to the Andes was not merely a means for Europeans to assimilate Andean history into the universalistic narrative of biblical history. It was also, more immediately, one of several channels through which local and regional actors — including Spanish missionaries, diocesan clerics, native converts, and indigenous shamans — disputed and negotiated the shape of the past and present. In order to understand how these various interests intersected and influenced each other on the ground, where these stories took root and even gave rise to new cultic objects, histories, and memories, it is worth examining the events in Carabuco in detail.

Communal conflict and the Cross of Carabuco

In 1600, a Jesuit observer in La Paz explained how the cross had been discovered. According to the Jesuit Provincial Rodrigo Cabredo, who compiled this anecdote and many others in his annual report to his Roman superior about the state of affairs in Peru, it had all begun with a 'solemn drinking bout'. During these communal festivals, local Andean leaders (called *caciques* by the Spanish) recounted recent struggles and heroic deeds of yore. These were also propitious occasions for consulting native religious specialists — 'demons in human form' for the Jesuit — for the discernment of 'hidden things' and other mysteries of this world and the beyond.[19] It was during one of these corn-alcohol-fuelled rituals festivals that the two moieties that constituted the community, known respectively as the Anansaya and Urinsaya, accused each other of violence, impiety, and murder. In short, as the caciques of each faction disparaged the other, the Anansaya leader boasted that at least *his* ancestors had not murdered Spaniards. The Urinsaya cacique retorted that his counterpart should 'shut up, because [the Anansaya] were sorcerers, and descended from those who had buried the cross'.[20]

When the parish priest of Carabuco caught wind of the intriguing rumour that half the community had murdered Spaniards, and the other half had destroyed a cross, he made inquiries, and soon enough was rewarded with the discovery of the cross itself. This prompted his superior, the Bishop of Charcas (modern Sucre), Alonso Ramírez de Vergara, to conduct an investigation into the cross, and to appropriate one of its nails — and, later, a significant portion of the holy wood itself — for his cathedral. The bishop's inquiry revealed — or perhaps helped create

— an ancient narrative that explained the genesis of the cross, and which the community's 'oldest Indians' professed to have heard from their forefathers; they, in turn, were supposed to have learned the story from their *quipus*, knotted cords used by Andeans for record-keeping in the pre-colonial period.

According to this oldest kernel of the narrative, a long time ago, a bearded man who resembled an apostle came to town. He and his twelve companions attempted to convert residents to his holy and exemplary life by carving a large cross in the town's central plaza. Once the cross was erected, the local 'demon' who had previously provided divination services to the community during their drinking rituals suddenly ceased his ministrations. The shaman also refused to return until the cross and its creators were gone. One cacique tried to handle the situation diplomatically by inviting the bearded outsiders to join the community in celebration, but they refused based on their principled opposition to ritual drinking. Thereupon the shaman and villagers set upon the bearded man, his followers, and their cross. They successfully murdered the twelve disciples and tried to incinerate the cross; but they were stymied by its indestructible wood, which immediately reconstituted itself into a cross from the ashes. Angry villagers tried to cut it into pieces with axes, but the miraculous wood repelled their blades. The frustrated Carabucans dispatched the object to a deep grave, where it remained hidden until the last years of the sixteenth century. In the meantime, they crucified the apostle by tying him to three large stones (one of which was later displayed as a relic in Carabuco's parish church).[21] Here again they were defied: the bearded man untied himself, escaped through a gap in the reeds on the shores of Titicaca, and sailed upon his cape until he was out of view. At the time of the bishop's report, the path through the reeds, as well as the three boulders that formed the shape of a cross, were still visible.[22]

While seventeenth-century chroniclers would soon make much hay out of these traces and hints of an Andean apostolic relic, our source is rather reticent on this count. The Carabuco story was just one anecdote in a longer report about the state of Peruvian Jesuit missions. Cabredo lifted passages from an earlier dossier assembled by Bishop Ramírez de Vergara (now lost), to which he appended only a few inconclusive observations about the possible veracity of the story. For example, he noted that the apostle in this story closely resembled a holy figure named 'Tumcapa' who, he had heard in a native 'fable or story', had nearly been crucified upon three stones before a wondrous escape. 'All of which', Cabredo conceded, 'seems to confirm that this [story] is quite ancient'. He also averred that the man could have been an early Church Father, but not an apostle, since 'there is no trace whatsoever in any of the ecclesiastical histories that Saint Thomas ever arrived in these parts, and we know that he preached in the East Indies, from which to these [Indies] there is a very great distance'.[23]

Neither the bishop nor Cabredo seems to have reflected on the role that their presence — and, more generally, that of Spanish colonial and religious administrations — might have played in exacerbating factional divisions in Carabuco and other indigenous communities, and in making the cross an object of communal discord. From our perspective, it seems clear that both the ancient and modern accounts of communal conflict did not necessarily record memories of actual events, but were metanarratives describing contemporary tensions around religious, political, and social change under colonial rule. By the time Cabredo wrote in 1600, over seven decades had passed since the Spanish arrived in the high Andean plains near Titicaca, but it had only been thirty years since the fifth Viceroy of Peru, Francisco Toledo, installed enduring systems of royal and ecclesiastical administration, such as in forcibly relocating many natives into new settlements (*reducciones*).[24] Scholars of the colonial Andes have demonstrated that this reshuffling from above prompted a reconfiguration of social and political arrangements at the level of the local indigenous community (*ayllu*), as pre-existing native dynasties were increasingly challenged by new players. In some cases, this meant that ascendant political factions were overthrown by previously disenfranchised parties who, in turn, had come to power by allying themselves with Spanish interests.[25] As local hierarchies were reformed and reconstituted, social memories were also renegotiated to align with the new order of things.

It seems clear that a similar conflict had arisen in Carabuco due to the Spanish conquest and evangelisation. In the process, traditional native elites and upstart caciques alike engaged in the reconstitution of memory; as factions jockeyed for power, they revised narratives of communal origins and identities to align with the current state of affairs. Since 'the power of the caciques derived its legitimacy from heavily reconstituted collective memory', narratives about the past could serve mnemonically to prompt retellings of the story for many years to come, to ensure that the wounds of the most recent intra-communal conflict would endure and remain fresh.[26] In these struggles for communal prestige and control, memory was a 'strategic resource'; so, too, were material remnants of this memory, such as the cross.[27]

We see this process in both the ancient and modern narratives regarding events in Carabuco, where intra-communal tensions attained new meanings due to the presence of outsiders. In the frame story — which recounted the most recent conflict between the factions in Carabuco — the leaders of the community seem to have been revising their own communal memories. The two moieties of the village blamed each other for driving out two different types of outsiders at two different times — the 'Spaniards' murdered in an (unspecified) earlier conflict in the frame story, and in the ancient narrative, the bearded apostle and his followers. This primeval event had most likely been preserved in oral traditions, and then reinterpreted from within the new idiom of Christianity, which privileged martyrdom. In the frame story regarding the most recent dispute about which faction had been more hostile to Christian outsiders, we see also as an internal reckoning of who would find favour and co-operate with the new actors in the region, and who would be shut out. In the process, members of the community (re)created and (re)formed the ancient narrative, and the apostolic visit became a primeval event, an etiological myth that would explain why and how the population was divided into two mutually antagonistic halves — and why one half was more powerful and prestigious than the other. If one group 'killed Spaniards', at least they had not been hostile to the messenger of Christ, nor buried his cross.

In sum, old tensions between the Urinsaya and Anansaya took on a new pungency thanks to the arrival of new actors — Spanish colonists and missionaries — who were personified in the ancient narrative by the apostle. This exemplifies how the battle for local primacy and legitimacy was being waged in actuality through political man-oeuvring, but also through retrospective narratives in which memories of communal conflicts were filtered through the prism of apostolic Christianity by pragmatic caciques who understood the practical advantages of allying with the Spanish. Only faintly echoed here are the dissonant voices of the so-called demons, the shamanistic figures who communicated with the beyond through divination rituals, and who, after the arrival of the missionaries, began to quite literally compete with Catholic religious specialists for the devotion and attention of the community.[28] They disappear com-pletely in the twentieth-century histories of Carabuco, in which the jagged edges of local conflict are sanded down to depict a smooth and continuous local order across different political and religious regimes. According to contemporary local scholars, a single dynasty — the Siñani family — led the community for several centuries, from before the time of the Incan conquest, to the Spanish arrival. In fact, the dominant Siñani cacique was the first in Carabuco to convert to Christianity; he was baptised 'Fernando', at the behest of don Francisco de Caravajal, the vicious conquistador known as the 'devil of the Andes', in 1538. Thereafter, the Siñani sons continued to serve as caciques and parish priests, in loyalty to Crown and Church, until the mid-eighteenth century, when the last Siñani was cut down in cold blood as he fought to defend the king's lands against neo-Incan rebels.[29]

The Cross as history, relic, and medical remedy

In the short term, matters were more complicated. News of the Cross of Carabuco moved quickly along the channels of communication that connected indigenous communities on the eastern shore of Titicaca with the broader commercial, poli-tical, and religious worlds of the colonial Andes. Soon indigenous and creole chroniclers — especially from the Jesuit and Augustinian religious orders — were listing the cross as one of several other clues of a pre-Hispanic apostolate. In his c.1615 manuscript history of the world, the Quechua notable Felipe Guaman Poma de Ayala protested the abuses of Spanish colonial agents, and the recent inversions that had displaced traditional communal leaders, such as his own father, in favour of greedy *arriviste* caciques who cavorted with corrupt parish priests and Spanish secular officials.[30] As part of his defence of the inherent goodness of the natives of the Andes, and particularly of the established, Incan-era social order (which had been disrupted by the Spanish arrival), Guaman Poma emphasised that Christianity had been introduced long before the Europeans by Christ's apostle, whom he identified as St Bartholomew. After having been chased out of the hos-tile town of Cacha, the apostle met with success in Carabuco, where he made the Americas' first convert, and left behind his cross as a 'sign of that holy miracle and baptism', an event that Guaman Poma also commemorated in a sketch in his own hand [Fig. 10. 1].[31]

FIGURE 10.1 The Cross of Carabuco, in Felipe Guaman Poma de Ayala, *El primer nueva crónica y buen gobierno* (1615), 73.
Royal Danish Library, GKS 2232.

The Augustinian friar Alonso Ramos Gavilán also cited the Cross of Carabuco as one among many possible clues of an early Christian presence in the New World. In his 1621 history of the nearby shrine of the Virgin at Copacabana, Ramos Gavilán referred to this early Christian visitor as the 'Holy Disciple'. Although he was sceptical that non-literate peoples could have maintained accurate records over so many centuries, the friar was nonetheless convinced that there had been a pre-Hispanic evangelisation, perhaps by one of Thomas' followers instead of the apostle himself, and that local narratives of the mysterious visitor captured actual memories, dimly but persistently transmitted across the generations.[32] For Ramos Gavilán, the need to preserve a written memory of these objects and narratives was particularly pressing in light of the destruction of these items, not by the ravages of time, but by zealous Spanish officials who were ignorant of their historical significance. Ramos Gavilán bemoaned a lost stone in Collao, near Lima. It was engraved with the image of a hatted and serious man, whom Ramos Gavilán was certain must have been the same man who had left the cross in Carabuco, and whose body had ended up in Lake Titicaca. However, since 'in that time there was not as much knowledge of the Holy Disciple', Viceroy Toledo mistook the image for a native idol, and had it destroyed.[33]

The predations of their fellow Spaniards gave Ramos Gavilán and his Augustinian continuator, Alonso de la Calancha, a sense of urgency. As objects continued to disappear, and memories faded, these Augustinian books of history became important repositories of evidence for a lost history of early Andean Christianity. We can see this in the case of a stone found near Calango, a short distance from Lima, imprinted with a single footprint and mysterious symbols and letters which, Ramos Gavilán reckoned, 'were in a language that must be either Greek or Hebrew'.[34] The oldest Indians affirmed that a tall white blue-eyed man with a long beard, who preached about a powerful God, had made the prints on the stone with his finger. Ramos Gavilán admitted that he had not seen the stone himself, but that he had received a description from friars of great credit and authority.[35] By the time Calancha wrote about the same stone (with scarcely more clarity or erudition) in his own history of Copacabana (1638), it was too late [Fig. 10. 2]: it had been destroyed by an ecclesiastical inspector who mistook it for a site of ritual veneration by the natives, known in Quechua as a *huaca*. From these details we can deduce that the stone must have been destroyed, along with thousands of other *huacas*, as part of a general ecclesiastical campaign against native 'idolatry' in the early seventeenth century.[36]

To these suggestive, complex, and fluid catalogues of local Andean memories, materials, and practices, we must append that of the Jesuit chronicler and mystic Antonio Ruiz de Montoya. His 1639 *Spiritual Conquest* described Carabuco as the end of the apostle's itinerary, which wound from India to Brazil, up the River Plate into Paraguay, and finally to Titicaca, where his route was still visible in an anomaly in the natural landscape, that is, in a distinctive parting of the reeds along the lakeshore.[37] These collections of local memories and objects served, in turn, to generate new memories and devotional materials in the long-term. In the 1680s, the parish priest of Carabuco commissioned a local artist to produce an elaborate series of murals on the topic of the Last Judgment. Below each mural is a sequence of images depicting the apostle's arrival, persecution, and escape; in the accompanying cartouches, the textual explanations specifically cite anecdotes from the texts of Ramos Gavilán and Calancha.[38]

While there is much still to be elucidated about the subsequent history of the cult and memory of Carabuco's cross, the church, the relic itself, as well as the

FIGURE 10.2 Antonio de la Calancha, *Coronica moralizada del Orden de San Augustin en el Perú con sucesos egenplares en esta Monarquía* (Barcelona: Pedro Lacavalleria, 1638), 328. Beinecke Rare Book & Manuscript Library, Yale University.

story of a primeval apostolate all survived, and are still commemorated annually on May 3, the festival of the invention of the cross by the mother of Constantine, St Helena. In practice, slivers of its wood were collected by visitors, who brought the cross far beyond its regional Andean context, and who were perhaps indifferent to the historical and apostolic thread of the story, and more acutely interested in the medicinal potency of the wood itself. In 1675, a parish priest reported from Cartagena de las Indias, a port on the Caribbean coast of modern Colombia, that several people, including the city's bishop, had been cured, not by means of an actual relic of the Carabuco cross, but by a piece of the same type of wood from which the cross had been made. The priest's reasoning was that the apostle must have granted natural healing qualities to all specimens of that tree, in honour of the first cross.[39]

Whose story?

It is tempting to imagine that these and other traces of a pre-Hispanic evangelisation were created and nourished by Spanish missionaries in their own image as part of a top-down 'colonizing discourse'.[40] It is true that, if the Spanish could have proven that the Americas had been Christianised, they could have used this history to legitimise their wars of conquest; by this logic, the invasion of the Indies would not, as Spain's domestic and foreign critics alleged, have been an illicit invasion, but instead a reconquest or recovery of formerly Christian territories for the faith.[41] Moreover, if it could be proven that the Americas were originally Catholic, this could have been a useful way of arguing that Catholic Spain should dominate for soteriological, and not just geopolitical, reasons as well. Some contemporaries came close to asserting that the conquest of the Americas did indeed possess a providential significance: as contemporaries were fond of observing, the many Catholics lost to Protestantism in Europe had a happy counterpart in the millions of souls gained for the Church in the Indies. Hence the urgent need to keep territories in Catholic — not Dutch or French or English — hands.[42]

Yet the potential of the pre-Hispanic evangelisation to serve as political propaganda remained unrealised. It was, instead, on a smaller scale, among regional actors that the story of an apostle and his cross took root. For Augustinian and Jesuit authors, it was important to demonstrate that their own respective religious orders were fulfilling the apostolic potential of the territories under their purview. They could achieve this, in part, by drawing parallels between the earliest Christian missions to the Andes and their own, as a way to argue for their own providential role in the salvation of the Indies. If the people of the Americas had been introduced to Christianity before the arrival of the Europeans, it was now time for the *right* missionaries to connect the natives with their own primeval Christian identities and convince them to abandon indigenous rites and beliefs.[43] This was not an abstract concern: after all, the Augustinians and Jesuits had only been granted these territories after the Dominicans had lost their monopoly of the lands around Titicaca, due to accusations of abuse, in 1569.[44]

Yet it was not only the Europeans' hopeful and pious imaginings that gave traction to the myth of the pre-Hispanic evangelisation. That broader story, and the material traces of its imagined history, proliferated thanks also to the interests of various indigenous communities in the Andes, Mexico, Paraguay, and Brazil. The case of Carabuco is admittedly unusual in that the surviving sources enable us to trace in great detail how local etiological legends were newly aligned with the history of apostolic Christianity. Yet when apostolic relics such as crosses and footprints were identified elsewhere, they may have also shaped local memory and identities in creative and enduring iterations, although scholars have yet to trace this in any systematic manner.[45] For a suggestive example we may look toward the Aymara-speaking regions below Lake Poopó (south of Titicaca), where, in the late twentieth century, the anthropologist Thomas Abercrombie found that the notion of a primeval visit from Jesus had become completely intertwined with communal origin myths among the K'ulta people, who attributed their ethnogenesis to a cosmic battle involving Jesus, also known as Tatala.[46]

Even as the notion of an apostolate to the Indies began to fall away from mainstream intellectual trends in eighteenth-century Europe, the implication of an autochthonous Christian identity and history for the Americas would prove immensely appealing for those American-born Spaniards known as creoles. This was especially true in Mexico, where in 1794, the Dominican friar Fray Teresa Servando de Mier delivered a sermon before an astonished Spanish viceroy in which he asserted that St Thomas had preached the Gospel to the people of New Spain over a millennium and a half before the European arrival. More controversially, he also asserted that the image of the Virgin of Guadalupe was not created in the sixteenth century, but actually dated to the first century, when it had been impressed upon the cape of the apostle St Thomas by the Virgin herself, only to be forgotten during a long epoch of apostasy. Therefore when the Virgin appeared to the native convert Juan Diego in 1531, it was to reveal the existence of her image, and to restore Mexico to its pristine and direct relationship with God.[47] In other words, the conquistadors had not introduced Christianity, nor was the Spanish presence necessary — in the first place, nor any longer — for the institution of good morals and Catholic faith in Mexico.[48]

In modern scholarship, the fact that the pre-Hispanic evangelisation underwrote Mexican nationalism on the eve of independence has effectively eclipsed the earlier part of this story, in which the myth flourished in particular local contexts and in unexpected ways. It is often assumed that this legend would have appealed inherently and exclusively to creole authors, when in fact, not everybody who advocated or documented the notion was creole; nor were they, as another author has erroneously asserted, only mestizo or indigenous.[49] As this essay has argued, it is important to recover the local circumstances and conversations that created the Carabuco relic and narratives, before the various Spanish, creole, and mestizo interpreters codified them in written histories. Local conflicts and conversations — among and between rival factions, missionaries, caciques, and Andean 'devils,' *inter alia* — generated the cross as well as memories and narratives of its genesis. Scholars of the history of ideas would do well to remain attentive to the potential for such disparate actors to create intellectual change in colonial contexts, as well as in the European metropole itself.[50]

As this closer look at the context in which tales and relics of the primeval Christianisation of the Indies arose in the sixteenth and seventeenth centuries has suggested, the theory was not just a dead-end in European intellectual history, nor simply a vehicle for nascent 'creole consciousness'. Rather, the search for an early Christian past, which preoccupied Catholic antiquarians throughout Europe, also informed the shape of memory among indigenous and Spanish inhabitants of the New World. In both the Indies and Spain, the early Church's history was believed to have been obscured by infidels and idolaters. On both sides of the Atlantic, clerics confronted the difficulty of how to harmonise dissonant elements within their own regional pasts with the normative narrative of Catholic reform, renewal, and recovery. Although the fact that parallel efforts were underway in Spain and its overseas territories was mostly unnoticed by these highly parochial authors themselves, from this distance we can see that both sets of authors confronted related heuristic and historical dilemmas, and they resolved them in similar manners. As the middlemen between local and universal cultures, cleric-chroniclers such as Ramos Gavilán and Ruiz de Montoya attempted to reshape memories of change into evidence of continuity. Spanish authors in the New World, like antiquarian-historians in Spain, sought evidence for their own social memories in physical objects, natural phenomena, and other 'clues' of a broader and even providential significance; they did so not just in texts, and not always in ways that conformed to evolving norms of critical historical thought. Somewhere in this effort, alchemy occurred, and hitherto hidden footprints, crosses, and memories emerged from the mists of the forgotten and obscure non-Christian periods of Spanish and American history. In these ways did local conflicts and preoccupations help reshape memory, in what was arguably a universal impulse in the world the Reformations had created: namely, to reshuffle the variegated strands of memory, imagination, and erudition in order to reform the Christian past, present, and future.

Notes

1   For reform in Spain, Lu Ann Homza, *Religious Authority in the Spanish Renaissance* (Baltimore, 2000); John E. Longhurst, *Luther's Ghost in Spain (1517–1546)* (Lawrence, KS, 1969); Stefania Pastore, *Una herejía española conversos, alumbrados e inquisición (1449–1559)*, tr. Clara Álvarez Alonso (Madrid, 2010), (originally published in Italian, *Un'eresia spagnola*, 2004). For anti-Luther imagery in the Spanish Americas: Lucila Iglesias, 'Naves, herejes y luteranos', *Avances* 23 (2013–2014), 205–20; Alicia Mayer, 'Política contrarreformista e imagen anti-luterana en Nueva España', *Hispania Sacra* 68, no. 137 (2016), 31–43; Mayer, *Lutero en el paraíso: La Nueva España en el espejo del reformador alemán*, 2nd ed. (México, 2012). A recent analysis of Jesuit theatre as history in New Spain and Brazil is Nicole T. Hughes, 'Stages of History: New World Spectacles and the Theater of the World in the Sixteenth Century' (PhD Thesis, Columbia University, 2017).

2   Antonio Urquízar-Herrera, *Admiration and Awe: Morisco Buildings and Identity Negotiations in Early Modern Spanish Historiography* (Oxford, 2017). See also Katherine Elliot Van Liere, 'Renaissance Chroniclers and the Apostolic Origins of Spanish Christianity', in *Sacred History: Uses of the Christian Past in the Renaissance World*, ed. Katherine Elliot Van Liere, Simon R. Ditchfield, and Howard Louthan (Oxford, 2012): 121–44; Katrina B. Olds, *Forging the Past: Invented Histories in Counter-Reformation Spain* (New Haven, 2015).

3 Simon R. Ditchfield, 'What Was Sacred History? (Mostly Roman) Catholic Uses of the Christian Past after Trent', in Van Liere, Ditchfield, and Louthan, *Sacred History*, 72–97. For Spain, Richard L. Kagan, 'Clio and the Crown: Writing History in Habsburg Spain', in *Spain, Europe and the Atlantic World: Essays in Honour of John H. Elliott* (Cambridge, 1995), 73–99; José Miguel Morán Turina, *La memoria de las piedras: anticuarios, arqueólogos y coleccionistas de antigüedades en la España de los Austrias* (Madrid, 2010); Katrina B. Olds, 'Local Antiquaries and the Expansive Sense of the Past: A Case Study from Counter-Reformation Spain', in *Local Antiquities, Local Identities: Art, Literature, and Antiquarianism in Early Modern Europe*, ed. Kathleen Christian and Bianca de Divitiis (Manchester, 2018): 167–89.

4 Giuliano Gliozzi, *Adamo e il nuovo mondo: la nascita dell'antropologia come ideologia coloniale: dalle genealogie bibliche alle teorie razziali (1500–1700)* (Florence, 1977); Lee Eldridge Huddleston, *Origins of the American Indians: European Concepts, 1492–1729* (Austin, 1967).

5 Anthony Pagden, *The Fall of Natural Man: The American Indian and the Origins of Comparative Ethnology* (Cambridge, 1986); Pagden, *European Encounters with the New World* (New Haven, 1993).

6 Verónica Salles-Reese, 'The Apostle's Footprints in Ancient Perú: Christian Appropriation of Andean Myths', *Journal of Hispanic Philology* 16, no. 2 (1992), 185–93.

7 Jacques Lafaye, *Quetzalcóatl and Guadalupe: The Formation of Mexican National Consciousness, 1531–1813* (Chicago, 1976).

8 Thérèse Bouysse-Cassagne, 'De Empédocles a Tunupa: evangelización, hagiografia y mitos', in *Saberes y memorias en los Andes: in memoriam Thierry Saignes*, ed. Thérèse Bouysse-Cassagne (Lima and Paris, 1997), 157–212.

9 A pre-Adamite creation was not postulated until later: see Carlos Cañete, 'Ambivalent Origins: Isaac La Peyrère and the Politics of Historical Certainty in 17th Century Europe', (Unpublished paper presented at UCLA conference 'The Quest for Certainty in Early Modern Europe: From Inquisition to Inquiry, 1550–1700', 2016).

10 José de Acosta, Jane E. Mangan, ed., and Walter D. Mignolo, intro., *Natural and Moral History of the Indies*, tr. Frances M. López-Morillas (Durham, 2002), Bk I and V.

11 Seville, Archivo General de las Indias, Charcas, 143. See also Guillaume Candela, *Entre la pluma y la cruz: el clérigo Martín González y la desconocida historia de su defensa los indios del Paraguay: documentos inéditos (1543–1575)* (Asunción, 2018).

12 Antonio Ruiz de Montoya, *The Spiritual Conquest Accomplished by the Religious of the Society of Jesus in the Provinces of Paraguay, Paraná, Uruguay, and Tape*, tr. C. J. McNaspy (St. Louis, 1993), 79.

13 For one synthesis of these traditions, see Pedro de Ribadeneira, *Flos sanctorum, o libro de las vidas de los santos* (Madrid: Luis Sanchez, 1616), 879 (St Thomas).

14 Ines G. Županov, '"One Civility, but Multiple Religions": Jesuit Mission among St. Thomas Christians in India (16th–17th Centuries)', *Journal of Early Modern History* 9, no. 3 (2005), 303. See also Liam Matthew Brockey, 'Doubting Thomas: The Apostle and the Portuguese Empire in Early Modern Asia', in Van Liere, Ditchfield, and Louthan, *Sacred History*, 231–49; and for his tomb in Mylapore, Jorge Cañizares-Esguerra, *How to Write the History of the New World: Histories, Epistemologies, and Identities in the Eighteenth-Century Atlantic World* (Stanford, 2001), 222.

15 Louis-Andre Vigneras, 'Saint Thomas, Apostle of America', *Hispanic American Historical Review* 57, no. 1 (1977), 88.

16 Klaus Hilbert, 'A descoberta a partir da "Nova Gazeta da Terra do Brasil"', *Estudos ibero-americanos*, edição especial Brasil 500 anos (2000), 39–56.

17 Serafim Leite, ed., *Cartas do Brasil e mais escritos do P. Manuel da Nóbrega (opera omnia)*, Acta Universitatis Conimbrigensis (Coimbra, 1955), 441.

18 Hilbert, 'Descoberta', 52.

19 For the social function of drinking, see Thierry Saignes, 'The Colonial Condition in the Quechua-Aymara Heartland', in *The Cambridge History of the Native Peoples of the Americas*, ed. Stuart Schwartz and Frank Solomon (Cambridge, 1999), 73; more broadly,

Rebecca Earle, 'Indians and Drunkenness in Spanish America', *Cultures of Intoxication*, ed. Phil Withington and Angela McShane, *P&P* issue suppl. 9 (2014), 81–99; William B. Taylor, *Drinking, Homicide and Rebellion in Colonial Mexican Villages* (Stanford, 1979).

20 Antonio de Egaña and Enrique Fernández, eds., *Monumenta peruana (1600–1602)*, 8 vols. (Rome, 1981) VII: 94–100, letter of Rodrigo Cabredo to Claudio Aquaviva, Lima, 20 April 1600.

21 Astrid Windus, 'Putting Things in Order: Material Culture and Religious Communication in the Seventeenth Century Bolivian Altiplano', in *Image - Object - Performance: Mediality and Communication in Cultural Contact Zones of Colonial Latin America and the Philippines*, ed. Astrid Windus and Eberhard Crailsheim (Münster, 2013), 255.

22 Egaña and Fernández, *Monumenta peruana*.

23 Ibid., 95.

24 Jeremy R. Mumford, *Vertical Empire: The General Resettlement of Indians in the Colonial Andes* (Durham, 2012).

25 Saignes, 'Colonial Condition', 69, 85–6.

26 On these and other functions of oral traditions, see Thomas V. Cohen and Lesley K. Twomey, eds., *Spoken Word and Social Practice: Orality in Europe (1400–1700)* (Leiden, 2015).

27 Cohen and Twomey, *Spoken Word*, 73.

28 Kenneth Mills, *Idolatry and Its Enemies: Colonial Andean Religion and Extirpation, 1640–1750* (Princeton, 1997); Mills, 'The Naturalization of Andean Christianities', in *The Cambridge History of Christianity: Re-Formation and Expansion, c.1500–1660*, ed. Ronnie Po-chia Hsia (Cambridge, 2007), 504–35.

29 Estéban Goyzueta Mariaca, *Origen y reseña histórica de Carabuco* (La Paz, 1992); Manuel Rigoberto Paredes, *Los Siñani: tradiciones y crónicas del pueblo de Carabuco* (La Paz, 1968).

30 Rolena Adorno, 'Felipe Guaman Poma de Ayala: Native Writer and Litigant in Early Colonial Peru', in *The Human Tradition in Colonial Latin America*, ed. Kenneth J. Andrien (Lanham, MD, 2002), 140–63.

31 Felipe Guaman Poma de Ayala, *El primer nueva crónica y buen gobierno*, ed. Rolena Adorno, John V. Murra, and Jorge L. Urioste, 4th ed. (Madrid, 2006), 72–5, and see also 606–7.

32 Alonso Ramos Gavilán, *Historia del celebre santuario de Nuestra Señora de Copacabana, sus milagros, e invencion de la cruz de Carabuco* (Lima: Geronimo de Contreras, 1621), 52.

33 Gavilán, *Historia*, 51.

34 Ibid, 51.

35 Gavilán, *Historia*, 52.

36 Antonio de la Calancha, *Coronica moralizada del orden de San Augustin en el Peru con sucesos egenplares en esta monarquía* (Barcelona: Pedro Lacavalleria, 1638), (Bk 2, chapter 3), 325–9. For another treatment, Verónica Salles-Reese, *From Viracocha to the Virgin of Copacabana: Representation of the Sacred at Lake Titicaca* (Austin, 1997), 150–2. On these and other Andean chronicles, see Sabine MacCormack, *Religion in the Andes: Vision and Imagination in Early Colonial Peru* (Princeton, 1991); MacCormack, *On the Wings of Time: Rome, the Incas, Spain, and Peru* (Princeton, 2006).

37 Ruiz de Montoya, *The Spiritual Conquest*.

38 Sebastián Ferrero, 'La escritura y los procesos de occidentalización del mito y legitimación de la imagen en *Las postrimerías* de Carabuco', *Revista de indias* 75, no. 265 (2015): 645–80; Teresa Gisbert, *Iconografía y mitos indígenas en el arte* (La Paz, 1980), 659. To see the images: Teresa Gisbert, José de Mesa, and Carlos Rúa Landa, *Restauración de cuatro lienzos monumentales, serie de 'Las postrimerías': 'el purgatorio', 'el juicio final', 'el infierno', y 'la gloria', templo de Carabuco* (La Paz, 2005).

39 'Certificación de Doctor D. Gregorio de Lara, cura del pueblo de Timiribaco de los milagros que hacia la cruz de Carabuco', Madrid, Biblioteca Nacional, Ms. 18719–34, 384r-385v, who cites Hernando Castrillo, *Magia natural, o ciencia de filosofia oculta, con nuevas noticias de los mas profundos misterios y secretos del universo visible* (Trigueros, 1649), 81v-86v.

40 Salles-Reese, *From Viracocha to the Virgin of Copacabana*, 150.

41 Lewis Hanke, *The Spanish Struggle for Justice in the Conquest of America* (Dallas, 2002). For Anglophone critiques, J. N. Hillgarth, *The Mirror of Spain, 1500–1700: The Formation of a Myth* (Ann Arbor, 2000).

42 Luke Clossey, *Salvation and Globalization in the Early Jesuit Missions* (New York, 2008), 232.

43 Vigneras, 'Saint Thomas, Apostle of America', 88.

44 Adolph F. Bandelier, 'The Cross of Carabuco in Bolivia', *American Anthropologist* 6, no. 5 (1904), 615.

45 For Augustinian reports of crosses in Mexico: Iván González de la Puente, 'Primera parte de la choronica augustiniana de Mechoacan, en que se tratan, y escriven las vidas de nueve varones apostolicos, augustinianos (1624)', in *Colección de documentos inéditos y raros para la historia eclesiástica mexicana*, ed. Francisco Plancarte y Navarrete (1907) I: 308–10, and for a cross at Tepique and a stone in Jalisco; Bouysse-Cassagne, 'De Empédocles a Tunupa', Figure 2, at https://books.openedition.org/iheal/docannexe/image/812/img-3.jpg.

46 Thomas A. Abercrombie, *Pathways of Memory and Power: Ethnography and History Among an Andean People* (Madison, 1998), 131–2.

47 David Brading, *First America: The Spanish Monarchy, Creole Patriots and the Liberal State, 1492–1866* (Cambridge, 1991), 583–7.

48 After Lafaye's influential study (*supra*), a new generation of scholars has documented the 'patriotic epistemology' of late-colonial Latin American scholars: see Brading; Cañizares-Esguerra. For these chronicles as part of a 'creole archive', Anna H. More, *Baroque Sovereignty: Carlos de Sigüenza y Góngora and the Creole Archive of Colonial Mexico* (Philadelphia, 2013).

49 Jeffrey L. Klaiber, 'The Posthumous Christianization of the Inca Empire in Colonial Peru', *Journal of the History of Ideas* 37, no. 3 (1976), 507–20.

50 One step in this direction is Andy Wood, *The Memory of the People: Custom and Popular Senses of the Past in Early Modern England* (Cambridge, 2013).

11

THE BRITISH INVENTION OF THE WALDENSES

Stefano Villani

Medieval Waldensianism and the Reformation

The beginning of the preferential relationship between the Waldenses and the British dates back to 1655, when Charles Emmanuel II, Duke of Savoy, massacred hundreds of Protestant valley dwellers in an attempt to impose religious uniformity in Piedmont. The international Protestant community reacted with indignation and Oliver Cromwell launched a diplomatic offensive that made a decisive contribution to stopping the carnage. John Milton dedicated a famous sonnet to this event in which the Waldenses are celebrated for having 'kept' 'truth so pure of old, / when all our fathers worshiped stocks and stone'.[1]

Milton's words are key to understanding why the Waldenses played such an important part in Protestant imagery. The Waldenses were not only a Protestant group persecuted by Catholics, like the Huguenots or the Dutch Calvinists; they were a people who through their very existence answered the question of where the church of Christ had been during the long night of apostasy. Since the times of the apostles, these valleys had been inhabited by Christians renouncing the corruption of Rome and keeping the flame of the true faith alight.

It is now established by historiography that the medieval Waldenses originated with Waldo of Lyon, who organised a religious movement — the Poor of Lyon — in approximately 1170. Waldo and his followers were excommunicated in 1184 and he probably died between 1205 and 1207.[2] In the *Liber electorum*, an account of the history of the Waldenses written in the mid-fourteenth century, the name Peter is added to Valdo for the first time (Petrus Valdus). It was probably a symbolic choice juxtaposing Peter of Rome with Waldo, a true Peter, the restorer of the true Church of Jesus Christ.[3]

This origin was disputed for centuries by the Waldenses, who dated their foundation back to a much earlier era.[4] Indeed, three founding myths were developed over time in Waldensian culture and historiography. The first traced the origins of the Waldensian Church to the apostolic age (as referred to in Milton's verse), the second referenced the Constantinian era and the third mentioned the Carolingian period with Claudius, Bishop of Turin. These narratives have always been contested by the Catholic Church and were abandoned by the Waldenses in the 1880s.

Before investigating these foundation myths, it is worth highlighting that an intense heated historiographical debate has developed — above all since the mid-1980s — about relations between the community gathered around Waldo, the medieval Waldenses, and the post-Reformation Waldensian communities. As Peter Biller recently pointed out in a brilliant historiographical article in *Past and Present*, a real historical turning point concerning these issues occurred in 1984 with the almost simultaneous publication of two books.[5]

The first, *Valdesi e Valdismi Medievali* by the Italian medievalist Giovanni Grado Merlo underlined the wealth of influences of the various heretical movements of the fourteenth century on the movement created by Waldo. The second, *The Reformation of the Heretics* by the British early-modernist Euan Cameron, demolished many of the legends that developed around Waldensian history.[6]

For the first time Cameron explicitly questioned the continuity between the medieval Waldenses and the Geneva-inspired churches founded in what were later called the Waldensian valleys. Both volumes have been decisive in radically changing the historiographical perspective of scholars working on these issues. Until the 1980s all historians took it for granted that there were Waldensian 'communities' who lived a secretive life in the valleys in Piedmont and in some areas of Puglia and Calabria, where the immigration of Piedmontese Waldensian groups in the Middle Ages led to the establishment of churches.[7] In recent years, although without Cameron's iconoclastic straightforwardness, a new generation of historians seem to believe that no formal or structured Waldensian congregations existed in the valleys of Piedmont. On the contrary, they emphasise that these places were essentially a radical milieu from the Middle Ages onwards, with Waldensian *barbes* playing a major role as itinerant preachers up to the first few decades of the sixteenth century. It was this radical underground tradition that favoured the adhesion to Reformed ideas by whole villages in the 1550s. From the very beginning, the Protestant churches established in the valleys based their identity on the memory of the medieval Waldenses. The direct continuity between medieval Waldensianism and the Waldenses of the early modern age was therefore an identity myth constructed to claim the 'national' origin of the Calvinist churches of the valleys.[8]

The sources at our disposal show that the initial contact between the Piedmontese *barbes* and the French reformers dates back to at least 1526, when, according to seventeenth-century reports, a certain '*barbe* Martin' of the Val Luserna brought Reformed books to the Piedmontese valleys.[9] In the autumn of 1530, two Waldensian *barbes* from Provence, Georges Morel and Pierre Masson, were sent to Switzerland to establish a link with the Reformed leaders, meeting with Oecolampadius and Martin Bucer.[10]

After this initial contact, the first Protestant missionaries arrived in the valleys in the early 1530s, including Guillaume Farel in 1532. Waldensian historiography described the meetings between these missionaries and the valley dwellers as real assemblies of people where they decided that the Waldensian churches would adopt the principles of the Reformation. There was special focus on a synod supposedly held in Chanforan in Val d'Angrogna on 12 September 1532. The outcome of this discussion was said to be a declaration of faith, which was later published in the seventeenth-century official stories of the Waldensian Church, based on a manuscript currently preserved in Dublin. Although the sources at our disposal unequivocally show numerous traces of missionary action by French and Swiss reformers in the valleys, it is feasible to doubt that a proper council was ever held. Once again it is more logical to interpret this narrative as an attempt to emphasise the Italian origin of the Protestant churches that were later established in the valleys.[11]

Protestant proselytism continued throughout the 1530s. A French translation of the Bible by Olivétan published in Neuchâtel in 1535 directly addressed the Waldenses in the preface.[12] Between the end of 1537 and the beginning of 1538, the government of the valleys of Angrogna, Luserna, Perosa, and Germanasca was entrusted to Guillaume Farel's brother for a few months. In this role he favoured the sympathisers of the Reformation who lived there. They duly proselytised the valley dwellers, taking advantage of the end of persecution and the difficulties in controlling the area faced by the local aristocracy.[13]

It would be a mistake, however, to think that most of the population of the valleys adhered to Protestantism. It is indeed extremely significant that no mention is made of either Waldenses or heretics in Cardinal Innocenzo Cibo's reports of his 1545 pastoral visit, demonstrating that the parishes were, at least formally, still Catholic.[14] It was only when the first Calvinist preachers arrived in the valleys in 1555 that preaching became public and conversions multiplied. The first Protestant temples were built in Angrogna, Pellice and Luserna, and ministers were sent from Geneva for these congregations. The ministers sent by the *Vénérable Compagnie des Pasteurs* included the Neapolitan Scipione Lentolo, who became the minister in Angrogna in 1559 (expelled in 1566, he spent the last years of his life in Valtellina).[15] As far as is known, at the time of his arrival only two ministers of the Waldensian Church had been *barbes*, Gillio de Gillio and François Laurens.[16]

On 15 February 1560, Emanuele Filiberto of Nice issued an edict that forbade his subjects from listening to 'Lutheran' preachers in the Lucerne valley (in Catholic documentation of the time, the term 'Lutheran' indicated generically any Protestant). The Protestants of the valleys armed themselves and successfully opposed the execution of the edict: the Peace of Cavour of 1561 guaranteed the free exercise of Waldensian worship in certain defined places in the valleys.[17]

Starting in 1563, synods were organised to coordinate the actions of the individual churches. A synod at Villar Pellice in 1564 established that the *Ordonnances* of Geneva should be followed as closely as possible. From that point onwards, the Waldensian Church in the valleys was to all effects Calvinist.

However, the continuity between Waldensianism and Protestantism was the pivot around which the construction of the early modern Waldensian identity revolved. According to this narrative, the Protestant congregations were not founded as a result of the preaching of foreign ministers. Instead, it was the Waldenses themselves who first established contact and decided to adhere to Protestantism.

Early modern Protestant and Waldensian historiography

The symbolic value of the claimed continuity between medieval Waldensianism and Protestantism was fully grasped by both the Catholic and Reformed churches. On the one hand, the Holy Office issued a decree on 2 February 1554 against the 'memory and the reputation' ('contra memoriam et famam') of Peter Waldo.[18] On the other hand, the battle over memory nurtured Protestant historiography. Jean Crespin spoke of Waldensian persecution in his martyrology of 1554, presenting the medieval heretics as precursors to the Reformation.[19] In his 1556 catalogue of witnesses to the truth, Flacius Illyricus published a long article on the Waldenses in which he reconstructed Waldo's biography and narrated their persecution in Provence.[20]

In around 1568, the aforementioned Scipione Lentolo completed a first draft of a history of the Waldenses in Italian which was essentially based on Flacius and Crespin for the part preceding his arrival in the valleys as pastor of Angrogna. Probably because of his pastoral duties, publication of this work never came to fruition, even if Lentolo returned to work on his text several times. The final draft was completed in 1595 and the following year Lentolo expressed his desire to have it published in Latin. However, his book was not published in the original Italian or the Latin version and remained in manuscript form until 1906.[21]

Another manuscript history, the *Historia breve e vera de gl'affari de i Valdesi delle Valli*, was written in January 1587. Largely based on Flacius, the text is divided into two distinct parts. The first of these consists of a series of 'Twenty questions and answers over the vicissitudes and religion of the Waldenses of the Valleys', outlining a history of Waldensian persecution and doctrines (with a brief history of the Val d'Angrogna). The second part is a list of 62 'Names of *barbes*, that is Waldensian Ministers' to underline the continuity between medieval Waldensianism and the Reformed Waldensian Church. The anonymous manuscript was attributed to Gerolamo Miolo, a former Dominican turned Waldensian pastor in Angrogna who had collected documents on the history of the Waldensian churches during his ministry.[22]

During the religious wars in France in November 1585, the Huguenots conquered Embrun and came into possession of some inquisitorial documents against the Waldenses of the Dauphine and the valley of Pragelato. The Protestant Synod of Embrun in 1603 decided to publish a history of these medieval heretics using these manuscripts. In 1605 the work was entrusted to the Lyonnais Jean-Paul Perrin, then a minister in Nyons.[23] His history of the Waldenses and the

Albigensians was published in Geneva in 1618.[24] This is the first printed history specifically dedicated to the Waldenses and although it is the product of a Huguenot Reformed environment, it is the founding moment of Waldensian historiography. The narrative of their history covers the period up to the end of the sixteenth century with extensive references to Morel and Masson's meetings with Oecolampadius.[25]

In September 1620, a year after the publication of the second volume of Perrin's history, the Synod of the Waldensian churches in Pramollo commissioned pastor Pietro Gillio (Pierre Gilles) to write an official history of the Waldenses continuing from where Perrin's narrative had stopped. Although the initial project was to write it in Italian, the author opted for the French language. The work took a long time to complete and was only published in 1644 with the title *Histoire ecclésiastique des Églises Réformées recueillies en quelques Vallées de Piedmont, autrefois appelées Églises Vaudoises.* [26] After briefly summarising the vicissitudes of medieval Waldensianism, the text focused on the sixteenth and seventeenth centuries up to the years immediately preceding the publication.

In 1646 another synod commissioned a new history of the Waldenses from the *modérateur* Jean Léger. It is possible that the need for a second work, written just two years after the publication of Gillio's volume, indicates some level of dissatisfaction amongst the Waldensian pastors. However, it is more likely that the main reason was that, beyond the history itself, the Waldenses were interested in publishing a collection of original theological and historical documents, a sort of reasoned anthology of Waldensian history and doctrine. They entrusted Léger with some late-medieval theological manuscripts and the inquisitorial reports from Embrun, which Perrin had probably returned after the publication of his history. Léger almost certainly concluded a large part of his work in 1655, the fatal year when the valleys were devastated by the Duke of Savoy's troops. He escaped the massacre and took refuge in France, where he wrote an appeal to Oliver Cromwell. To solicit English intervention in favour of the persecuted Waldenses, Léger made explicit reference to the apostolic origin of their churches: 'We ought not to forsake those Churches who can prove their succession from the very time of the Apostles'.[27]

In England, the history of the Waldenses was well known long before the tragic events of 1655 largely thanks to the chapter on them in John Foxe's *Book of Martyrs* (from the 1583 edition). Furthermore, the theologian James Ussher had carried out research on the Waldenses for his *De Christianarum Ecclesiarum successione & statu*, published in 1613, in which he argued that even before Luther there had been continuity of a visible church of true Christians on earth.[28] Ussher had obtained some fifteenth-century Waldensian theological manuscripts and copies of the inquisitorial trials, probably from the same source used by Jean-Paul Perrin. In 1624 Samson Lennard translated Perrin's history into English with the significant title *Luthers Fore-Runners or a Cloud of Witnesses, deposing for the Protestant Faith, Gathered Together in the Historie of the Waldenses.* [29] It was this familiarity with Waldensian history combined with Cromwell's desire to present himself as the leader of the Calvinist International that prompted direct English interest in events in the valleys. After the tragic events of 1655, the English translation of Perrin's book was republished thanks to the input of the Protector under the title *Matchlesse Crueltie declared at large in the ensuing History of the Waldenses*.[30] Newsbooks, ballads, pamphlets, and leaflets were distributed in the streets of London. Fasting was proclaimed and a national collect was promoted. Milton wrote his famous sonnet.[31]

Cromwell decided to send a diplomatic representative to France, Switzerland, and Savoy, and duly appointed Samuel Morland, a young intellectual with previous major diplomatic experience in Sweden.[32] Before leaving England, he had a meeting with Archbishop Ussher, who encouraged him to take advantage of his mission in continental Europe to collect documents on Waldensian history.[33] Morland played a decisive role in the peace between the Waldenses and the Duke of Savoy, remaining in Piedmont from May to July 1655. He then moved to Geneva, where he remained until December 1656.[34] There, Jean Léger entrusted him with the Waldensian theological and historical manuscripts he had used to write his history of the Waldensian churches, as well as the first draft of his historical introduction.[35]

Upon his return to England, Morland translated all this material into English, undoubtedly with Léger's consent, and in 1658 published the two volumes of his *History of the Evangelical Churches in the Valleys of Piedmont*, which presented the aforementioned theological and historical primary sources (often with parallel original text).[36]

In 1669 Jean Léger published his *Histoire générale des Eglises Evangeliques des vallées du Piemont ou Vaudoises*, in which he essentially reproduced the same texts used by Morland eleven years earlier. The texts were published in roughly the same order in which they had featured in the English book, even though, in this case, there was a French translation and slightly different editorial criteria. The final part of the volume narrated events following Morland's mission and was therefore completely new. Both Catholic and Protestant historiography has tended to consider Léger's text as completely dependent on Morland's history, if not a form of outright plagiarism. However, it is much more natural to think, as we have said, that Léger had given the English diplomat a manuscript of his history at an advanced stage with the French translation of the original documents.[37]

Cromwell's interest established a connection between the Waldenses and England that lasted for centuries. Since the battle in favour of the Waldenses was also played out at the level of historical memory, Morland deposited the documents he had received at Cambridge University Library and published a list of the 19 volumes that contained them to dispel any doubt about their authenticity.[38] The manuscripts owned by Ussher were later deposited at Trinity College Library in Dublin,[39] while others were left in Geneva by Antoine and Jean Léger.[40] Together with those held in Paris, these are the major collections of medieval Waldensian manuscripts.[41]

In response to Bossuet's *Histoire des variations*, Pierre Allix, a Huguenot minister who had found asylum in England after the Revocation of the Edict of Nantes, published *Some Remarks upon the ecclesiastical History of the Ancient Churches of Piedmont* in 1689 and *Remarks upon the ecclesiastical History of the Ancient Churches of the Albigenses* in 1692.[42]

From the eighteenth century onwards there was an increase in the number of histories of the Waldenses both in French and English. The main reason for the interest shown towards the Waldenses was precisely the idea that they were the living answer to the question of where the church of Christ had been before Luther. It was therefore central to Waldensian historiography not only to enhance the continuity between medieval and Reformed Waldensianism but to antedate its origin to the apostolic age. For this reason, starting with Flacius Illyricus, the foundation myth was developed whereby the pure and uncorrupted original form of Christianity was always professed in the isolation of the valleys, which were supposedly Christianised by the same St Paul that stopped in the Cottian Alps to preach the gospel on his journey to Rome. Alternatively, the valleys could have been Christianised by those fleeing Rome during the third-century persecution by Decius and Valerian. Numerous Waldensian and Protestant works refer to the apostolic origins of the Waldenses. The matter is discussed by Jean-Paul Perrin in his *Histoire des Albigeois et des Vaudois* of 1618, Jacques Brez in his *Histoire des Vaudois* of 1796,[43] Pierre Boyer in the *Abrégé de Histoire des Vaudois* of 1691, and finally in all the historical works by the Waldensian pastor Alexis Muston in the 1830s and 1840s, as well as his 1854 *The Israël des Alpes*, which for decades was considered the official and standard history of the Waldenses.[44]

The myth that attributed the birth of the Waldenses to the Constantinian era claimed that at the time of the imperial donation which awarded the Bishop of Rome civil jurisdiction over the Western Roman Empire, a certain Leo warned his friend Pope Sylvester of the serious consequences that power and wealth could have for the Church. His appeal fell on deaf ears and he was banished from Rome. He reached the valleys of Piedmont and supposedly originated the movement of the Waldenses. This would be the reason why the Waldenses were also called Leonists (in all likelihood, however, the term comes from Lyon, Waldo's place of origin).[45] This opinion circulated widely among the medieval Waldenses and was reported and refuted by the Inquisitor Raniero Sacconi in around 1250.[46] A document drafted by the Inquisition of Passau already pointed out in 1266 that some people claimed that the Waldenses originated at the time of Pope Sylvester, while others claimed that they dated back to the times of the apostles.[47] This narrative is found in the aforementioned *Liber electorum* and is summarised in the *Epistola fratrum de Italia*, written by some Italian Waldenses and addressed to the Austrian brothers.[48] In the sixteenth century this Waldensian theory was reported by many Catholic authors, starting with the Bishop of Turin Claude de Seyssel in his *Disputationes adversus errores ... Valdensium* (1520), in order to deny that it had any basis.[49]

The third foundation myth attributed the Waldensian doctrine to Claudius, the ninth-century Bishop of Turin. He was an iconoclast and an opponent of the cults of the Virgin Mary, the saints, and relics. Although a native of Catalonia, some historians argued wrongly that he was Scottish.[50] The myth was supported by Morland, Léger, and the Calvinist Jacques Basnage De Beauval in his *Histoire de la religion des églises reformées* (Rotterdam, 1690).[51] This theory became extremely widespread in the 1800s. It was referenced by pastor Peyran when questioned about Waldensian origins by Napoleon and openly endorsed by Amedeo Bert in 1849.[52] The Waldensian publishing house, which still exists, was named Claudiana in 1855 in honour of this bishop.[53]

The three myths intertwine with a mutually enhancing effect. From the apostolic age, the Piedmontese valleys were home to a purer Christianity. From time to time they provided shelter for people fleeing from the corruption of Rome, like Leo at the time of Pope Sylvester or Claudius at the time of Charlemagne. Finally, Waldo's followers sought refuge in the Alpine valleys. Waldo was presented as a learned man and an inspired preacher. He was therefore attributed with a central role, but was not seen as a founder.

These incredible genealogies are interwoven in the twin works of Léger and Morland, and have long influenced the imagery of European Protestantism. This historiographical Protestant and Waldensian narrative was openly attacked by Catholic historians. To cite an example, the myth of Waldensianism predating the twelfth century was attacked by Bossuet in his *History of the Variations of the Protestant Churches*, published in 1688.[54] With the emergence of historical criticism, however, there were even historians in the Protestant field who demolished the foundation of these pious legends. The mythical past was debunked in the 1920s by the Lutheran historians August Neander and Johann Karl Ludwig Gieseler, and later by the Reformed historians Charles Schmidt and Johann Jakob Herzog. Nevertheless, these historiographical works were not well received by either the Waldensian historians of the time or the British evangelicals who, as we shall see, took the Waldensian cause to heart after the Restoration in 1815. Not surprisingly, Muston opened his *Histoire des Vaudous des vallées du Piémont* in 1834 with an open protest against Protestant historiography, which traced the origins of the Waldenses back to Peter Waldo.[55]

The Archbishop of Pinerolo, André Charvaz, replied to Muston's work with his *Recherches historiques sur la véritable origin des Vaudois* in 1836, triggering a real historiographical war.[56] It was only with the 1880 publication by Waldensian pastor and historian Emilio Comba, *History of the Waldenses of Italy, from their origin to the Reformation* (*Valdo e i valdesi avanti la Riforma*), that it was openly admitted that the Waldenses did not predate Waldo of Lyon.[57]

The second British discovery of the Waldenses

We have dwelt on the Waldensian founding myths and the heated historiographical debate that developed around them because they played a fundamental role in the construction of an imaginary Waldensianism in Britain. This directly influenced the growing interest in the Waldenses among the British churches and the English crown, as well as the attempt to invent the Waldensian Church as an Italian 'national' church.

Starting with the Glorious Revolution, England regularly paid subsidies to support the Waldensian valleys. Although most of these were suspended during the French Wars, the Waldenses attempted to have them restored immediately after the fall of Napoleon. At this time the Waldenses needed political support from their foreign friends in addition to financial assistance, because Victor Emmanuel I restored all the *ancien régime* anti-Waldensian legislation in 1814. England did not restore the 'royal subsidy' forthwith but was extremely active in helping the Waldensian cause in the diplomatic sphere, making sure that the persecution was not compounded.

At the same time as the British diplomatic action in their favour there was an explosion of pro-Waldensian mania in England. Numerous British clerics travelled to the Waldensian valleys during the nineteenth century and published accounts of their experiences on returning.[58] The first in a long line of visitors and friends of the Waldenses was Thomas Sims who, after visiting the valleys in 1814, played a decisive part in the renewed attention. Born into a wealthy Welsh family, Sims was a Church of England cleric who lived most of his life in Bristol and actively participated in the activities of both the Church Missionary Society and the Bible Society.[59]

As soon as Sims returned to Britain, he (anonymously) published a *Brief Memoir Respecting the Waldenses*, 'to interest British Christians in favour of our unnoticed and almost forgotten fellow-Christians of the Valleys of Piedmont'.[60] Sims recounted the history of the Waldensians in his booklet, taking their apostolic origins for granted. It is highly significant that he presented the figure of the *modérateur de la Table vaudoise* ('moderator' of the Table) as a bishop and the original structure of the Waldensian ecclesial government as episcopal in nature.

This is a fundamental theme in what can be defined as an 'invention' of the Waldenses in the nineteenth-century British imagination. It was in this period that the question of apostolic succession took shape as a major identity factor of the Church of England. If the moderator was a bishop, the Waldensian Church could boast not only that it had been the only flame burning during the long night of apostasy that started with Constantine, but also that its ministry was based on the uninterrupted transmission of spiritual authority from the Apostles. In 1826 Sims published a collection of writings by the Waldensian pastor and intellectual Jean-Rodolphe Peyran. In his introduction, Sims identified the origin of the Waldenses as the opposition to the decrees of the Second Council of Nicea by the Bishop of Turin. The episcopal function of the Waldensian Church moderator was once again emphasised and the Waldensian confession of faith was presented as essentially equivalent to the Articles of the Church of England. Despite his evangelical views, Sims presented both the Church of England and the Waldensian Church as third ways between continental Protestantism and Roman Catholicism.[61]

In the winter of 1822, the Anglican Reverend William Stephen Gilly went to the valleys. On his return to England he published an extensive account of his trip, which also included a short history of the Waldenses: *Narrative on an Excursion to the Mountains of Piedmont … and Researches among the Vaudois or Waldensians* (London 1824). The book was a huge success, leading to multiple re-editions. Gilly's exceptional organisational skills enabled him to mobilise the attention of the British public towards the Waldenses and he became the reference point for all British initiatives in their favour. It was thanks to his fundraising that a hospital and neighbourhood or rural schools were built in the valleys. He then managed to arrange the resumption of payments of the British subsidies. Once again, a key element in Gilly's historical narrative was the idea that Waldo had not been the founder of the Waldensians but had joined a pre-existing church.[62]

Gilly's book was decisive in arousing the interest of John Charles Beckwith, a British-Canadian former officer that had been wounded at Waterloo. After reading it, he first went to the valleys in 1828 and returned every year until 1850, generally in the autumn to spend the whole winter there.[63]

Like Sims, Beckwith was convinced of the episcopal nature of the office of moderator and wrote to the Waldensian pastors in the autumn of 1837, inviting them to transform it into an office for life. In 1850 he suggested that they adopt a liturgy he had drafted in imitation of the Anglican rite. Both proposals fell on deaf ears, but the streams of money from Great Britain mostly thanks to his work did not dry up. The extremely poor valleys became filled with hospitals, schools, and places of worship built in a sober North-European style. Every little village in the valleys had its own small fully-equipped school as a result of Beckwith's work.

Anglican activism brought the situation of the Italian Waldensians to the attention of all the British with an interest in religious matters (we can find an ironic reference to this pro-Waldensian mania, for example, in George Eliot's *Middlemarch*).[64] Soon, the Free Church of Scotland, born out of a schism of the Presbyterian Church in 1843 on the crucial question of the relationship between churches and state, began to deal with them specifically. Robert Stewart, who had been in Livorno since 1845, was the coordinator of all activities of the Free Church in Italy and the Mediterranean. He made contact with the Waldensian pastors, emphasising how Calvinist theology and the Presbyterian form of his church were much closer to Waldensianism than the doctrines and structure of the Church of England.[65]

The pastors of the valleys skilfully managed to maintain good relations with everyone, obtaining funds from multiple sources. When the revolts of 1848 led to the emancipation of the Waldensians of the Kingdom of Sardinia, they managed to 'enjoy all the civil and political rights along with the Catholic subjects'.[66]

Emancipation took place after thirty years of intellectual exchange and economic support from British Protestantism. Beginning with Sims, who started this renewed British interest in the Waldenses, the main motivation behind the actions of people like Beckwith, Gilly, and Stewart (as well as the many dozens of lesser known benefactors and missionaries) was the idea that the Waldensian Church had been preserved to convert the whole of Italy. During these decades of the discovery and re-invention of Waldenses, the British — both Anglicans and Presbyterians — gradually managed to convince the prudent Waldensian pastors that their duty was to spread the gospel outside the valleys.

The margins of freedom in 1848 finally allowed this project to unfold. Since the Waldensians of Calabria had been massacred in 1561, there had been only thirteen Waldensian parishes in the valleys. The temple of Turin was consecrated in 1853. As it was the first temple built outside the valleys, it symbolically marked the drive towards the missionary commitment of the Waldenses. Another temple was opened in Genoa in 1855. Following the Unification of Italy, practically every urban centre in the country had its own Waldensian congregation.

The history of the Waldenses was constructed around their mythical memory, exalting both their antiquity and their independent origin from Protestantism. As the 'pure remnant' of the primitive Church, the Waldenses became central to Protestant memory and imagination from the very beginning of the Reformation. They were not simply a Calvinist church: as we have seen, the early modern conversion of the inhabitants of the Piedmontese valleys to Protestantism was considered only as a 'moment' in their long history and not a real beginning. Waldenses were protestants before Protestantism, so their sixteenth-century encounter with Reformation was regarded as the recognition of a common identity. Their mythical apostolic past sparked intense interest in the medieval Waldenses and nourished the memory battles between the conflicting Protestant and Catholic historiographies.

The foundation myths of the Waldensian Church were fundamental to fostering interest and economic support from British churches. This contributed enormously to what we have defined as the second British rediscovery of the Waldenses at the end of the Napoleonic Wars in the early 1800s. At the time, continental Europe was a missionary field for British Protestantism and streams of money poured into the valleys in an attempt to 'invent' what could be termed Anglican Waldensianism.[67] Due to a 'heterogenesis of ends', the Anglican commitment placed Italy and the Waldenses at the centre of the European missionary endeavours of the Free Church of Scotland. The competition between Anglicans and Presbyterians contributed decisively to the Waldensian decision to leave their valleys and become a national church.

However, we know, Italy did not convert to Protestantism. This diminished gradually the British interest in Italian religious life.[68] But the nineteenth-century period of intense Anglo-Waldensian exchanges was absolutely decisive in pushing the Waldensian Church to abandon its Piedmontese identity and become an Italian church. It was therefore the memory of a past that to some extent never existed which built the identity of the Waldensians of today.

Notes

1 Enea Balmas and Grazia Zardini Lana, eds., *La vera relazione di quanto è accaduto nelle persecuzioni e i massacri dell'anno 1655*; Balmas and Lana, eds., *Le 'Pasque Piemontesi' del 1655 nelle testimonianze dei protagonisti* (Turin, 1987); Martino Laurenti, *I confini della comunità: Conflitto europeo e guerra religiosa nelle comunità valdesi del Seicento* (Turin, 2015).

2 Peter Biller, *The Waldenses, 1170–1530: Between a Religious Order and a Church* (Burlington, VT, 2001); Euan Cameron, *The Reformation of the Heretics: The Waldenses of the Alps 1480–1580* (Oxford, 1984); Cameron, *Waldenses. Rejections of Holy Church in Medieval Europe* (Oxford, 2000); G. G. Merlo, *Eretici e inquisitori nella società piemontese del Trecento* (Turin, 1977); Merlo, *Valdesi e valdismi medievali I: Itinerari e proposte di ricerca* (Turin, 1984); Merlo, *Valdesi e valdismi medievali II. Identità valdese nella storia e nella storiografia: Studi e discussioni* (Turin, 1991); Gabriel Audisio, *The Waldensian Dissent: Persecution and Survival* (Cambridge, 1999); Audisio, *Preachers by Night: The Waldensian Barbes* (Leiden, 2007).

3 Grado G. Merlo, *Valdo: L'eretico di Lione* (Turin, 2010).

4 Peter Biller, 'Medieval Waldensians' Construction of the Past', *Proceedings of the Huguenot Society* 25 (1989), 39–54, now in Biller, *The Waldenses 1170–1530*, 191–206. Albert de Lange, 'Dalla Riforma al Valdismo in Val Pragelato: 1555–1564', in *Presenze religiose, migrazioni e lingua occitana nell'alta Val Chisone tra il '400 e il '500 dai conflitti alla convivenza*, ed. Raimondo Genre (Villaretto–Roure, 2011), 55–126.

5 Peter Biller, 'Goodbye to Waldensianism?' *P&P* 192, no. 1 (2006), 3–33.

6 See 'Goodbye to Waldensianism?' note 2.

7 In 1561 a crusade completely eradicated the 'Waldensian' communities of southern Italy, see Pierroberto Scaramella, *L'Inquisizione romana e i valdesi di Calabria (1554–1703)* (Napoli, 1999); Alfonso Tortora, *Presenze valdesi nel Mezzogiorno d'Italia (secoli XV–XVII)* (Salerno, 2004). For the bibliography on the Waldenses of southern Italy see the review-article by Simone Maghenzani, '"Valdesi nel Mediterraneo" e Riforma italiana: Contributi per una discussione', *Bollettino della Società di Studi Valdesi* (hereafter *BSSV*) 207 (2010), 181–91.

8 de Lange, *Dalla Riforma al Valdismo in Val Pragelato: 1555–1564*, 55–126; Susanna Peyronel Rambaldi, ed., *Identità valdesi tra passato e presente* (Turin, 2016).

9 Cameron, *The Reformation of the Heretics*, 131–2, 134; Giovanni Gonnet, 'Rapporti tra i valdesi franco-italiani e i riformatori d'Oltralpe prima di Calvino', in *Ginevra e l'Italia, Raccolta di studi promossa dalla Facoltà Valdese di Teologia di Roma*, D. Cantimori, L. Firpo, and G. Spini (Firenze, 1959), 1–63 (6, 12).

10 Cameron, *The Reformation of the Heretics*, 135–6, 202–3, 205. See Giovanni Gonnet, *Rapporti tra i valdesi franco-italiani*, 7–9

11 Cameron, *The Reformation of the Heretics*. See also S. Peyronel Rambaldi, 'I riformatori di lingua francese e 'les eglises dressées' delle valli valdesi: Gli anni del silenzio', in *Riformati, cattolici e organizzazioni ecclesiastiche nelle valli nella seconda metà del Cinquecento: Dai conflitti alla convivenza*, ed. P. Pazé (Perosa Argentina, 2015), 15–47.

12 Georges Casalis and Bernard Roussel, eds., *Olivétan, traducteur de la Bible* (Paris, 1987).

13 Laurenti, *I confini della comunità*.

14 A. Pascal, 'Comunità eretiche e chiese cattoliche nelle valli valdesi, secondo le relazioni delle visite pastorali del Peruzzi e del Broglia', *BSSV* 30 (1912), 62; see Cameron, *The Reformation of the Heretics*, 146.

15 Augusto Armand-Hugon, 'Popolo e Chiesa alle valli dal 1532 al 1561', *BSSV* 110, (1961), 16; Cameron, *The Reformation of the Heretics*, 157–8, 173–4, 179–80; Emanuele Fiume, *Scipione Lentolo 1525–1599: 'Quotidie laborans evangelii causa'* (Turin, 2003).

16 Cameron, *Waldenses*, 270. On the passage from Waldensian *Barbes* to Calvinist Pastors see Daniele Tron, *Un profondo mutamento: Da barba a pastori*, in *Valdismo e cattolicesimo prima della Riforma (1488–1555): Dai conflitti alla convivenza*, ed. Raimondo Genre (Villaretto–Roure, 2010), 253–92.

17 Pierpaolo Merlin, 'Dal Piemonte all'Europa: I risvolti antiereticali di Emanuele Filiberto di Savoia, in *Frontiere geografiche e religiose in Italia: Fattori di conflitto e comunicazione nel XVI e XVII, BSSV* 177 (1995), 74–86.

18 Scaramella, *L'Inquisizione Romana*, 34.

19 J. Crespin, *Actes des martyrs* (Geneva, 1554); see Cameron, *The Reformation of the Heretics*, 199–200, 237–9.

20   Matthias Flacius Illyricus, *Catalogus Testium Veritatis* (Basel, 1556), 712; see Cameron, *The Reformation of the Heretics*, 244.

21   S. Lentolo, *Historia delle grandi e crudeli persecutioni fatte ai tempi nostri in Provenza, Calabria e Piemonte contro il popolo che chiamano valdese e delle gran cose operate dal Signore in loro aiuto e favore*, ed. T. Gay (Torre Pellice, 1906). See also Cameron, *The Reformation of the Heretics*, 230; G. Gonnet, 'Su un Nuovo Manoscritto della "Historia delle grandi e crudeli persecutioni" di Scipione Lentolo', *BSSV* 163 (1988), 41; Jean-François Gilmont, *Aux origines de l'historiographie vaudoise du XVIe Siècle: Jean Crespin, Etienne Noël et Scipione Lentolo*, in *I Valdesi e l'Europa* (Torre Pellice, 1982), 169; Federico Zuliani, 'Scrivendo e riscrivendo "ad meam historiam locupletandam": La Historia delle grandi e crudeli persecutioni tra Scipione e Paolo Lentolo', *Bibliothèque d'Humanisme et Renaissance* 79, no. 1 (2017), 169–85.

22   Cambridge, Cambridge University Library, Dd. 3.35, cc. 31–41v; see Gerolamo Miolo, *Historia breve & vera de gl'affari de i valdesi delle valli*, ed. Enea Balmas (Turin, 1971); Cameron, *The Reformation of the Heretics*, 233–4. See also Giovanni Gonnet, 'Note sulla storiografia valdese dei secoli XVI e XVII', *Rivista di storia e letteratura religiosa* 10 (1974), 335–66.

23   Marina Benedetti, *Il 'santo bottino': Circolazione di manoscritti valdesi nell'Europa del Seicento* (Turin, 2006), 21–2, 25–8, 34, 40–1, 54–5.

24   Cameron, *The Reformation of the Heretics*, 234–5; A. Muston, 'Note sur l'origine des deux premières histoires des vaudois (Perrin et Gilles)', *Bulletin de la Société d'Histoire Vaudoise* 1 (1884), 23–6; Benedetti, *Il 'santo bottino'*, 10–6, 19–23.

25   Cf. Miolo, *Historia Breve*, 8–13.

26   P. Gilles, *Histoire ecclésiastique des églises vaudoises* (Geneve, 1644); see Laurenti, '"Les vrays vaudois originaires": La nascita dell'identità valligiana nelle comunità valdesi del Piemonte Seicentesco', in Rambaldi, *Identità Valdesi tra Passato e Presente*, 108–9; Laurenti, *I confini della comunità*, 74, 125; J. Jalla, 'Les historiens Perrin et Gilles', in J. Jalla, *Glanures d'histoire vaudoise* (Torre Pellice, 1936).

27   Benedetti, *Il 'santo bottino'*, 77.

28   See Cameron, *The Reformation of the Heretics*, 247. Earlier, in 1611, Ussher had asked Isaac Casaubon about some Waldensian manuscript that would have been in the possession of Joseph Juste Scaliger; see Benedetti, *Il 'santo bottino'*, 54–5.

29   Another edition was published with a different title: *Bloudy rage of that great Antechrist of Rome and his superstitious adherents, against the true Church of Christ and the faithfull professors of his Gospell* (London: [Richard Field, John Beale, Eliots Court Press, and Thomas Snodham] for Nathanael Newbery, 1624); see Enea Balmas and Ester Menascé, 'L'opinione pubblica inglese e le "Pasque Piemontesi": Nuovi documenti' *BSSV* 150 (1981), 3–26 (8); Balmas and Lana, *Vera Relazione*, 158–9. On the translator see J. Broadway, 'Sampson Lennard (d.1633)' *ODNB*.

30   Balmas-Menascé, *L'opinione pubblica inglese*, 9; Laurenti, *I confini della comunità*, 201.

31   Balmas-Menascé, *L'opinione pubblica inglese*, 9; Tullio Contino, 'L'intervento diplomatico inglese a favore dei valdesi in occasione delle Pasque Piemontesi del 1655', *BSSV* 94 (1953), 35–43; William Mc Comish, 'Reazioni inglesi alla "primavera di sangue" valdese del 1655', *BSSV* 149 (1981), 3–10; Giorgio Vola, 'Cromwell e i Valdesi: Una Vicenda non del tutto chiarita', *BSSV* 149 (1981), 11–37; Vola, '"Oche selvagge" nelle valli valdesi: La presenza e il ruolo dei mercenari irlandesi nelle Pasque Piemontesi', *BSSV* 181 (1997), 234–65.

32   Vola, *A proposito di Samuel Morland*; Pierre Lombart, 'Sir Samuel Morland (1625–1695)' *ODNB*; H.W. Dickinson, *Sir Samuel Morland: Diplomat and Inventor, 1625–1695* (Cambridge, 1970); E. Menascè, 'L'autobiografia inedita di Samuel Morland', *BSSV* 158 (1986), 3–22; Giorgio Vola, 'A proposito di Samuel Morland, i suoi inediti e i suoi biografi: Alcune considerazioni', *BSSV* 160 (1987), 47–52.

33   Cameron, *The Reformation of the Heretics*, 241–2.

34   Benedetti, *Il 'santo bottino'*, 74.

35 Mario Viora, 'Notizie e documenti sulle assistenze diplomatiche prestate dall'Inghilterra ai valdesi durante il regno di Vittorio Amedeo II', *Studi Urbinati* 2 (1928), 81–135, particularly 84–91. See Martino Laurenti, 'Jean Léger: Pastore resistente e storico valdese', in *Eretici, dissidenti, inquisitori: Per un dizionario storico mediterraneo*, ed. Luca Al Sabbagh, Domizia Weber, and Daniele Santarelli (Ariccia, 2016), 353–61.

36 Laurenti, *Jean Léger*, 359. See Benedetti, *Il 'santo bottino'*, 86.

37 Marina Benedetti is the first scholar who hypothesised that Morland's text derived from Léger's work (*Il 'santo bottino'*, 89–90). We can supplement her arguments by saying that it is highly improbable that Jean Léger would know any English (a language that very few could speak in seventeenth-century Italy) while Morland, of course, knew French very well. For a precise comparison between Morland's and Léger's histories, see Teofilo Pons, 'Giovanni Léger e Samuel Morland', *BSSV* 113 (1963), 27–64; Daniele Tron, 'Jean Léger e la storiografia valdese del Seicento', *BSSV* 172 (1993), 82–90. On the importance of Léger for the definition of the Piedmontese valleys as 'Waldensian' see M. Fratini, 'Una frontiera confessionale: La territorializzazione dei valdesi nella cartografia del Seicento', in *Confini e Frontiere in età moderna un confronto fra discipline*, ed. Alessandro Pastore (Milano, 2007).

38 Cambridge, Cambridge University Library, Dd. 15.29–15.34; Dd. 3.25–3.38.

39 Dublin, Trinity College Library, mss. 258–67, 269. See Todd, *The Books of the Vaudois;* Benedetti, *Il 'santo bottino'*, 9, 45, 52–3, 55; Anne Brenon, 'The Waldensian Books', in *Heresy and Literacy, 1000–1530*, ed. Peter Biller and Anne Hudson (Cambridge, 1994), 137–59; M. Esposito, 'On some Waldensian Mss Preserved in the Library of Trinity College Dublin', *Journal of Theological Studies* 18 (1917), 177–84; M. Esposito, 'Sur quelques manuscrits de l'ancienne littérature religieuse des vaudois de Piémont', *Revue d'histoire ecclésiastique* 46 (1951); Peter Biller, *The Waldenses, 1170–1530* (Routledge, 2001), 237–69.

40 Ginevra, Bibliothèque Publique et Universitaire, mss. 206–209, 209a. See E. Balmas and M. Dal Corso, *I manoscritti valdesi di Ginevra* (Turin, 1977); Benedetti, *Il 'santo bottino'*, 87–8. On Antoine Léger, uncle of Jean, see Albert de Lange, 'Antoine Léger, un "internazionalista" calvinista del Seicento', *BSSV* 181 (1997), 202–32; Laurenti, *I confini della comunità*, 328.

41 A. Hugon, 'A proposito di Manoscritti e di Storici Valdesi', *BSSV* 143 (1978), 87–9; Andrea Giraudo and Luciana Borghi Cedrini, eds., *Sermoni valdesi medievali: I e II domenica di Avvento* (Turin, 2016).

42 Benedetti, *Il 'santo bottino'*, 91–101; Benedetti, '"De patria Spolitana": Due Predicatori Itineranti di fine Quattrocento', *Franciscana: Bollettino della Società internazionale di studi francescani* 2 (2000), 259–78.

43 Jacques Brez, *Histoire des Vaudois* (Paris, 1796), xii–xiii, 47.

44 This work was translated into English (1852, 1853, 1857, 1875), German (1875), Danish (1898), and Swedish (1865). On Muston see M. R. Fabbrini and S. Pasquet, *Alexis Muston (1810–1888): Radici valdesi e storia europea di un pastore e intellettuale dell'Ottocento* (Turin, 2004); G. Gonnet, 'Muston e Charvaz: Una memorabile polemica sulle origini valdesi', *BSSV* 161 (1987), 3–18.

45 G. Gonnet, 'La donazione di Costantino presso gli eretici medioevali', *BSSV* 132 (1972), 17–29; Alberto Cadili, *Il Veleno di Costantino: La Donazione di Costantino tra Spunti Riformatori ed Ecclesiologia Ereticale* in *Costantino I*, ed. P. Brown, J. Helmrath et al., 3 vols. (Roma, 2013) II: 621–43.

46 Raniero Sacconi, *Summa de Catharis et Leonistis seu Pauperibus de Lugduno* (Paris, 1548).

47 *Quellen zur Geschichte der Waldenser*, 73, quoted in Peter Biller, *Medieval Waldensian Followers' Construction of the Past: Jaqueta, Peroneta, the Old One zum Hirtze and Peyronette*, in *'Una strana gioia di vivere': A Grado Merlo*, ed. M. Benedetti and M. L. Betri (Milan, 2010), 181–98.

48 On the *Liber Electorum* see Peter Biller, 'The "*Liber electorum*"', in Biller, *The Waldenses*, 207–24; Cameron, *Waldenses*, 118–25. On the *Epistola fratrum de Italia* see G. Gonnet, 'I valdesi d'Austria nella seconda metà del secolo XIV', *BSSV* 72 (1962), 5–41.

49 A. Caviglia, 'Claudio di Seyssel (1450–1520)', in *Miscellanea di Storia d'Italia*, 3rd series, 23 (1928), 397–421.
50 Emilio Comba, *Claudio di Torino with an Introduction by Carlo Papini* (Turin, 2004).
51 Laurenti, '*Les Vrays Vaudois Originaires*', 105.
52 Amedeo Bert, *I valdesi ossiano i christiano-cattolici secondo la Chiesa Primitiva abitanti le così dette valli di Piemonte* (Torino, 1849).
53 Carlo Papini and Giorgio Tourn, *Claudiana, 1855–2005: 150 anni di presenza evangelica nella cultura italiana* (Turin, 2005), 24.
54 J.-B. Bossuet, *Oeuvres* (Versailles, 1816–1817) XX: 176–8. See Cameron, *The Reformation of the Heretics*, 201. Bossuet worked on two manuscripts collected by Jacques-Auguste de Thou now in the Bibliothèque Nationale of Paris (Paris, Bibliothèque Nationale, mss. Lat. 3375 I-II); see Benedetti, *Il 'santo bottino'*, pp. 61–72.
55 Muston, *Histoire des vaudois des vallées du Piémont* (Paris, 1834).
56 See Gonnet, *Muston e Charvaz: Una memorabile polemica*; Merlo, *Valdesi e Valdismi Medievali*, 30.
57 G. Spini, *Italia liberale e protestanti* (Turin, 2002), 128.
58 John Pinnington, 'La scoperta dei valdesi da parte degli anglicani', *BSSV* 126 (1969), 63–74; Randolph Vigne, '"The Sower will again cast his seed": Vaudois and British Interaction in the 19th century', in *Dall'Europa alle valli valdesi: Atti del XXIX Convegno Storico Internazionale: Il Glorioso Rimpatrio (1686–1989)* (1990), 439–63; Giorgio Tourn, ed., *Viaggiatori britannici alle valli valdesi* (Turin, 1994).
59 Stefano Villani, 'Dal Galles alle valli: Thomas Sims (1785–1864) e la riscoperta britannica dei valdesi', *BSSV* 215 (2014), 103–71.
60 *Brief Memoir Respecting the Waldenses or Vaudois Inhabitants of the Vallies of Piedmont. The Result of Observations Made During a Short Residence Amongst that Interesting People in the Autumn of 1814*, by a Clergyman of the Church of England (London, 1815).
61 *An Historical Defence of the Waldenses or Vaudois, Inhabitants of the Valleys of Piedmont, by Jean Rodolphe Peyran*, … with an introduction and appendixes by the rev. Thomas Sims (London, 1826).
62 Enrico Peyrot, 'I grandi benefattori dei valdesi: William Stephen Gilly', *BSSV*, 129 (1971), 25–70; Augusto Comba, *Gilly e Beckwith fra i valdesi dell'Ottocento* (Torre Pellice, 1990).
63 Franco Giampiccoli, *J. Charles Beckwith: Il generale dei valdesi (1789–1862)* (Turin, 2012).
64 George Eliot, *Middlemarch* (Toronto, 2004), 42. See also Marco Fratini, *Englische Reisende in den Waldensertälern und die Schaffung von 'Erinnerungsorten'*, in *Wandern auf Hugenotten- und Waldenserwegen vom 19. bis zum 21. Jahrhundert*, ed. Albert de Lange and Renate Buchenauer; Vorträge der wissenschaftlichen Tagung am 5./6. Oktober 2018 in Ötisheim-Schönenberg (Neu-Isenburg, 2019), pp. 87–117.
65 J. Wood Brown, *An Italian Campaign; or, the Evangelical Movement in Italy: 1845–1887, from the letters of the late rev. R.W. Stewart, D.D., of Leghorn* (London, 1890); Albert Glenthorn MacKinnon, *Beyond the Alps: The Story of the Scottish Church in Italy and Malta* (London and Edinburgh, 1937).
66 Gian Paolo Romagnani, ed., *La Bibbia, la coccarda e il tricolore: I valdesi fra due emancipazioni (1798–1848)* (Turin, 2001).
67 Simone Maghenzani and Stefano Villani, eds., *British Protestant Missions and the Conversion of Europe, 1600–1900* (New York, forthcoming).
68 Sergio Pace, *L'Ultima impresa del generale: Il progetto e la costruzione del tempio valdese in Torino (1850–1853)*, in Paolo Cozzo, Filippo De Pieri, and Andrea Merlotti, *Valdesi e protestanti a Torino (XVIII-XX Secolo)* (Turin, 2005), 43–57.

PART VI

Migrating memory

12

ON THE ROAD

Exile, experience, and memory in the Anabaptist diaspora

Kat Hill

Fashionable crowds of the film world at the 2007 Cannes Film Festival saw the Jury Prize go to a film from Mexican director Carlos Reygadas called *Silent Light*. Set in a Mennonite community on the Mexican border, it narrates a story of a married Mennonite man who falls in love with a woman not his wife.[1] Not only was the film shot in a colony close to Cuauhtémoc with non-professional Mennonite actors, characters also conversed in *Plautdietsch*, the Low German dialect spoken by 400,000 individuals in some Mennonite communities.[2] Despite declining use, *Plautdietsch* retains its significance for Mennonites; it is a verbal link to a European past and a sign of belonging. Conversations at the Mennonite archives in Winnipeg sometimes break into the dialect, whilst greeting cards in the gift shop in the Mennonite Heritage Village Museum in Steinbach make *Plautdietsch* word puns.[3] This linguistic remnant in Mennonite culture is an evocative reminder of the power of memory amongst modern-day successors of the Anabaptist movement who migrated from Europe and Ukraine across the Atlantic and beyond. Connections to their past, evoked by language in this instance, have shaped and sustained a distinct communal identity bound to experiences of migration and exile.

Descendants of sixteenth-century Anabaptism — Mennonites, Hutterites, and Amish — retain vivid recollections of their Reformation past. For these communities, memories of persecution, exile, and withdrawal from the world bolster a sense of distinction from contemporary society. The degree of disconnection varies: integrated, open Mennonites in Manitoba differ from stricter communities who still practice traditional ways of life, such as Mennonite colonies in Mexico, the Hutterite Bon Homme Bruderhof in South Dakota, or Amish communities in Lancaster County Pennsylvania whose 'Plain' lifestyle draws on historical traditions (and is also a major tourist attraction).[4] Differences in convention and practice separate the communities, yet all share an affinity with their past and its traditions which evoke connections to the early modern world. Histories and literature recall martyrdom, persecution and migration, and these memories are embedded in cultural practices such as speaking *Plautdietsch*.

Scholarship has often considered Reformation memoryscapes in recent years but has tended to focus on mainstream institutional churches such as Lutheranism and Calvinism[5] and has neglected non-conformist legacies which evolved from the 'left-wing' of the Reformation.[6] Memories of the Reformation are both vividly alive and also unique for descendants of Anabaptism. These non-conformist communities, often dispersed, did not focus memory-making on the on establishment, success and the growth of the institutional church but migration, fragmentation, and suffering. Different experiences resulted in different ways of looking back. Anabaptist memory culture focused on its own heroes, it existed in specific forms which had to be sustained across distance, and it narrated the memory of exile and dispersion. This memorial culture has astounding geographical and chronological breadth but is little understood in the broader context of Reformation histories.

Migration and dispersion shaped Anabaptism from the movement's inception. Persecution in the sixteenth century fragmented communities. Some sought out refuge in safer, more accepting havens, such as Strasbourg or established settlements in lands which offered tolerance, such as Moravia.[7] Mennonites, the followers of Menno Simons, an erstwhile Catholic priest from Friesland who converted to Anabaptism in 1536, formed communities scattered across the Netherlands, Germany and Switzerland spreading east to tolerant Polish Prussia in the sixteenth and seventeenth centuries. In the eighteenth century communities moved again to New Russia, and from the nineteenth century began migrations to North America.[8] In similar but distinct patterns, Hutterites, followers of Jakob Hutter, formed communities in Moravia, with subsequent persecution forcing them across central and eastern Europe, then to the Russian Empire, and finally America and Canada.[9] The Amish were followers of Jakob Amman, who split from Swiss Mennonites in the seventeenth century, and moved to Pennsylvania in the early eighteenth century following South German Mennonites who had already migrated west. Such a brief survey cannot encapsulate the diversity of migratory experiences amongst Anabaptists and their descendants, but dispersion is deeply ingrained in Anabaptist culture.[10]

However, little scholarship exists on memory-making in the Anabaptist diaspora. The persecution narrative is fundamental to memory cultures among these confessional groups, although exile and martyrdom was never the complete story of Anabaptist history, nor was a commitment to peace or opposition to worldliness.[11] Communities both forgot and remembered as they constructed memoryscapes which emphasised the ongoing quest for a place to be 'die Stillen im Lande' (the Quiet in the Land), the search for somewhere to pursue non-engagement with the world in peace. Anabaptist histories continue to draw a direct link between persecution of the sixteenth century and withdrawal from society, although the era of martyrdom has long since passed.[12] Collective memory, the term coined by Maurice Halbwachs, gave Mennonites a sense of shared identity as they created the 'sites of memory' which passed down generations.[13] The theory of collective processes of remembering and forgetting has been refined by Jan Assmann who points to the canonical, cultural memories consciously selected by people and by Aleida Assmann who underscores the importance of functional memories drawn from a large bank of archival memories.[14] This provides a convincing framework for thinking about the reciprocal processes of individual and collective memory, although scholars such as David Berliner argue that only individuals can truly remember. He critiques the overuse of memory by anthropologists who label every social enactment of recalling and recollection as memory.[15] However, this over-simplifies the complexity of memory culture, and the practices of recollections which allow individuals and communities to retain memories of events, people and places across generations and beyond living memory.

But diasporic memory presents particular challenges. How were memories shared across distance? How did individual memories in dispersed communities shape collective cultural memories? How did a shared memoryscape operate at distance and across time to help fashion identity? Scholarship on contemporary diasporas has explored the 'de-territorialised' identities separated from the rootedness of nation and land, where memory can be 'hybrid, displaced, split'.[16] But memory is also particularly important because of this absence of territory since it creates continuities across space and time; it connects dispersed groups to the immediate community; to the diaspora around the world; and to places of origins.[17] Forgetting translocal connections would mean the end of the community embedded in the intangible bonds of memory across distance. This essay examines how Anabaptist groups and their descendants produced memories of the Reformation era and beyond, which sustained diasporic communities. A growing literature on exile has examined the experience of dislocation for Jewish, Protestant, and Catholic exiles.[18] However, understandings of memory in these contexts are limited,[19] and Anabaptist traditions have barely featured at all.[20] Dagmar Freist argues that we need new parameters to address the production of fragmented memories in dispersed early modern communities outside the framework of the nation-state. 'Glocal memoryscapes' in diasporas connect time, space, and things in the practice of memory.[21]

Confronting Anabaptist diasporic memory, therefore, allows us to explore important questions in early modern cultural and confessional history. Anabaptist memories of the Reformation do not just reside in official histories and institutional structures but more intangible places such as landscapes and language, producing long-lasting associations connecting transnational identities across generations. Shared investment in the memory of separation, for example, and a desire to find a place free from the constraints of the state to live, worship and farm, spurs migration to this day, as recent reports about the movement of Mennonites from Ontario to Prince Edward Island suggest.[22] Anabaptist memory allows us to confront the dynamic between individual and collective memories and how local reproduction of memory cultures produced translocal belonging. Thus, the spread and survival of Mennonite, Amish, and Hutterite communities suggest new ways of thinking about the act of remembering the Reformation in the *longue durée* of a confessional diaspora. It reveals new perspectives on both our histories of confessional diasporas and on how memories of religious change have shaped global trajectories.

Memory and time

About an hour's drive from the Mennonite archives in Winnipeg is the Mennonite Heritage Village and Museum in Steinbach. The museum's permanent gallery tells the history of the Reformation, including figures like Huldrych Zwingli and Thomas Müntzer but focusing on the key figures of Anabaptism many of whom were persecuted or exiled: Felix Manz, Conrad Grebel, Balthasar Hubmaier, and Menno Simons, amongst others. The era of bitter persecution in the sixteenth century provides the cornerstone for Anabaptist memory cultures, similar to the way that migration during the Dutch revolt created a 'grand narrative of persecution and exile' for Dutch Protestants.[23] Anabaptist memories are deeply embedded in the era of early modern confessional change, although the figures celebrated are not the conventional stalwarts of the Reformation. The sixteenth century is labelled the era of peace, a surprising title for a period of violent confessional conflict but here the contrary and specific memory of the Reformation is evident: Anabaptists emphasised peace and non-violence at a time of conflict. These chronologies connect modern Mennonites to their early modern pasts.

Memory is intimately related to time. Writing the history of the Reformation or relating stories of martyrs involved thinking about time and chronology.[24] Studies of diasporic memory, however, have often been expansive in geographical scope but less so in chronological range. Perhaps this is the apparent tendency for diasporic memory to appear simply nostalgic, longing for a lost homeland, rather than creating dynamic chronologies. More broadly, critics of influential memory studies of the 1970s to 1990s argue that the nostalgia for any trace of past in the present and the sanctification of memory is a form of 'presentism'.[25] Both studies of remembering and forgetting become nothing more than the construction of culture in the present.[26] It could be argued that Anabaptist attempts to capture a distant past are not memory but nostalgic presentism. But a dynamic understanding of nostalgic memory is a particularly useful way to think about diasporic memory.

Recent studies have rehabilitated the notion of nostalgia within diasporic memory studies. Scholars see it as a way of dealing with trauma and both chronological and temporal dislocation so that such nostalgia 'produces postcolonial identity and has the power to create utopias'.[27] The dynamism of nostalgic memory amongst dispersed communities gives new force to how we understand the longing for a Golden Age of the early modern world or the veneration of the era of steadfast martyrs amongst Anabaptist communities. These communities look back with this nostalgic vision of history, but they are also concerned about preserving heritage for future generations since the past is something to be passed down. Nostalgia is not simply a passive longing for the past but a dynamic force which allows us to see how memory is translated into an active heritage and even heritage tourism, such as the Steinbach museum and village. Thus, the way in which Mennonites, Hutterites or Amish constructed temporal frameworks as they remembered the Reformation was essential to their existence and survival, providing continuity and a rootedness in the past, but also hope for the future in the face of dispersion. As Esther Peeren argues, diasporas share in chronotopes which intermingle past and present as well as home and exile.[28]

Early modern Anabaptists did not always leave explicit historical records but gathered letters, confessions of faith and martyr stories into collections which have been preserved. Hutterites produced the most explicit historical writing, and their flourishing book and literary culture from the 1560s to 1660s generated 300 surviving manuscripts, including historical chronicles, which record their understanding of the past.[29] The Great Chronicle was probably started by Kaspar Braitmichel on the suggestion of Elder Peter Walpot in Moravia in the mid-sixteenth century, then copied by the clerk Hauptrecht Zapff, and added to by six further annalists.[30] Writers had access to archives in Austerlitz which kept materials relating to the Hutterite communities as well as probably a small library with works by authors such as Eusebius and Sebastian Franck.[31] Other Anabaptist traditions were less systematic in their historical collections but the martyr stories, shared across groups and collected into volumes such as the *Ausbund*, look back to the past.[32] These histories and martyrologies all evolved in the context of dislocation, telling a different story from the standard Reformation narrative.

The Hutterite chronicles adopt a distinctive approach to chronologies and memories of the Reformation.[33] The Great Chronicle started with a conventional account of biblical history, running through the Old Testament, the age of Christ, and the Apostles, and then related the persecutions of the early church, the Donation of Constantine and late medieval corruption and heresy. After a cursory account of Luther and Zwingli, the chronicle narrates the beginning of Anabaptism through the lives of Conrad Grebel, Felix Manz and Georg Blaurock, and other early martyrs. Although the chronicle opens the section on the Reformation in 1517, it is clear that the history of the true church does not start until the 1520s with these Anabaptists. Subsequent history is divided into ages: an age of beginnings, the emergence of the brotherhood, persecution, a good age, a golden age, renewed persecution, tribulations and difficult times.[34] There are several intriguing features in this composition. In these sections on the Reformation era and the narrative of the Hutterites' own history, the chronicle is devoid of almost all wider outside context, such as the Schmalkaldic Wars, or religious conflicts in France and the Netherlands. The destruction and suffering caused by the Thirty Years' War are given more room but remains limited. With this internalised perspective, there is also very little narrative to explain why and when things happen, or how one age moves to the next. But although the chronicle is enclosed within the Anabaptist world, focused on ebbs and flows of persecution, it is also part of a universal narrative of the true church, placed in a biblical context.

The Reformation that Hutterites remembered was very different from many of the narratives of the Lutheran or Reformed churches. Anabaptist history which linked diasporic communities could not be focused on the same events, and the growth of the institutional church, but instead looked to shared experiences of dispersion across territories but also through time. The effect of the Hutterite visions of history was to bring the past into touching distance and to emphasise the continuity of experiences of suffering, even though there were also better times. This was also true of the great martyr collections like the *Ausbund* or Van Braght's *Martyrs' Mirror* (*Het Bloedig Tooneel Der Doops-gesinde*), first published in 1660 but perhaps best known from the second edition of 1685 which included engravings by Jan Luyken.[35] Martyrologies never started as explicitly historical pieces of writing, but collections of contemporary accounts developed into bound parts of martyr stories which bore witness to the past and, in the case of the *Martyrs' Mirror*, linked this to biblical histories. The *Martyrs' Mirror* was split into two volumes. The first begins with Jesus's crucifixion, persecution in his lifetime and the age of the Apostles, lists early Christian martyrs, and then witnesses who suffered century by century. The second recounts martyrs of the sixteenth and seventeenth centuries, starting with Hans Koch and Leonhard Meister.[36] Although a new volume ushers in the sixteenth century, the Reformation is not a distinctive caesura, but a continuation of the story of persecution. Once contemporary accounts had become indirect recollections beyond living memory, but connections existed between the experience of the Apostles, the martyrs of the seventh century, Anabaptists in the sixteenth century, or communities singing songs in the eighteenth or even the twenty-first century. Time narrowed as past, present, and future became linked.

Martyr stories were integral to communities as they moved. Aside from the Bible, martyr hymns and narratives were the most central texts to Anabaptist piety, and they are frequently mentioned in letters or bibliographies.[37] When Mennonites migrated to America, martyrologies mattered. In 1742 Mennonites in Pennsylvania wrote to the Committee of Foreign Needs of the Dutch Mennonite Church to request a German translation of the *Martyrs' Mirror*.[38] The Skippack Mennonites wrote again in 1745, and although the migratory enterprise had been largely untroubled, they emphasised that the situation in colonial America was now dangerous and that the 'cross and tribulation may … [soon] fall to the lot of the non-resistant Christian'.[39] The texts were of crucial importance to maintain faith in difficult times. When no response was forthcoming, they turned to the German-language press in the frontier community of Ephrata, where the first North American edition of the *Martyrs' Mirror* was printed in 1748–1749.[40]

The centrality of these texts elucidates important ways in which the Anabaptist memoryscape functioned. Nostalgia for the era of martyrdom was more than a wistful glance back but a fundamental way in which piety based in suffering was reinterpreted in ways that comforted and connected communities. More broadly, the shared diasporic and collective memory of martyr stories from the sixteenth century underscores the critical importance of the connection to the past and histories of dislocation. Past, present, and future are linked in chronological networks across generations and place. The importance of temporal connections is evident in the records kept by individual communities. From the eighteenth century, Mennonite communities who had migrated to Prussia from the Netherlands started keeping their own church books. The records of the Przechówko congregation in the Vistula Delta (modern-day Poland) were started in the late eighteenth century by Elder Jacob Wedel. The records, however, date back to 1661 and must have been based on older records or oral knowledge within the community.[41] The sense of the importance of the past was bolstered by chronicles, family records, and genealogies. Heinrich Donner, an elder of Orlofferfelde in Marienburg, West Prussia and his son and successor Johann Donner wrote community chronicles, two of which are integrated into the Orlofferfelde church books.[42] Community history also intersected with family history. In these closely connected groups, church books preserved family histories, and families kept their individual genealogies which also told community history. The diary of the Lehn family which dated back to the seventeenth century was a record of the Danzig and West Prussian Mennonites but was also a family history continued by subsequent generations, remaining in their possession to this day.[43] Generational transmission of memory in these records was essential to diasporic identity, sustaining the community in both space and time.[44] The importance of cross-generational bonds is evident too amongst the Hutterites. They were voracious letter writers whose epistles have been preserved in remarkable codices.[45] These ranged in size from folio editions to 32, tricesimo-secondo, mere centimetres high which could be slipped into a pocket or carried in a hand, and they were living, mobile documents, detailing experiences of prison, tribulations, suffering or conflict, which were written down, shared, read, and stored.

The copying and the sharing of histories, from great chronicles to manuscript histories of individual communities, emphasised collective memory. In some ways, writing genealogies, letters, or chronicles was deeply conventional but in the face of displacement, the practices of writing and rewriting constructed a shared interest in the continuity of time and shared chronologies. These histories often looked back to the era of persecution and martyrdom but were also constantly reshaped. Not everyone had to experience persecution to share in it. According to Johannes Waldner, an elder of the Hutterite community that had settled in Wischink, north of Kyiv, it was necessary to start a new chronicle in 1794 and write out excerpts from the old 'Gemeingeschichtsbuch', a treasure of faith, full of songs and tales which were a model of their steadfastness in the face of suffering.[46] Anabaptist memories recorded in martyrologies and histories were more than inert recollections but relational narratives which were performed and shared in a network of communities. The nostalgic memoryscapes emphasised the connection to the present, not in a negative or static sense, but in a way that sustained the diaspora across space and time.

People

A long-standing exhibition dedicated to the *Martyrs' Mirror* which opened in 1990 explores themes of suffering and persecution based on the 1685 edition of the matryrology; it is currently at its permanent home at the Kauffman Museum in North Newton, Kansas, but since its creation has travelled around 21 states and 55 Canadian provinces.[47] Its success underscores the centrality of martyrs to Anabaptists' conception of themselves. Martyr stories established genealogies of those considered true persecuted servants of the faith. The Hutterite chronicles, the

Ausbund and the *Martyrs' Mirror* named particular figures in a clear lineage, such as Hans Koch and Leonhard Meister, Felix Manz, Michael Sattler and Georg Blaurock, whose pasts were not just transcribed but sung or narrated again and again.[48] The repetition of names established tradition and belonging, and the singing of the songs reflected the continuous reproduction of eras of confessional significance amongst these communities. Martyr stories were embedded in a literary, oral, and performative culture which was shared across communities and media.

Martyrdom, however, did not continue into later centuries, nor did it provide a sustainable vision for an ongoing future, apart from one that perhaps pointed to the apocalypse. The *Martyrs' Mirror* appeared at a moment of security and prosperity for Mennonites in the Dutch Golden Age. The indulgent second edition which included Luyken's engravings was a reminder of intolerance at a time of comparative tolerance, produced amidst concerns that Mennonites had forgotten what past suffering meant.[49] Martyrdom was a collective memory, but with the passing of generations, it passed out of living memory. Yet new meanings emerged with these remembered narratives of persecution, such as the Skippack Mennonites' reliance on the *Martyrs' Mirror* to comfort them on the colonial frontier. The narratives continue to play a pivotal role in memory production, for both communities and individuals. The Harlem Doopsgezinde community celebrated their 300th year anniversary with a reprinting of the 1685 edition of the *Martyrs' Mirror*.[50] In a more intimate engagement with histories of suffering, Elder Isaak Dyck described the deadly flu virus of 1918 that hit his Sabinal Mennonite community as a time of sorrow but also beautiful spirituality. His wife was disappointed not to suffer God's punishment and remain unscathed.[51] For this traditional Old Order Colony in Chihuahua, the *Martyrs' Mirror* is central to their faith. Memories of martyrs created cultural associations that could be reproduced in different contexts, and Dyck's wife reinterpreted the macro narrative at the local level with new meanings.

Martyrological genealogies functioned as a form of diasporic memory in both translocal and local contexts. Membership books and family histories also produced memories through people and genealogies. The Przechówko church book is far more than a list of members. The opening pages establish heritage by recording the surnames of families in the community, including a short history of where the name first originated. The first name on the list is Becker. Johan Becker came from Lutheran parents apparently of questionable morality, but Johan became a minister in the community.[52] Lineage matters in the record books of the Przechówko Mennonites, but these lineages were being reinvented in new contexts, as the migrant community sought to root themselves in a translocal environment. Origins were necessarily messy. Some were Lutherans who had converted such as Becker, some such as Tobias Schnellberger came from the Moravian Brethren, forced out by Catholic persecution, and in some cases, there is no information. Once someone had accepted believer's baptism, he founded a new line and the individual's family was marked in the record. The church book proceeds to list all church members in tabled columns, male and female, with an accompanying number. Going along the row from one name and number, the next two columns list numbers which correspond to other names indicating the father and mother of the individual. Subsequent columns give the date and place of baptism, first, second and even third marriages, children, and the date of death. The records are sequenced (at least initially) according to family — the Ratzlaffs, then the Beckers, and so on — recording family genealogies across generations, all linked to a founding father. The records are even covered in annotations and scribbled notes which provide further detail about the community and its members. In one record, the compiler Wedel notes that Jacob Ratzlaff was his grandfather, scrawling 'Grossvater' next to the record, as personal memory intersected with communal memory.

The Przechówko books are just one example amongst numerous church books compiled by Mennonites, all of which differ slightly in format and composition. Church books were very different from martyr stories and remind us that communal memory-making amongst Anabaptists was not just about martyrdom, but the texts performed comparative functions in the way they created genealogies that grounded communal memory in people and networks. Whether martyrs or family members, memories of individuals were fundamental to Anabaptist culture since such lineages of people bridged diasporic spaces. Contemporary Mennonites can do their family histories by using the Mennonite database, 'GRANDMA' (The Genealogical Registry and Database of Mennonite Ancestry), accessed through the website 'Grandma's Window'. The emphasis on lineage has even spurred controversial conversations about whether Mennonites can be considered an ethnic group.[53] Intimate connections enacted across distance enabled a resilient transnational network, and the methods used to maintain 'glocal' memoryscapes have continued to evolve. Newspapers and periodicals were established to share recollections and news, trace origins, and keep the diaspora connected throughout the world. For example, the *Mennonitische Rundschau*, an American German-language Mennonite periodical, was started in 1878 and remained active until 2007,[54] whilst the *Mennonitische Post* founded in 1977 recently celebrated its 40th anniversary as one of the last German-language publications amongst North American Mennonites.[55] These publications have created not simply an imagined but very tangible global community.[56]

Continuity of language is a crucial cultural practice which allows dispersed Anabaptist communities to maintain connections across distance. The Przechówko congregation, renamed the Alexanderwohl community in New Russia, used German for records, even in Ukraine and Kansas, though English has subsequently been adopted. Particular regional dialects have also endured such as the form of *Plautdietsch* heard in Reygadas' film.[57] Hutterisch is a mix of German and Austrian, Moravian, Slovakian and Transylvanian, spoken by Hutterites, containing within its structure the origins but also the migratory past of the Hutterite communities.[58] Language is also about ways of speaking as collections of Amish, Mennonite, or Hutterite proverbs suggest.[59] Attachment to language is more than a nostalgic remnant, but a way of drawing boundaries between the sacred and non-sacred, though the struggle to keep languages alive is an ongoing concern for Anabaptist elders. Prairieleut Hutterite descendant Delbert Wiens remarked, 'Once the mental stranglehold of our mother tongue is broken, new ways of speaking and seeing come more quickly... A way of speaking is a way of seeing'.[60]

Things and places

The Przechówko church book is a delicate document with thin fragile pages and tattered edges, the loose binding still holding together folios of hundreds of names.[61] Though kept by the Mennonite archives in North Newton, Kansas since 2008, where its custodian is archivist John Thiesen it remains the property of the Alexanderwohl Mennonite Church who left the Ukrainian Molotschna communities in 1874 and migrated to Kansas.[62] The church remains an active congregation in the prairie lands of middle America. Relating histories back to the sixteenth century, the church book has survived each movement of the community from the Vistula Delta to New Russia and then the journey across the Atlantic. It stayed with the Mennonites as they lived in temporary accommodation for at least two years in communal huts provided by the Santa Fe railroad company.[63] Similarly, the Hutterites venerate the Great Chronicle which the community sheltered throughout years of exile and persecution. Today it is kept in a special wooden box by the Bon Homme colony in South Dakota, which was the first Hutterite community to settle in North America in 1874.[64]

Such documents and records are embodied material memories which connect times and places. Recent scholarly conversations between the history of emotions and material culture offer new ways of thinking about these objects in the context of diasporic memory, not simply as inert entities but actors that produce and shape human responses.[65] The power of their experience as things which had travelled and which invoked emotions and memories, speaks to the way in which they were entangled with the communities who used and owned them.[66] Their tangible materiality embodied memories of dislocation, while their continued use shaped memory practices across generations. Objects also reflected change and transition in their material substance. We can see generational shifts in the church records when the hand of the scribe changes, or when the community started a new membership book. The first page from the earliest church book of the Alexanderwohl church after the emigration to Kansas is a remarkable snapshot of a community in transition. The names of members are listed and then follow registers which record baptisms that had happened in Ukraine. Past and present, Eurasia and America, collide in one document.

The shifting emotional valences of objects illustrate how they functioned in diasporic memory by negotiating the gap between personal and collective memory, as well as local and transnational spaces. The *Ausbund*, for example, contains hymns sung all over the world, shared by communities, but as material objects, copies of this book travelled across land and sea in personal family collections.[67] Material possessions kept by a family throughout generations suggested permanence, but their journeys also recalled experiences of migration and preserved communal and family memories. One folder in the archives in Bethel has a single page from the front of a Bible commentary which was owned by the Krehbiel family entitled 'Pro Memoria'.[68] It is a little potted history, telling how Jacob Krehbiel bought the volume in 1791 in Krimmerhof which then passed to one of his sons, Johannes and then to Johannes' brother, Jacob. When the family emigrated to America in 1831, the book remained in Weierhof in the Palatinate as it was too difficult to transport. However, it was so important to Jacob that in 1836 he wrote to ask friends to bring it with them when they too came across the Atlantic. Christian Danner obliged and transported the Bible commentary to Clarence, New York State. Jacob records fondly that at the time of writing in 1837 the book had been in his family's possession for 46 years and asks his 'Dear descendants' to preserve it. The memorial slip has been archived separately from the book, though the memory of its history is evident on the page. Once I ordered up the volume, it quickly became clear why the book was unwieldy to transport but also how important it was as a physical object. Rather than a single volume, it is an eight-section commentary bound in four volumes printed in the 1720s and 1730s, each one substantial in size.[69] Memories of early modern pasts are enacted by continued use of these objects.

The materialities of everyday life such as ceramics, clothing, furniture, and personal items also evoked chronological and geographical connections. Many contemporary Hutterites, Amish and conservative Mennonites maintain distinctive forms of dress and culture which suggest simplicity and humility, and some domestic objects like books have survived migrations. Clockmaking evolved as a specialist technique amongst the Vistula Delta Mennonites from the eighteenth century, most notably the Kroeger family but also the Mandtlers, who made simple wall clocks without casements and with little decoration. As Mennonites moved from Poland to Ukraine and then North America, they took not only skills and craftsmanship with them but also the clocks, which hung on walls of homes, marking out the passage of time.[70] Families went to great lengths to save their clocks and the daily tick of the timepiece marked the continuity of daily time even as years passed and places changed. Despite their size, clocks or multivolume books were precious enough to be taken across oceans. As objects, they combined a dynamic tension of the comfort of domestic settled life and the reality of migration. This spatial dialogue between both settlement and travel, and the past and present is dramatically evident in the decision by Canadian Mennonites in the 1960s and 1970s to move from Ukraine the monuments to Johann Bartsch and Jakob Höppner, the delegates who negotiated the migration of Mennonites from Prussia to New Russia with the Tsarist government in the late eighteenth century. Their graves remain in Ukraine, but their stone memory is part of the Steinbach heritage centre in Canada.[71] Material practices of memory have created a powerful public heritage.

Spatial connections to the past underpinned the practice of transporting books, objects and even graves, and materiality of place and the landscape was important to memories amongst Anabaptists. Because exiles are in motion, memories necessarily involve the construction and inhabitation of diaspora space.[72] Spatial connection to the diaspora does not necessarily equate to nostalgia for a homeland to which Anabaptists wish to return, although communities often have a profound sense of connection to migration as well as the Swiss, German, Dutch, Polish, Ukrainian, or Russian parts of their past. Communities even took parts of the landscape with them. Mennonite communities across North America have planted acorns from the great Chortitza oak which grew in the lands settled in Ukraine, whilst Manitoba Mennonites carried seeds when they migrated to replant grasslands. Place and environment were integral to community memory.[73] There was always tension in diasporic memory connected to space between the attachment to one location and the connection with the wider community, the local and the translocal, as well as the reality that even exile communities often did settle in their new locations. However, this constant dialectic between movement and settlement was also productive in the way it expressed the local community's particular place within a broader diaspora.

Conclusion

For descendants of the Anabaptist tradition, the Reformation and the early modern period is a time of martyrdom and exile. They remember this period in a unique way which has shaped and continues to shape the Anabaptist diaspora. As communities or individuals went through hardship, resettlement, persecution or migration, the collective memories of exile, pacifism and martyrdom, connected to the Reformation era, were integral to identity. Tensions existed in these memories: in the attempt to make the lived present recreate the past; in the notion of global space as the diaspora spread and people migrated but also the highly specific memories of individual locations; in the expansive genealogies of martyrs but the deeply personalised records of family and community membership. The ability to manage this tension is at the core of Anabaptist diasporic memory. Memories of persecution and pacifism have been shaped to tell a particular narrative, which forgets, excludes and obscures more violent early modern pasts in Münster or the military service of Prussian Mennonites. Indeed, the dissonance between the collective memories of martyrdom versus the reality of prosperity in the Dutch Golden Age or migration and survival in the twenty-first century is not without its problems.[74] But the power of these memoryscapes which have allowed the Anabaptist diaspora to evolve is unquestionable. They must be part of our accounts of memories of the Reformation and its legacies and cannot remain peripheral.

Interrogating these histories is not always easy. It involves travel across the dispersed locations associated with Anabaptists. Visits to the heat of Kansas in the summer or bitterly cold Poland in winter have made me feel that I am inhabiting the diasporic spaces of Anabaptists. But the parallel is also problematic. Driving to archives and around cemeteries in the comfort of a car and archiving records with an iPhone is very different from the experiences of exiles and displaced persons. However, there is a productive tension since being aware of this difference draws attention to the material remains of Anabaptists, to the material conditions of the production of history and sources, the contexts which shaped it and the distances of space and time in these dispersed communities.

The diasporic memories of Anabaptists explode understandings of the meaning of legacies of the Reformation, as well as making us reconsider the concept of diasporic memory itself across places and times. The history of Amish, Mennonite and Hutterite communities is connected to questions about the rise of democracies and nations, obedience to the state, refugees, and global connections before the era of globalisation.[75] Both local and transnational contexts shaped experience and memory in the Anabaptist diaspora as communities responded to communal and individual problems but also large scale historical phenomena such as eighteenth-century Prussian militarism, Russian Tsarist reforms, North American migrations, or the 2017 Luther anniversary. Memories amongst these communities underscore the importance of uncovering the diverse legacies of confessional cultures and of understanding the experience of non-conformity, exile, and migration in global or translocal contexts.

Notes

1 *Stellet Licht*, directed by Carlos Reygadas (2007; USA: Palisades Tartan). See also Rebecca Janzen, *Liminal Sovereignty: Mennonites and Mormons in Mexican Culture* (Albany, 2018); Steven P. Carpenter, *Mennonites and Media: Mentioned in It, Maligned by It, and Makers of It: How Mennonites Have Been Portrayed in Media and How They Have Shaped Media for Identity and Outreach* (Eugene, OR, 2015), 54–6.

2 Reuben Epp, *The Story of Low German and Plautdietsch: Tracing a Language Across the Globe*, 2nd ed. (Hillsboro, Kansas, 1999).

3 Informal conversations and visits to the Mennonite Heritage Centre in Winnipeg and the Mennonite Heritage Village, Steinbach, July 2018.

4 See James Urry, *Mennonites, Politics, and Peoplehood: Europe – Russia – Canada, 1525–1980* (Winnipeg, 2006); Harold S. Bender, ed., *Hutterite Studies: Essays by Robert Friedman - Celebrating the Life and Work of an Anabaptist Scholar*, 2nd ed. (MacGregor, MB, 2010); John A. Hostetler, *Hutterite Society*, 2nd printing paperback, (Baltimore, 1997); John A. Hostetler, *Amish Society*, 4th ed. (Baltimore, 1993); Rod Janzen, *The Prairie People: Forgotten Anabaptists* (Hanover and London, 1999). See also the tourist guide to Amish: Donald B. Kraybill, *The Amish of Lancaster County* (Mechanicsburg 2008).

5 See for example Susan R. Boettcher, 'Late Sixteenth-Century Lutherans: A Community of Memory?', in *Defining Community in Early Modern Europe*, ed. Michael James Halvorson and Karen E. Spierling (Aldershot, 2008), 121–41; C. Scott Dixon, 'Luther's Lost Books and the Myth of the Memory Cult', in *Cultures of Lutheranism*, ed. Kat Hill, *P&P* issue suppl. 12 (2017), 262–89; Dixon, 'Luther's Ninety-Five Theses and the Origins of the Reformation Narrative', *EHR* 132, no. 556 (2017), 533–69; Peter Marshall, *1517: Martin Luther and the Invention of the Reformation* (Oxford, 2017); Philip Benedict, 'Divided Memories? Historical Calendars, Commemorative Processions and the Recollection of the Wars of Religion During the Ancien Régime', *French History* 22, no. 4 (2008), 381–405. See also the 2017 issue of the *Archiv für Reformationsgeschichte*. For 2017 Luther celebrations see 'Luther2017. 500 Jahre Reformation', accessed 20 June 2018, https://www.luther2017.de/. This is the official website of the 500-year anniversary supported by the EKD: Evangelische Kirche in Deutschland.

6 Anabaptists were included in this problematic notion of the 'left-wing' by Ronald H. Bainton, which has homogenised but also marginalised these groups. Ronald H. Bainton, 'The Left Wing of the Reformation', *Journal of Religion* 21, no. 2 (1941), 124–34.

7   For a good overview of sixteenth century Anabaptism see John D. Roth and James M. Stayer *A Companion to Anabaptism and Spiritualism, 1521–1700* (Leiden, 2007).

8   An excellent study of one family's migration is Arlette Kouwenhoven, *The Fehrs: Four Centuries of Mennonite Migration* (Leiden, 2013), tr. Lesley Fast and Kerry Fast.

9   Emese Bálint, 'Anabaptist Migration to Moravia and the Hutterite Brethren', in *Religious Diaspora in Early Modern Europe: Strategies of Exile*, ed. Timothy G. Fehler, Greta Grace Kroeker, Charles H. Parker and Jonathan Ray (Abingdon and New York, 2014).

10 For locations of communities see William Schroeder and Helmut T. Huebert, *Mennonite Historical Atlas*, 2nd ed. (Winnipeg, 1996).

11 Kat Hill, *Baptism, Brotherhood, and Belief in Reformation Germany: Anabaptism and Lutheranism, 1525–1585* (Oxford, 2015), especially chapter 2; James M. Stayer, *Anabaptists and the Sword*, Rev. ed., (Eugene, OR, 2002); Urry, *Mennonites, Politics, and Peoplehood*. For tensions in Mennonite identities see also Michael D. Driedger, *Obedient Heretics: Mennonite Identities in Lutheran Hamburg and Altona During the Confessional Age*, New ed. (Abingdon and New York, 2017).

12 For some history on this phrase see Isaias J. McCaffery, *Mennonite Low German Proverbs from Kansas* (Goessel, KS, 2008). See for example Laura L. Camden and Susan Gaetz Duarte, *Mennonites in Texas: The Quiet in the Land* (College Station, TX, 2006).

13 Pierre Nora, 'Between Memory and History: Les Lieux de Mémoire', *Representations* 26 (1989), 7–24.

14 Jan Assmann, 'Communicative and Cultural Memory', in *A Companion to Cultural Memory Studies*, ed. Astrid Erll and Ansgar Nünning (Berlin, 2008), 109–18; Jan Assmann and John Czaplicka, 'Collective Memory and Cultural Identity', *New German Critique* 65 (1995), 125–33; Aleida Assmann, *Erinnerungsräume: Formen und Wandlungen des Kulturellen Gedächtnisses* (Munich, 1999).

15 David Berliner, 'The Abuses of Memory: Reflections on the Memory Boom in Anthropology', *Anthropological Quarterly* 78, no. 1 (2005), 197–211.

16 Andreas Huyssen, 'Diaspora and Nation: Migration into Other Pasts', *New German Critique* 88 (2003), 147–64 (152); Vijay Agnew, 'Introduction', in *Diaspora, Memory and Identity: A Search for Home*, ed. Vijay Agnew (Toronto, 2005), 3–18 (5).

17 Marie-Aude Baronian, Stephan Besser, and Yolande Jansen, 'Introduction', in *Diaspora and Memory: Figures of Displacement in Contemporary Literature, Arts and Politics*, ed. Marie-Aude Baronian, Stephan Besser, and Yolande Jansen (Leiden, 2016), 9–16 (11–12); Avtar Brah, *Cartographies of Diaspora: Contesting Identities*, repr. (London and New York, 2005), esp. p. 16.

18 Ole Peter Grell, *Brethren in Christ: A Calvinist Network in Reformation Europe* (Cambridge, 2011); Fehler et al., *Religious Diaspora in Early Modern Europe*; David van der Linden, *Experiencing Exile: Huguenot Refugees in the Dutch Republic, 1680–1700* (Abingdon and New York, 2016); Geert Janssen, 'The Counter-Reformation of the Refugee: Exile and the Shaping of Catholic Militancy in the Dutch Revolt', *JEH* 64, no. 4 (2012), 671–92; Jesse Sponholz, *The Tactics of Toleration: A Refugee Community in the Age of Religious Wars* (Newark, 2011); Yosef Kaplan, ed., *Early Modern Ethnic and Religious Communities in Exile* (Newcastle upon Tyne, 2017); Giovanni Tarantino and Charles Zika, eds., *Feeling Exclusion: Religious Conflict, Exile and Emotions in Early Modern Europe* (Abingdon and New York, 2019).

19 On early modern diasporic memory see Liesbeth Corens, 'Dislocation and Record Keeping: The Counter Archives of the Catholic Diaspora', in *The Social History of the Archive: Record Keeping in Early Modern Europe*, ed. Alexandra Walsham, Kate Peters, and Liesbeth Corens, *P&P* issue suppl. 11 (2016), 269–87; Dagmar Freist, 'Lost in Time and Space? *Glocal* Memoryscapes in the Early Modern World', in *Memory before Modernity: Practices of Memory in Early Modern Europe*, ed. Erika Kuijpers, Judith Pollmann, Johannes Müller, and Jasper van der Steen (Leiden, 2013), 203–22; Johannes Müller, *Exile Memories and the Dutch Revolt: The Narrated Diaspora, 1550–1750* (Leiden, 2016); David J. B. Trim, ed., *The Huguenots: History and Memory in Transnational Context: Essays in Honour and Memory of Walter C. Utt* (Leiden, 2011).

20 See for example isolated chapters: Emese Bálint and Christopher Martinuzzi, 'Composite Religions and Ideas in Exile: Encounters between Saxon Reformers and the First

Anabaptists', in Kaplan, *Ethnic and Religious Communities*, 218–41 and Bálint, 'Anabaptist Migration'.

21 Freist, 'Lost in Time and Space', 206–13.

22 Greg Mercer, '"No land for love or money": How Gentrification hit the Mennonites', *The Guardian*, 26 July 2018, accessed 3 August 2018, https://www.theguardian.com/cities/2018/jul/26/no-land-for-love-or-money-how-gentrification-hit-the-mennonites.

23 Müller, *Exile Memories*, 5.

24 C. Scott Dixon, 'The Sense of the Past in Reformation Germany: Part 1', *German History* 30, no. 1 (2012), 1–21 and 'The Sense of the Past in Reformation Germany: Part 2', *German History* 30, no. 2 (2012), 1–23.

25 Lynn Hunt, *Measuring Time, Making History*, The Natalie Zemon Davis Annual Lecture Series (Budapest, 2008), 16–18; Nora, 'Between Memory and History'.

26 Berliner, 'The Abuses of Memory'.

27 Anette Hoffmann, 'Comparing to Make Explicit: Diasporic Articulations of the Herero Communities in Namibia', in Baronian et al., *Diaspora and Memory*, 37; Pamela Sugiman, 'Memories of Internment: Narrating Japanese-Canadian Women's Life Stories', in Agnew, *Diaspora, Memory and Identity*, 48–80 (63–4); Huyssen, 'Diaspora and Nation', 149–51.

28 Esther Peeren, 'Through the Lens of the Chronotope: Suggestions for a Spatio-Temporal Perspective on Diaspora', in Baronian et al., *Diaspora and Memory*, 67–77 (74).

29 Martin Rothkegel, 'Anabaptism in Moravia and Silesia', in Roth and Stayer, *Anabaptism and Spiritualism*, 163–215 (204–6); Robert Friedmann, 'Hutterite Chronicles', in *Hutterite Studies: Celebrating the Life of an Anabaptist Scholar*, ed. Harold S. Bender, 2nd ed. (MacGregor, MB, 2010), 157–62 (157–8).

30 The historical writings have a complex history and although the Great Chronicle is the most famous and standard account of Hutterite history, there are many other chronicles in existence. 'Hutterite Chronicles', *Global Anabaptist Mennonite Encyclopedia Online*, accessed 20 August 2018, https://gameo.org/index.php?title=Hutterite_Chronicles.

31 Friedman, 'Hutterite Chronicles', 157.

32 Peter Burschel, *Sterben und Unsterblichkeit: Zur Kultur des Martyriums in der frühen Neuzeit* (Munich, 2004), 117–95.

33 Twentieth-century printed German editions include: Rudolf Wolkan, *Geschicht-Buch der Hutterischen Brüder* (Macleod, AB, and Vienna, 1923) and A. J. F. Zieglschmid, *Die Älteste Chronik der Hutterischen Brüder: Ein Sprachdenkmal aus Frühneuhochdeutscher Zeit* (Philadelphia, 1943). An English translation was prepared in the 1980s, *The Great Chronicle of the Hutterian Brethren* (Rifton, NY, 1987). Josef Beck also produced an edition of smaller chronicles or *Denkbücher*, Josef Beck, *Die Geschichts-Bücher der Wiedertäufer in Oesterreich-Ungarn* (Vienna, 1883; repr. Nieuwkoop, 1967).

34 *Great Chronicle of the Hutterian Brethren*.

35 The first known extant edition of the *Ausbund* is from 1583; it has been reprinted many times with several additions, though it is still used today by the Old Order Amish in America substantially unaltered from the 1583 edition. Selected hymns have been translated: *Songs of the Ausbund: History and Translations of Ausbund Hymns* (Millersville, OH, 1988).

36 Tieleman Jansz. van Braght, *Het bloedig tooneel, of Martelaers spiegel der doops-gesinde of weereloose christenen* (Amsterdam, 1685); Brad Gregory, 'Anabaptist Martyrdom: Imperatives, Experience and Memorialization', in Roth and Stayer, *Anabaptism and Spiritualism*, 467–506.

37 Robert Friedmann, *Mennonite Piety Through the Centuries: Its Genius and Its Literature* (Goshen, IN., 1949), 96–7.

38 John C. Wenger, *History of the Mennonites of the Franconia Conference* (Telford, PA, 1937), 311.

39 David L. Weaver-Zercher, *Martyrs Mirror: A Social History* (Baltimore, 2016), 130.

40 Weaver-Zercher, *Martyrs Mirror*, 130–42.

41 North Newton, KS, Mennonite Library and Archives, Bethel College, CONG. 15, Box 11, ['Alexanderwohl original Przechowka book']. For a modern and translated edition see *Church Book of the Alexanderwohl Mennonite Church in the Molotschna Colony of South*

Russia, tr. Velda Richert Duerksen and Jacob A. Duerksen (Goessel, KS, 1987). Scans of the original book are also available through the archives at Bethel College.

42 Bolanden-Weierhof, Mennonitische Forschungsstelle Weierhof, KB.OR.01 ['Geburten, Taufen, Trauungen, Todesfälle 1727–1857'], 77–146 and KB.OR.02 ['Chronik (Donner), Geburten, Trauungen, Taufen, Kirchenzucht 1800–1899'], 1–85; Mennonite Heritage Centre Archives (MHCA), Winnipeg, MB, Small Archives, 4355, Box 2 ['Heinrich Donner's Chronik']. Donner was a keen record keeper. His own meticulous 'Hausbuch' survives in the archives in Bethel; North Newton, KS, Mennonite Library and Archives, Bethel College, SA-II-1906 [Heinrich Donner's Hausbuch].

43 The MS of this text is still kept by the family, but a translated word-processed version is held by the MHCA, Winnipeg, MB.

44 Müller, *Exile Memories*, 124–46. On generations and religious change see also Alexandra Walsham's 2018 James Ford Lectures in British History at the University of Oxford: 'The Reformation of the Generations: Age, Ancestry, and Memory in England c. 1500–1700'.

45 Robert Friedmann, 'The Epistles of the Hutterian Brethren: A Study in Anabaptist Literature', in *Hutterite Studies*, 163–89.

46 Harmut Kegler, 'Das "Dicke Buch" der Gemeinde Gottes: Zur Literarischen Selbstdarstellung der Huterischen Täufergemeinschaft', in *Literatur und Laienbildung im Spätmittelalter und in der Reformationszeit*, ed. Ludger Grenzmann and Karl Stackmann (Stuttgart, 1984), 152–72 (168).

47 'The Mirror of the Martyrs', Exhibition at the Kauffman Museum, Bethel College, North Newton, KS.

48 *Chronicle of the Hutterian Brethren*, I: 43–7.

49 Mary S. Sprunger, 'The Dutch Golden Age: Prosperity and the Martyr Tradition', *Mennonite Life* 45, no. 3 (1990), 28–31.

50 Nanne van der Zijpp, Harold S. Bender, and Richard D. Thiessen, 'Martyrs' Mirror', *Global Anabaptist Mennonite Encyclopedia Online*, accessed 10 Sep 2018, http://gameo.org/index.php?title=Martyrs%27_Mirror&oldid=145854.

51 Kouwenhoven, *The Fehrs*, 194, 212.

52 'Alexanderwohl original Przechowka book'. There are no folio numbers on the document but scans can be accessed here: https://mla.bethelks.edu/archives/cong_15/prz/IMG_1816.JPG.

53 Grandma's Window is a paid service available at https://www.grandmaonline.org/, accessed 21 July 2018. On ethnicity see Royden Loewen, 'The Poetics of Peoplehood: Ethnicity and Religion among Canada's Mennonites', in *Christianity and Ethnicity in Canada*, ed. Paul Bramadat and David Seljak (Toronto, 2008), 330–64.

54 Centre for Mennonite Brethren Studies, accessed 29 July 2018, https://cmbs.mennonitebrethren.ca/publications/mennonitische-rundschau-die/.

55 Rachel Bergen, 'Die Mennonitische Post celebrates 40th anniversary', *Mennonite Central Committee*, 23 June 2017, accessed 25 May 2019, https://mcccanada.ca/stories/die-mennonitische-post-celebrates-40th-anniversary.

56 Robyn Sneath, 'Imagining a Mennonite Community: The *Mennonitische Post* and a People of Diaspora', *Journal of Mennonite Studies* 24 (2004), 205–20.

57 Epp, *Story of Low German and Plautdietsch*; Mark L. Louden, 'Anabaptists and Minority Languages', 16 May 2019, *Anabaptist Historians. Bringing the Anabaptist Past into a Digital Century*, accessed 30 August 2019, https://anabaptisthistorians.org/2019/05/16/anabaptists-and-minority-languages/.

58 Rod Janzen and Max Stanton, *The Hutterites in North America* (Baltimore, 2010), 147.

59 McCaffery, *Mennonite Low German Proverbs*; Suzanne Woods Fisher, *Amish Proverbs: Words of Wisdom from the Simple Life* (Grand Rapids, 2012).

60 Janzen, *Prairie People*, 226–9

61 'Alexanderwohl original Przechowka book'.

62 David C. Wedel, *The Story of Alexanderwohl 1874–1974: Profile of a Heritage* (North Newton, KS, 1974); J. A. Duerksen, 'Przechowka and Alexanderwohl: Beginnings of

Alexanderwohl, Tabor, Hoffnungsau and Other Churches', *Mennonite Life* 8 (1955), 78–82; Abram Teichrib, *Alexanderwohl-600 Jahr danach* (Lemgo, 2007).

63 Norman E. Saul, 'The Migration of the Russian-Germans to Kansas', *Kansas Historical Quarterly* 40, no. 1 (1974), 38–62; Cornelius Krahn, 'Santa Fe Railroad Company', *Global Anabaptist Mennonite Encyclopedia Online*, accessed 2 September 2018, http://gameo.org/index.php?title=Santa_Fe_Railroad_Company&oldid=102652.

64 Hostetler, *Hutterite Society*, 305–6.

65 Jane Bennett, *Vibrant Matter: A Political Ecology of Things* (Durham, NC, 2009); Stephanie Downes, Sally Holloway, and Sarah Randles, eds., *Feeling Things: Objects and Emotions Through History* (Oxford, 2018); Catherine Richardson, '"A very fit hat": Personal Objects and Early Modern Affection', in *Everyday Objects: Medieval and Early Modern Material Culture and its Meanings*, ed. Tara Hamling and Catherine Richardson (London, 2016), 289–98; Sasha Handley, 'Objects, Emotions and an Early Modern Bed-sheet', *History Workshop Journal* 85, no. 1 (2018), 169–94; Catherine Richardson, Tara Hamling, and David Gaimster, eds., *The Routledge Handbook of Material Culture in Early Modern Europe* (Abingdon and New York, 2017); Sarah Randles, 'Materiality', in Susan Broomhall, *Early Modern Emotions: An Introduction* (Abingdon and New York, 2017), 17–9.

66 Ian Hodder, *Entangled: An Archaeology of the Relationships Between Humans and Things* (Oxford, 2012).

67 The only known surviving copy of the 1564 edition of the *Ausbund* for example is now at the Mennonite Historical Library in Goshen, Indiana, bought by Harold S. Bender in 1928 in Harrisburg, Pennsylvania. Ervin Beck, 'Goshen alumnus restores rare 1564 Ausbund', 3 May 2017, *Canadian Mennonite*, accessed 5 October 2019, https://canadianmennonite.org/stories/goshen-alumnus-restores-rare-1564-ausbund.

68 North Newton, KS, Mennonite Library and Archives, Bethel College, Small Archives I, Box 13, 249 ['Page from a Bible commentary owned by Jacob Krehbiel'].

69 North Newton, Mennonite Library and Archives, Bethel College, M 220.531, H363b, Rare Bk. Coll.

70 Arthur Kroeger, *Kroeger Clocks* (Steinbach, MB, 2012); James O. Harms, 'The Search for Jacob Mandtler, Clockmaker', *Mennonite Life* 64 (2010).

71 James Urry, 'Memory: Monuments and the Marking of Pasts', *Conrad Grebel Review* 25, no. 1 (2007).

72 Brah, *Cartographies of Diaspora: Contesting Identities*, chapter 8.

73 On the Chortitza oak see Schroeder, *Mennonite Historical Atlas*, 116, 120; Preface in Robert Zacharias, *Rewriting the Break Event: Mennonites and Migration in Canadian Literature* (Winnipeg, 2013). Susie Fisher, '(Trans)planting Manitoba's West Reserve: Mennonites, Myth and the Narrative of Place', *Journal of Mennonite Studies* 35 (2017), 127–48. See this issue of the journal more broadly on Mennonites and landscape.

74 Rebecca Plett, 'From Martyr Narrative to Medical Discourse: Writing a Contemporary Mennonite Subject', *Journal of Mennonite Studies* 35 (2017), 339–55.

75 See also Urry, *Mennonites* and Driedger, *Obedient Heretics*, 3.

13

THE LEGACY OF EXILE AND THE RISE OF HUMANITARIANISM[1]

Geert H. Janssen

The memory cultures of the Reformation are intrinsically connected to stories of migration. This is true in the sense that religious tensions sparked the movement, either voluntary or coerced, of thousands of dissenters across early modern Europe. The Reformation has even been blamed for causing the first European 'refugee crisis'.[2] Yet the linkage of the Reformation and migration is also true in the sense that migratory experiences generated powerful memories that would shape the confessional mentalities of the following generations. As Johannes Müller has argued, memories of persecution, flight and displacement stimulated a 'narratisa-tion' of the concept of exile and diaspora among various denominational groups and became a popular tool of religious expression in post-Reformation Europe.[3] Just like martyrs' tales and conversion stories, migration histories defined the rival confessional canons of Protestants and Catholics alike.

Memories of migration, and the notion of exile in particular, served particular purposes in early modern Europe. First, they provided a frame of reference that could be invoked to address the challenges of the times. When, for example, large numbers of Huguenots left France during the 1680s, Protestant audiences else-where in Europe were duly reminded that the Huguenot diaspora was just the latest example of a well-known history of Catholic tyranny.[4] Second, memories of persecution and flight were used to underpin calls for action in the present. In his study of the Thirty Years' War, Ole Grell has noted that the military conflict in the German Empire triggered large-scale relief efforts and church collections in sur-rounding countries. Many of these built on transnational refugee networks that had emerged in the sixteenth century and employed a rhetoric of exile history with which many Protestant communities could identify.[5]

The 'cult of exile' in post-Reformation Europe has received some attention in recent scholarship, but a cross-confessional analysis of its significance, popularity, and functions among different denominations is lacking.[6] More specifically, few

attempts have been made to assess the impact of exile memories on shifting charitable mentalities and emerging humanitarian sensibilities in Europe. Still, such an
endeavour seems pertinent because most scholars situate the origins of modern
humanitarianism in human rights thinking, which would only gain ground during
the eighteenth-century Enlightenment.[7] By addressing the relationship between
memory practices and the rise of long distance advocacy in post-Reformation
Europe, this essay seeks to rethink this common Enlightenment narrative and
gauge the agency of religious minorities in forging early humanitarian cultures.

Migrations of the Reformation

Forced migration and displacement have been common throughout history, but
recent scholarship contends that the refugee first emerged as a mass phenomenon
in the early modern period. In his wide-ranging overview, *Religious Refugees in
the Early Modern World*, Nicholas Terpstra explains how the bureaucratisation of
states, shifting economic structures and, above all, increasing religious tensions
fostered anxieties about uniformity in late-medieval Europe.[8] Partly inspired by
Robert Moore's thesis about the formation of a persecuting society and David
Nirenberg's work on communities of violence, Terpstra asserts that from the late
fifteenth century onwards European elites sought to establish more cohesive and
pure communities of faith.[9] The removal of religious dissenters was a common
means to achieve a more purified *corpus christianum*. According to this line of
argument, the notable rise in the number of displaced persons in the sixteenth
century was not kick-started by Reformation disputes as such, but rather found
its origins in broader concerns and earlier attempts to purge and cleanse European
societies of dissent.

Challenging the notion of a single, exclusively Protestant 'refugee Reformation',
Terpstra urges scholars to include Jewish diasporas and Muslim expulsions in traditional Reformation historiographies. Thus, his analysis of the early modern refugee crisis starts with the expulsion of Jews from German and French towns in the
mid-fifteenth century and the forced migration of New Christians or Sephardim
from the Iberian Peninsula after 1492. These diasporas were followed by the displacement of 'Morisco' minorities from Spain in the early seventeenth century.
Meanwhile, the rise of Protestantism and its subsequent persecution generated
waves of evangelical refugees across sixteenth-century Europe. Countervailing
Catholic migrations were generally smaller and were mostly concentrated in
northern Europe. Although precise numbers are not available for any of these
groups, estimates suggest that several hundred thousands of men and women were
driven away as a result of repressive confessional policies.[10] The effects of religiously informed migrations were tangible in the development of hubs of asylum,
including Emden and Cologne in the Holy Roman Empire, London and Norwich
in England, Geneva and Zurich in the Swiss Confederation, Venice and Rome in
the Italian peninsula, and Tunis and Istanbul in the Ottoman Empire.

The Reformation's refugee crisis generated paradoxical consequences. Despite the hardship and misery, diasporic communities were able to forge new international networks of correspondence, media, and business. Economic historians have pointed to the impact of Protestant refugees for the revitalisation of draperies in sixteenth-century England and the advancement of printing industries in Geneva and Emden. The expulsion of Sephardim likewise fostered the development of innovative trading networks in the Mediterranean and the Atlantic world.[11] Yet the experience of displacement borne by so many would have particularly profound consequences for European thinking about religious identity and confessional allegiance. The growing number of displaced communities fuelled a greater appetite for politicised confessional mentalities among all religious groups. Scholars have noted how in places such as Emden, Geneva, and London many evangelical refugees became receptive to strands of Reformed Protestantism.[12] Something similar happened to Catholics who escaped Protestant regimes in the British Isles and the Low Countries in the later sixteenth century. In safe havens such as Douai and St Omer, many expatriate Catholics for the first time encountered Counter-Reformation doctrine and experimented with more militant forms of Tridentine spirituality.[13]

Recent scholarship contends that the galvanising effects of exile was not a specifically Calvinist or Tridentine phenomenon. The experience of diaspora also triggered a re-judaisation among expelled Sephardic communities and forged more cohesive Jewish identities in major host cities such as Venice and Amsterdam.[14] Scattered evidence about expelled 'Moriscos' likewise suggests that many of them became part of the dedicated, confessional forces of the Islamic Ottoman regime in the early seventeenth century.[15] This is not to claim that all religious refugees went through a similar 'radicalising' process. Several scholars, notably Liesbeth Corens, Jesse Spohnholz, and Mirjam van Veen have pointed to the variety of responses to displacement and to the many forms of religious mobility that coexisted. In some areas, the experience of exile in fact encouraged experiments with religious toleration.[16] All the same, the rise of parallel, confessional mentalities in post-Reformation Europe cannot be separated from the formative experiences of its various migrating minorities.

The rise of the refugee

If migration was a driving force behind religious identity formation, it also nurtured the discursive invention of the refugee as a distinct social category in European society. In their search for meaning and their wish to distinguish themselves from common migrants, displaced dissenters eagerly looked to classical and, particularly, biblical precedents. The Old Testament offered a number of role models in this regard, including Abraham, Moses, and the exiled prophets from the time of the Babylonian captivity. These edifying examples were appropriated by displaced Protestants and Catholics alike. Martin Luther and his adherents drew on Matthew 10:23 ('when they persecute you in this city, flee ye into another') as well as a catalogue of biblical blueprints to argue that exile — either physically or spiritually — was part of a venerable Christian experience, a sign of steadfastness, and means towards spiritual salvation.[17] Calvinists of a following generation claimed Old Testament analogies in even bolder ways. The Panhuys family from Antwerp, for one, commissioned a large imaginary group portrait (c. 1575) in which the dispersed relatives were re-united as ancient Israelites on their way from Egypt to the Promised Land. Moses himself was included to the evocative *portrait historié* [Fig. 13.1].[18]

The Catholic publicist Joannes Costerius, in turn, asserted in 1580 that it was Catholic refugees who were the true victims of Pharaoh who relived the wandering fate of the biblical Jews.[19] As the religious conflict in sixteenth-century Europe hardened, confessional parties on both sides styled their respective displaced communities as reenactors of a long biblical tradition and consisting of quasi-martyrs of the faith.

The term exile (or *exul, exulant*) became a popular catchphrase for those who justified their migration along such confessional lines. As Alexander Schunka and Jesse Spohnholz have observed, narratives of biblical exile were often applied with hindsight and obscured the very different incentives and experiences behind the various migrations during the Reformation.[20] This observation is also pertinent for our understanding of the emergence of the concept of refugee in the same period. Although its semantic origins have never been fully studied, the term refugee first gained ground in the context of expelled religious

FIGURE 13.1 Maarten de Vos, *Moses Showing the Tablets of the Law to the Israelites, with Portraits of Members of the Panhuys Family, their Relatives and Friends* (c. 1575). Collection Mauritshuis, The Hague.

minorities and their exile discourses. The Latin *refugium* (place of shelter) and the French verb *se réfugier* (to seek shelter) had long existed, but the person of the refugee as a noun was unknown, as sixteenth-century dictionaries demonstrate.[21] In a letter to Cardinal Antoine Perrenot de Granvelle of October 1572, provost Maximilian Morillon referred to 'ung monde des bien réfugiés' when he discussed the fate of escaping Catholics in the Dutch Revolt.[22] The expression 'les réfugiés' was subsequently adopted by the Habsburg administration in the 1580s to single out 'bonnes catholicques' who had fled sites of Protestant rebellion in the Low Countries.[23] Being a refugee thus implied a particular type of migrant who had become the victim of religious repression and deserved solidarity and support from co-religionists. Distinctions between the terms exile, refugee, fugitive, and expelled were often blurred though. Contemporaries used them in a variety of senses and sometimes even interchangeably. The usage of refugee vocabulary became more widespread in different European languages after the Huguenot *refuge* of the later seventeenth century. Dictionaries published after 1685 generally listed 'refugee' and privileged it for French Protestants, thereby ignoring its sixteenth-century, Catholic origins. Well into the eighteenth century, refugee retained its confessional connotations and was applied almost exclusively to victimised Protestants.[24] Forced displacements during the Reformation thus encouraged the development of a richer and more nuanced vocabulary of migration, but they also generated the myths of exclusive victimhood, which have long coloured our understanding of the phenomenon.[25]

The agency of religious minorities in distinguishing between types of migrants and framing the concepts of 'exile' and 'refugee' becomes particularly clear when we compare them to other early modern victims of forced migration. For example, men and women who fled war violence, economic deprivation, or climate change in early modern Europe never adopted the language of biblical exile to explain their experiences, nor did they conceptualise their flight in analogous semantic categories. Hence they were not seen, or indeed did not see themselves, to be akin to refugees. It was the language of religion that first provided displaced minorities in Europe with a distinct identity, which aligned their experiences with venerable precedents and could be used as a badge of social respectability. For numerous other migrants, such a categorisation may not have been feasible or useful, for example if they were aiming for social assimilation or economic integration into host communities.

The emergence of the refugee as a distinct social category in pre-modern Europe was not, then, solely the result of the rising number of displaced minorities. Its conceptualisation also stemmed from the activism and the discursive strategies of particular groups who sought religious freedom, legal protection, and international solidarity from co-religionists. By defining their displacement in terms of persecution, religious migrants effectively reinvented themselves: rather than unprivileged strangers, they were honourable victims who deserved a special status in civilised societies.

Exile memory politics

The growing respectability of the religious refugee translated into the memory politics of Europe's rival churches. Protestants and Catholics all cultivated their respective histories of persecution and exile as evidence of the religious commitment and sacrifice of their forebears.[26] Still, there were notable differences in the meanings attached to the exile past and their popularity among different denominations. For Reformed Protestants, exile narratives reinforced the notion of an elect community, whose members had relived the biblical script set by the people of Israel. In the seventeenth century, identifications with Israel became a trope within puritan and Reformed circles and the idea that Calvinism was a religion born out of exile experiences was widely disseminated in sermons, songs, chronicles, and published histories.[27] Lutherans too developed a didactic and devotional exile genre, which included histories of persecution and migration and biographical accounts of exemplary Lutheran ancestors.[28] As Liesbeth Corens has shown, within the Church of Rome the theological concept of exile was less popular and the idea of an embattled minority church did not sit well with Counter-Reformation teachings. To be sure, English Catholics cultivated memories of persecution and migration during the Reformation but these fused into a broader framework of religious mobility, which also included missionary activity and pilgrimage. In this way, the migratory past of Catholic minorities could be integrated into general Tridentine models.[29] In the Dutch Republic, a sense of religious competition contributed to exile being claimed as a founding experience by Calvinists, Protestant dissenters, and Catholics alike.[30]

Publicists and publishers, sometimes labelled the 'memory brokers' of the period, fuelled and channelled these different scripts of exile. It is telling that many of them shared a migration past. In his overview of exile and expatriate culture, Peter Burke remarks that history-writing and publishing have long been a powerful tool and resource for refugees. Indeed, numerous religious migrants of the sixteenth and seventeenth centuries later became chroniclers and historians who could write and have disseminated a particular image of their troubled past. Several popular histories of the Dutch Revolt, for instance, were composed by former exiles, who claimed that the history of flight and displacement had been instrumental to the rise of a newborn Protestant state.[31] The English Jesuit Robert Persons sought to frame and publicise his experience of exile as part of a wider missionary effort to retake England for the Church of Rome.[32] A cyclical reading of history characterised many of these works. The *Historia persecutionum* (1648), for one, was styled after books of martyrs and presented the migrations of Protestants from Bohemia as a recurring story of persecution of 'true Christians', which had existed since the Christianisation of the region in the ninth century.[33]

Memories of exile were also promoted through selective record-keeping, collections of memorabilia, and the construction of public monuments. The opening lines of the notes of the Reformed Church of Amsterdam stated dramatically that the congregation had been established on 24 May 1578 'after the return from exile'. The diverse migrations of some of its members were thus rewritten into a founding myth of the entire Reformed community.[34] In Emden, the local church capitalised on its heroic past by installing a memorial plaque as late as 1660 — almost a century after the exile of Netherlandish Protestants in the town. It proudly claimed that 'God's church, persecuted and expelled, has received God's consolation here'.[35] The relevance of the exile past was remembered in Counter-Reformation circles, too. In seventeenth-century Antwerp, for example, the expulsion and subsequent return of Catholics in the Dutch Revolt were commemorated in a dedicated chapel of the Cathedral of Our Lady.[36]

In the later seventeenth century, French Huguenots would exploit these different and rivalling scripts of exile. Of all persecuted groups in early modern Europe, they were arguably most successful in shaping a particular image of their diaspora by adapting and recycling established Protestant tropes. Through prints, illustrated histories and pamphlets, Huguenot authors retold the story of their *refuge* in the darkest possible colours and infused their written histories with suggestive historical parallels. The *History of the Jews* (1706–1707), written by Jacques Basnage, is a case in point. His narrative of the dispersion of the chosen people clearly echoed recent stories of Huguenots.[37] In the popular news prints of Romeyn de Hooghe, analogies between forced migrations during the sixteenth-century Reformation and the current situation in France were skilfully made by reusing familiar images of earlier Protestant suffering.[38]

Collective memories of exile could serve confessional, political, and social purposes. In areas where religious refugees had been instrumental in advancing the Reformation, stories of displacement became arguments for social mobility. In the United Provinces, the history of the Dutch Revolt encouraged the development of a patriotic discourse about the aristocracy of exile suffering during the war. Numerous urban elites in Holland capitalised on their familial histories of migration — real or imagined — and presented themselves as natural standard-bearers of the new Protestant regime.[39] In Amsterdam, a clan of former Emden exiles was able to stay in power throughout the seventeenth century. In England, too, exile credentials were used, with various degree of success, to further political and ecclesiastical careers under the regimes of Elizabeth I and James I.[40] As for Catholic elites in Protestant areas, exile pedigree could be useful as well. References to an ancestral history of flight appear in requests for patronage to the authorities in Rome or at the court of the King of Spain and the German Emperor.[41]

The cult of exile even appeared as an argumentative strategy in diplomatic circles. In 1612, for example, the town of Emden sought relief for its many financial troubles. One of their main creditors, the Dutch States General, received a letter in which the magistrates of Emden asked to have their debts waived because the town had offered hospitality to Dutch refugees in the sixteenth century. Now, they argued, their descendants should in turn show their generosity and solidarity. The English ambassador in The Hague, Dudley Carleton, expressed a similar reasoning a decade later.[42] The significance of exile memories in post-Reformation Europe is perhaps best illustrated in its use by men and women whose refugee past was, in fact, unclear or even non-existent. Johannes Müller and Jesse Spohnholz have uncovered how the appreciation of exile encouraged later generations to rewrite their family histories.[43]

A seemingly paradoxical aspect of confessional exile narratives concerns their transnational character. From the start, the refugee crisis of the sixteenth century had forged international communities of faith. In hubs of asylum such as Geneva and Emden (for Reformed Protestants), Cologne and Paris (for Catholics) and Venice and Amsterdam (for Sephardic Jews), refugees of various national backgrounds had interacted and often shared the same religious facilities, patronage resources, and devotional media. International group-bonding also bred a charitable mentality along confessional yet transnational lines. In Protestant circles these long-distance solidarities have been dubbed 'International Calvinism'. But among expelled (crypto-) Jews the expansion of international bonds and a heightened sense of Sephardic community have been observed as well. More recently, scholars have pointed to Catholic variants of the same transnational support networks that had been strengthened by the rise of a militant, confessional brand of International Catholicism in the 1580s.[44] The experience of displacement thus fed a charitable mentality among rivalling churches and stimulated a continuing interest in new 'refugee crises'. In the seventeenth and eighteenth centuries, international aid to repressed co-religionists abroad became a popular tool of religious expression among Protestants, Catholics, and Jews alike. This proto-humanitarian spirit was particularly visible in transnational charity campaigns and forms of public diplomacy.

International charity

The informal webs of correspondence, business, and media that had developed in sixteenth-century refugee communities provided the basis for an enduring charitable network. From the early seventeenth century onwards, Protestant congregations in England, France, and the Dutch Republic regularly organised church collections for oppressed and dispersed brethren elsewhere in Europe. Ole Grell has highlighted the scale of some of these campaigns during the Thirty Years' War. In the United Provinces, for example, about 64,000 *thaler* were raised between 1626 and 1645 for refugees from the troubled German Palatinate. Successive collections in England, Scotland, and Ireland generated even larger total sums for the same cause.[45] The end of the war in the Holy Roman Empire did not diminish this charitable zeal directed beyond one's own borders. Growing tensions between Catholics and Protestants in Ireland triggered a widely publicised campaign in Dutch Reformed churches in 1643–1644. Erica Boersma has estimated that no less than 300,000 guilders were given in aid of Irish Protestants.[46]

Charity to the needy had of course long been part of Christian culture. What seemed to distinguish the fundraising practices of (post-) Reformation Europe from established charitable giving traditions, concerned their geographical scope, confessionalised agenda, particular focal groups, and sophisticated use of media. By campaigning for fleeing and persecuted co-religionists abroad, the organisers of transnational support networks advocated a new type of long-distance solidarity and encouraged a sense of identification with the suffering of distant others. Politicised, confessional media furthered these sensibilities and disseminated a vocabulary of empathy, which showed similarities with later humanitarian discourses.[47]

The engagement with persecuted refugees in distant lands may have been particularly pronounced in Reformed circles, but it was by no means limited to supporters of 'International Calvinism'. Scattered evidence suggests a similar sort of transnational solidarity among Lutheran, Anabaptist as well as Catholic communities, which set-up their own competing charitable schemes in the early decades of the seventeenth century.[48] Sephardic Jews in Hamburg and Amsterdam likewise started to organise support for oppressed Ashkenazi Jews in Central and Eastern Europe. Despite tensions between the denominations, Yosef Kaplan has revealed the considerable sums collected by the Sephardic community in Amsterdam during the pogroms in Poland in 1648.[49] While these different initiatives have usually been seen and interpreted in the context of particular Jewish or Protestant attitudes, a more comparative perspective allows us to appreciate that each of these transnational support networks were local variants of a broader European pattern.

Exile memories fuelled these identifications with refugee-victims abroad and stimulated a continuing popularity for long-distance aid. Indeed, the cult of exile neatly fit the emerging cult of transnational 'humanitarian' charity. In the United Provinces church collections for international refugees of Protestant colouring were generally justified by a rhetoric about barbarian Catholic persecution and earlier Protestant refugee experiences during the sixteenth century. The notion of a shared history of exile and the responsibility of Protestant communities elsewhere in Europe to support their brethren underpinned the aid campaigns for the Palatinate and Bohemia in the 1620s and 1630s. During their meeting in Dordrecht in 1637, the Dutch Reformed Synod typically reasoned that the current sufferings of German Protestants affected their Dutch co-religionists, too, because they were all 'parts of the same body'.[50] A circular letter by English Puritan minsters in 1627 likewise referred to German refugees as 'Brethren in Christ'.[51] Published chronicles and other media kindled such identifications. In the funeral sermon for the London alderman John La Motte in 1655, the local minister told his flock that John's benevolence towards oppressed Calvinists abroad had been informed by his readings of the 'Histories' of his age, 'especially such as treated of the Persecutions and Deliverances of the Church of God, and the Propagation of the Gospel'.[52]

As Judith Pollmann has shown, early modern contemporaries generally believed that remembering the past was useful because it could teach something about the present. Identifying historical analogies was therefore a common argumentative strategy in printed media such as newspapers and illustrated broadsheets.[53] During the Thirty Years' War, Protestant publishers skilfully re-used well-known images of alleged Spanish atrocities in the Americas and religious violence in the Dutch Revolt to draw comparisons with more recent victims of 'Catholic barbarity' and 'Habsburg tyranny'.[54] International propaganda during the English Civil War of the 1640s, the Waldensian crisis of the 1650s, and the Huguenot diaspora of the 1680s recycled these and other iconic images.[55] The history of the Waldensians in Piedmont in particular had long been revered in Protestant circles because they were regarded as a kind of forerunners of the Reformation. When the dukes of Savoy renewed their persecutions of the community in the seventeenth century, an international Protestant outcry followed.[56] Calls for financial aid and relief operations for the Waldensian refugees were bolstered by references to the renowned past of this proto-Protestant community. The media war of the 1680s employed similar historical scripts. Huguenots may have left France for a variety of reasons, but they were keen to portray themselves as traditional confessional exiles. By fusing their sufferings into recognisable Protestant categories of exile, Huguenot publicists sought to persuade host countries such as England, Brandenburg-Prussia, and the Dutch Republic to fulfil their obligation of charity towards fellow Protestants in need.[57]

Narratives of exile remained an important frame of reference for charity campaigns of the early eighteenth century. When in 1731–1732 the Lutheran minority of Salzburg was expelled by the local prince-archbishop, Protestant publishers seized the opportunity to frame the migration as the latest chapter in a long tradition of persecution and exile. Thus, the 'exodus' of Salzburg Lutherans was compared to the exilic wanderings of the ancient Israelites and readers were duly reminded that Protestants had been victims of similar forced migrations since the start of the Reformation.[58] An orchestrated international media campaign for help eventually elicited some 34,000 *thaler* from European donors, including the kings of Sweden and Great Britain and leaders of several Protestant cities in the Holy Roman Empire. Brandenburg-Prussia in particular presented itself as the generous safe haven for the wretched Salzburg Lutherans.[59]

As the example of Brandenburg suggests, transnational charity often interacted with the interests of states. But religiously informed long-distance solidarities could also cause friction between churches and government officials, who were anxious about the wider repercussions of aid to refugees. The eagerness with which the Reformed Church of the United Provinces presented itself as a rescuer of repressed brethren abroad regularly worried Dutch diplomats. In 1629, the States of Holland opposed a new collection for German refugees because it feared large-scale migrations of foreign Protestants to the Netherlands.[60] In England, the royal government was hesitant to fully endorse Puritan initiatives during the Thirty Years' War when they seemed to damage dynastic interests or heighten domestic religious tensions.[61]

Europe's rivalling churches were key in defining the focus groups and organising the infrastructure of this proto-humanitarian activism. Still, the emphasis taken by historians, concentrating on these institutional players and their archives, has obscured the agency of individual families. Numerous charitable initiatives were, in fact, kick-started and promoted within family networks whose members cultivated their own ancestral histories of refuge. The Courten dynasty in London, for example, was made up of powerful entrepreneurs who were instrumental in raising international attention and support for refugees during the Thirty Years' War. The

Courtens typically descended from Protestant refugees from the sixteenth-century Low Countries. In Counter-Reformation Antwerp, the Van der Cruyce family had likewise suffered exile during the Calvinist regime of the early 1580s and became ardent advocates for Catholics displaced from the Northern Netherlands.[62] As conscious descendants of sixteenth-century refugees, these families were both the stakeholders of the collective cult of exile as well as the informal agents and stewards of the humanitarian spirit that emerged out of it.

Humanitarian diplomacy

Media coverage of persecutions and refugee crises in the seventeenth-century have recently been interpreted as part of 'public diplomacy' and lobby for foreign intervention.[63] Already in the sixteenth century, religious refugee communities had called upon authorities abroad to step in and use their power in the service of these communities' interest. Elizabeth I, for one, had received petitions from Dutch rebels and exiles in London, asking for protection and military help in their fight against the Habsburg monarchy. Catholic refugees, for their part, had sought to interest Philip II of Spain in their cause. In the 1580s, Catholic émigrés in Cologne even designed an ambitious plan for a Counter-Reformation league of princes that would eliminate the Protestant threat in northern Europe. While most of these ambitious schemes never materialised, the Thirty Years' War would show the disastrous effects of a rhetoric of transnational confessional solidarity. In the later sixteenth century, the preservation of 'the Church' became an accepted legal argument to justify military interventions abroad. Not only was it employed by Philip II to defend his military involvement in France in the 1590s, but traces of the same reasoning about foreign intervention as an act of 'collective defence' can be found in Protestant writings of the following decades as well.[64]

In the seventeenth century, calls for intervention on 'humanitarian' grounds were, it seems, directed particularly towards England and the Dutch Republic.[65] As a self-styled bastion of Protestant resistance against Catholic persecution, the United Provinces received numerous petitions for help from German Protestants in the 1610s and 1620s. While the States General was reluctant to become involved in religious troubles in the Empire, they did occasionally provide money and loans to displaced German communities from places such as Paderborn and Aachen and wrote pleading letters to German princes.[66] The flight of the Waldensian minority in Piedmont in the 1650s prompted similar calls for foreign intervention. Oliver Cromwell's government applied strong diplomatic pressure on Louis XIV and the Duke of Savoy in favour of the community.[67] Actual military involvement on behalf of refugees was rare, though, and the available examples should be seen in the context of wider strategic concerns. In the United Provinces, the arrival of thousands of Huguenots in the 1680s was marshalled rhetorically as a justification of Dutch military campaigns against Louis XIV.[68] Many Huguenot refugees were also recruited into Dutch, English, and Prussian armies to fight their repressive French monarch. In 1689, the Dutch East India Company (VOC) even planned an attack on French-held islands in the Indian Ocean, allegedly with the aim of compensating Huguenot refugees for their confiscated properties in France.[69] The Spanish-Habsburg monarchy did something similar on behalf of Catholics who escaped 'Protestant aggression' elsewhere in Europe. After the battle of Kinsale (1601), for example, a considerable number of Irish Catholics settled in Spain. Some of the Irish émigrés were recruited for the Habsburg armies, but even those who were considered unfit for military tasks were eventually offered asylum. King Philip III reportedly refused to send back 'useless' men, women, and children because of his charitable responsibilities as a Catholic monarch.[70]

Although little studied in the context of early modern international relations, calls for humanitarian intervention often coincided with the charity campaigns discussed earlier. They also built on the same memory culture of exile. During the Thirty Years' War a dedicated stream of pamphlets targeted Protestant audiences across Europe. Written by local ministers, residents or anonymous agents, these printed media sought to influence public opinion by reporting events in the Palatinate and Bohemia within a framework that recalled well-known histories of the sixteenth century. The *Humble Request* of 1637 reminded Dutch readers of the hospitality that the Palatinate had offered to Protestant exiles during the Dutch Revolt and encouraged the Dutch to put pressure on their authorities to help the afflicted former host.[71] Some authors signed their appeal letters as 'exules', emphasising the links between past and present suffering. Immigrant communities in the United Provinces employed similar argumentative strategies in their negotiations with governments. When a group of Sephardic Jews submitted a petition to the authorities in Amsterdam in 1616, they stressed their entrepreneurial importance for the city, but also presented themselves as 'being refugees of the fire of the Spanish inquisition and other cruelties'. The Sephardim knew how to kindle sympathy by using a vocabulary with which Dutch elites were keen to identify.[72]

Pre-modern humanitarianism

Although the scale and effectiveness of early modern 'humanitarian' activity remains understudied, the examples given here prompt some larger questions about its character and origins. First, it is notable that forms of transnational refugee support already used a language of empathy and even humanity, which scholars have traditionally attributed to the eighteenth-century Enlightenment. Lynn Hunt has famously shown how human rights thinking gained currency in the eighteenth century as a result of what she called a new emotional regime, which centred on imagined empathy. A legal regime of human rights eventually followed from this development.[73] While it is undeniable that the Enlightenment project defined the concept of human rights, it appears that a rhetoric of empathy and long-distance solidarity already characterised the refugee aid networks of the preceding two centuries. Religiously forced migrations of the sixteenth century had confronted all denominations with the question of what it actually meant to be persecuted and expelled, and whether particular migrants deserved their help and protection.

These embryonic humanitarian sensibilities were furthered by the ways in which memories of the Reformation's refugee crisis were cultivated by different confessional groups in the following decades.

Second, by evoking memories of a shared exile past, pre-modern humanitarian mentalities challenge accepted readings about agency. Within the rapidly expanding historiography on the topic, most scholars situate the roots of humanitarianism in external pressure groups that became particularly popular in the nineteenth century.[74] The examples from post-Reformation Europe, by contrast, largely stem from the activism of the victims themselves. Indeed, the very concept of 'refugee' was invented by religious minorities in their search for protection, aid, and respectability. Sceptics of this reading might argue that the examples of early modern 'humanitarian' culture are still quite different from their modern counterparts in their strict confessional colouring. Indeed, rival refugee networks rarely offered the prospect of solidarity with each other, let alone lobbied for equal privileges to be extended to all repressed minorities. Early modern humanitarianism was firmly confessionalised.[75] But this observation does not imply that there existed a clean break between the confessional world views of early modern Europe and more secular, enlightened, or 'modern' ones. The work of Caroline Shaw and Abigail Green has revealed that the notion of an international Protestant brotherhood was still an important frame of reference in nineteenth-century humanitarian networks, but it coexisted with more religiously neutral, general Christian discourses.[76]

In recapturing early forms of long-distance advocacy, this essay has finally sought to demonstrate that the refugees of Reformation Europe were not mere marginalised victims of conflict, as contemporary images and later historiography often suggest. Displaced religious minorities were also agents of change who made a significant impact on early modern society, be it as the inventors of refugee vocabulary, the promoters of exile memory cultures, or as the initiators of transnational humanitarian attitudes. This was a legacy on which the Enlightenment project would build.

Notes

1 This essay is part of the NWO-VICI project 'The Invention of the Refugee in Early Modern Europe' (016.Vici.185.020).

2 Peter Burke, *Exiles and Expatriates in the History of Knowledge, 1500–2000* (Waltham, MA, 2017), 39–64; Susanne Lachenicht, 'Refugees and Refugee Protection in the Early Modern World', *Journal of Refugee Studies* 30, no. 2 (2017), 261–81; Nicholas Terpstra, *Religious Refugees in the Early Modern World: An Alternative History of the Reformation* (Cambridge, 2015).

3 Johannes Müller, *Exile Memories and the Dutch Revolt. The Narrated Diaspora, 1550–1750* (Leiden, 2016), 203–5.

4 David van der Linden, *Experiencing Exile: Huguenot Refugees in the Dutch Republic, 1680–1700* (Farnham, 2015); Ulrich Niggemann, *Immigrationspolitik zwischen Konflikt und Konsens: Die Hugenottenansiedlung in Deutschland und England, 1681–1697* (Cologne, 2008); Anne Dunan-Page, ed., *The Religious Culture of the Huguenots, 1660–1750* (Aldershot, 2006).

5 Ole P. Grell, *Brethren in Christ: A Calvinist Network in Reformation Europe* (Cambridge, 2011).

6 Liesbeth Corens, *Confessional Mobility and English Catholics in Counter-Reformation Europe* (Oxford, 2018); Müller, *Exile Memories*; Scott Oldenburg, *Alien Albion: Literature and Immigration in Early Modern England* (Toronto, 2014), 45–71; Alexander Schunka, 'Constantia im Martyrium: Zur Exilliteratur zwischen Humanismus und Barock', in *Frühneuzeitliche Konfessionskulturen*, ed. Thomas Kaufmann et al. (Gütersloh, 2007), 175–200; Jesse Spohnholz, *The Convent of Wesel: The Event that Never was and the Invention of Tradition* (Cambridge, 2017).

7 Michael Barnett, *Empire of Humanity: A History of Humanitarianism* (Ithaca, 2011); Lynn Hunt, *Inventing Human Rights: A History* (New York, 2007); Fabian Klose, ed., *The Emergence of Humanitarian Intervention: Ideas and Practice from the Nineteenth Century to the Present* (Cambridge, 2015).

8 Terpstra, *Religious Refugees*.

9 Robert I. Moore, *The Formation of a Persecuting Society: Authority and Deviance in Western Europe 950–1250* (Oxford, 1987); David Nirenberg, *Communities of Violence Persecution of Minorities in the Middle Ages* (Princeton, 1996).

10 Overviews in Burke, *Exiles*; Terpstra, *Religious Refugees*; Lachenicht, 'Refugees'; Timothy Fehler et al., ed., *Religious Diaspora in Early Modern Europe: Strategies of Exile* (London, 2014).

11 Classic examples include Heinz Schilling, *Niederländische Exulanten im 16. Jahrhundert: Ihre Stellung im Sozialgefüge und im religiösen Leben Deutscher und Englischer Städte* (Gütersloh, 1972); Jonathan I. Israel, *European Jewry in the Age of Mercantilism, 1550–1750* (Oxford, 1985).

12 Henning P. Jürgens and Thomas Weller, eds., *Religion und Mobilität: Zum Verhältnis von raumbezogener Mobilität und religiöser Identitätsbildung im frühneuzeitlichen Europa* (Göttingen, 2010); Andrew Pettegree, *Emden and the Dutch Revolt: Exile and the Development of Reformed Protestantism* (Oxford, 1992); Heinz Schilling, *Niederländische Exulanten*.

13 Katy Gibbons, *English Catholic Exiles in Late Sixteenth-Century Paris* (Woodbridge, 2011); Geert H. Janssen, *The Dutch Revolt and Catholic Exile in Reformation Europe* (Cambridge, 2014).

14 Miriam Bodian, *Hebrews of the Portuguese Nation: Conversos and Community in Early Modern Amsterdam* (Bloomington, 1997); David Graizbord, *Souls in Dispute: Converso Identities in Iberia and the Jewish Diaspora, 1580–1700* (Philadelphia, 2003); Jonathan I. Israel, *Diasporas Within a Diaspora: Jews, Crypto-Jews and the World of Maritime Empires (1540–1740)* (Leiden, 2002); David B. Ruderman, *Early Modern Jewry: A New Cultural History* (Princeton, 2010), 23–40.

15 Tijana Krstić, 'The Elusive Intermediaries: Moriscos in Ottoman and Western European Diplomatic Sources from Constantinople, 1560s–1630s', *Journal of Early Modern History* 19, no. 2–3 (2015), 129–51.

16 Corens, *Confessional Mobility*; Jesse Spohnholz and Mirjam van Veen, 'The Disputed Origins of Dutch Calvinism: Religious Refugees in the Historiography of the Dutch Reformation', *Church History* 86, no. 2 (2017), 398–426.

17 Hans B. Leaman, 'Count Every Step in my Flight. Rhegius's and Luther's Consolations for Evangelical Exiles, 1531–3', in *Exile and Religious Identity, 1500–1800*, ed. Jesse Spohnholz and Gary K. Waite (London, 2018), 9–24; Alexander Schunka, 'Lutheran Confessional Migration', in *European History Online*, accessed 8 August 2019, http://www.ieg-ego.eu/schunkaa-2012-en; Vera von der Osten–Sacken, 'Lutheran Exiles of Christ in the Sixteenth Century', *Journal of Early Modern Christianity* 3, no. 1 (2016), 31–46.

18 Müller, *Exile Memories*, 56–7.

19 Janssen, *Dutch Revolt*, 48–50.

20 Spohnholz, *Convent of Wesel*; Schunka, 'Constantia im Martyrium'. Also Christopher d'Addario, *Exile and Journey in Seventeenth-Century Literature* (Cambridge, 2007); J. Seth Lee, *The Discourse of Exile in Early Modern English Literature* (London, 2018).

21 Examples in Latin, French, German, English, and Dutch consulted at https://logeion.
    uchicago.edu/lexidium;https://www.lexilogos.com/;https://artfl-project.uchicago.edu/
    content/dictionnaires-dautrefois;https://www.etymonline.com/;https://www.dwds.de/;
    http://etymologiebank.nl/, accessed 13 August 2019.
22 *Correspondance du cardinal de Granvelle, 1565–1583*, ed. Edmond Poullet and Charles Piot
    (Brussels, 1884), IV: 458.
23 Brussels, Algemeen Rijksarchief Brussels, Staat en Audiëntie, 809–7, 809–9, 809–13
    [Nominations for office in Bruges, Ghent, and Antwerp, 1584–1585].
24 Burke, *Exiles*, 2–4, 62–64; John M. Hintermaier, 'The First Modern Refugees? Charity,
    Entitlement, and Persuasion in the Huguenot Immigration of the 1680s', *Albion* 32, no.
    3 (2000), 429–49.
25 Geert H. Janssen, 'The Republic of the Refugees: Early Modern Migrations and the
    Dutch Experience', *HistJ* 60, no. 1 (2017), 233–52.
26 Müller, *Exile Memories*, 1–26; Judith Pollmann, *Memory in Early Modern Europe, 1500–
    1800* (Oxford, 2017), 38. Also Rachel L. Greenblatt, *To Tell Their Children: Jewish
    Communal Memory in Early Modern Prague* (Stanford, 2014), 86–117.
27 Müller, *Exile Memories*; Heiko A. Oberman, *John Calvin and the Reformation of the Refugees*
    (Geneva, 2009); Spohnholz, *Convent of Wesel*.
28 Schunka, 'Lutheran Confessional Migration'; Vera von der Osten-Sacken, 'Erzwungenes
    und selbsgewähltes Exil im Luthertum: Bartholomäus Gernhards Schrift De Exiliis
    (1575)', in *Religion und Mobilität: Zum Verhältnis von raumbezogener Mobilität und religiöser
    Identitätsbildung im frühneuzeitlichen Europa*, ed. Henning P. Jürgens and Thomas Weller
    (Göttingen, 2010), 41–58.
29 Corens, *Confessional Mobility*, 24–9.
30 Judith Pollmann, 'Met grootvaders bloed bezegeld. Over religie en herinneringscultuur
    in de zeventiende-eeuwse Nederlanden', *De Zeventiende Eeuw* 29 (2013), 154–75.
31 Burke, *Exiles*, 70–72; Janssen, 'Republic of the Refugees'.
32 Corens, *Confessional Mobility*, 24–8, 164–90.
33 Alexander Schunka, 'Lutheran Confessional Migration'.
34 Amsterdam, Stadsarchief Amsterdam, Archief van de Hervormde Gemeente, kerkenraad,
    1, 1.
35 Müller, *Exile Memories*, 172.
36 Janssen, *Dutch Revolt*, 131–79; Judith Pollmann, *Catholic Identity and the Revolt of the
    Netherlands, 1520–1635* (Oxford, 2011), 139–42.
37 Burke, *Exiles*, 70–1; Van der Linden, *Experiencing Exile*, 228.
38 Henk van Nierop, *The Life of Romeyn de Hooghe, 1645–1708* (Amsterdam, 2018), 89–
    138; Van der Linden, *Experiencing Exile*, 225–7.
39 Jonathan I. Israel, *The Dutch Republic: Its Rise, Greatness and Fall, 1477–1806* (Oxford,
    1998), 180, 341–4.
40 Andrew Pettegree, *Marian Protestantism: Six Studies* (Aldershot, 1996). A fine reassess-
    ment is offered by Frederick E. Smith, 'Life After Exile: Former Catholic Émigrés and
    the Legacy of Flight in Marian England', *EHR* 133, no. 563 (2018), 806–34.
41 Gibbons, *English Catholic Exiles*; Janssen, *Dutch Revolt*, 131–79; A. J. Loomie, *The Spanish
    Elizabethans: The English Exiles at the Court of Philip II* (New York, 1963).
42 *Resolutiën der Staten-Generaal 1576–1630*, 12 December 1612 and 13 December 1622,
    Huygens ING, accessed 15 August 2019, http://resources.huygens.knaw.nl/retroboeken/
    statengeneraal/#page=0&accessor=toc&view=homePane.
43 Müller, *Exile Memories*, 124–46; Spohnholz, *Convent of Wesel*, 121–54.
44 Israel, *European Jewry*; Janssen, *Dutch Revolt*, 104–28; Menna Prestwich, ed., *International
    Calvinism, 1541–1715* (Oxford, 1985).
45 Grell, *Brethren*, 178–273.
46 Erica Boersma, 'Yrelandtsche traenen gedroogd: Transnationale solidariteit en lokale
    politiek in Zeeland, 1641–1644', *Tijdschrift voor Geschiedenis* 128, no. 2 (2015), 201–22.

47 Compare Barnett, *Empire of Humanity*; Matthew Hilton et al., 'History and Humanitarianism: A Conversation', *P&P* 241, no. 1 (2018), 1–38; Peter Stamatov, *The Origins of Global Humanitarianism: Religion, Empires, and Advocacy* (Cambridge, 2013).

48 Kat Hill, *Baptism, Brotherhood and Belief in Reformation Germany: Anabaptism and Lutheranism, 1525–1585* (Oxford, 2015); Janssen, *Dutch Revolt*, 104–28; Erika Kuijpers, *Migrantenstad: Immigratie en sociale verhoudingen in 17e-Eeuws Amsterdam* (Hilversum, 2005), 293–9.

49 Yosef Kaplan, *An Alternative Path to Modernity: The Sephardi Diaspora in Western Europe* (Leiden, 2000), 52–63; Tirtsah Levie Bernfeld, *Poverty and Welfare among the Portuguese Jews in Early Modern Amsterdam* (Oxford, 2012).

50 *Acta der Particuliere Synoden van Zuid-Holland 1621–1700, Huygens ING*, accessed 15 August 2019, http://resources.huygens.knaw.nl/retroboeken/actazh/#view=imagePane. Examples in I: 263–5, 299; II: 123–7.

51 Grell, *Brethren*, 184.

52 Quoted in Grell, *Brethren*, 293. Also Müller, *Exile Memories*, 124–5.

53 Pollmann, *Memory*, 71.

54 Erika Kuijpers, 'The Creation and Development of Social Memories of Traumatic Events: The Oudewater Massacre of 1575', in *Hurting Memories and Beneficial Forgetting: Posttraumatic Stress Disorders, Biographical Developments, and Social Conflicts*, ed. Michael Linden and Krzysztof Rutkowski (London, 2013), 191–201; Erika Kuijpers and J. Pollmann, 'Why Remember Terror? Memories of Violence in the Dutch Revolt', in *Ireland: 1641: Contexts and Reactions*, ed. Micheál Ó Siochrú and Jane Ohlmeyer (Manchester, 2013), 176–96; Benjamin Schmidt, *Innocence Abroad: The Dutch Imagination and the New World, 1570–1670* (Cambridge, 2001), 111–22.

55 Andrew Thompson, 'The Protestant Interest and the History of Humanitarian Intervention, c. 1685–1756', in *Humanitarian Intervention: A History*, ed. Brendan Simms and D. J. B. Trim (Cambridge, 2011), 67–88; Boersma, 'Yrelandtsche traenen'.

56 Pollmann, *Memory*, 181

57 Corens, *Confessional Mobility*, 25. Philip Benedict, *Christ's Churches Purely Reformed: A Social History of Calvinism* (New Haven, 2002), 373–83.

58 Mack Walker, *The Salzburg Transaction: Expulsion and Redemption in Eighteenth-Century Germany* (Ithaca, 1992), 197–205; Benjamin J. Kaplan, *Divided by Faith: Religious Conflict and the Practice of Toleration in Early Modern Europe* (Cambridge, 2007), 58–60. For a sophisticated assessment of exile narratives in eighteenth-century pietistic circles see Müller, *Exile Memories*.

59 Walker, *Salzburg Transaction*, 197–9.

60 A.Th. van Deursen, *Mensen van klein vermogen. Het kopergeld van de Gouden Eeuw* (Amsterdam, 1991), 48.

61 Grell, *Brethren*, 178–9, 184–7.

62 Grell, *Brethren*, 192–3; Janssen, *Dutch Revolt*, 70, 85–7, 131–55.

63 Helmer Helmers, 'Public Diplomacy in Early Modern Europe: Towards a New History of News', *Media History* 22, no. 3–4 (2016), 401–20; D. J. B. Trim, '"If a Prince use Tyrannie towards his People": Interventions on Behalf of Foreign Populations in Early Modern Europe', in Simms and Trim, *Humanitarian Intervention*, 29–66.

64 Randall Lesaffer, 'Between Faith and Empire: The Justification of the Spanish Intervention in the French Wars of Religion in the 1590s', in *International Law and Empire: Historical Explorations*, ed. Martti Koskenniemi et al. (Oxford, 2017), 101–22 (117–9).

65 Trim, 'If a Prince', 29–66.

66 *Resolutiën der Staten-Generaal 1576–1630, Huygens ING*, accessed 15 August 2019, http://resources.huygens.knaw.nl/retroboeken/statengeneraal/#page=0&accessor=toc& view=homePane. Examples: 1 December 1604, 31 January 1605, 9 January 1612, 15 March 1616, 1 and 23 February 1617, 10 May 1617, 19 December 1617, 4 and 15 June 1618, 25 July 1621, 9 September 1621, 10 February 1623, 11 November 1625.

67 Trim, 'If a Prince', 54–62.

68 Donald Haks, *Vaderland & vrede, 1672–1713: Publiciteit over de Nederlandse Republiek in oorlog* (Hilversum, 2013), 62–64, 95.

69 Owen Stanwood, 'Between Eden and Empire: Huguenot Refugees and the Promise of New Worlds', *American Historical Review* 118, no. 5 (2013), 1319–44 (1337).

70 Ciaran O'Scea, *Surviving Kinsale: Irish Emigration and Identity Formation in Early Modern Spain, 1601–1640* (Manchester, 2015), 44–8.

71 Matthias Nahum and Andreas Wosius, *Ootmoedighe Requeste van alle de teghenwoordighe inwoonders …* (1637). I am grateful to Lotte van Hasselt for pointing me to this reference.

72 Amsterdam, UB Amsterdam, Bijzondere Collecties, MS ROS 350/1. I am grateful to Marc de Wilde for this reference. See also Marc de Wilde, 'Offering Hospitality to Strangers: Hugo Grotius's Draft Regulations for the Jews', *The Legal History Review* 85, no. 3–4 (2017), 391–433.

73 Hunt, *Inventing Human Rights*. See also Siep Stuurman, *The Invention of Humanity: Equality and Cultural Difference in World History* (Cambridge, MA, 2017); John Witte Jr., *The Reformation of Rights: Law, Religion and Human Rights in Early Modern Calvinism* (Cambridge, 2008).

74 Barnett, *Empire of Humanity*; Abigail Green, 'Humanitarianism in Nineteenth-Century Context: Religious, Gendered, National', *HistJ* 57, no. 4 (2014), 1157–75; Klose, *The Emergence*; Stamatov, *The Origins*.

75 Lachenicht, 'Refugees'. Compare Benjamin J. Kaplan, 'The Legal Rights of Religious Refugees in the "Refugee-Cities" of Early Modern Germany', *Journal of Refugee Studies* 32, no. 1 (2019), 86–105.

76 Caroline Shaw, *Britannia's Embrace: Modern Humanitarianism and the Imperial Origins of Refugee Relief* (Oxford, 2015); Green, 'Humanitarianism'.

PART VII
Extended memory

14

THE STONES WILL CRY OUT

Victorian and Edwardian memorials to the Reformation martyrs

Andrew Atherstone

During the nineteenth and early twentieth centuries, the visual landscape of Britain and the Empire was populated with a plethora of monuments to the nation's heroes — monarchs, soldiers, politicians, inventors, explorers, artists, poets, and many more besides. Thousands of memorials, of every shape and size, honoured the illustrious dead and recommended their virtues to succeeding generations. The contested status of the Reformation in forging modern British identities, especially debates over the ongoing relevance of Protestantism to public life, stimulated campaigns to remember the sixteenth-century martyrs alongside more recent luminaries. In the centuries immediately following the Reformation, the martyrs had often been memorialised in Protestant print, but not usually in stone. Their bodies had been consumed by the flames and their ashes discarded, so there were no tombs or tombstones. Early Protestant commentators argued that their martyrs did not need earthly monuments, and that 'shrines' and 'pilgrimages' to gravesites were abhorrent to Protestant principles. John Strype's *Memorials of Thomas Cranmer* (1694) was typical:

> His Body was not carried to the Grave in State, nor buried, as many of his Predecessors were, in his own Cathedral Church, nor enclosed in a Monument of Marble or Touchstone. Nor had he any Inscription to set forth his Praises to Posterity: No Shrine to be visited by devout Pilgrims, as his Predecessors S. Dunstane, and S. Thomas had.

Strype observed that 'the Rewards of God's Elect are not Temporal, but Eternal. And Cranmer's Martyrdom is his Monument, and his Name will outlast an Epitaph, or a Shrine'.[1] Yet during the nineteenth century this rhetoric was directly reversed, as Protestants began to proclaim that it was a reproach upon the church and nation for allowing the martyrs to be forgotten by failing to build permanent monuments.

The peak of memorialising activity in honour of the martyrs spanned the Victorian and Edwardian eras, from 1837 to 1910. Scores of monuments were erected, ranging from the simple to the extravagant — obelisks, crosses, mural tablets, stained-glass windows, busts, statues, churches, chapels, lecture halls. Many were fixed in communal public spaces such as town squares or municipal parks. Perhaps the most utilitarian was the memorial erected in 1909 on the village green at Pembury in Kent to Margery Polley (martyred in 1555) — a drinking fountain for thirsty travellers on the London to Hastings road, with smaller and larger troughs for their dogs and cattle [Fig. 14.1].[2] Some memorials were funded by public subscription, others donated by wealthy individuals or campaigning organisations such as the Protestant Alliance and the National Protestant Federation. A few were national initiatives, but most were local affairs. Some were strictly denominational, others aimed to be broadly inclusive of all Protestant perspectives. Anti-Catholic agendas predominated, but some campaigners distanced themselves from theological polemic and emphasised instead civic pride and the virtues of liberty and tolerance. This populating of England's landscape with martyrs' memorials sheds significant light on the ways in which Victorian and Edwardian communities remembered, reinterpreted,

FIGURE 14.1 Memorial to Margery Polley, in the form of a drinking trough, erected at Pembury, Kent, in 1909.
Photograph: Author.

and reappropriated their Reformation heritage. Each memorial campaign deserves close investigation for what it reveals about the evolution of religious and political identities in specific local contexts, but this essay instead offers a macro-level analysis, sampling some of the principal examples in multiple locations over a ninety year period, thus encompassing the whole memorialising phenomenon.

The Victorian era

The market town of Hadleigh in Suffolk was the memorial pioneer. Uniquely, the site of Rowland Taylor's execution at Aldham Common in 1555 had been marked, perhaps since the sixteenth century, by a rough stone with a simple inscription, 'D. TAYLER IN DEFENDING THAT WAS GOOD AT THIS PLAS LEFT HIS BLODE'. But in 1818 Hadleigh's rector E. A. Hay Drummond and physician Nathan Drake combined their energies to bring renewed attention to the martyr's legacy, erecting a grander monument to their local hero on the same spot.[3] His memory was hymned in *The Suffolk Garland*, a collection of poetry, but it was not merely a Romantic endeavour.[4] Theological motivations loomed large as Drummond explained to his parishioners that Taylor had suffered 'for the Truth of our Holy Religion':

> History hath Recorded Him as a most Distinguished and able Advocate for the Protestant Faith. He was one of the Brightest Ornaments of which the Church of England can Boast. He was an Uniform and inflexible Defender of the Reformation and He Resisted even unto Death the Idolatry, the Superstition, and the false Doctrines of the Church of Rome. He was an Unspeakable Honor to, & the Glory of our Parish.[5]

This combination of anti-Catholicism, antiquarianism, and local civic pride (in varying proportions) catalysed many martyrs' memorials erected across England and Wales in the succeeding century. Hanoverian Hadleigh set a pattern which other local communities began to emulate.

With the burgeoning of Roman Catholicism from the late 1820s, at last freed from its civil disabilities, and with Tractarianism soon on the march in the national church, the theological battles of the Reformation were renewed with vigour.[6] Memories of the Reformation martyrs were especially emotive, and the burnings under 'Bloody Mary' in 1555–1558 were recalled by Victorian Protestants as proof of the inherent brutality of Rome, the church that was 'always the same' (*semper eadem*).[7] John Foxe's *Acts and Monuments of These Latter and Perilous Days* was reissued in eight volumes between 1837 and 1841, the first complete edition since 1694.[8] Foxe's martyrology, announced the evangelical clergyman Edward Bickersteth, 'should never be forgotten by British families' because it was a vital bulwark against the 'subtle' snares and 'seductive' temptations of Rome.[9] He compared England to Palestine as 'a holy land' in which every place associated with the martyrs was 'hallowed',[10] listing 54 locations from St Albans in Hertfordshire and Ashford in Kent to Wotton-under-Edge in Gloucestershire and Yoxford in Suffolk. Bickersteth urged local communities:

> LET EACH PLACE WHERE THE MARTYRS SUFFERED RAISE A LASTING MEMORIAL to shew their children, and lead them to inquire into the principles and actions of those to whom, under God, we are so deeply indebted for our present privileges and blessings: an Ebenezer of help which may strengthen us in holding fast the lively truths of God's word. It is high time for us to awake out of the torpor and indifference into which we were sinking.[11]

Bickersteth was increasingly convinced of 'the great duty and absolute necessity of bringing back again to the recollection of the present day, the bitter trials and sufferings through which our Reformers passed'.[12] Memorial tablets began to multiply in local churches — at Lutterworth in 1837, where John Wycliffe died, depicting the Reformer preaching from the Bible while worried friars looked on;[13] at Thurcaston in 1843, where Hugh Latimer was born, praising him as a 'great champion of the Protestant Faith';[14] at Carmarthen in the same year, where Bishop Robert Farrar was martyred 'for adhering to the Protestant religion';[15] and to the 'blessed martyrs for Christ' at Colchester, executed 'for their firm adherence to the Protestant Faith'.[16] At Oxford a much more ambitious monument was erected, modelled on the Eleanor Crosses, containing large statues of Cranmer, Latimer, and Nicholas Ridley, paid for by Protestant subscribers nationwide. It inevitably became identified as an anti-Tractarian protest, in the city where the Oxford Movement was born, though alarm at the growth of Roman Catholicism was a central motivation.[17]

Popular histories which grouped the martyrs geographically, rather than chronologically, helped to generate local interest, such as *Footprints of Popery; or, Places Where Martyrs Have Suffered*, published by the Religious Tract Society in 1844. Charles B. Tayler's *Memorials of the English Martyrs* (1853), which began as a series of articles in *The Christian Guardian* in 1844–1845, also encouraged evangelical pilgrimage to martyrdom sites. Tayler's curiosity in the Marian martyrs had been piqued during his years as curate under Drummond in Hadleigh in the 1820s, and then as a vicar in Chester where he was shocked to discover that most of his congregation had never heard of their local martyr George Marsh (burned in 1555).[18] He wanted to 'sound aloud the trumpet of alarm' by calling attention to 'the frightful persecutions of popery' and 'the dangers that are threatening the Church of Christ on every side'. Tayler was aware that the concept of 'pilgrimage' was suspect to Protestant ears, and criticised the tens of thousands of Catholic pilgrims who had recently visited Trier in Germany for the exhibition of the Holy Coat, rebuking the Church of Rome for daring 'to impose such absurd and lying legends upon the weak-minded and the credulous'. He was promoting 'pilgrimage of a very different character', to locations where the Reformation martyrs suffered for 'the truth as it is in Jesus', spots which 'in these days of error, must not, and shall not be forgotten!'[19] But Protestant pilgrims, like their Catholic counterparts, needed material objects to view. Shakespeare's birthplace in Stratford-upon-Avon was purchased in 1847, to be restored as a national monument, signalling the start of the Shakespeare heritage industry, but Tayler professed that he would far rather visit houses where the martyrs had lived.[20] The growing number of martyrs' memorials across England and Wales helped to supply the need for tangible, visible mementos. As the secretary to the Canterbury memorial campaign observed in the 1890s, Victorian visitors expected to see 'suitable monuments', so a martyrs' memorial would act as 'an additional inducement to travellers', thus stimulating local economic prosperity through the religious tourist trade.[21]

Material relics associated with the martyrs also helped to enhance the pilgrim's experience — such as Wycliffe's chair at Lutterworth, Latimer's pulpit at Cambridge, the door of the Bocardo prison cell at Oxford, and the surviving fragment of John Hooper's stake at Gloucester. But pilgrims were not to be hood-winked, Tayler warned. Visitors to Smithills Hall, near Bolton, were shown an unusual mark on the floor where George Marsh was said to have stamped his foot when faced by his persecutors — here, in the analysis of Alexandra Walsham, was 'the ancient trope of the indelible sacred footprint' reintegrated into a Protestant context.[22] The story was often retold by Victorian martyrologists, but Tayler dismissed it as 'an idle legend', belief in which might be 'excusable in a Papist' prone to 'superstitious credulity', but not in a clear-thinking Protestant.[23] A more respected relic was Deryk Carver's Bible, said to have been carried to the stake at Lewes in 1555, now smoke-stained and splashed with the martyr's blood. It was displayed in the early twentieth century to excite interest in martyrs' memorial campaigns, though it was later proved to have been published in the reign of Elizabeth I.[24]

High points of ecclesial conflict helped to stimulate memorialisation. For example, the restoration of the Roman Catholic hierarchy in September 1850 by Pope Pius IX's bull *Universalis Ecclesiae* stoked Protestant ire, and the Reformation martyrs were drawn into the fight. According to Edward Girdlestone (evangelical vicar of Deane, near Bolton) the 'papal aggression' had 'stirred up from John o'Groat's house to the land's end, such a loud and hearty Protestant outcry, as has had no parallel since the glorious days of the Reformation'. As a riposte, Girdlestone chose Deane's local martyr, George Marsh, as the subject for his advent sermons.[25] In many local communities the annual bonfire celebrations took on renewed anti-papal fervour, as Denis Paz has shown.[26] Dartford in Kent had a lively, and sometimes riotous, bonfire tradition and in November 1850 they organised an elaborate procession to the place where Christopher Waid had been martyred in 1555. Banners urged 'Britons, down with popery', as six men carried an over-sized effigy of the pope in tiara and fake jewels, sitting in a coffin. It was accompanied by a ten-foot crucifix, two thurifers, a lad in a surplice carrying a mocked-up version of the papal bull, and imitations of Nicholas Wiseman (the new Archbishop of Westminster) in cardinal's hat and his twelve new bishops each with mitre, crosier, and rosary. At the martyrdom site, the pope was the first to be burned in front of a jeering crowd, as mock devils threw squibs and fire crackers.[27] The following year a memorial to Waid was unveiled on the same spot. Significant anniversaries, like the tercentenary of the Marian burnings in the mid-1850s, also kept the martyrs in the spotlight. During the widespread commemorations there were frequent calls for permanent monuments.

At Gloucester, there had been a modest pedestal memorial on the site of Bishop Hooper's martyrdom since 1826, erected by a private benefactor. But it was criticised in 1851 by Richard Roberts, the local Wesleyan minister, as 'very unworthy of the Gloucester people, and very unworthy of the immortal martyr'. A grander monument was needed because 'Popery' and 'Puseyism' were spreading like an 'infection' at an alarming rate. 'The very sod of Gloucester is hallowed, because Hooper trod it', Roberts proclaimed; 'his blood speaks, his ashes speak! they speak woe to every pulpit where the doctrines for which he bled and died are not preached'.[28] It took a further decade for the idea to gather momentum and the foundation stone was laid in September 1861, with full Masonic rites, for a neo-gothic monument sufficiently ambitious in style to rival even that in Oxford.[29] At its centre was a statue of the bishop, standing 8 feet tall, in the act of preaching with Bible in hand. It was inaugurated in 1863, on 9 February, the anniversary of his martyrdom, and the sermon at the event by Anglican vicar H. C. Minchin asserted that the great principle for which Hooper willingly suffered was 'an open Bible, and the right of every man and woman to read that Bible for themselves'. Minchin warned that Satan was now assailing the Word of God in many Protestant denominations not with 'Romish superstition' but with 'infidelity', and that Victorian 'men of science' had begun a 'crusade' against Scripture.[30] In other memorial campaigns the Reformation blessing of the Bible in English was also the chief focus. At Brentwood an obelisk was erected in February 1862 in honour of the teenager William Hunter, the first Marian martyr in Essex [Fig. 14.2]. The inscription exhorted: 'Christian reader, learn from his example to value the privilege of an open Bible, and be careful to maintain it'.[31] A grander monument — a tower standing 111 feet tall — was inaugurated in honour of William Tyndale on Nibley Knoll in Gloucestershire in November 1866 after a national campaign which downplayed the martyr's strident evangelicalism in favour of his unitive role as a Bible translator, merging the motifs of anti-Catholicism, English patriotism, and religious liberty. 'No greater calamity can befall a nation', urged the *Daily Telegraph*, 'than irreverence for the memory of its illustrious dead'.[32]

Local pride was at stake as communities, or counties, sought to out-do one another by the manner of their commemorations. Smithfield in the City of London witnessed more Protestant martyrdoms than anywhere else (43 in Mary's

FIGURE 14.2 Memorial to William Hunter at Brentwood, Essex, erected in 1862. Photograph: Author.

reign alone) but lagged behind in the race to memorialise. Initial plans for a monument in 1851 in response to the papal aggression came to nothing.[33] There were difficulties in securing an appropriate site in the bustling metropolis. During the 1850s Smithfield became a major railway junction and its famous meat market was rebuilt on an impressive scale, so real estate was highly prized. But Protestant Londoners were goaded into action by public shaming. The American biographer of John Rogers declared of Smithfield in 1861:

> In every quarter of the overgrown city that now surrounds this hallowed place, are to be seen mementos erected to the memory of statesmen, warriors, scholars, and philanthropists; but no tall shaft, or even humbler cenotaph, directs the curious visitor or the anxious pilgrim to this spot … This neglect is unpardonable, on the part of Church or State, or both.[34]

Likewise, in an 1867 lecture entitled 'Why Were Our Reformers Burned?' the evangelical tract-writer J. C. Ryle (vicar of Stradbroke in Suffolk) proclaimed:

> Honour be to those who at Oxford, Gloucester, Carmarthen, and Hadleigh, have raised stones of remembrance and memorials to the martyrs! Shame be to the great

metropolis of London that, in all her expenditure of money she has never raised a memorial to those who were burned in Smithfield. There is to be a dead-meat market and a railway-station there; but as yet there is no martyrs' memorial![35]

The shame was too great to bear and soon there was a memorial tablet at Smithfield, erected by the Protestant Alliance and unveiled in March 1870 by Lord Shaftesbury. As the First Vatican Council in Rome debated papal infallibility, the Smithfield memorialists emphasised the close connection between Protestantism and national and religious liberty. Thomas Chambers (MP for Marylebone and the Common Serjeant) declared that he was 'a free man whom truth made free' and that the 'best security of freedom of conscience' was 'the free and open pages of the Bible'. Shaftesbury concurred that 'all civil liberty must rest upon the doctrines and the principles of the Gospel', the theological foundation of 'true freedom', in opposition to Roman thralldom.[36] The dogma of papal infallibility, declared *The Record* newspaper, 'must still more indelibly seal the Antichristian character of that apostate Church, against whose errors and usurpation our glorious Reformers protested even to the death'. It contrasted the courage of the English martyrs in their anti-papal protests with the timidity of the Gallican party in the 1870s such as Félix Dupanloup, Georges Darboy and Jacques Ginoulhiac, who it predicted would 'submissively succumb' to the forces of Ultramontanism. Thus these prelates would return to France after defeat at the Vatican Council, 'not as men of the stamp of our Ridleys, our Latimers, our Hoopers, or our Smithfield Martyrs, but as men vanquished and cowering to usurped authority, although vexed and sorrowful'.[37] Jingoism was never far from the martyrs' memorial campaigns, fusing Protestantism with proud patriotism, and freedom of conscience with English liberty from unwanted European interference.

In parallel with the Smithfield monument, a new mission church was erected in the nearby overcrowded parish of Clerkenwell, known colloquially as the Martyrs' Memorial Church, with statues and bas-reliefs of the Smithfield martyrs — or, as one ritualist commentator rudely put it, 'decorated with effigies of the principal Zuinglian heretics who had been executed according to the law of the land'.[38] Thomas Hugo, a high church clergyman, complained that very few deserved the title of 'martyr', because most of these 'culprits' were 'Atheists, Socinians, Munster Anabaptists, and members of other wild and obscure sects which have no connection whatever with the existing Church of England'.[39] Yet Benjamin Oswald Sharp (missionary curate in Clerkenwell) insisted that the martyrs of Smithfield had been 'murdered by the Church of Rome' and must never be forgotten. The memorial church was

> our protest to an age which has allowed its mouth and ear to be shut. Our memorial in stone is intended to stir up every man to be his own sculptor, and restore the memorials, dark and dim, once burnt in upon his very heart and brain, we did once think deep enough to out-last time itself.[40]

Those seeking to erase memory of the martyrs he rebuked as 'Iconoclasts', an inversion of the usual Protestant language against image makers.[41] Lord Shaftesbury, who laid the foundation stone, called it a public protest against the 'abominations' of the Church of Rome and a celebration of Reformation rescue from 'the domination of a soul-destroying religion', though he also hit out at parallel examples of 'tyranny and oppression', like Victorian rationalism and ritualism.[42] 'Will not every true Protestant desire to have at least a brick in such a building?' asked the vicar of Clerkenwell, Robert Maguire, in his appeal for donations.[43] Bishop Jackson of London was caught in the crossfire. His diocesan building fund had given £2000 towards the scheme and he was abused in the ritualist *Church Times* for identifying himself with 'intolerant Puritans' who 'degrade the name of martyrdom' by associating it with Smithfield.[44] But the new church was formally dedicated to St Peter, not to the Reformation martyrs, so at its consecration in 1871 the bishop carefully explained that it must be not only 'thoroughly Protestant' (avoiding 'the corruptions of Rome') but also 'truly Catholic', taking its stand upon 'the rock of primitive truth' and modelling a 'primitive form of worship'. Such nuances went either unnoticed or deliberately overlooked by the main campaigners, for whom Protestantism *versus* Catholicism was the primary motif.[45]

The form of monuments was an additional source of contention. Protestants were especially alert to Catholic iconography being smuggled into martyrs' memorials. *The Rock*, an Anglican evangelical newspaper, refused to support the campaign for a monument at Stratford-le-Bow in East London (unveiled by Lord Shaftesbury in 1879) until guarantees were made about its final form. It alluded to the Smithfield Martyrs' Church, 'covered with effigies', before adding darkly: 'That style of treatment is best left to the other side'.[46] Monumental crosses — as seen, for instance, in Oxford's neo-gothic design — were also viewed with suspicion and many martyrs' memorials took the form of a simple obelisk, popular among Protestants since the seventeenth century as 'neutral Christian ornament' free from idolatrous associations.[47]

At Canterbury, where the Protestant societies felt deliberately excluded from the memorial campaign, the design of the monument was a particular focus of angst. The city had witnessed 41 burnings in Mary's reign, more than any other location except Smithfield. Nevertheless, at the inauguration of the monument in June 1899 reference to Protestantism was conspicuous by its absence. The celebrations began in Canterbury cathedral with a sermon by Canon A. J. Mason (Lady Margaret Professor of Divinity at Cambridge) whose recent biography *Thomas Cranmer* (1898) portrayed the martyred archbishop through an Anglo-Catholic lens. In his sermon he praised the Canterbury martyrs for breaking 'the tyranny of mediaeval abuses' and for bringing the Church of England 'back from custom and tradition to the authority of the teaching of Scripture'. Yet the professor cautioned that the martyrs were not professed theologians, and were not all perfect people. Some of them held strange opinions, some called their judges by opprobrious names, some used coarse and shocking language regarding things held sacred by other people; we were by no means bound to admire everything they said and did ...

This was hardly the ringing endorsement expected by Protestant campaigners more used to reading Foxe. Mason's sermon was derided by D. S. Hyslop (organising secretary of the Protestant Alliance), who thought it 'a farce' that the organisers had invited a preacher known to hold doctrines which the martyrs gave their lives to oppose.[48] There was vocal protest at the unveiling of the memorial. The inscription proclaimed 'Lest We Forget', but avoided all mention of Protestantism and spoke only of the martyrs' 'heroic fidelity' in helping 'to secure for succeeding generations the priceless blessing of religious freedom'. It took the form of an obelisk surmounted by a 'Canterbury Cross', modelled on a Saxon brooch unearthed at Canterbury in 1867 and a symbolic connection with pre-Reformation English Christianity.[49] After the official speeches, Hyslop and H. R. Knight (secretary of the Canterbury Protestant Union) handed the Dean of Canterbury, F. W. Farrar, a written protest rebuking the organisers for 'desecrating' the memorial with a 'Pagan and Popish Cross', an 'insult' to the martyrs' memory; but Farrar scornfully brushed away their concerns with the retort, 'It is very silly'. As the crowd dispersed, Hyslop tried to address them, warning that the image of the cross had been worshipped by the Babylonians many centuries before Christ, and that Canterbury was 'in great danger of going back to Rome'. Another Protestant agitator lamented that it might easily be mistaken for a Roman Catholic memorial, especially since the word 'Protestant' had been 'sedulously excluded'. The cross was 'a desecration', he complained, and he would have no hesitation in putting up a ladder and knocking it off.[50] In the fierce contest to define the martyrs' legacy, memorials had the potential to repel local Protestants as much as attract them.

The Edwardian era

At the turn of the twentieth century anti-Catholic agitation showed no immediate signs of abating. The Reformation martyrs remained rhetorically potent for Protestant orators like John Kensit, founder in 1889 of the Protestant Truth Society which campaigned vociferously against Catholicism in both its Roman and Anglican guises. Kensit was killed in 1902 by an iron file thrown by a Catholic mob near Liverpool, thus demonstrating to his followers that martyrdom for the faith was as much a reality in the modern age as it had been in the days of Tyndale or Cranmer. 'Another witness is slain', mourned the *English Churchman*; 'Another martyr is added to the noble army of the past'.[51] The first decade of the new century saw a crescendo in memorialising activity, as local communities without a martyrs' monument hurried to catch up with their neighbours. The National

Protestant Federation (founded in 1899) took a national perspective, aiming to supply memorials wherever they were missing, while the three hundred and fiftieth anniversary of the Marian burnings in 1905–1908 was a further stimulus. At Exeter, for example, the idea for a memorial was brought forward at a lecture in 1907 by Emma Miller (mission secretary for the Protestant Reformation Society in Devon and Cornwall) to mark the martyrdom in 1557 of Agnes Prest.[52] Monuments already erected by many other towns and cities were acknowledged as 'an incentive to Exonians to have one also'.[53] It was unveiled by Sir John Kennaway, evangelical MP and father of the House of Commons, who recalled how as an undergraduate in the 1850s he had looked out upon Oxford's martyrs' memorial every morning from his rooms at Balliol College, 'and why should Exeter be behind Oxford?'[54] However, as Edwardian memorials multiplied, new questions began to emerge, about broadening the category of martyrdom beyond the Protestant Reformation, and about the intrinsic relationship between Protestantism, freedom of conscience, and civil liberty.

At Lewes in Sussex, where 17 Protestants were burned during the Marian persecution, the town council refused to allow a memorial at the town hall because it would be a 'slap in the face' to local Roman Catholics and was inappropriate on municipal property.[55] Campaigners had to settle for a private plot outside the town, where a memorial obelisk was unveiled by the Countess of Portsmouth in May 1901.[56] At Colchester in Essex, where 23 were burned under Mary, the town council took a different approach. Their town hall was rebuilt between 1898 and 1902, decorated with marble statues depicting local heroes ranging from Queen Boadicea, scourge of the Romans, to Bishop Samuel Harsnett, scourge of the puritans. A martyrs' monument was funded by Samuel Fennell Hurnard, a prominent local Quaker, but to the long list of Marian martyrs he added the names of two seventeenth-century Quakers, the evangelist James Parnell (who died in Colchester Castle in 1656 after cruel treatment by his puritan captors) and Edward Graunt (who died in 1664 after being beaten by royalist soldiers sent to break up a Quaker meeting). The inclusion of Quaker martyrs, observed the *Essex County Standard*, showed that modern Colchester recognised all 'victims of religious fanaticism', whether slain by Catholics or Protestants. The new memorial was thus 'no ebullition of mere Kensitism, for the Protestants have plenty to be ashamed of in the matter of religious persecution'.[57] Nonetheless, the line was drawn at including Thomas Beche, the last abbot of Colchester, who was hanged, drawn and quartered in 1539 for his opposition to the royal supremacy. Beche had recently been beatified by Pope Leo XIII in 1895, but his credentials as a religious 'martyr' were disputed, leading local Roman Catholics to protest that a town hall built with tax-payers' money should be inclusive of all religious opinions.[58]

Similar dispute over the category of 'martyrdom' was evident in Suffolk. Local enthusiasm was reignited by Nina Frances Layard's *Seventeen Suffolk Martyrs* (1902), drawing extensively on Foxe's *Acts and Monuments*. Their histories might 'lie buried in ancient libraries, covered with the dust of centuries', wrote evangelical clergy-man Samuel Garratt, but none would be 'missing from the book of God's remembrance. … It is well to read of them: "Lest we forget! Lest we forget!"'[59] A meeting in Ipswich town hall in November 1902 resolved to erect a public monument to these local heroes 'who died for the Protestant faith and the testimony of Jesus Christ'. Garratt asserted that for more than half a century, since the rise of the Oxford Movement, there had been a growing 'spirit of coldness, and then of avowed hostility, to the very name of Protestant'. Yet it was a glorious title which belonged to those 'who believed in the blessed work of the Reformation, and one which, by God's grace and help, they would never give up. (Hear, hear.)'. The newly-elected mayor, W. J. Catchpole, emphasised instead the Reformation blessing of freedom of worship, 'without interference from any authority, spiritual or temporal'. Another speaker predicted that a wealthy town like Ipswich should have no difficulty in raising funds for a monument, especially when they recalled that 'this prosperity was due to the liberties which were purchased by the blood of the martyrs', an explicit causality between Protestantism and economic growth.[60] The *East Anglian Daily Times* welcomed the proposal but reminded its readers that 'there were martyrs on both sides', and that 'liberty of conscience' was the Reformation's chief legacy to the twentieth century. It applied this lesson to the notorious 1902 Education Act, brought in by Balfour's Conservative government, which forced Nonconformists to subsidise denominational schools (mostly Anglican and Roman Catholic) through the rates. Religious freedom was constantly being exposed to 'subtle attacks', the newspaper warned.[61] The memorial therefore had anti-Tory and anti-Anglican dimensions, entwined with the dominant anti-Catholicism [Fig. 14.3].

If the Ipswich memorial was a genuine celebration of religious freedom, however, then why limit it to Protestants? One critic recommended that the names of Catholic martyrs be added: 'let us put into practice that broadminded, tolerant spirit which sees good in all creeds and in all sects, irrespective of denominations'. He hoped to see Protestants and Catholics standing side-by-side at the unveiling ceremony, 'in the spirit of mutual love and forgiveness'.[62] Some wanted to broaden the scope even further. If toleration was the dominant motif, then what about the scores of East Anglian women cruelly executed during Matthew Hopkins' witch-hunts of 1645–1647? Anglican rector H. N. Grimley chimed in: 'let us not forget the poor witches. They were martyrs; poor, mute martyrs. They have had no one to idealise them; no one to turn them into heroes and heroines of romance. But they suffered grievously … from Puritan tyranny'. A martyrs' memorial presented an opportunity for a 'grand act of reparation' by the evangelical successors of puritanism.[63] Nevertheless, these calls for a catholicity of approach fell on deaf ears. The Ipswich memorial was unveiled in December 1903 by Henry Wace (the new Dean of Canterbury), a prominent Protestant spokesman. A week later he was in nearby Bury St Edmunds to unveil their martyrs' monument, which also stirred up significant controversy among the local populace. When ritualist vicar Thomas Stantial preached against the scheme as 'foolish to rake

FIGURE 14.3 Martyrs' memorial at Ipswich, unveiled by Dean Wace in 1903.
Photograph: Author.

up the ashes of a bad past', the *English Churchman* mocked that he would probably prefer a
monument to Guy Fawkes.[64] Another activist offered to contribute £50 for the memorial, on condition that 'the aggressive word Protestant' in the inscription be replaced by
'the peace-giving word Christian', and that a cross be substituted for 'the Pagan obelisk'.
The committee refused, determined not to repeat the mistakes made at Canterbury.[65]

The intertwining of anti-Catholicism with agitation over civil liberties was
repeated in the village of Heathfield in Sussex, where an obelisk was erected in
September 1905 in the grounds of the Congregational Chapel to commemorate
four local martyrs burned at Lewes in 1557. Anti-Catholic motivations were made
explicit by the inscription which announced that the martyrs were burned 'by the
Roman Catholics … because they dared to worship God as the Word of God
directs'. 'Sacerdotalism was rampant', warned General Sir William Stirling (former
Lieutenant of the Tower of London) as he unveiled the monument, 'and everything was being done by the Romanising party to crush the Word of God'.[66]

Seven hundred schoolchildren took part in the celebration and David Catt (secretary of the Calvinistic Protestant Union) presented each of them with a copy of *Turn or Burn*, an illustrated history of the Sussex martyrs.[67] Yet the Heathfield memorial doubled as a vindication of Nonconformist 'passive resistance' against the 1902 Education Act — indeed, it was first proposed at the local branch of the Liberation Society, of which Heathfield's Congregational minister, Josephus Lemm, was secretary.[68] The great lesson of the Reformation martyrs, announced James Green of Hailsham, was the need to 'stand firm for Christ and religious liberty'. At the unveiling, he urged all men who possessed a vote to use that privilege very carefully at the next General Election, 'to vote for the cause of liberty, liberty of citizenship and liberty of religion. The two must go together. Nonconformity had been sleeping long enough, and Nonconformity must awake'. Likewise Charles Hutchinson (MP for Sussex East), a member of the resurgent Liberal Party, declared that the Marian martyrs had 'fought, bled, and died' for the 'the great blessings of liberty' which their successors in the twentieth century must fight to hand down to the next generation 'untarnished and unsullied'. Although it was no longer fashionable to burn people for their religious convictions, Christians in 1905 were still suffering under 'oppressive laws', being dragged before the magistrate for refusal to pay the rates. These conscientious men and women, Hutchinson averred, were 'martyrs of another sort'.[69] Such politically-motivated comparisons offended Anglican clergyman J. J. Coxhead, who dismissed the Heathfield memorial as 'cant'. It was 'very wicked' to suggest that the treatment of Nonconformists by Balfour's government was equivalent to the sufferings endured under Mary Tudor, he protested. English liberty meant freedom of worship not freedom to refuse to pay taxes.[70] Yet Sussex liberals continued to reinforce the martyrdom parallels: 'Passive Resisters are fighting the same battle today'.[71]

The recurrent motifs of anti-Catholicism and liberation comingled also at Rayleigh, in Essex, where a memorial obelisk was erected in September 1908, an ecumenical initiative led by T. W. Moss of the Peculiar People, a Wesleyan offshoot. Alexander Roger (secretary of the National Protestant Federation) saw the monument as an antidote to ritualism in the Church of England, while other speakers called for more vocal Protestantism in the House of Commons and told the crowd that 'The Bible and Popery could not live together'. But the event was chaired by Edmund Wright Brooks, a Quaker businessman and philanthropist, who drew attention instead to the martyrs' sacrifice for 'religious liberty' and spoke more about the sufferings of Margaret Fell, the 'mother of Quakerism', than about the Reformation. The memorial was unveiled by Rowland Whitehead (Liberal MP for South East Essex) who declared that 'truth is a most precious jewel, but it has many facets … no individual is entitled to claim that he alone sees truth in its entirety'. The chief lesson of the Marian burnings, he observed, was 'the abiding need of toleration'.[72]

At Coventry, where eleven Lollards and Reformers were executed between 1510 and 1555, doctrinal questions were deliberately excluded. The memorial committee was led by the mayor, Alderman William Lee (a ribbon manufacturer and Baptist deacon), who insisted that their motivation was civic duty, desiring to honour their 'fellow citizens' without reference to 'creeds and parties'. They appealed for help from 'men of all religions, and even those of no religion at all'.[73] Why should Coventry hang back when 'almost every town in England' had memorialised its martyrs?[74] The monument, in the form of a Celtic Cross, was unveiled in September 1910 and its inscription was firmly neutral, noting only that the martyrs 'suffered death for conscience sake'. Concerning their theological principles, Alderman Lee feigned agnosticism:

> What was the reason of their martyrdom? Were they religious or political, scientific or philosophical martyrs? I must confess I do not know. I do not know that they belonged to any sect or party. That is of very little importance. The point of interest to me is that some of them were resident in this city.

Instead he explicitly connected Coventry's martyrs with others willing to suffer for their religion or philosophy, like Socrates executed in Athens, and Baruch Spinoza expelled from the Jewish community in Amsterdam in the 1650s. The martyrs had courage, the mayor declared, to die for the 'liberty to think and speak', and their memorial would stand for many centuries as 'a witness to the truth that error must be met by argument and not by force'. It was a reminder, said another speaker, to the inhabitants of Coventry that their convictions must never be sacrificed 'for personal convenience or to public conventionality'.[75] Here was a keynote strikingly different from the robust religiously-motivated Protestantism of many earlier memorials.

The ecumenical era

The civic monument at Coventry marked the close of two generations of memorialising fervour in honour of the Reformation martyrs between 1837 and 1910. After the horrors of the First World War, local communities were absorbed in remembering their recent dead, not those from the distant past. Furthermore, the demise of anti-Catholicism and the dwindling power of Protestantism as a national and communal rallying cry, left the martyrs increasingly out of vogue.[76] There were some notable exceptions, such as the substantial monument unveiled at Amersham in 1931 in memory of seven Lollards burned between 1506 and 1521. It was organised by the Protestant Alliance and the gathered crowd was exhorted to do all they could to maintain 'a Protestant King on a Protestant throne, and be ruled by a Protestant Parliament'.[77] Existing memorials became the focus of annual commemorations by the Protestant societies, for preaching and wreath-laying. At Exeter in 1931, for example, on the quartocentenary of Thomas Benet's martyrdom, a 'remembrance day' celebration was held at the memorial attended by about a thousand people. The obelisk was illuminated with red and yellow electric lights, and the remains of Benet's stake (dug up in 1849) was displayed as a precious Protestant relic.[78] The Sussex Martyrs Commemoration Council was particularly active in keeping the story of its local martyrs alive, and memorial tablets multiplied throughout the county.[79] Gaps were filled in the memorial record elsewhere too, for example by the Protestant Alliance at the Lollards' Pit in Norwich in 1984, making up for a failed attempt to erect a martyrs' memorial in the city a century earlier.[80] It proclaimed that the Norwich martyrs all died 'in the cause of Biblical Evangelical Christianity and in denial of the unscriptural doctrines of the Church of Rome', a significant shift in nomenclature at the end of the twentieth century away from the bygone language of 'Protestantism' towards a preferred 'Evangelical' identity. But by now these were minority interests, raising barely a flicker in the local press, and the memorials were much more modest compared with the architectural glories of the Victorian and Edwardian eras. The nadir was reached in 2007 when John Hullier (martyred in 1556) was commemorated on Jesus Green, Cambridge, with the planting of a copper beech tree and a small plaque fixed to a nearby bench.[81] It presented a pathetic contrast with Oxford's major monument.

In an ecumenical age, there was more appetite for memorials which bridged historic animosities. There had been radical calls at the turn of the twentieth century (as at Colchester and Ipswich) for Protestants and Catholics to be honoured together, though the status of the Catholic martyrs, technically executed for treason, remained hotly contested. Even as late as 1970, despite the spirit of *aggiornamento* ushered in by the Second Vatican Council, the canonisation of the Forty English Martyrs by Pope Paul VI caused ecumenical embarrassment.[82] However, in 1977 Westminster Abbey pioneered a new policy, with a modest tablet near the tomb of queens Mary and Elizabeth, which exhorted: 'Remember before God all those who, divided at the Reformation by different convictions, laid down their lives for Christ and conscience' sake'.[83] This ecumenical pattern was soon repeated at Chester. Reformation preacher George Marsh was commemorated there by a Protestant obelisk, erected in 1898, but Roman priest John Plessington (one of 'the Forty') had been hanged, drawn and quartered on the same spot in 1679 during the 'Popish Plot' hysteria. At his tercentenary in 1979, there was a grand Catholic procession through the streets of Chester from the place of execution, carrying the martyr's relics (a lock of hair and a piece of bloodstained garment), and the Apostolic Delegate to Great Britain celebrated pontifical high mass robed in Plessington's own vestments before a crowd of 6,000 people.[84] Shortly afterwards Chester city council added Plessington's name alongside Marsh's on the monument, despite protests from the Protestant Alliance at this act of 'desecration'.[85]

Eton College indicated a similar rapprochement with a memorial tablet to its six Reformation martyrs, both Protestant and Catholic, dedicated in 2003 by Cardinal Cormac Murphy-O'Connor (Roman Catholic Archbishop of Westminster) and Simon Barrington-Ward (former Anglican Bishop of Coventry).[86] Stimulated by Eton's example, another ecumenical memorial was erected at Oxford's University Church in 2008, unveiled by Lord Patten (Chancellor of the University and a lay Roman Catholic), at the initiative of Sir Hugo Brunner (Lord Lieutenant of Oxfordshire).[87] It named not just Cranmer, Latimer, and Ridley but twenty other 'martyrs of the Reformation' associated with Oxford or Oxfordshire, including Edmund Campion and Archbishop Laud. Professor Diarmaid MacCulloch, an adviser to the project, called it 'a new sort of memorial', distinct from the 'tribal' monuments of Victorian England. It was designed to reconcile Christians, not to 'celebrate separation' but to 'create common memory' and encourage meditation upon 'the sincerity of faith held by both sides'. MacCulloch linked this ecumenical initiative to the efforts by Tony Blair's government to legislate against the incitement of religious hatred, in a twenty-first-century context where anti-Catholicism had now been substituted in popular polemic by Islamophobia.[88]

Conclusion

Memorials to the Reformation martyrs, which populate England's visual landscape, speak with multivalent voices. Mostly built in stone, they appear fixed and rigid, standing unmoved and unbending for generations to come. They appear mute, often with only the briefest inscription. Yet, as this essay has shown, there is an inherent plasticity in the martyrs' monuments. They are highly malleable objects, flexing to fit a variety of ambiguous and conflicting messages about the Reformation. Subscribers did not sign a doctrinal statement; they paid for a stone. Therefore, paradoxically, theological interpretations remained fluid and always contested. Indeed the meaning of the memorials was often deliberately massaged and shaped, by the campaigning committee or the local press, to legitimise multiple interpretations and thus win as broad support as possible. To one audience, a memorial might be received as an explicit anti-Catholic statement, a protest against the spread of contemporary Roman Catholicism and its Tractarian and ritualist offshoots. To another audience, the same memorial might be invested with a message about civic pride and the virtues of tolerance, deliberately eschewing theological polemic — freedom of conscience, freedom to think, freedom from ecclesial authority, became the keynotes. In memorial campaigns the rhetoric of Protestantism, patriotism, and liberty jostled for attention. The same monument might stand for an open Bible or an open mind, anti-Romanism or anti-Anglicanism, a desire to throw off the shackles of the pope or the Tory party, or all of these competing agendas at the same time. Conflicting ideologies were brought together under the same Reformation banner in an uneasy alliance. These ambiguities inevitably led to misunderstandings, as men in public office — whether bishops, mayors, or parliamentarians — tried to avoid being caught in party schemes. Arguments about the nature of martyrdom, and the incompatibility or otherwise of Protestant and Catholic teaching, provoked febrile controversy in newspapers and pulpits. These Reformation monuments demonstrate the deep potency and potentiality of communal memory with its emotive tales of trauma, heroism, persecution, and sacrifice. The martyrs' memorials of Victorian and Edwardian England allowed local communities to rediscover, reappropriate, and reimagine that Reformation heritage for their many different contemporary needs.

Notes

1 John Strype, *Memorials of the Most Reverend Father in God, Thomas Cranmer, Sometime Lord Archbishop of Canterbury* (London, 1694), 391.
2 *Kent and Sussex Courier*, 30 July 1909.

3 *Suffolk Chronicle*, 10 October 1818.

4 Nathan Drake, 'Lines, Written at the Stone, near Hadleigh', in *The Suffolk Garland: or, A Collection of Poems, Songs, Tales, Ballads, Sonnets, and Elegies, Legendary and Romantic, Historical and Descriptive, Relative to that County* (Ipswich, 1818), 251–4.

5 Bury St Edmunds, Suffolk Record Office, FB81/E/1/3 [Address to the Hadleigh Committee, 25 June 1818].

6 Among an extensive literature, see for example, John Wolffe, *The Protestant Crusade in Great Britain, 1829–1860* (Oxford, 1991); D. G. Paz, *Popular Anti-Catholicism in Mid-Victorian England* (Stanford, CA, 1992); Michael Wheeler, *The Old Enemies: Catholic and Protestant in Nineteenth-Century English Culture* (Cambridge, 2006).

7 Judith Richards, 'Defaming and Defining "Bloody Mary" in Nineteenth-Century England', in *Reinventing the Reformation in the Nineteenth Century: A Cultural History*, ed. Peter Nockles and Vivienne Westbrook, *Bulletin of the John Rylands Library* 90, no. 1 (2014), 287–303.

8 Andrew Penny, 'John Foxe's Victorian Reception', *HistJ* 40, no. 1 (1997), 111–42; Penny, 'John Foxe, Evangelicalism and the Oxford Movement', in *John Foxe: An Historical Perspective*, ed. David Loades (Aldershot, 1999), 182–237.

9 Edward Bickersteth, 'Introductory Remarks', in *The English Martyrology, Abridged from Foxe*, ed. Charlotte Elizabeth Tonna, 2 vols. (London, 1837) I: xii.

10 Bickersteth, 'Introductory Remarks', xiv.

11 Bickersteth, 'Introductory Remarks', xv.

12 Bickersteth, 'Introductory Remarks', xix.

13 J. H. Gurney, *A Sermon, Preached in Lutterworth Church, on Wednesday, December 20, 1837, upon Occasion of the Erection of a Monument to the Memory of Wiclif* (Leicester, 1838).

14 *Leicester Journal*, 12 January 1844.

15 *North Wales Chronicle*, 26 September 1843.

16 *Essex Standard*, 8 September 1843.

17 For detailed analysis, see Andrew Atherstone, 'The Martyrs' Memorial at Oxford', *JEH* 54, no. 2 (2003), 278–301.

18 C. B. Tayler, *Memorials of the English Martyrs* (London, 1853), 2–3, 60–1, 311–2.

19 Tayler, *Memorials of the English Martyrs*, 2–3.

20 Tayler, *Memorials of the English Martyrs*, 103.

21 *Canterbury Journal*, 5 February 1898.

22 Alexandra Walsham, *The Reformation of the Landscape: Religion, Identity, and Memory in Early Modern Britain and Ireland* (Oxford, 2011), 520.

23 Tayler, *Memorials of the English Martyrs*, 304.

24 *Kent and Sussex Courier*, 19 February 1909. On the authenticity of Carver's Bible, see J. A. Erredge, *Brighthelmstone, Sussex: The Ancient and Modern History of Brighton* (Brighton, 1867), 122–3; Frederick Harrison, 'Deryk Carver's Bible', *Sussex Notes and Queries* 7, no. 3 (1938), 72–3.

25 Edward Girdlestone, *George Marsh, the Martyr of Deane* (London, 1851), iii.

26 'Bonfires, Revels, and Riots', in Paz, *Popular Anti-Catholicism*, 225–47.

27 *Maidstone Journal*, 12 November 1850.

28 Richard Roberts, *Tract for the Times: Bishop Hooper's Character and Martyrdom, in A Sermon Preached on the Anniversary of his Death* (Gloucester, 1851), 22–3, 25.

29 *Gloucester Journal*, 21 September 1861.

30 *Gloucester Journal*, 14 February 1863.

31 *Essex Standard*, 14 February 1862.

32 *Daily Telegraph*, 12 November 1866. For detailed analysis, see Andrew Atherstone, 'Memorializing William Tyndale', in Nockles and Westbrook, eds., *Reinventing the Reformation in the Nineteenth Century*, 155–78.

33 *The Standard*, 29 August 1851.

34 Joseph Lemuel Chester, *John Rogers* (London, 1861), 211.

35 J. C. Ryle, *Why Were Our Reformers Burned? A Lecture* (London, 1867), 18. For Ryle's didactic use of Protestant history, see Andrew Atherstone, 'J. C. Ryle and Evangelical

Churchmanship', in *Making Evangelical History: Faith, Scholarship and the Evangelical Past*, ed. Andrew Atherstone and David Ceri Jones (London, 2019), 81–101.

36 *The Record*, 14 March 1870.

37 *The Record*, 14 March 1870.

38 W. H. B. Proby, *Annals of the 'Low-Church' Party in England, Down to the Death of Archbishop Tait*, 2 vols. (London, 1888) II: 289. The Martyrs' Memorial Church was destroyed in the Blitz.

39 *Church Times*, 30 June 1871.

40 B. O. Sharp, *Anne Askew, Martyr, A.D. 1545* (London, 1869), 3.

41 Sharp, *Anne Askew*, 14.

42 *Clerkenwell News and London Times*, 30 June 1869.

43 *The Record*, 29 April 1870.

44 *Church Times*, 7 July 1871.

45 *London Daily Chronicle and Clerkenwell News*, 1 July 1871.

46 *The Rock*, 9 March 1877. See further, W. J. Bolton, *The Stratford Martyrs of the Reformation: A Sermon* (London, 1868); W. J. Bolton, *The Story of the Stratford Martyrs* (Stratford, 1879).

47 Margaret Aston, *Broken Idols of the English Reformation* (Cambridge, 2016), 857.

48 *Canterbury Journal*, 17 June 1899.

49 *Kentish Gazette and Canterbury Press*, 24 June 1899.

50 *Canterbury Journal*, 17 June 1899.

51 *English Churchman*, 9 October 1902, quoted in Martin Wellings, 'The First Protestant Martyr of the Twentieth Century: The Life and Significance of John Kensit (1853–1902)', in *Martyrs and Martyrologies*, ed. Diana Wood (Oxford, 1993), 349. See also, John C. Wilcox, *John Kensit: Reformer and Martyr* (London, 1903).

52 *Devon and Exeter Daily Gazette*, 12 May 1908.

53 *Devon and Exeter Daily Gazette*, 12 July 1909.

54 *Devon and Exeter Daily Gazette*, 21 October 1909.

55 *Sussex Agricultural Express*, 20 March 1896.

56 *Sussex Agricultural Express*, 10 May 1901.

57 *Essex County Standard*, 3 June 1899.

58 *Essex County Standard*, 10, 17, and 24 June 1899.

59 Samuel Garratt, 'Preface', in Nina Frances Layard, *Seventeen Suffolk Martyrs* (Ipswich, 1902). For an overview of the Suffolk memorials, see Peter Wickins, *Victorian Protestantism and Bloody Mary: The Legacy of Religious Persecution in Tudor England* (Bury St Edmunds, 2012), 37–64.

60 *East Anglian Daily Times*, 27 November 1902.

61 *East Anglian Daily Times*, 27 November 1902. See further, N. R. Gullifer, 'Opposition to the 1902 Education Act', *Oxford Review of Education* 8, no. 1 (1982), 83–98.

62 *East Anglian Daily Times*, 1 December 1902.

63 *East Anglian Daily Times*, 3 December 1902.

64 *English Churchman*, 22 January 1903.

65 *Bury and Norwich Post*, 5 and 19 May 1903.

66 *Sussex Express*, 30 September 1905.

67 F. J. Hamilton and W. Stanley Martin, *Turn or Burn: The Lewes Protestant Martyrs' Memorial Volume* (London, 1901).

68 *Sussex Express*, 7 November 1903. See further, J. E. B. Munson, 'A Study of Nonconformity in Edwardian England as Revealed by the Passive Resistance Movement Against the 1902 Education Act' (DPhil thesis, University of Oxford, 1973); D. R. Pugh, 'English Nonconformity, Education and Passive Resistance 1903–6', *History of Education* 19, no. 4 (1990), 355–73.

69 *Sussex Express*, 30 September 1905.

70 *Sussex Express*, 30 September 1905.

71 *Sussex Express*, 7 October 1905.

72 *Southend Standard*, 24 September 1908.

73 *Coventry Herald*, 5 September 1908. The Coventry martyrs' memorial committee minutes (1908–1910) survive at Coventry Archives, PA120/1.
74 *Coventry Herald*, 23 April 1909.
75 *Coventry Herald*, 16 September 1910.
76 S. J. D. Green, *The Passing of Protestant England: Secularisation and Social Change, c.1920–1960* (Cambridge, 2011).
77 *Middlesex Advertiser and County Gazette*, 12 June 1931.
78 *Western Morning News*, 12 January 1931. On the discovery of the relic, see *Morning Advertiser*, 6 October 1849; photograph in Mary E. T. Stirling, *The Story of the Exeter Protestant Martyrs* (Weston-super-Mare, 1913), 14.
79 Sussex Martyrs Commemoration Council, accessed 24 August 2019, www.sussexmartyrs.co.uk; E. T. Stoneham, *Martyrs of Jesus: The Story of the Sussex Martyrs of the Reformation* (Lewes, 1935; new editions 1953, 1967, and 1983).
80 *Norfolk Chronicle*, 15 November 1884; *Eastern Daily Press*, 1 October 1984.
81 'Cambridge Martyr Remembered', *Evangelical Times* 41 (June 2007), 11.
82 Andrew Atherstone, 'The Canonisation of the Forty English Martyrs: An Ecumenical Dilemma', *Recusant History* 30, no. 4 (2011), 573–87.
83 *Church Times*, 21 October 1977.
84 'St John Plessington Tercentenary', *The Universe*, 20 July 1979, 16.
85 'Chester Martyrs' Memorial', *The Reformer* (July/August 1979), 15; 'Rev. George Marsh Martyrdom Remembered', *The Reformer* (July/August 1980), 4.
86 Charles DesForges, 'Old Etonian Martyrs', *The Chronicle* no. 4053 (May 2003), 26–7.
87 *Oxford Times*, 20 June 2008.
88 Diarmaid MacCulloch, 'History Against Hatred', *BBC History Magazine* 7 (April 2006), 52.

15

RELIGIOUS HERITAGE AND CIVIC IDENTITY

Remembering the Reformation in Geneva from the sixteenth to the twenty-first century

Philip Benedict and Sarah Scholl

Geneva, the 'Protestant Rome', offers an exceptionally interesting case for exploring how the Reformation and the people and events associated with it were remembered in holidays, commemorations, and memorials from the sixteenth century to the present. No city in Europe, not even Wittenberg, had its development and historical experience more profoundly shaped by the Reformation. No city except Wittenberg is accorded more attention in histories of the Reformation. Geneva's Reformation was also closely tied to the consolidation of the city's independence and gave rise to a new myth of urban identity that cast the town as a bastion of the Gospel where morals and manners were reformed as nowhere else; preserving its liberty and prosperity was said to depend on remaining true to this heritage.[1] For over 250 years, Geneva remained the mono–confessional free city, affiliated through treaties of protection with the chief Protestant cantons of the Swiss Confederation, which it became between 1526 and 1536. Then, around 1800, its territorial situation and religious composition were scrambled in ways that would complicate recalling the Reformation. In 1798 it was incorporated into France. Between 1814 and 1816 it was re-attached to the expanded and restructured Swiss Confederation as a full-fledged canton. At the same time, its boundaries were enlarged to encompass a number of previously Savoyard and French, hence Catholic, rural communes, whose religious status quo was guaranteed by the Treaty of Vienna. In 1847, after considerable debate, a new liberal constitution established freedom of worship. By the end of the 1850s, as a result of the border changes and immigration, Catholics formed a majority of the cantonal population, although not of the urban elite.

Surprisingly, far from diminishing the scale or importance of Reformation commemorations, these changes gave them new urgency, although they also obliged the secular authorities to withdraw from sponsoring them. The century from 1814 to 1914 that saw the advent of religious pluralism and a decline in the

Protestant percentage of the population also proved to be the century of Reformation commemorations and monuments par excellence. In part, this was because of general trends across Europe and North America in this century of grandiose centennial celebrations and 'statuemania'. In part, it stemmed from local causes: faced with a population containing many Catholic immigrants, fractions within the local elite found it politically and pedagogically useful to recall the Reformation's role in shaping Geneva. Ultimately, commemorating fifty- and one-hundred-year anniversaries finally became such a routinised practice that the period from 1918 to 2017 saw more Reformation-related 'jubilees' than ever before, but these engaged less of the population and were marked by a growing sense of historical distance from the events and personalities commemorated, as ecumenism advanced, confessional tension abated, religious practice waned, and a new urban identity as an international center of peace and humanitarianism overlaid, without entirely effacing, the old image of 'la cité de Calvin'.

Reviewing Geneva's evolving political memory of the Reformation over nearly five centuries shows us how one changing city recalled this epoch-making event across the ages. It also enables us to explore a question foregrounded in the current literature about the history of memory, that of the extent to which the Age of Revolutions marked a rupture in commemorative practices and memory regimes. The great surge of interest in the history of memory that has taken place over the past thirty years initially focused on the centuries since 1789, said to be characterised by new memory practices and a changed relationship to the past. In the third and concluding volume of the seminal *Realms of Memory*, Pierre Nora argued that the French Revolution invented the practices of public commemoration through anniversary and centennial celebrations that are so familiar to us today. Such celebrations, he asserted, were directed by and focused upon the nation for most of the next two centuries. Then in the late twentieth century they fragmented as regional and group identities came to the fore.[2] But Judith Pollmann has recently challenged the idea that memory cultures underwent a fundamental transformation around 1800.[3] Already in 1995, the anthropologically-inspired Australian historian Charles Zika wrote a pathbreaking article on the Reformation jubilees of 1617 that identified these as 'the first significant public celebration of a centenary in European history'.[4] Since then, Winfried Müller has pushed the first centennial or bicentennial celebrations further back in time, to commemorations held by German universities from 1578 onward to recall their foundation one hundred or two hundred years previously.[5] Thomas Slettebo found state-sponsored centennials of specifically political or constitutional events prior to the French Revolution, notably Denmark's 1749 tercentenary celebration of the accession of the Oldenburg dynasty and 1760 centenary of the establishment of royal absolutism.[6] To say that the centennial has a longer history than Nora or even Zika imagined, however, is not to say that such commemorations did not multiply in frequency or adopt new forms or practices in the nineteenth or twentieth centuries. What seems essential now is for historians of public holidays, commemorations, and other public memory practices to scrutinise the patterns of continuity versus change over the *longue durée*. We can do that for Geneva because local historians have already explored many aspects of the story that we will synthesise here.[7]

The *ancien régime*

In the late Middle Ages, Geneva was subject to the authority of a prince-bishop, with the Duke of Savoy also exercising limited judicial rights in the city. Then an urban revolution occurred. Between 1526 and 1534, the municipality formed a pact of *combourgeoisie* with Bern and Fribourg, reshaped its governing councils, assumed judicial and regalian powers previously belonging to the bishop and duke, and declared the episcopal see vacant. The bishop, the duke and their local partisans threatened retaliation, but the Bernese conquest and occupation of the surrounding Savoyard territories in early 1536 brought a measure of breathing room, even if the Savoyard dynasty would claim the city and scheme to conquer it for decades to follow. Concurrently, evangelical ideas spread within the city. In August 1535, six months before the Bernese incursion, the evangelical faction installed Guillaume Farel in the cathedral by force and pressured the municipality to abolish the mass and seize church wealth. The revenue thus obtained helped pay troops protecting the city. The Reformation and the establishment of urban independence were closely linked.

Just as they were in reality, so too would they be in civic memory. How closely is shown by a plaque whose erection in two places — on the facade of the Hôtel de Ville and on the city wall — is the first known memorialisation of the Reformation. Voted by the Council just after the definitive triumph of the pro-Calvin faction in 1555, the text as finally engraved read, 'In 1535, after the tyranny of the Roman Antichrist was toppled and its superstitions abolished, Christ's holy religion was restored here in its true purity and the church put in better order through an extraordinary blessing of God. The city, once its enemies were repelled, miraculously reconquered its liberty. In consequence, the council and people of Geneva decided to carve this inscription and erect it in this spot that its memory may be perpetuated and in testimony of their gratitude to God'.[8] The plaque could be considered a Protestant *ex voto*.

From circa 1560 onward, the year 1535 — specifically, the date August 27, 1535 — would also be recalled in the historical calendars that Genevan printers began to insert in the front of psalters and prayer books. Where previously the moveable feasts and saints' days had figured, these calendars listed great dates of sacred and profane history. In addition to 'the Reformation according to the truth of the Gospel in the most renowned city of Geneva', other Reformation-related red-letter dates highlighted in these calendars included October 31, 1517, when '101 years after the burning of Jan Hus Martin Luther began to issue propositions against papal indulgences in the city of Wittenberg', as well as the death dates of Luther, Zwingli, Calvin, Bucer, and Edward VI.[9] But although historical calendars recalled these dates, neither the moment of Geneva's Reformation nor the day of Calvin's death were marked annually by any sort of special sermons or church ceremonies in Geneva — in striking contrast to what quickly began to be done in many cities and principalities of Lutheran Germany, whose governing authorities variously decreed that special sermons each year mark the date of Luther's baptism, his death, or the date of the introduction of the new Protestant church order.[10] Notoriously, the Genevan ecclesiastical order involved a particularly thoroughgoing purge of Catholic holy days, including even Christmas. Preaching throughout the year was organised around the *lectio continua* of consecutive books of the Bible. Calvin's hostility to any sort of cult of the dead had been so strong that he had insisted that nothing indicate the place of his own burial. All this differentiated the Genevan from the Lutheran Reformation and discouraged formal remembrance of special dates.

The particularly strong allergy to any chronological practices hinting of Popery may also explain why the coordinated 'jubilee' celebrations held across Protestant Germany to mark the hundredth anniversary of Luther's posting of the Ninety-Five Theses were far more elaborate affairs than the sole public recognition of the centennial to take place in Geneva. The German celebrations, decreed by the secular authorities after consultation with the leading organs of church government, commonly included multi-day sermon cycles, the distribution of special prayers of thanksgiving, and the striking of commemorative medals.[11] Geneva saw no special church events, but only a Latin oration delivered by the rector of the Academy, Theodore Tronchin, on the occasion of the annual ceremony in May to celebrate the promotion of students from one grade to the next. In his speech, Tronchin reminded his audience of what had happened a century ago, reviewed the sweep of Christian history, and lauded the role of that divinely inspired hero, Martin Luther, in unmasking the impostures of the Roman Church that had grown so in the centuries prior to 1517.[12]

While Zika's claim that the extensive commemorations of 1617 constituted the first significant public celebration of a centennial in European history needs modification in light of Müller's demonstration that several German universities earlier celebrated their hundred years with special orations, banquets and theatrical performances, the ceremonies of 1617 certainly publicised the idea that major foundation dates or caesuras in history deserved special recall at hundred year intervals and encouraged the spread of the practices associated with these ceremonies in Germany. Eighteen years later, when the hundredth anniversary of the Genevan Reformation came around, Geneva still avoided special church services (in contrast to Basel's 1628 Reformation centennial), but several of the memory practices of the German Reformation centenaries were adopted. Again, a Latin oration by the rector was the central event. At this mid-point in the Thirty Years' War in Germany, Frederick Spanheim prayed that the miraculous providences that had ensured Geneva's 'protection and the security ... amid so many intrigues, dangers, troubles and fears' would continue so that the city would forever remain 'the miracle and prodigy that it is in our time' — a perfect illustration of the post-Reformation myth of Geneva. What was new was that his discourse was printed, a special commemorative medal was struck, and a second vernacular *pièce de circonstance* was also published: Jacob Laurent's *The Rejoicing Genevan*. This work, which linked political independence and spiritual freedom, also urged the city's inhabitants to rejoice 'inwardly, moderately, and in a Christian fashion'. The outward display of a few 'small sparks that show the fire that burns beneath' might be permitted, but only to promote a renewed dedication to serve God, '*notre patrie*', duty, and the civic authorities.[13]

A century later, in 1735, Geneva's celebrations conformed more to what had become the standard model of Reformation centennials in Protestant central Europe. Now there were special prayers of thanksgiving and sermons on the topic in the city's churches, as well as another commemorative medal. Not coincidentally, the old liturgical austerity had faded by this time, and Christmas had returned as a holiday.[14] Illuminations and banquets also now marked the day, with the public authorities and churchmen walking together through the streets from one event to the next.[15]

Although the centennials of 1617 and 1635 involved less ceremony than in other Protestant territories, by the time these anniversaries rolled around one event associated with the Reformation had become the occasion for annual recollection and rejoicing in a manner that would only grow more elaborate over the next century. Indeed, the way in which this event was already being celebrated each year probably helps explain Laurent's preoccupation with the dangers of excessive outward jubilation. The event in question was the failed attempt by the Duke of Savoy to recapture the city by a surprise escalade on night of December 12, 1602. Its commemoration can be situated squarely within the widespread late medieval and early modern practice of celebrating great deliverances through annual processions and religious ceremonies, with the distinction that where such acts of remembrance in Catholic cities mixed sermons with processions, the formal celebration in Geneva retained only the sermon.[16] What is especially interesting about Geneva's Escalade celebrations is how rich and varied a range of unofficial rituals of rejoicing came to be associated with them, rituals that worried pious men like Laurent and still today seem decidedly un-Genevan in light of the city's general reputation and prevailing civic ideology.

No sooner had the Savoyards been repulsed than the city enacted three measures of commemoration: a public fast of thanksgiving, the engraving of commemorative inscriptions on the spot where the attackers placed their scaling-ladders and on the Hôtel de Ville, and the commissioning of a funerary monument for the seventeen inhabitants who died defending the city. Even though this monument was a simple list of names on a tablet, the pastors protested, fearing that it could inspire prayers for the dead or a cult in their honour. Their objections were overridden. A year later, the city council enacted a measure ordering that 'commemorations and acts of thanksgiving (*actions de grace*)' be held every year on December 12 in the city's three churches. Other manifestations of rejoicing quickly appeared. Within a year, twelve songs celebrating the deliverance, some inspired by canticles, others completely profane, were printed.[17] A clause in the 1603 treaty that resolved the

tensions with Savoy required that 'the memory of everything that has occurred …
be forever extinguished', so the city fathers forbade the publication of songs
mocking the beaten Savoyards, but this did not prevent Genevans from composing, singing and writing more; by the nineteenth century, local manuscript com-
pilations preserved some 150.[18] Those injured defending the city also soon began
to gather for a banquet each year. From this, a larger tradition of family and group
banquets emerged. Farces and tragi-comedies began to be privately staged. From
1631 onward the day became a non-working day for many. Beginning in 1673,
the public authorities took the day off too. The consistory attempted to enforce
restraint in the commemoration, but by the 1660s it was losing the battle. 'For
several years now, […] a day of thanksgiving and sanctification has been given over
to debauches and amusements in large gatherings', it fulminated in 1673. In 1701 it
complained that 'masked and costumed people go through the streets making
merry, singing and making loud noise with violins and sticks that they beat against
doors … which is totally contrary to Christian propriety and a horrible example in
a reformed city such as this'.[19] So integral to Genevan identity by the eighteenth
century were joyous banquets on the occasion that expatriates living in Paris
formed a Société de l'Escalade, whose annual gatherings involved such excess that a
mid-twentieth-century historian of the holiday felt obliged for modesty's sake to
spare the reader the details. As so often happens with special days, ludic practices
developed spontaneously alongside the officially sponsored commemoration, took
on a life of their own, and became deeply rooted in popular culture despite
attempts to control them. Those familiar with English history and customs will
immediately see parallels with the celebrations commemorating an almost exactly
contemporaneous event, the failure of the Gunpowder Plot, with the difference
that where the English feted Guy Fawkes Day with bonfires and bells, the Genevans preferred more discreet indoor banquets, living as they did in the immediate
vicinity of the much larger Savoyard state.[20]

As the political and diplomatic context changed, the city authorities sought to
uncouple from religion the patriotic element that had always been present in this
and other Reformation commemorations, and then to end sponsorship of Escalade ceremonies altogether. The sermons delivered on the occasion were initially
a time for ministers to compete to see who could serve up the most stirring anti-
Catholic rhetoric. In 1680 and 1699, amid the wars of Louis XIV, the magistrates
asked the pastors to tone down the anti-Catholicism. 'Should their text [the
biblical passage on which they were preaching] lead them to speak of the Antichrist, they [the ministers] should not equate him with the pope in light of the
current situation'.[21] In 1739, with reconciliation with Savoy a priority, the Small
Council instructed the city pastors to refrain from long history lessons about the
event; instead, they should 'insist principally on the love of country'.[22] In 1754,
after the treaty of Turin finally settled Geneva's longstanding disputes with what
was now the kingdom of Sardinia over sovereignty and boundaries, the Council
voted to end the holiday. Popular outrage forced it to backtrack immediately, but
a generation later, as the aristocratic government tightened its alliances with

Sardinia and France in response to the abortive democratic revolution of 1781, it successfully put a stop for a decade to the formal portion of the annual commemoration. After the French Revolution, the local revolutionary clubs, determined to 'teach youth that devotion to one's *patrie* is among the highest republican virtues', spearheaded the reintroduction in 1793 of a 'pure Genevan holiday' of 'the Escalade and equality'. The restored commemoration involved both sermons and a parade of militiamen and club members to the tomb of the 'citizens who died as martyrs for Liberty on the 12th of December 1602'.[23] After France annexed Geneva in 1798, official celebration of the Escalade ceased again. A pure Genevan holiday was now inappropriate for citizens of *la grande nation*.

From the Restoration to 2017

One might expect that the Restoration would revive the celebration anew, but now Geneva's political status, its territorial borders, and its religious composition had changed. In a canton that the 1822 census would reveal to be thirty-nine per cent Catholic, the political challenge of the day was to inspire loyalty to Geneva in the formerly Savoyard or French rural communes and to the Confederation among all. Official commemoration of the defeat of the Savoyards two hundred years previously seemed inappropriate. It would take several generations and significant changes in the non-state-supported ways of marking the date for the governmentally sanctioned commemoration of the Escalade to return. Yet because the festive traditions associated with the Escalade had sunk such deep roots among the population, the day was not forgotten. Family banquets continued, and children went door-to-door singing Escalade songs.

More generally, once Geneva stopped being a monolithically Protestant confessional state, the public authorities had to be conscious of Catholic sensibilities. As a result, the local government grew reticent of directly sponsoring anything to do with the Reformation. At the same time, the old families that continued to dominate the political class remained deeply aware of their Protestant heritage and still believed that it had been essential to making the city what it was. The tension between these two impulses cut right through the breast of many civic leaders.[24]

Further complicating commemoration of the Reformation, but also making it seem to many more imperative than ever, were the ways in which this new age of religious pluralism also became a second age of religious schism and confessional rivalry. Evangelising tendencies gained ground within Protestantism. Catholicism experienced a post-revolutionary and anti-revolutionary revival. Accelerating urban growth attracted Catholics from other parts of Switzerland and neighbouring Catholic lands. Debate arose about the place of religion in education and the extent of freedom to be granted to different faiths. Although political struggles about the place of religion in society would not truly die down until the separation of church and state in 1907, Protestant-Catholic conflict was particularly intense in two periods: the 1830s and 1840s, and the *Kulturkampf* of the 1870s. The former era saw Liberal agitation for generalised freedom of worship, broader national struggles over a new constitution that ultimately produced the 1847 Sonderbund civil war, and the emergence locally of a secret, militant Protestant Union dedicated to defending Geneva's Protestant character and opposing Catholic immigration. The Swiss hot spots of the latter were the mixed confessional cantons such as Geneva.

In these contexts, the centennials or demi-centennials of the Genevan Reformation or of its iconic personality John Calvin, appeared to Protestant opinion leaders to be so many teaching moments to remind and instruct an increasingly diverse and foreign population about the events and ideas that in their eyes had determined Geneva's character, and ensured its eminent rank among the cities of the world. The period from 1835, the tercentenary of the Genevan Reformation, to 1909, Calvin's four-hundredth birthday, consequently saw unprecedented organisational efforts devoted to commemorating the heritage of the Reformation. They were spearheaded not by the public authorities, but by what was now known as the Protestant National Church, evangelical leaders, and private committees composed of leading members from the old Protestant elite. For those involved in their planning, determining what in the city's Reformation legacy deserved to be honoured was not controversy-free, with the growth of evangelicalism having engendered splits and secessions and one wing of liberalism having become hostile to clericalisms of all stripes. Historical understanding of the Reformation also deepened and changed over this century of great interest in history. As this happened, the themes highlighted in the commemorations changed as well.

The first commemorative high point was the three-hundredth anniversary of the Genevan Reformation in 1835. Planned by a committee of pastors, professors and lay notables, its commemoration included several features typical of Reformation centennials under the ancien régime, notably special sermons, commemorative medals, and the preparation of didactic histories. The scale of the event was nonetheless far larger than previous Genevan Reformation centennials and included a far more varied menu of activities. The central four days of the commemoration (August 21–24) combined speeches, sermons, a *grande fête musicale* (planned by the pastor of the local Lutheran church), illuminations, and banquets. Hot air balloons were launched, and a shooting contest was staged. To pass the message along to the next generation, special assemblies were held in the city's churches open to children of all faiths, who received a small version of the commemorative medal and a history of Geneva's Reformation and its significance.[25]

One unquestionable novelty of the nineteenth century was the vogue for erecting statues in public places to great men who were not rulers or saints. In the run-up to this tri-centennial, Count Jean-Jacques de Sellon, a pacifist, politician and philanthropist, proposed a monument to Calvin in the form of a stele engraved '*la patrie reconnaissante*' topped by a bust of the reformer. Even after suggesting that it be sited inside the cathedral 'so as not to offend the sight of our Catholic fellow citizens' (the cathedral had been reserved for Protestant use ever since the Reformation), neither the political nor the ecclesiastical authorities could be convinced to support it, for the conviction that Calvin himself would not have wanted such memorialisation was simply too strong.[26] Sellon had to content himself with erecting a large pyramidal tomb honouring Calvin on the terrace outside his house on the rue des Granges.[27] Instead, the organisers of the centennial raised funds to re-install the plaque of 1555–1558 commemorating the recovery of spiritual and temporal liberty, that had been taken down from the Hôtel de Ville after French annexation in 1798. It was now placed inside the cathedral, where it remains to this day. The displacement suggests that the post-Reformation myth of Geneva was no longer that of the entire 'République et Canton', but only of the Protestant community.

'Tolerance' was a watchword of the planning of the 1835 jubilee, and the organisers sought to involve Genevan citizens of all faiths, yet the celebration retained an emphatically Protestant cast. By the turn of the nineteenth century, a liberal, non-dogmatic faith had come to dominate the national church. The all-Protestant organising committee consequently spoke of 'promoting the grand principles of tolerance which are those of true Protestantism'. But the centrality of the Reformation to the city's destiny and identity remained a key theme. 'Geneva owes all it was and could still be to the Reformation: its independence, its institutions, its men, its laws, its national character, its monuments', the organisers proclaimed. Speakers expressed the hope that this moment of historical instruction might inspire all in the city to 'pass on to your children … the heritage of … family, religion and patriotism that constitute the soul of a people and alone can guarantee its continuation'. One even dared hope that it might yield 'a new covenant between the Almighty and his people'. For the first — but hardly the last — time, the event was given a substantial international dimension. Sixty foreign delegates representing many different Protestant denominations made the trip to Geneva, although several determinedly orthodox institutions such as Scotland's General Assembly and the Presbytery of Ulster failed to send representatives, an absence deplored in the official account of the Jubilee as a symptom of Protestant 'separatists' seeking to impose a straitjacket on consciences. Not all Genevans joined the celebration either. One local evangelical wrote a lively dialogue suggesting that amid the entire commemoration just one thing was missing: attention to Christ's saving message. A Catholic pamphleteer wrote that it was very nice of the organisers to invite Catholics to join the festivities, but 'we … have not forgotten that French and Savoyard blood runs through our veins and have no inclination to … play the hypocrite'. Still, the event touched a chord among the Protestant majority and perhaps even drew some Catholics. One estimate, perhaps exaggerated, claimed that 50,000 people took part in the various events. (The total population at the time was only 56,000). After a public banquet in the parish of Saint Gervais, three hundred attendees accompanied their pastors back to their houses with cries of 'Vive la Reformation! Vive l'Eglise nationale! Vivent nos pasteurs!'[28]

Over the next thirty years, evangelicalism sunk deep roots in Geneva. Local churchmen linked up with international Protestant associational networks and enhanced their place in these by recalling Geneva's historical importance to the

Reformation. Francophone Protestantism, or at least currents thereof, rediscovered the historical Calvin and his ideas, largely forgotten in the eighteenth century.[29] As the three-hundredth anniversary of Calvin's death in 1564 approached, feeling was stronger than before that a significant monument to him should be erected. The leader in promoting this idea was Jean-Henri Merle d'Aubigné, at once a free church pastor active in international evangelical associations and a renowned historian of the Reformation. He initially dreamed of a statue of Calvin atop a pillar on the shore of Lake Geneva, but soon abandoned this idea in favour of a much more practical construction, an auditorium that could serve as 'a tribune for the exposition and defense of the Gospel truths'. The project was launched in 1864. Money was raised from evangelical banking families in the city and internationally. By 1867, a two-thousand seat auditorium had been constructed known alternatively as the Calvinium or the Salle de la Reformation.[30] The top floor was given over to a Bibliothèque Calvinienne that built up a remarkable collection of books and objects concerning the reformer and served as a little Calvin museum. (Its ever-expanding collections would subsequently be transferred to the Musée Historique de la Réformation, founded in 1897, then put to academic use by the University of Geneva's Institut d'histoire de la Réformation, created in 1969). On completion, the Salle de la Réformation became Geneva's largest auditorium and turned out to have excellent acoustics. It therefore had a long and eventful life until its demolition in 1969, used not only for revival meetings and lectures on religious topics, but also for the first meetings of the League of Nations and, in the 1960s, rock concerts. Before its doors closed, Johnny Halliday played there.

The national church also marked the anniversary with a cycle of sermons about Calvin, the first known commemoration by the Geneva church linked to an event of his life. Five leading lights of local intellectual life, all professors of theology known for their speaking ability, mounted the pulpits of the Protestant parishes. Their sermons, soon published, were strikingly historical in character and not without ambivalence about the idea of honouring a mortal man rather than the eternal Word he served. One refrain ran: we are celebrating Calvin, but he was not the sole figure of importance in the Genevan Reformation, nor do we wish to make him into a saint. Another: Calvin had many great virtues, most notably his iron will and self-sacrificing dedication to his reforming mission, but he also had his flaws, notably intolerance for those who disagreed with him and an inclination toward theocracy.[31]

Forty-five years later, in 1909, the commemoration of Calvin reached its monumental apotheosis on the occasion of the four-hundredth anniversary of his birth with the laying of the foundation stone for the massive, 100-meter-long International Reformation Monument, or Reformers' Wall, that still looms over the Parc des Bastions just below the Old City. This was just the most ambitious and consequential project in a spate of activities held that year.

Before any positive celebration of Calvin's four-hundredth birthday could be attempted, however, his champions felt compelled to erect a smaller monument, expiatory rather than celebratory, to confront the great blot on his reputation that the growth of Free Thought and the polemics of the debate over the separation of church and state had made notorious, the execution of Michael Servetus. In the run-up to 1909, a group led by the Calvin biographer and professor of church history at the Protestant theology faculty of Montauban, Emile Doumergue, spearheaded the erection of such a monument on the site of the gallows where the Anti-Trinitarian had been burned — a location, it might be observed, well away from the centre of town and from any crossroad or square of symbolic importance or high visibility. This took the form of a massive boulder with plaques on either side recalling the event and expressing atonement through a convoluted formula that so manifestly downplayed Calvin's personal responsibility for Servetus' arrest and condemnation that many questioned whether it truly served the purpose. The wording read:

> As grateful and respectful sons of our great reformer Calvin, condemning an error typical of his era, and firmly attached to liberty of conscience in keeping with the true principles of the Reformation and the Gospel, we erected this monument on October 27 1903.[32]

An ironic epilogue can be added to this story. By the turn of the twenty-first century, the expiatory monument had become an overlooked bit of the cityscape, half-hidden between a bus shelter and encroaching bushes in an awkward space behind the University hospital complex. In 2011 the Mayor of Saragossa visited for a conference of mayors and learned that the monument did not include a figurative representation of his region's famous native son. He offered to donate a copy of the sculpture of Servetus initially cast for a monument erected by French free-thinkers in Annemasse and later reproduced in Saragossa. Geneva's left-wing mayor unhesitatingly accepted the offer. Thus, with virtually no local initiative and little ceremony, did an image of the poor, imprisoned doctor shivering in rags come to be placed just beneath the expiatory boulder [Fig. 15.1].[33]

The planning that went into the Calvin jubilee of 1909 was done by a committee that included representatives of the different Protestant tendencies of the time, but one man, Charles Borgeaud, emerged as its driving spirit. In the preceding decades, the *Kulturkampf* had cemented the view that Protestantism was the religion of modernity and Catholicism that of reaction. Borgeaud, an internationally educated law professor and proto-political-scientist, was one of the most important early expositors of the sophisticated academic version of that view according to which Calvinist Protestantism was the matrix of modern democracy. For a Geneva that Borgeaud believed had been more profoundly shaped by the Reformation than by any other event but was 'no longer the Huguenot republic of former times' but instead 'one of the capitals of the modern world', he envisaged a monument not to Calvin alone, but instead to a certain idea of Calvin's and the Genevan Reformation's world-historical importance. Deferring to the concern expressed by the speakers of 1864 that Calvin not be seen as sole shaper of the Genevan Reformation, his sculptural programme placed 30-foot-high statues of

FIGURE 15.1 Expiatory monument (upper right) and statue (lower left) of Michael Servetus. Photograph: Judith Benedict.

Farel, Beza, and Knox alongside Calvin in the centre. Flanking them were smaller statues of carefully selected Protestant heroes from other lands such as William the Silent, Oliver Cromwell, and Roger Williams, alternating with bas-reliefs depicting events such as the promulgation of the Edict of Nantes, William and Mary accepting the English Bill of Rights, and the Great Elector welcoming Huguenot refugees to Brandenburg. This was a representation in stone of what the cutting edge of international social science then considered to be the Calvinist Reformation's essential role in promoting the modern, universal values of toleration and human rights — a legacy the entire city could be proud of and that, as an international monument for a city that was now the seat of the International Red Cross, could be largely financed by donations from abroad. Theodore Roosevelt served as the honorary chair of the American fundraising committee. Kaiser Wilhelm II contributed. After Hungarian Protestants made particularly generous gifts, Istvan Bocksai was added to the tableau.[34] An international competition resulted in the selection of a group of Swiss architects to design the monument and of the French artists Henri Bouchard and Paul Landowski (later responsible for the Christ of Rio de Janeiro) to sculpt it [Fig. 15.2].

Special church services, concerts, banquets, a parade in historical costumes, fireworks, and children's events were also on the programme for 1909, while the *Journal de Genève* saw fit to publish a special issue devoted to the centennial.

Doumergue opened the festivities with a lecture in the cathedral entitled 'Calvin, Geneva's Preacher'. At the University, Nathanaël Weiss, the guiding spirit of the Société de l'Histoire du Protestantisme Français, spoke on 'The Reformation and Modern Thought'. The participation of prominent academic figures charged with explaining the historical significance of the Reformation had been a constant in local centennial observations since 1617. Now, in an age of increased mobility, the featured speakers came from abroad.[35]

Meanwhile, the nineteenth century did not forget the Escalade. During the 1840s, the Protestant Union made December 12 a date on which to rally its members and 'all true Protestants' at the cathedral to recall the event. In 1857, a fountain with bas-reliefs depicting the defence of the city was erected in the commercial heart of town, although inaugurated without ceremony because the subject was still confessionally marked and considered politically inflammatory. In the 1860s and 1870s, and then again from 1898 onward, prominent pastors spoke about the event at the Salle de la Reformation. But it would be by de-confessionalising and folklorising the form of remembrance that public commemoration of the Escalade would be enduringly reinvented at the century's end. In 1898 the 'Geneva Patriotic Association for the Renewal of the Escalade' was founded to prepare for the upcoming three-hundredth anniversary. The major citywide celebration it mounted for 1902 included forms of church-based remembrance that show, through their evocation of the event during Catholic and Jewish services alongside sermons in the Protestant temples, that the non-Protestant religious groups were now well enough integrated into the body politic to associate themselves with its commemoration so long as this was cast chiefly as a manifestation of civic patriotism and historical recollection. The bishop even issued a dispensation allowing Catholics to eat meat on the Friday on which the anniversary fell. But the central element of the public commemoration designed by the association was a historical cortege: men and women dressed in period costume and impersonating figures of 1602 marched through the streets in solemn procession, stopping regularly to read out the names of those who died defending the city. This form of ceremony proved so successful that it was soon made an annual event. It was taken in hand in 1926 by a private association, the Compagnie de 1602, which flourishes to this day, as does the annual procession. Five years after the tri-centennial, the Department of Public Instruction decreed that special lessons about the event be given in every school on the date. Related rituals subsequently grew up, the most famous being the ritual shattering of a chocolate soup kettle by the youngest and eldest person present as all intone 'thus perish the enemies of the republic'. A hugely popular foot race through the Old City was initiated in 1978 that now draws 30,000 participants. The holiday has increasingly become a high point in Geneva's annual calendar, an occasion for the long-time Genevans who eagerly seek membership in the Compagnie de 1602 to remind a globalised city with a large component of recent arrivals working for high-turnover international organisations and corporations of the distinctiveness of the place in which they find themselves.

While this folklorised and deconfessionalised celebration of the city's distinctive past flourished in the twentieth- and twenty-first century, the zeal for other Reformation-related commemorations diminished even while their frequency increased. When the Reformers' Wall was completed on schedule in 1917, Europe was three years into a murderous war pitting some Protestant countries whose heroes were depicted on the wall against others. The monument's inauguration was a discreet local affair that contrasted sharply with the gathering of international eminences for the laying of the cornerstone. The chiming of temple bells in unison, topical sermons and a few historical brochures also soberly noted the four-hundredth anniversary of the posting of the Ninety-Five Theses that year.[36] In the war's aftermath, the choice of Geneva as the seat of the League of Nations decisively accelerated the shift in its civic identity from Protestant Rome to international centre of peace and human rights. As clashing secular ideologies of the left and right came to dominate political debate, the question of religion receded in importance. Confessional rivalry gave way to ecumenism. Religious practice declined. Historians of the Reformation ceased to think that Calvinist Protestantism constituted the high road to modernity. In this context, major monuments to the reformers or their legacy were no longer proposed, although a minor change was made to the Reformers' Wall in 2002 to include the name of a woman of importance in the local Reformation, Marie Dentière. More generally, it became harder and harder to muster wide support for the commemorations or make them

FIGURE 15.2 Design sketch by Alphonse Laverriere and Eugène Monod for the Reformers' Wall, incorporating Charles Borgeaud's programme, from *The International Studio*, 1909.

(https://archive.org/stream/internationalstu00newy10#page/160/mode/1up).

do the kind of political work they had done between 1835 and 1909. Recalling the most important events of the past at every fifty-year and hundred-year anniversary had nonetheless become such a deeply ingrained practice that more centenary events were staged over the century following the end of the Great War than ever before: the 400th anniversary of the Genevan Reformation in 1936, Calvin's 450th birthday in 1959, the 400th anniversary of Calvin's death in 1964, the 450th anniversary of the Genevan Reformation in 1986, Calvin's 500th birthday in 2009, and most recently the 500th anniversary of the Reformation in 2017. As each date approached, the church, the University's theology faculty, and in 2009 and 2017 the university's non-confessional Institute of Reformation History saw that the anniversary offered useful opportunities: for the church, to try to renew a commitment to the faith or simply remind the population of Protestantism's historical place in the city; for the theologians, to re-examine Calvin's work to see what remained of contemporary relevance; for the historians, to present the fruits of their academic research to a wider public than normal. They consequently responded to the solicitation of each date by mounting a panoply of events that typically included a special church service (now often broadcast via radio or television), an academic conference, the publication of one or more commemorative histories, and a component aimed at a broader public that might vary from a 'Huguenot village' to historical dramas to comic book contests.

The four-hundredth anniversary of the Genevan Reformation was celebrated in 1936, not 1935, because under Borgeaud's prodding Geneva had chosen since 1909 to foreground as the decisive moment in the local Reformation an event that seemed less insurrectionary and more democratic than the outlawing of the mass and expropriation of church property in August 1535: the formal adoption of the Reformation by oath at a general assembly of citizens in May 1536. One high point of the 1936 commemoration was a ceremony in which a crowd estimated by its organisers at 25–30,000 gathered at the Reformers' Wall to swear the oath anew. (The total population of the Socialist-governed canton by then had risen to 170,000 people). The lectures and sermons by pastors that the church gathered into a book entitled *The Reformed Faith that We Promised to Uphold* continued to cast the Reformation as the event that forged the city's destiny, but in the sombre atmosphere of the times, with Fascism and Communism both on the rise internationally and the industrial city in the grip of economic crisis, the essence of the Reformation legacy was understood differently than in 1909. Younger pastors influenced by Karl Barth grappled more deeply with Calvin's actual teachings than had been the case in prior jubilees, finding in them an ethic of responsibility and a source of consolation that they hoped could offer solutions to a troubled world.[37]

By 1986, a significant fraction of Genevans of Protestant ancestry was beginning to fall away from the faith and identify as areligious. In the 1980 census, only thirty per cent of the population checked the 'Protestant' box. As the church leaders felt their hold over the public diminishing, they gave the occasion a more festive character in an effort to draw in as much of the population as possible. A comic book contest, children's books, guided tours and exhibitions, a party in historical dress, a reconstitution of a market square, and an international village were all on the agenda. With ecumenism now strong in Geneva, an official ceremony involving the civic authorities and the president of the Confederation included an address by a Catholic curé in the name of an ecumenical working group, the Rassemblement des Eglises de Genève. Yet the fun-filled programme for the *grand public* could not hide the anxious uncertainty of the most perceptive Protestant leaders about the relevance and posterity of the Reformation in an increasingly de-Christianised and ecumenical Europe. The professor of church history at the University's theology faculty, Olivier Fatio, the scion of an old and distinguished Genevan family who subsequently become the faculty's dean and director of the Institut d'histoire de la Réformation, asked in a provocative paper: does Protestantism have a future? A collective volume written with several colleagues sought to define the relevance of the Reformation message for the present, without really succeeding in articulating a clear answer. The uncertainty and disagreement expressed in the essays revealed how much the local and international religious landscape had changed since 1909, when the Reformation's significance seemed so clear, positive, and wide-reaching.[38]

The five-hundredth anniversary of Calvin's birth in 2009 came around just before the 2010 census revealed that declared Protestants were only twelve per cent of the population. It brought two large outreach events, one chiefly academic and international, the other more ecclesiastical and locally oriented, as well as issues of local magazines with leading personalities commenting on what Geneva owed to Calvin.[39] The scale, however, was small in comparison with a hundred years previously. The city's engagement was minimal by comparison with Rousseau's 300th birthday three years later. With the Barthianism that was growing in the 1930s now on the wane, the awkward theological position in which the spokesmen of the mainline Reformed found themselves as they sought to expound Calvin's legacy was summed up by the title of a short book by the Lausanne theology professor Bernard Reymond, *Protestantism and Calvin: What's To Be Done with such a Bothersome Ancestor?* [40] The international academic conference explored Calvin's legacy across the centuries as so many episodes from a now bygone era.[41]

Geneva still houses guardians of the flame of Protestant identity, the clearest proof being the ambitious new Musée International de la Réformation, opened in 2005 in an elegant eighteenth-century residence next door to the cathedral. Fatio was the guiding force behind the museum's creation. Financing came from private sources, chiefly old Protestant families and foundations. One can speculate that the museum's creation responded in part to a belief in these circles that something needed to be provided to satisfy the demand of tourists who come to Geneva looking for the cradle of Calvinism. Text within the museum made it clear that it sought to illustrate with state-of-the-art museology the tradition of historical mainline Protestantism, especially in its francophone variants, for both residents and visitors unfamiliar with it and inclined to associate Protestantism with mega-churches and Pentecostalism. While the MIR quickly established itself as one of

Geneva's five most visited museums, it seems symbolic of the Reformation's place in present-day Genevan memory and identity that its current annual attendance of roughly 20,000 people is just a fourth of that of the Red Cross Museum.[42]

Conclusion

This examination of Genevan public memory practices across the early modern/ modern divide has provided us an interesting mix of continuity and change. The new religious order so powerfully imprinted on the city at the Reformation was marked by exceptional liturgical austerity and led by a man insistent that a cult of personality not grow up around him. In keeping with this original character, the earliest forms of public commemoration of the Reformation were modest: an *ex-voto*-like plaque placed on the Hôtel de Ville; mention of the event in calendars; more plaques, a tomb to the victims, and services of thanksgiving in the city's churches after the 1602 repulsing of the Savoyard escalade; nothing more than a history lesson at the annual school promotion ceremony on the hundredth anniversary of the posting of the Ninety-Five Theses. After the more elaborate jubilee celebrations held in many German territories in 1617 publicised the practice of celebrating centennials of major historical events, Genevan centennials of the local Reformation gradually incorporated such conventional components of these as commemorative medals, publications, and special sermons. In the changed circumstances of the nineteenth century, after the dramatic reshaping of both Geneva's political status and its religious composition, centennial and half-centennial celebrations increased in frequency and grew in scale, even while the state withdrew from sponsoring them, contrary to what Pierre Nora's remarks about modern commemoration would lead us to expect. Concerts, academic conferences, and historical re-enactments were added to the mix of commemorative practices, along with hot-air balloon rides or comic book contests. The blend of celebration, reflection, education, and recreation varied each time, but the trend was clearly to increase the last element as public outreach became a growing priority of the organising committees. If the nineteenth- and twentieth-century commemorations can be seen as attempts by the leadership of the Protestant fraction of the population to compensate for the Reformed loss of confessional exclusivity and influence by reminding a changing population of what the city owed to the Reformation, a clear shift can also be seen in where they located this legacy. Under the ancien régime, it lay with the recovery of the Gospel, the reformation of manners, and the establishment of urban independence, all of which were interconnected. The nineteenth century placed more emphasis on toleration and the liberation of minds from the tyranny of authority. At the turn of the twentieth century, the finest fruits of the Genevan Reformation were seen as its promotion of stable representative government, human rights, and the humane treatment of refugees. As the twentieth century advanced, however, uncertainty about where to locate the positive legacy of the Reformation grew. At the same time, the rise of secular ideologies, ecumenism, declining religious practice, and the shift in urban identity toward '*La*

Genève internationale' made that legacy, whatever it might be, less salient to either politics or personal identity for much of the population. More commemorations than ever were held, but their importance dwindled.

Already by the later seventeenth century, one event, the annual commemoration of the Escalade, belied Geneva's otherwise deserved reputation for sobriety. The public authorities decreed an annual sermon of thanksgiving in the immediate aftermath of the event. Alongside it, much to the dismay of churchmen, a series of festive forms of celebratory commemoration sprang up including banquets and public singing. The more formally organised component of the annual celebration changed in character in an oscillating fashion over the centuries. Born in the confessional age and initially marked by a heavy dose of anti-Catholicism, it became more focused on patriotic themes in the eighteenth century, took on a renewed, if more sublimated, confessional character for most of the nineteenth century after the secular authorities stepped away from supporting it lest they offend the ex-Savoyard portion of the population, and finally became folklorised and stripped of its anti-Catholic components at the beginning of the twentieth century in a manner that allowed the public authorities to embrace it anew. The precise mix of such popular practices as banquets, nocturnal noise-making, singing special songs, and children going door-to-door may also have altered over time, although we lack the evidence to trace the waxing and waning of each of these with precision. Whatever their mix, they were what ensured the perpetuation of the celebration from the eighteenth century to the present. Historians of holidays overlook the place of *homo ludens* in their story at their peril.

Geneva did not escape the statuemania of the nineteenth century, but as monuments to a range of benefactors and heroes began to dot the cityscape, statues of Geneva's greatest Reformation hero remained all but totally absent. This was not because of enduring Calvinist iconophobia; it was because so many of those most inclined to honour Calvin knew that to do so with a statue contradicted his thought. When Charles Borgeaud proposed a symbolisation in stone of Geneva's central place in Calvinism's larger world-historical role, a vast bas-relief in which the reformer was just one figure among many, he inspired the construction of what was almost certainly the largest Reformation monument anywhere in Europe at the time. This was a true discontinuity of form in Geneva's commemoration of its Reformation.

Meanwhile, if one continuity stands out throughout our tale, it is the recurring role of academic historians in articulating the significance of the events commemorated. In the seventeenth century, Theodore Tronchin and Frederick Spanheim, both professors of theology but also historians in their spare time, explained on centennial occasions why the Reformation was important for both the city and the wider world. From 1865 through 2005, Jean-Henri Merle d'Aubigné, Charles Borgeaud, Emile Doumergue, and Olivier Fatio not only spoke at the major commemorations and wrote the books and brochures produced for the occasion; they shaped the most important constructions of each epoch. Social memory and academic history are communicating realms.

Notes

1 Alain Dufour, 'Le Mythe de Genève au Temps de Calvin', *Revue Suisse d'Histoire* 9 (1959), 489–518.
2 Pierre Nora, 'The Era of Commemoration', in *Realms of Memory: Rethinking the French Past*, ed. Pierre Nora (New York, 1996; original French ed., Paris, 1988–1992), III: 609–637. John Gillis, 'Memory and Identity: The History of a Relationship', in *Commemorations: The Politics of National Identity*, ed. John Gillis (Princeton, 1994), 3–20, also posits a distinctive post-Revolutionary era of commemoration focused on the nation.
3 Pollmann, *Memory in Early Modern Europe 1500–1800* (Oxford, 2017).
4 Charles Zika, 'The Reformation Jubilee of 1617: Appropriating the Past in European Centenary Celebration', first published in D. Kennedy, ed., *Authorized Pasts: Essays in Official History* (Melbourne, 1995), reprinted in Charles Zika, *Exorcising our Demons: Magic, Witchcraft and Visual Culture in Early Modern Europe* (Leiden, 2003), 199.
5 Winfried Müller, 'Erinnern an die Gründung: Universitätsjubiläen, Universitätsgeschichte und die Entstehung der Jubiläumskultur in der frühen Neuzeit', *Berichte zur Wissenschaftsgeschichte* 21, no. 2–3 (1998), 79–102.
6 Thomas E. W. Slettebo, 'In Memory of Divine Providence: A Study of Centennial Commemoration in Eighteenth-Century Denmark-Norway (1717–1760)' (PhD thesis, University of Bergen, 2015), chapters 6–7.
7 Notably Jean-Pierre Ferrier, 'Histoire de la Fête de l'Escalade', in *L'Escalade de Genève—1602: Histoire et Tradition*, ed. Paul Frédéric Geisendorf (Geneva, 1952), 487–530; Olivier Fatio, 'Quelle Réformation? Les Commémorations Genevoises de la Réformation à travers les Siècles', *Revue de Théologie et de Philosophie* 118, no. 2 (1986), 111–30; Mireille Lador, 'Le Jubilé de la Réformation de 1835 à Genève: "Religion-Patrie-Tolérance"', *Bulletin de la Société d'Histoire et d'Archéologie de Genève* 25 (1995), 97–110; Sarah Scholl, '"Nous sur notre montagne…" Le Jubilé de 1917 et l'Identité Réformée Helvétique', *Chrétiens et Sociétés* XVIe–XXIe siècles 23 (2016), 47–64; Antony Ardiri, *Les Enjeux du Souvenir: Calvin et les Jubilés de Genève en 1909* (Geneva, 2017); Christian Grosse, 'Célébrer la Providence Divine: Jubilé et Culture Commémorative Réformée (Genève, XVIe-XVIIe Siècle)', *Études Épisté* 32 (2017), 1–18.
8 Grosse, 'Célébrer la Providence Divine', 9.
9 Francesco Maiello, *Histoire du Calendrier: De la liturgie à l'Agenda* (Paris, 1996), esp. 155–66; Max Engammare, *L'Ordre du Temps: L'Invention de la Ponctualité au XVIe Siècle* (Geneva, 2004), chapter 4; Philip Benedict, 'Divided Memories? Historical Calendars, Commemorative Processions and the Recollection of the Wars of Religion during the Ancien Régime', *French History* 22, no. 4 (2008), 381–405 (385–8).
10 Zika, 'Reformation Jubilee', 200; Michael Mitterauer, 'Anniversarium und Jubiläum: Zur Entstehung und Entwicklung Öffentlicher Gedenktage', in *Der Kampf um das Gedächtnis: Öffentliche Gedenktage in Mitteleuropa*, ed. Emil Brix and Hannes Stekl (Vienna, 1997), 23–89 (54).
11 Zika, 'Reformation Jubilee', 197–236; Thomas Albert Howard, 'Remembering the Reformation, 1617, 1817 and 1883: Commemoration as an Agent of Continuity and Change', in *Protestantism after Five Hundred Years*, ed. Thomas Albert Howard and Mark A. Noll (Oxford, 2016), 25–46; Christopher W. Close, 'Reawakening the "Old Evangelical Zeal": The 1617 Reformation Jubilee and Collective Memory in Strasbourg and Ulm', *SCJ* 48, no. 2 (2017), 299–321.
12 'Discours du recteur Théodore Tronchin prononcé à l'occasion de la cérémonie des promotions du Collège de Genève' (May 7, 1617), *Registres de la Compagnie des Pasteurs de Genève*, vol. XIII, ed. Gabriella Cahier, Nicolas Fornerod, and Matteo Compagnolo (Geneva, 2001), 330–43.
13 Fatio, 'Quelle Réformation?', 111–3.
14 Maria-Cristina Pitassi, *De l'Orthodoxie aux Lumières: Genève 1670–1737* (Geneva, 1992), 55–61; Pitassi, 'Entre Liberté et Nostalgie: Noël à Genève aux XVIIe et XVIIIe Siècles', in *C'est la faute à Voltaire, c'est la faute à Rousseau*, ed. R. Durand (Geneva, 1997), 321–30.
15 J.-M. Paris, *Le jubilé de la Réformation célébré à Genève le 21 août 1735* (Geneva, 1870).

16 On which see Benedict, 'Divided Memories?', 383–4, 390–7, and the literature cited there.

17 François Ruchon, 'Les Chansons de l'Escalade', in Geisendorf, ed., *L'Escalade de Genève*, 323–64.

18 Ruchon, 'La Littérature de l'Escalade', 321–77, in Geisendorf, ed., *L'Escalade de Genève*, esp. 324, 325, 336.

19 Ferrier, 'Histoire de la Fête de l'Escalade', 498. Unless otherwise noted, this deeply researched article is the basis for all statements about the Escalade celebrations in this and subsequent paragraphs.

20 On Guy Fawkes day, see David Cressy's pioneering *Bonfires and Bells: National Memory and the Protestant Calendar in Elizabethan and Stuart England* (London, 1989); Cressy, 'The Fifth of November Remembered', in *Myths of the English*, ed. Roy Porter (Cambridge, 1993), 68–90.

21 Ferrier, 'Histoire de la Fête de l'Escalade', 500.

22 Ferrier, 'Histoire de la Fête de l'Escalade', 503.

23 Ferrier, 'Histoire de la Fête de l'Escalade', 519.

24 Irène Herrmann, *Genève entre République et Canton: Les Vicissitudes d'une Intégration Nationale (1814–1846)* (Geneva, 2003), esp. 227–58.

25 *Jubilé de la Réformation à Genève. Août 1835. Historique et conférences* (Geneva, 1835); Fatio, 'Quelle Réformation?', 116–20; Lador, 'Jubilé de la Réformation de 1835', 98–104.

26 J.-J. Sellon, *Notice sur le monument proposé par le comte de Sellon, fondateur de la Société de la paix de Genève, à l'occasion du jubilé de l'an 1835* (Geneva, 1835), 2.

27 David Ripoll, 'Un Hommage Contrarié: Le Monument à Calvin du comte Jean-Jacques de Sellon', in *Une Question de Goût: La Collection Zoubov à Genève*, ed. Frédéric Elsig (Milan, 2013), 34–41.

28 *Jubilé de la Réformation à Genève. Août 1835*, 6, 23, 74; Fatio, 'Quelle Réformation?', 116–123, esp. 117, 122 (citing the contemporary *Dialogues sur le jubilé annoncé par les ministres de Genève, entre un élève catholique du collège de Carouge et un élève protestant du collège de Genève*); Lador, 'Jubilé de la Réformation de 1835', 104–8.

29 André Encrevé, 'Lost, Then Found: Calvin in French Protestantism, 1830–1940', in *Calvin and His Influence, 1509–2009*, ed. Irena Backus and Philip Benedict (Oxford, 2011), pp. 224–54.

30 Luc Weibel, 'Un Rêve de Merle d'Aubigné: La Salle de la Réformation à Genève', *Bulletin de la Société de l'Histoire du Protestantisme Français* 152 (2006), 245–63; Weibel, *Croire à Genève: La Salle de la Réformation (XIXe Siècle–XXe Siècle)* (Geneva, 2006).

31 *Calvin. Cinq discours prêchés à Genève le 29 mai 1864 par MM. Oltramare, Coulin, Tournier, Bungener et Gaberel* (Geneva, 1864).

32 Ardiri, *Enjeux du souvenir*, 61–74; Valentine Zuber, 'Servetus vs. Calvin: A Battle of Monuments during the Secularization of the French Third Republic', in *Sober, Strict and Scriptural: Collective Memories of John Calvin, 1800–2000*, ed. Herman Paul, Johan de Niet, and Bart Wallet (Leiden, 2009), 167–94.

33 'Une Statue Réhabilite Michel Servet, Humaniste Condamné au Bûcher', *Tribune de Genève*, October 4, 2011, 23.

34 *Monument international de la Réformation à Genève/ International Monument of the Calvinian Reformation/ Internationales Denkmal der Genfer Reformation. Guide-Mémorial* (Geneva, [1909?]); *Monument internationale de la Réformation à Genève* ([Geneva?], [1909?]), Alexandre Claparède, *Les voix magyares au Jubilé de Calvin, Genève 1909* (Geneva, 1910); Ardiri, *Enjeux du souvenir*, 158–161. On the prominent place of Calvin and Calvinism in Hungarian nationalism c. 1900, see Botond Gaál, '"Calvin's Truth" and "Hungarian Religion": Remembering a Reformer', in Paul, de Niet, and Wallet, eds., *Sober, Strict and Scriptural*, 97–124.

35 *Jubilé de Calvin à Genève: juillet 1909: allocutions, adresses, lettres et documents* (Geneva, 1910); *Actes du Jubilé de 1909, Université de Genève* (Geneva, 1910).

36 Scholl, 'Nous sur notre montagne…', 47–64.

37 Fatio, 'Quelle Réformation?', 124–8.

38 Alain Dufour et al., *1536: Quelle Réforme!* (Geneva, 1986).

39 International Congress 'Calvin and His Influence 1509–2009' sponsored by an ad hoc Association Calvin 2009, the Musée Historique de la Réformation, and the University of Geneva's Institut d'Histoire de la Réformation and Faculté Autonome de Théologie Protestante; '1509–2009 Jubilé Calvin Genève' sponsored by the Association Jubilé Calvin-Genève; 'Calvin revient!', *Tribune de Genève*, 17–18 January 2009; 'Un Homme Nommé Calvin. L'Héritage de la Réforme. Son Influence sur Genève. Témoignages de Romands', special issue of *L'Hebdo*, 2009; 'Que reste-t-il de Calvin?', *Campus* no. 94 (April–May 2009).

40 Reymond, *Le Protestantisme et Calvin: Que faire d'un Aïeul si Encombrant?* (Geneva, 2009). Cf. Martin Ernst Hirzel and Martin Sallmann ed., *John Calvin's Impact on Church and Society, 1509–2009* (Grand Rapids, 2009), a volume of essays commissioned by the Federation of Swiss Protestant Churches; 'Jean Calvin à Genève', 3 volume c.d. produced by www.Calvin09.org.

41 Backus and Benedict ed., *Calvin and His Influence* (see note 29).

42 Information kindly provided by Gabriel de Montmollion, director of the MIR, telephone conversation, April 6, 2018.

16

AFTERWORD

Memory practices and global Protestantism

Dagmar Freist

This afterword analyses the memory practices in Germany around the commemoration of the 500th anniversary of the Reformation. It argues that memory cultures generated by the 2017 Reformation anniversary in Germany mixed various economic, political and religious interests as well as the local and the global, although each followed a completely different logic. It will be shown that there was, on the one hand, a professional, top-down orchestration of memory cultures of the Reformation strongly supported by the media, and, on the other hand, a struggle from within the churches to create a bottom-up local, European, and even global awareness of the Reformation. The dilemma that we witness is not only one of organising a stunning commemorative event; it also has to do with the different ways in which cultural memories are constructed and the often conflicting roles of memory activists and historians. The heated debates in Germany over the relationship between history and memory culture which broke out between historians and state and church representatives over the design of the Reformation anniversary of 2017 bear witness to the different understandings of the past.

The essay contextualises these debates by setting them in dialogue with historic controversies over Reformation memory. Taking the memory practices of the Moravians as a case study, it explores how a Protestant group imbued with missionary zeal was obliged to rethink the relationship between space, memory, and religious identity in the late seventeenth and eighteenth centuries in cultures beyond the borders of Europe which could not directly relate to the sites, national heroes, symbols, or artefacts of the Reformation. This fuelled the emergence of global Protestantism. But what exactly do we remember when we relate the Reformation to global Protestantism in the past and the present? The changing European attitude towards the Moravian contribution to the Reformation over the centuries foregrounds this question. In the eighteenth century the Moravians were one of the first Protestant groups to launch missions around the world.

Simultaneously, in Europe they were accused of nonconformity by the Lutheran orthodoxy. In 2016, however, Herrnhut, the centre of the Moravian mission in eighteenth-century Germany, was proclaimed a 'Reformation city' during the commemoration of the Lutheran Reformation. This afterword thus considers whether a global perspective on memory can help explain the conflicting and dividing visions of the Reformation, today and yesterday.

From marginalisation to embracement: Herrnhut as Reformation city

In 1795, the Moravian missionary Catharina Borck sent the following lines from Paramaribo, Surinam, to her parents in Christiansfeld, Denmark.

> Over here, we are hardly aware of the times we live in, therefore, we do not celebrate Maundy Thursday or Good Friday, the poor negroes can only come in the evenings to listen to the story of suffering, the reading assigned for Thursday has to be read on Wednesday because holy communion has to be celebrated on Thursday. The Sabbath lovefeast is also celebrated in the evening.[1]

Catharina Borck and her husband were members of the second generation of Moravians in the Paramaribo mission station in Surinam which had been set up in 1735, initially without much success, by order of the Dutch West India Company. The couple stayed connected with the Moravian 'world community' through the official Moravian handwritten manual *Gemeine Nachrichten* ('parish news'), which had been founded in 1747. It addressed Moravians and other Protestant groups alike, and it advised and supported them in their struggle for a godly life and the promotion of a Protestant transconfessional piety around the world. Robert Beachy has pointed to the dual nature of the *Gemeine Nachrichten* as both a medium which 'maintained and extended these early networks of correspondence' and as a means to support 'the communal reading practices of Moravian congregations'.[2] Its composition and contents as well as its manuscript nature were based on detailed instructions and editorial guidelines designed to foster a strong confessional identity and codes of conduct among a widely dispersed religious community. These new Moravian 'world communities' were tied together by the movement of people, by the promotion of a powerful sense of religious belonging, by a missionary calling to promote the Protestant faith without necessarily including the converts within their tight-knit Moravian communities, and by a highly organised communication network.[3] In addition, Moravians corresponded privately with friends and family using the postal services of the many ships that sailed between Europe and the Caribbean. Besides the requirement for clear religious commitment, the everyday challenge for Moravian men and women lay in adapting to local circumstances within the context of migration and missionary work. Only traces of these adaptation strategies can be found in the official correspondence of the Moravians, but they are expressed clearly in thousands of extant letters transported by ships that were seized when they were captured during the numerous naval wars of the eighteenth century. The letters were taken to the High Court of Admiralty in London, where they are still stored today, largely untouched and unsorted.[4] These letters provide compelling insights into the adjustment of Moravian religious practices to habitual routines and local cultural features in ways that clearly differentiated them from orthodox Lutheran identity as promoted in Europe.

It is therefore striking that in 2016, the year before the 500th anniversary of Luther's alleged posting of Ninety-Five theses on the door of the Castle Church in Wittenberg in 1517, the Moravians (the German term is 'Herrnhuter') were celebrated as a central element of the Protestant Reformation. A movement marginalised in its own time was embraced in the twenty-first century as an important dimension of globalising Protestantism. On Thursday, 21st of June 2016, the *Süddeutsche Zeitung*, one of Germany's leading newspapers, announced 'Herrnhut ist Reformationsstadt Europas': the former village of Herrnhut, where a group of religious refugees from Moravia had found shelter in 1722 with the support of Count Ludwig von Zinzendorf was declared a 'City of the Reformation'. The title had been granted by the Community of Protestant Churches in Europe, an ecclesiastial body which goes back to the so called Leuenberg agreement of 1973 which bound the Protestant churches of Europe — Lutheran, Reformed, and Unitarian — together on the basis of a shared understanding of 'faith, recognising that the remaining doctrinal differences among the churches of the Reformation were no longer of a church-dividing nature'.[5] With this in mind, the Community of Protestant Churches in Europe had created the programme 'Europa reformata: 500 years of Reformation in Europe' in order to complement the German Reformation anniversary celebrations of 2017 with a European perspective.

Herrnhut is one of more than ninety cities across Europe which received the title 'City of the Reformation'.[6] In a specially designed website the public was informed about the aims and objectives of the campaign.[7] In order to qualify for this title, a briefing on how to participate points out that towns and cities had 'to possess historical evidence from the era of the Reformation, demonstrate European charisma and have a well-developed tourist infrastructure'.[8] The Community of Protestant Churches in Europe invited cities to apply for the title and explained: 'The initiative supported the rich interplay of art, culture and spirituality, promoting journeys of historical discovery and tourism in the cities of the Reformation'.[9] The overall project was underpinned by the idea that these cities would 'create a European-level public awareness of the principles of the Reformation right across the entire Continent'. Cities chosen by a specially commissioned academic advisory panel formed partnership agreements with municipal authorities, city offices and district councils as well as tourism offices and cultural organisations in order to create 'a fitting presentation of [their] particular role in the historical course of the Reformation'. The website provided information on the events and activities on offer and explained the Reformation heritage of these cities and towns. Most of the designated 'Cities of the Reformation' were integrated into a mobile 'Reformation show truck' initiated by the Evangelical Church in Germany (EKD) and the German Protestant Kirchentag. Under the heading 'public attention' the website advocating this event stated:

> Past events will come to life again in surprising dramatic presentations at each stop-over. Encounters with local people will bring out the relevance of the Reformation for today. Personal story-telling will testify to the contemporary nature of Reformation viewpoints. Every way-station will then send along a memento to the World Reformation Exhibition in Wittenberg. The European Reformation Roadmap will enable the cities – those in Germany having been proposed by their regional Protestant churches – to propel the Reformation issues relevant to them to the forefront of media and public attention. A show-truck ("storymobile") will stand on a central square as an eye-catcher. The regional media will report on the events and encounters before, during and after the visit.[10]

Four years previously, in December 2013, the general secretary of the Lutheran World Federation, Martin Junge, had declared that 'The Reformation is a World Citizen'.[11] This statement was repeated by the EKD council chair, Heinrich Bedford-Strohm, in 2017, and he continued to explain that Luther's message of the freedom of a Christian knows no national or cultural boundaries. That is why the international dimension of the Reformation anniversary was central. The European Reformation Roadmap would illustrate this particularly vividly by collecting regional Reformation histories and bringing them to Wittenberg.[12]

In what I have presented so far, key elements of the build up to the '500 year Reformation anniversary' can already be recognised: European Reformations, Reformation as a World Citizen, Luther, Wittenberg, history and memories, personal stories, tourism. Likewise, key 'memory activists' — to use Aleida Assmann's terminology — are mentioned: representatives of the Evangelical Church in Germany, the Lutheran World Federation, the Community of European Reformed Churches, municipal authorities, city offices, district councils, tourism offices, cultural organisations and Lutheran, Reformed, or United Church parishes.

However, the picture becomes even more complex when we move from the year 2017 just ten years back to the launch of the so called 'Luther decade' in Germany. This event stretched over a period of ten years from 2008 through to 2017. It had a thematic focus for each year, and it created an emblem with an image of Martin Luther alone. The decade was jointly sponsored by the German state and the Church, and it was financed by the Federal Ministry of Culture and Media. A key criterion for funding project proposals was to demonstrate 'the influence of the Reformation on education, music, art and languages, as well as politics, tolerance, and the understanding of freedom'.[13] In April 2014, the German government launched a position paper in which it confirmed its institutional and financial support of the Reformation anniversary celebrations of 2017, emphasising the national significance and the historical role of the Reformation for the development of the modern, tolerant, free, and democratic society which constitutes Germany today.[14] What we observe here is the official formation of a memory culture of the Reformation, initiated by and supported by the German state and jointly organised with the Evangelical Church in Germany, driven by both economic incentives and political imperatives as well as Protestant identity politics. But what we can also observe is a struggle from within the churches to create a bottom-up local, European and even global awareness of the Reformation as both a clear identity marker of 'my reformation', my story, my church in my reformation city, and a series of plural and colourful Reformation movements.

Conflicting memory strategies

The memory cultures engendered by the 2017 Reformation anniversary in Germany mixed these various economic, political and religious interests with the local and the global although for different reasons. At the same time, memory activists from the church, state and municipalities found themselves entangled with all of these conflicting interests due to the architecture of events and their respective players. They felt a pressure to deliver in superlatives, to rock the world, to produce large audiences and mind-puzzling stunning effects, to attract, sustain, and control attention. Despite the lip service that was paid to a global perspective, the Reformation anniversary of 2017 in Germany made the nation state and national historiography the focal point of memory formation. Over the centuries the commemoration of the German Reformation has produced strong images and ideals: the hammer,[15] the Ninety-Five theses, the statement 'Hier stehe ich, und kann nicht anders' ('Here I stand, I can do not other') as an expression of resistance and freedom, and places and buildings of high recognition value — Wittenberg, the Wartburg, and the blotted ink on the wall. It has also created Luther as a supreme hero. Recent biographies have resurrected him as a human being and child of his own time, different yet almost familiar, made of flesh and blood, with bodily pains, sexual desires, neuroses, and obsessions, anything but perfect, but a strong and charismatic personality.

Following Aleida Assman's definition, cultural (and political) memory is a form of collective memory in the sense that it is shared by a number of people, based on powerful symbols, and conveys to people the idea of a shared identity.[16] The transmission of memory from generation to generation is a prerequisite for the emergence, continuity, and change of memory cultures.[17] Collective memory-building relies on top-down constructed memory cultures and the mythologisation of the past rather than a critical historical assessment of its plural voices and the unearthing of subjugated knowledge. Whereas memory activists need a legacy constructed around a set of core beliefs and strong symbols, historians do not. Since the 1990s, historians in Germany, the Netherlands, Italy, France, the US, and the UK have rejected earlier assumptions about the Reformation as a coherent and monolithic event which paved the way to modern European society. The conflicts in Germany that flared up between historians and political and ecclesiastical officials around the planning of the Reformation anniversary of 2017 reflect the tensions between history and memory culture and different perceptions and uses of the past.[18] However, in order to highlight the world dimension of the Reformation, we need to be attentive to the more fragmented perceptions, adaptions, translations and changes which constitute the focal point of global memory formation and memory transmission of the Reformation. We need to explore the creation of Reformation memory cultures which were not grounded within the confines of the nation-state but generated in a dynamic between translocal developments and local circumstances.

The emerging global turn in memory studies is a comparatively recent phenomenon, which had been inspired by works focusing on the twentieth century.[19] Studies of the Holocaust, for instance, have argued that a key to understanding the construction of transnational collective memory is demonstrating the competing cultural uses of the Holocaust in film, popular history, and social theory. According to these scholars, memories of the Holocaust have been de-contextualised from the original event and thus offer a framework for interpreting contemporary acts of injustice such as ethnic cleansing and genocide. Building on this idea, Aleida Assmann and Sebastian Conrad have argued in *Memory in a Global Age* that the nation is no longer the 'natural container of memory debates'.[20] Instead, the interconnections of global frameworks and national memory discourses have to be analysed. In other words, memory has to be studied from the angle of *histoire croisée* in its global entanglements. In their edited volume on memory and migration, Julia Creet and Andreas Kitzmann point out that 'migration rather than location is the condition of memory': they emphasise the connections between memory, place, and displacement.[21]

Global Protestantism and memory cultures

How can we make these observations fruitful for the study of global Protestantism and memory cultures? As I have argued elsewhere, the long Reformation within and outside Europe through the seventeenth and eighteenth centuries, was 'glocal' for a number of reasons.[22] The conflicts between and within world religions, the definition of rituals and dogma, religious wars, the inquisitions and the prosecution of 'heretics', missionary programmes, the circulation of religious print media and objects, religious migrants, refugees and the emergence of transnational martyrologies all had a profound impact on the formation and spread of Protestantism and on the formation of Protestant memory across time and space.[23] Memory transmission itself must not only be approached from the perspective of *time* with reference to generational memory, but also from the perspective of *space* with reference to migration and the dispersion of people, written media, and artefacts. A decentred, global perspective on the Reformation and its memory cultures, however, lacks strong symbols.[24] This is certainly true of the 2017 anniversary. It is very hard to think of anything global with a high recognition value like the Ninety-Five theses or figures such as Wycliff, Calvin, Zwingli, or Luther. However, Protestant congregations around the world relate to their own founding fathers, myths, and material objects. Moreover, a decentred perspective on global Protestantism requires a focus on the spatial as well as the diachronic dimension of memory. And it requires a focus on memory practices rather than on objects and figures as infinite memory containers. What does this mean?

This brings me back to the proclamation of Herrnhut as a 'City of Reformation' in the wake of the 2017 Reformation anniversary. The official website of Herrnhut as a 'City of Reformation' introduces the Moravians as a 'World Community', which strongly identifies with the Reformation movement led by the reformer Jan Hus (c. 1370–1415), which 'also adopted the ideals of the Reformation',[25] and which, under the influence of Count Zinzendorf and the founding of the Moravian colony in Herrnhut, developed its own theology of pietism from the heart with the crucified saviour at the centre of spirituality and religious practices. Bonding different religious traditions through his theology, Zinzendorf defined the Moravians as an 'ecumenical and cross-confessional community' with the explicit aim of world mission.[26] In their own time, the Moravians were one of the most controversial religious groups under the umbrella of Protestantism, with their origin dating back almost fifty years before Martin Luther. Within two generations the Moravians had not only spread across western Europe but also created what has been called a pious world community with missionary settlements in North America, the Caribbean, India, and Africa.

Moravians were not the first Protestant missionaries who attempted to spread the gospel in the wake of European Reformation movements in other parts of the world,[27] but they were among the best organised before the evangelical world mission took off on a larger scale from the nineteenth century onwards.[28] The so-called long missionary century from 1790 to 1914 was characterised by awakening movements and the foundation of European-based missionary societies which shared a Protestant ecumenical outlook.[29] The twentieth and twenty-first centuries saw the formation of global confessional institutions such as the Lutheran World Federation, the World Communion of Reformed Churches, the Anglican Communion, and the World Methodist Council, all of which trace their roots back to the late nineteenth century. The foundation of these organisations was paralleled by the establishment of more ecumenical institutions, above all the World Council of Churches, founded in 1947.[30]

When we consider the expansion of Protestantism since the late sixteenth century a number of problems arise, especially the question of what we mean by 'Protestantism' and by 'global'? In the late 1990s Thomas Kaufmann and others not only pointed to the plurality of Protestantism, even within Lutheranism, and rejected fixed identities.[31] These researchers also focused on everyday practices and on 'living with religious diversity'.[32] They suggested an approach to questions of Protestant identity which takes into account processes of appropriation and the relevance of specific social and cultural milieux, as well as family ties, for religious subjectivation. There has been a shift away from an exclusive concentration on confessional dogma towards the central role of religious practices and the impact of the material world for identity formation, which is understood as a continuous process within an increasingly plural world.[33]

Global Protestantism obviously shares these characteristics on a larger geographical scale, which reaches beyond Europe. First of all, there is the question of the actors who have contributed to the spread of Protestantism beyond Europe. Secondly, the adoption of the Protestant faith varied from place to place and contributed to religious diversity within Protestantism. Thirdly, forms of religious coexistence and the relationship to non-Christians differed and were subject to local circumstances.

As far as the actors who spread Protestantism are concerned, research has tended to focus on the work of Protestant clergy and missionaries from the early eighteenth century onwards, above all the Moravians and Hallensian pietists. The fact that the first Protestants who left Europe mainly belonged to nonconformist religious groups raises the question of who they represented in terms of religious belief and ecclesiastical affiliation. They were not tolerated at home at a time when state and church struggled to form confessional subjects for the sake of order and governance. Yet these nonconformists were also far from being a homogenous group, as terms such as the 'Puritan paradigm' with reference to the founding years of the United States have implied.[34] In their studies, Wellenreuther, Häberlein, Dixon, and others have pointed to their inherent pluralism.[35] Nevertheless, these early religious migrants shared what Scott Dixon has diagnosed for the eighteenth century: a 'growing indifference to dogmatic distinctions and the constraints of the institutional church'.[36] While in most of continental Europe the emerging confessional churches struggled for confessional orthodoxy and homogeneity, in the New World we observe a more experimental and practice-oriented religious life with fluid religious boundaries.[37] More recent studies have focused on the role of colonial administrators and members of chartered companies, who functioned as multipliers of Protestantism. In the case of the Netherlands — in spite of its persistent image as a crucible of religious tolerance — colonial governors were expected to behave as godly magistrates and to refrain from religious disputes while the directors of the Dutch chartered companies oversaw religious policy.[38] However, as Haefeli has convincingly shown, in everyday contexts Dutch authorities were willing to overlook deviancy for the sake of peaceful religious and social coexistence.[39] Taking New England as a second example, here, too, religious life in the colonies differed from Anglican ideals of religious conformity.[40] Chartered companies played a role in 'crownsponsored initiative(s) for propagating the gospel among the native populations'.[41] After the expulsion of the Huguenots from France in the late seventeenth century, Protestants acquired a new role in French colonisation due to Huguenot religious and trading networks and their economic success despite the efforts of Catholics to bar them from French colonies.[42] Furthermore, in the wake of European overseas expansion, professionals such as traders, doctors, or craftsmen and their families migrated to regions outside Europe for a variety of reasons, and their religious practices had an impact on people around them. They usually belonged to one of the emerging confessional churches in Europe, and were interested in establishing ecclesiastical structures and practices in imitation of them, usually without any missionary intentions, in their new homes.

However, there is evidence of increasing conflicts and divergences between the priorities of ministers in Europe and those overseas. The picture of what we mean by 'global Protestantism' becomes even more complex when we consider the emergence of a 'circum-Atlantic Afro-Christian culture', the development of an Afro-Atlantic Christian identity, and the impact of evangelical networks that originated in a Caribbean and Black church and reached beyond the plantations and plantation societies.[43]

Secondly, how was the Protestant faith adopted? The ensuing diversity of Protestantism in practice and everyday life has provoked the question of how we actually analyse the adoption of the Protestant faith. The term 'conversion' has come under question because of its 'missionary mindset',[44] and there have been debates about the legitimacy of conversion practices.[45] To do justice to the diversity of the religious cultures that clustered under the umbrella of global Protestantism, terms such as hybridity have been introduced and the focus has shifted to processes of appropriation and translation and to the transactions that took place between European religious practices and locally distinct variations of the Protestant faith.[46]

This links to the third question, that of regional diversity. In his study of Dutch religious liberty Haefeli has compared the New Netherlands with Dutch Brazil and pointed to the impact that local contexts and the presence of other religious groups had on the formation of specific forms of Protestantism. Further microhistorical studies will be able to show how these developed under the influence of formal Lutheran, Anglican or Calvinist confessional identities, each of which claimed universal validity, and under the influence of the indigenous conditions that shaped processes of appropriation and hybridisation.[47]

Most studies of Protestantism outside Europe to date have relied chiefly on official letters, diaries, and theological treatises of ministers, or male missionaries.[48] They have struggled to fit these movements and communities into established narratives of Lutheran, Anglican or Calvinist faith and of the formation of confessional identities. However, the (re)discovery of about 160,000 letters dating from 1652 to 1815 among the prize papers in the High Court of Admiralty in London gives women, non-office holders, and less educated people a voice in the story of European overseas expansion.[49] A considerable number are written by the members of different religious groups, among them Jews and Moravians. What comes into focus in this correspondence is the complexity of religious, social, and ethnic life in colonial settings. This escapes both the clear-cut confessional categories and the fixed racial and social asymmetries mapped out by postcolonial discourses, providing evidence instead of the permeability of social and ethnic hierarchies and dependencies.

The emergence of global Protestantism as a new research theme in recent publications has already forged a new grand narrative. Three major developments have been identified since the late seventeenth century: the growth of religious diversity; the consolidation of religious institutions; and the emergence of revivalism as a major spiritual and social force.[50] Although these trends are helpful pointers, it is too early to offer macro, European centred explanations for what was going on outside Europe. It will be the task of further research to take a closer look at social and religious practices in colonial settings and their connectivities with European and African localities, and to ask, how religious ideas, artefacts and memories were transmitted across time and space, and how they were adapted to local circumstances. Protestant religious practices in global settings were simultaneously deeply localised as well as being extensive in their origin and reach.[51]

Remembering religious life across time and space

I close by returning to the correspondence of Catharina Borck and her Moravian brethren in Surinam. This example is not chosen for its representativeness, but for its value in illuminating the complexities of religious life within and across time and space. I have chosen Surinam, a Dutch colony, because it was characterised in the seventeenth and eighteenth centuries by the density of different ethnicities and religious groups, including Caribbeans, Arawacs, Warao, Dutch, Portuguese, French, English, German and Swiss, Sephardic Jews, Ashkenazi Jews, Huguenot, Dutch-reformed, Moravians, Lutherans, and Catholics, as well as indigenous faiths. The Jewish Purim was the biggest folk festival in Surinam with people from all religious and ethnic backgrounds dressing up and participating. In the midst of this was Catharina Borck, a Moravian shopkeeper in Paramaribo, who had arrived in 1792. Her letters are in themselves evidence of her efforts to stay connected with her brethren at home in Christiansfeld and of her engagement with the various social practices that constituted religious life and meaning in Paramaribo. Catharina was part of the densely woven Moravian communication and economic network of the pious world community described by scholars such as Gisela Mettele, Michele Gillespie, or Robert Beachy.[52] And she left traces in several of the official Moravian central archives, too.

Catharina Borck regularly read the diaries, letters, and reports which were sent with the *Gemeine Nachrichten*, and she was convinced that she shared the same news with her fellow believers around the world. She joined in liturgical practices of her congregation at set dates and times. She repeatedly expressed her intense emotions at the thought of Christ's suffering, commented on the hardships and sufferings of others as well as her own, and marvelled at the mystical joy 'our negroes' felt at the sight of Christ's wounds. She was, as expected, concerned with the spiritual well-being of the 'two-hundred negroes' who had joined the community.[53] But she was also aware of deviations from the liturgical year and from habitual religious practices due to local conditions. In several letters she described religious life in Paramaribo, not as a distant observer, but as someone in the midst of it, immersed in the soundscapes, smells and tastes which she conjured up in real-time for the inner eyes of her friends at home. She described these senses not simply as different, as loud or quiet, but always as embedded in social practices, from funeral rites and the rhythmic stamping of coffee to the sounds and colours of the Purim festival. Furthermore, in the course of her letters, the shifting arrangements of people of diverse origins, unfamiliar artefacts, and unintelligible social practices, together with the challenges posed by nature and the environment, were bundled up with the familiar features of Catharina Borck's immediate Moravian community.

The act of writing was an attempt to try to locate herself within these shifting social sites and to let her friends and family participate in her new world while she participated in the world at home. In a way, Catharina's letters connected these worlds by translating the nexus of social and religious practices and arrangements through her experiences and perceptions. Her letters also show how she situated herself in relation to other people by connecting a lived present, a memorised past, and an anticipated future.[54] A key objective of her letters was to keep the memory of herself alive among her brethren at home, and to remember her life there. She overcomes the long distance of time and space through memory practices. She remembered things of the past by recalling them in writing in her numerous letters. The practice of letter writing was both proof of and a prerequisite for staying connected; it was also vital to remembering where she belonged. Moravians related to people at home virtually, through writing, projecting themselves across time and space and creating the illusion of a bodily co-presence with friends, family, and fellow believers. In a letter from Paramaribo to her friend Anne Marie Richter in Christiansfeld in 1795, Catharina Borck asked her: 'Do you remember when we were roommates?'[55] She then shared various memories and talked about mutual acquaintances in Christiansfeld while giving her advice about how to deal with various problems. Numerous similar examples of remembering a world and a religious community far away have survived.

How can we integrate these variations of Protestant religious life and memories around the world into our understanding of global Protestant memory cultures? One way is to find these voices and listen to them, to tolerate and preserve their deviation, rather than to wrest their meaning for the sake of grand narratives or in keeping with strong religious symbols and identities. This is a challenge for research, for teaching, for the rewriting of text books for universities and schools, and for public history. It is also a challenge for our present perceptions of Protestant life in Europe and its memory cultures: it is easy to hear the loud voices of memory activists, and to analyse what seems to be a national memory culture. It is harder to hear the quiet voices of people who lacked strong visible symbols with a high recognition value because of their plurality and lack of a public stage. The emergence of international evangelical and migrant churches within our midst is fascinating evidence of how Protestantism is perpetually reinvented across time and space.

Notes

1 Kew, The National Archives, The High Court of Admiralty (HCA) 30/374.
2 Robert Beachy, 'Manuscript Mission in the Age of Print: Moravian Community in the Atlantic World', in *Pious Pursuits: German Moravians in the Atlantic World*, ed. Michele Gillespie and Robert Beachy (New York and Oxford, 2007), 33–49 (39).

3   Gisela Mettele, *Weltbürgertum oder Gottesreich: Die Herrnhuter Brüdergemeine als Globale Gemeinschaft, 1727–1857* (Göttingen, 2000), 124–90.

4   For more details of this archive see below, note 49.

5   Gottfried Locher, 'The Reformation: Remembering the Future', in *Reformation: Legacy and Future*, ed. Petra Bosse-Huber et al. (Geneva, 2015), 8–12 (9).

6   For a survey of cities that have been identified as 'City of Reformation' in the context of the commemoration of the Reformation in 2017, see 'European Cities of the Reformation', accessed 8 October 2019, https://reformation-cities.org/?lang=en.

7   'Welcome to the European Cities of the Reformation', accessed 8 October 2019, https://reformation-cities.org/?lang=en.

8   'Briefing on How to Take Part', accessed 8 October 2019, https://reformation-cities.org/wp-content/uploads/2015/07/Briefing-für-Teilnahme-ENG-jkt.pdf.

9   'Invitation to Participate', accessed 8 October 2019, https://reformation-cities.org/wp-content/uploads/2015/02/GEKE_Schmuckkarte_ENG_MAIL.pdf.

10 'European Reformation Roadmap Launch', accessed 8 October 2019, https://www.oikoumene.org/en/press-centre/events/european-reformation-roadmap-launch.   See also 'Stories on the Road', https://r2017.org/en/european-roadmap/.

11 I would like to thank Petra Bosse-Huber for this reference.

12 For the centrality of the freedom narrative across borders see 'Justification and Freedom: Celebrating 500 Years of the Reformation in 2017: A Foundational Text from the Council of the Evangelical Church in Germany' (Hannover, 2017), esp. 57–66. See https://archiv.ekd.de/english/download/justification_and_freedom.pdf.

13 https://www.luther2017.de/en/2017/luther-decade/, accessed August 21, 2017.

14 Beauftragte der Bundesregierung für Kultur und Medien, Projektgruppe Reformationsjubiläum, ed., *Die Bundesregierung und das Reformationsjubiläum 2017: Eine Positionsbeschreibung* (Bonn, 2014).

15 Aleida Assmann, 'Was ist so Schlimm an einem Hammer?', *Rotary Magazin* 1 (2017), accessed April 1, 2019, https://rotary.de/gesellschaft/was-ist-so-schlimm-an-einem-hammer-a-10106.html.

16 Aleida Assmann, *Der Lange Schatten der Vergangenheit: Erinnerungskultur und Geschichtspolitik* (München, 2006), 36–40.

17 Assmann, *Der Lange Schatten der Vergangenheit*, 15f., 27.

18 Matthias Pohlig, 'Vom Fremdeln mit dem Reformationsjubiläum 2017: Über die Rolle der Geschichtswissenschaft bei den Aktivitäten zum Luther-Gedenken', accessed April 1, 2019, https://www.uni-muenster.de/Religion-und-Politik/aktuelles/2014/okt/Ansichtssache_Reformationsgedenken_zu_sehr_auf_Luther_zentriert.html. See also a short summary of the debate in 2014 by Stefan Dege, 'Fremdeln mit dem Reformationsjubiläum', *Deutsche Welle*, accessed 13 September 2019, https://www.dw.com/de/fremdeln-mit-dem-reformationsjubiläum/a-18028043.

19 John Sundholm, 'Visions of Transnational Memory', *Journal of Aesthetics & Culture* 3, no. 1 (2011), 1–5. For the first influential studies see Daniel Levy and Natan Sznaider, *Holocaust and Memory in the Global Age*, tr. Assenka Oksiloff (Philadelphia, 2008). This was first published as *Erinnerung im Globalen Kontext: Der Holocaust* (Frankfurt, 2001).

20 Aleida Assmann and Sebastian Conrad, 'Introduction', in *Memory in a Global Age: Discourses, Practices and Trajectories*, ed. Aleida Assmann and Sebastian Conrad (Basingstoke, 2010), 1–16 (6).

21 Julia Creet and Andreas Kitzmann, 'Introduction', in *Memory and Migration: Multidisciplinary Approaches to Memory Studies*, ed. Julia Creet and Andreas Kitzmann (Toronto, 2011), 3–27 (9). See also Sundholm, 'Visions of Transnational Memory'.

22 Roland Robertson, 'Glocalization: Time-Space and Homogeneity-Heterogeneity', in *Global Modernities*, ed. Mike Featherstone, Scott Lash, and Roland Robertson (London, 1995), 25–44.

23 Dagmar Freist, 'Lost in Time and Space? Glocal Memoryscapes in the Early Modern World', in *Memory Before Modernity. Practices of Memory in Early Modern Europe*, ed. Erika Kuijpers et al. (Leiden, 2013), 203–21.

24 Already in 2004, Hans Medick and Peer Schmidt argued in favour of a decentred perspective on the Reformation. Hans Medick and Peer Schmidt, eds., *Luther zwischen den Kulturen: Zeitgenossenschaft – Weltwirkung* (Göttingen, 2004), 11–30.

25 Historically, neither in the kingdom of Bohemia nor in the margravate of Moravia did Lutheranism manage to act as a unifying theological force in a mainly pluralistic Protestant religious environment. The basis for this pluralism was the Confessio Bohemia (1575) which was based on the Confessio Augustana. Between 1627–1781 Lutheranism disappeared from the public space.

26 http://reformation-cities.org/cities/herrnhut/?lang=en, accessed August 22, 2017.

27 In the 1950s a number of articles appeared in leading German historical journals on the early stages of Protestant missions emphasising on the one hand the lack of any missionary impulse of the first Protestants but pointing on the other hand to individual missionaries already operating in the seventeenth century. See for instance Walter Holsten, 'Reformation und Mission', *Archiv für Reformationsgeschichte* 44 (1953), 1–31. Mark Häberlein has recently summarised some of the arguments: 'Protestantism Outside Europe', in *The Oxford Handbook of the Protestant Reformation*, ed. Ulinka Rublack (Oxford, 2017), 350–73.

28 Carola Wessel, 'Connecting Congregations: The Net of Communication among the Moravians in the late 18th Century', in *The Distinctiveness of Moravian Culture: Essays and Documents in Moravian History in Honor of Vernon H. Nelson on His Seventieth Birthday*, ed. Atwood D. Craig and Peter Vogt (Nazareth, 2003), 153–72; Gisela Mettele, *Weltbürgertum oder Gottesreich: Die Herrnhuter Brüdergemeine als Globale Gemeinschaft, 1727–1857* (Göttingen, 2009), 43–9.

29 Artur Bogner, Bernd Holtwick, and Tyrell Hartmann, eds., *Weltmission und Religiöse Organisationen: Protestantische Missionsgesellschaften im 19. und 20. Jahrhundert* (Würzburg, 2004).

30 Konrad Raiser, *500 Jahre Reformation: Weltweit* (Bielefeld, 2016).

31 Thomas Kaufmann, 'Die Konfessionalisierung von Kirche und Gesellschaft: Dammelbericht über eine Forschungsbdebatte', *Theologische Literaturzeitung* 122, no. 11–12 (1996), 1008–24, 1112–21.

32 Scott Dixon, Dagmar Freist, and Mark Greengrass, *Living with Religious Diversity in Early-Modern Europe* (Farnham, 2009).

33 For the central role of material culture in the Reformation see Alexandra Walsham, ed., *Relics and Remains, P&P* issue suppl. 5 (2010). For a practice theoretical approach see Dagmar Freist, *Glaube – Liebe – Zwietracht: Religiös-Konfessionell Gemischte Ehen in Deutschland in der Frühen Neuzeit* (München, 2017).

34 Charles L. Cohen, 'The Post-Puritan Paradigm of Early American Religious History', *The William and Mary Quarterly* 54, no. 4 (1997), 695–722.

35 See the contributions in Jonathan Strom, Hartmut Lehmann, and James Van Horn Melton, eds., *Pietism in Germany and North America, 1680–1820* (London, 2009).

36 Scott Dixon, *Protestants: A History from Wittenberg to Pennsylvania, 1517–1740* (Chichester, 2010), 223.

37 Dixon, *Protestants*, 93.

38 Evan Haefeli, *New Netherland and the Dutch Origins of American Religious Liberty* (Philadelphia, 2012), 89–91.

39 Haefeli, *New Netherland*, chapter 2.

40 See especially the articles in J. Gregory, ed., *The Oxford History of Anglicanism: Establishment and Empire, 1662–1829*, vol. 2 (Oxford, 2017) and Häberlein, 'Protestantism Outside Europe', 356.

41 Gabriel Glickman, 'Protestantism, Colonization, and the New England Company in Restoration Politics', *HistJ* 59, no. 2 (2016), 365–391 (365).

42 Gayle Brunelle, 'Ambassador's and Administrators: The Role of Clerics in Early French Colonies in Guiana', in *Spiritual Geopolitics in the Early Modern World*, ed. Susanne Lachenicht, Lauric Henneton, and Yann Lignereux, *Itinerario* 40, special issue 2 (2016), 257–77.

43 John W. Catron, *Embracing Protestantism: Black Indentities in the Atlantic World* (Gainesville, 2016), 79–80.

44 Katharine Gerbner, 'Theorizing Conversion: Christianity, Colonization, and Consciousness in the Early Modern Atlantic World', *History Compass* 13, no. 3 (2015), 134–47 (134).

45 Linford D. Fisher, 'Native Americans, Conversion, and Christian Practice in Colonial New England, 1640–1730', *Harvard Theological Review* 102, no. 1 (2009), 101–124 (103).

46 Hartmann Tyrell, 'Weltgesellschaft, Weltmission und Religiöse Organisationen – Einleitung', in *Weltmission und Religiöse Organisationen: Protestantische Missionsgesellschaften im 19. und 20. Jahrhundert*, ed. Artur Bogner, Bernd Holtwick, and Hartmann Tyrell (Würzburg, 2004), 13–133.

47 For religious practices see Robert Orsi, *Everyday Miracles: The Study of Lived Religion*, in *Lived Religion in America: Toward a History of Practices*, ed. David D. Hall (Princeton, 1997).

48 Repeating familiar names such as August Herman Francke, Heinrich Melchior Mühlenberg, Roger Williams, William Penn, Bartholomäus Ziegenbalg, Heinrich Plütschow, August Gottlieb Spangenberg, John Wesley, or George Whitefield.

49 For a description of this collection see Amanda Bevan and Randolph Cook, 'The High Court of Admiralty Prize Papers, 1652–1815: Challenges in Improving Access to Older Records', *Archives* 53, no. 137 (2018), 34–58, and Dagmar Freist, 'The Prize Papers – Uncurated Histories of Global Scope', in *Das Meer: Maritime Welten in der Frühen Neuzeit | The Sea: Maritime Worlds in the Early Modern Period*, ed. Peter Burschel and Sünne Juterczenka (Frühneuzeit-Impulse, 4), Köln/Weimar/Wien (forthcoming 2020).

50 Häberlein, 'Protestantism Outside Europe', 363; but more explicit with regard to the relevance of context and contingency in Dixon, *Protestants*, 5–6.

51 For a praxeological theoretical framework of global social sites and social practices see Dagmar Freist, 'A Global Microhistory of the Early Modern Period: Social Sites and the Interconnectedness of Human Lives', *Quaderni Storici* 155a. LII, n. 2 (2017), 537–55.

52 Michele Gillespie and Robert Beachy, eds., *Pious Pursuits: German Moravians in the Atlantic World* (New York and Oxford, 2007); Gisela Mettele, *Weltbürgertum oder Gottesreich: Die Herrnhuter Brüdergemeine als Globale Gemeinschaft, 1727–1857* (Göttingen, 2009).

53 The High Court of Admiralty (HCA) 30/374.

54 For a more detailed study of her sense of multiple belongings see Dagmar Freist, '"Wo wurdest Du geboren, und wo überall hast Du gelebt?" Mehrfachzugehörigkeiten und Selbstverortungen am Beispiel der Herrnhuter Weltgemeine im 18. Jahrhundert', in *Transkulturelle Mehrfachzugehörigkeiten als kulturhistorisches Phänomen*, ed. Dagmar Freist, Sabine Kyora, and Melanie Unseld (Bielefeld 2019), 83–101.

55 The High Court of Admiralty (HCA) 30/374.

INDEX

Page numbers in *italics* refer to figures.